W9-ABK-791

RICHELIEU
HIS RISE TO POWER

RICHELIEU

(From a painting by Ph. de Champaigne)

CARL J. BURCKHARDT

RICHELIEU

AND HIS AGE

HIS RISE TO POWER

TRANSLATED AND ABRIDGED
BY EDWIN AND WILLA MUIR

A HELEN AND KURT WOLFF BOOK

HARCOURT, BRACE & WORLD, INC.

NEW YORK

FIRST PUBLISHED IN ENGLISH IN 1940

SECOND IMPRESSION 1967

CONTENTS

LIST OF ILLUSTRATIONS

7

CHAPTER I

INTRODUCTION

Wherever the kings of France turned at the end of the sixteenth century the power of the Hapsburgs confronted them, the greatest power of that time, encircling the boundaries of their distracted realm with a pressure that was a standing threat to its still indeterminate frontiers. There were many weak, undefended, and open places in the body of the French territories, especially at that period, and the inner structure of the country was still far from stable. The idea of national unity, then emerging into consciousness, was at times the concern of the burghers merely and the townsfolk, who formed the main bulwark of the kingdom; the great feudal nobles, grown too powerful, played at high treason, while the petty nobles sold themselves to the highest bidder; as for the Protestants, they were a still greater danger: a State within the State. The King of France had to maintain himself against the Hapsburgs in Madrid and Vienna, whose empire was world-wide, and at the same time against the strongest nobles of his own country and the religious sectarians, who leagued themselves with foreign powers whenever they felt it expedient.

France in the sixteenth century had reached the same state of misery which Germany was to attain in the seventeenth during the Thirty Years' War. Laid waste, sunk from the rank of a continental power, reeling from plague to plague, from famine to famine, she was torn into factions. The realm staggered under a monstrous load of debt; law and order were quite in abeyance; the kingship as an institution was questioned; tyrannicide was not only tolerated as a legitimate means, but actually advocated. Complete anarchy, confusion, and exhaustion prevailed everywhere. Eight religious and civil wars had come and gone; four under Charles IX, four under Henry III and Henry IV. In the beginning they were waged passionately for the sake of truth, but soon, as everywhere else, they became a pretext for the murderous usurpation of power.

Henry IV, backed by the burghers of the towns, began the political rehabilitation of France; for the intellectual and spiritual renewal of the nation a group of theologians working in the closest collaboration with him was chiefly responsible. The mighty and resolute rise of France to consistent unity was to last for the whole of the seventeenth century, yet it did not proceed undisturbed; to picture that century as an age of majestically calm proportions is far too easy. From the conflagration of the unexampled sixteenth century men's spirits had emerged still burning, and a long time was to pass before they cooled. In the sixteenth century individuals had grown too strong in a State that was too feeble; now they had to be disciplined out of their endless misery and embroilments; they had to be pieced together into a unity; a closely-knit ruling class had to be devised, a new and strict régime, a new authority to be set up. The task was hard and unremitting to the point of desperation, involving set-backs all the time, and risking collapse at every moment. For it was conditioned—and that was the remarkable thing about it—by the need for continuous collaboration among the political, the intellectual, and the religious leaders of the country.

When Henry IV encouraged and favoured men of letters he was acting entirely in the tradition of the Renaissance, but he was also initiating a necessary and clearly apprehended policy. The intellectual élite had to be brought into the framework of his State. This became obvious from the very start of his work of reconstruction, when the best writers devoted themselves with such admirable enthusiasm to the tasks of the State. With the same success the spiritual powers were also deliberately enlisted. The Counter-Reformation in France was essentially an inner reform of the Church; in its own way the Church assimilated Humanism and the Renaissance, thus winning over and penetrating the whole intellectual élite, which had to be kept faithful to Church and State by being furnished with a profound new sense of responsibility.

How great was the task for which these men had to nerve themselves at the turn of the century! How vastly in their minds still loomed the power of their dangerous neighbour, Spain! Spain: that meant the Iberian peninsula, Castile, Navarre, and Portugal; a great part of Italy, Milan and the Kingdom of Naples, with Sicily and Sardinia; finally the ruins of ancient Burgundy, the Netherlands, and Franche Comté. To its immeasurable American colonies it had added those of Portugal, scattered round Africa and about the Indian Ocean. A Spanish chronicler of the time asserted that the empire of his King exceeded twenty times in extent the territory of the ancient Roman Empire. And all Europe knew the saying: "When Spain stirs the earth trembles." The Spanish kings were not only absolute rulers of an immeasurable empire on which the sun never set; they raised themselves to the like-ness of gods through the liturgy of their Court ceremonial, which was informed with the pious awe of their subjects. The administration of Spain was strictly centralized, and in that it was a pattern for France. All the business of the Empire was co-ordinated by a few royal committees. The State Council as the chief authority was presided over by the King. The holy Inquisition operated in the dark background of this great fabric of power, uncanny and omniscient; it served many curiously interlaced interests. Spain was never a military power in the proper sense of the term, and yet the huge fabric of its antique and world-wide State rested on an army that was world-famous. The two most powerful rulers òf the six-teenth century, Charles V and Philip II, had created the Spanish army, the infantry in particular, the Tercios, as they were called, in whose ranks the noblest and bravest were enlisted, where each soldier had a vested right in his post, was accorded equal respect with his officer, and like him was fanatically resolved to vindicate his honour. As for the Navy, even the destruction of "the invincible Armada" in 1588 had not succeeded in permanently damaging the naval prestige of Spain.

Against this mighty power France held its own and eventually overcame it. Eventually: after long and hard endurance and a still longer preliminary period of lying in wait. The task of France was to spy out the vulnerable spots in the greatest power in Europe of the sixteenth century, to estimate in Madrid and in Vienna the weaknesses of the Hapsburgs, to search for the Empire's hidden, self-generated poisons, of which the most violent were to be found in the struggle for German liberties.

A political genius, Cardinal Richelieu, beyond all others after the premature death of Henry IV, succeeded in spying out the frailties of the enemy during the century-long struggle between the houses of Bourbon and Hapsburg; more than anyone else he knew how to split the power of his opponent, how to rally new enemies against it, to stir up all that was most dangerous in it as a force for self-destruction, to encompass its downfall methodically and unremittingly through the encouragement he gave to the canker which long before had begun to invade the huge body of the Spanish Empire.

CHAPTER II

RICHELIEU'S EARLY LIFE

Richelieu was born on September 9th at the Château Richelieu in Poitou during the reign of the last Valois, Henry III,
the freakish grandson of Francis I, who was such a strange
blend of corruption, cunning, daring, and weakness, who
lived in men's memories as the murderer of the Duke of
Guise and himself was to fall by a murderer's hand, like the
great king whom he named on his death-bed as his successor,
Henry IV. That extraordinary genius ascended the throne
when Richelieu was four years old. For twenty-one years his
cheerful rule lasted, with its infallible gift for brilliant improvisation, which made a virtue of every necessity, and created
out of every glaring anomaly a workable compromise leading
to some future solution. A statesman of rare quality, Sully,
stood by him, as Richelieu was destined one day to stand by
his son and successor, Louis XIII; but if in the first generation
the ruler was greater than his servant, in the second the opposite was to be the case.

"The scandalous bloodbath," as the Emperor Maximilian
called the crime of St. Bartholomew's Night attributed to the
Italian, Catherine de' Medici, showed the fearful tension that
existed between Catholic and Protestant in France. It is quite
clear that in a State not yet grown to maturity and ringed
round with enemies the continuance of such a schism was
bound to bring destruction: all thoughtful observers of
France's destiny always recognized this and acted upon it,
sometimes against their deepest personal convictions. Henry
IV, the greatest of them, should be mentioned first; his well-

known phrase "Paris is worth a Mass" will be judged only by shallow minds as the frivolous, insolent utterance of an irresponsible and ambitious gambler. That brave monarch, who could estimate to a hair the slightest variation in the realities surrounding him, carried his burden of great political aims, a full knowledge of all the forces opposed to him, and the premonition of a bitter and premature death, with a gallantry of bearing, acknowledged for centuries as the pattern of knightly virtue, which had always in it something of the baffling lightness of a Saladin cutting a feather in two with his damascened blade. He had had a stern struggle to conquer his kingdom. The Catholic party had united against him and founded the so-called "League." He had experienced the bitterness of seeing the Council of Sixteen, after the Revolt of the Barricades in Paris, invite their allies the Spaniards to set up a garrison in the capital of France. Philip II of Spain was then within an ace of proclaiming his daughter Isabella Queen of France. On this piece of presumption the League began to split, and that was the moment when Henry informed the Archbishop of Bourges that he was prepared to become a Catholic in order to save the unity and independence of the country, to preserve France for the dynasty and the dynasty for France. On July 23, 1593, he abjured the Protestant faith and received the sacraments, and in 1594 entered Paris as the King of France. Philip II, who had been fighting in France merely as the ally of the League, now waged war on his own account, but victory evaded him; the fatal hour for Spain was approaching; the objective towards which the Spaniards had been striving ever since Charles V, since Pavia, the bringing of France to her knees, began to recede. Henry IV struck back vigorously, and battle succeeded battle until both sides were exhausted.

But while the King of France was heading this desperate struggle his Calvinistic subjects stood aside in hostile activity because of his conversion to the Catholic Church. So destructive, so blindly paralysing was the effect of religious division.

At last in 1598 the peace treaty of Vervins was signed between Spain and France. Neither had conquered. A month before the signing of the treaty Henry had succeeded, after difficult negotiations, in winning over the Huguenots by the Edict of Nantes. This Edict guaranteed the Protestants freedom of conscience in the entire kingdom and freedom of worship wherever Protestant services had been customary before 1597, as well as one church in each parish, either in a village or a suburb. Complete equality of rights with the Catholics was guaranteed, also eligibility for any and every profession. Several justiciary courts were set up in which Protestants were to have equal representation, involving the appointment of Protestant as well as Catholic judges. More than that, the Edict empowered Protestants to assemble in provincial or national synods, and for the duration of eight years Henry left some hundred fortified places at their disposal. The danger of this particular concession was yet to be painfully demonstrated. It was not merely from a deliberate policy of compromise that the King went so far on the road to appeasement, but because by his very nature he was genuinely tolerant. He had great trouble in getting the law courts to register the Edict. To some delegates from the Department of Toulouse, who stood out against it, he said: "I see you still have Spanish fanaticism in your bones," expressing himself, as he liked to do, with familiar bluntness.

When Henry's labours were crowned in 1598 by the Edict of Nantes and the peace with Spain, Richelieu was thirteen: at that time his father had been dead for eight years. Who was his father? From what stock did the great Cardinal spring? Under what conditions did he spend his youth?

The Du Plessis Richelieus were not very well-off country gentry from Poitou.

The social rise of the family resulted from the marriage of Louis du Plessis, Richelieu's grandfather, with the last representative of one of the greatest names in France, Françoise de Rochechouart. She is said to have been past her youth, poor and embittered, living as a companion with a relative, Anne de Polignac. Yet pride and assurance are powers, for good or for evil; and at that time such a family alliance was decisive both because of its actual influence and what it stood for, not only because of the new and extensive family connections it brought, all of them gravitating round the Court, but for its assured tradition of self-confidence which gave it specific weight. Louis de Richelieu du Plessis secured advancement at Court through the influence of his father-in-law; he became chamberlain and cup-bearer to the King; he fought in many battles and died young, leaving five small children. Years of war followed, of impoverishment, of hardship, but the pride, the passion, the faith of the family did not decay. Among smoking, pillaged villages, neglected fields, roads that were year in, year out a highway for fugitives, assassins, bandits, and troops of soldiery, again and again in a state of siege, often without food, two generations grew to manhood, that of Richelieu's father and that of the Cardinal himself, fatherless orphans brought up by women. But the sacred fastness of the family, that ultimate, integral cell in the general chaos, did not give way; not one right of self-assertion or prestige was abandoned by the Richelieus.

The eldest son of Françoise de Rochechouart, Louis du Plessis, grew up to serve as Lieutenant in the Company of the Duc de Montpensier. He came home on leave. Half a mile from Château Richelieu lay the strong castle of the Maussons, who had been the Richelieus' rivals from time immemorial, occasional marriages between the two families having only exacerbated the situation. A dispute between Louis du Plessis and Monsieur de Mausson concerning a question of precedence at church flamed up into a quarrel; Mausson lay in ambush for du Plessis, surprised him, and killed him.

At this time the second son of Françoise de Rochechouart was a page at the Court of Charles IX. His mother summoned him back to the paternal castle and fostered within him plans of revenge. As he grew to manhood, his neighbour began to take alarm and never left his castle except by an underground passage, which led to a ford on the road to Champigny. And so young Richelieu lay in wait for him at the ford. As Mausson's horse picked its way through the foaming shallows Richelieu bowled a cart-wheel at its fore-legs so that it reared and fell, bringing down its rider. At once young Richelieu and his confederates flung themselves upon the fallen man and did by him as he had done by the other.

Then a hurried farewell to his stern mother and a flight by way of England and Germany to Poland, where the French candidate for the Polish throne, the Duke of Anjou, later to be Henry III, had assembled many Frenchmen. François de Richelieu distinguished himself in the retinue of that subtle, ingenious, and very unsatisfactory Prince; he was employed on difficult missions; he was the first to inform Anjou of the death of Charles IX, he accompanied him on his adventurous flight from Poland, and securely in favour with the new King reached France, where he achieved a career of increasing eminence, becoming Grand Prévôt of France and Knight of the Order of the Holy Ghost. This vendetta murderer seems to have retained a character of his own even in the effeminate court of Henry VII with its serenades and its *mignons*; he is described as a strict and pious Catholic, a mild and respected administrator of his estates, a man of clear and quick intellect. At the same time the deed to which he had been incited in his youth by his mother seems to have weighed heavily upon him; his melancholy temper made him a solitary; people called him "Tristan the Hermit." This man was the father of the great Cardinal. To one principle he remained constant through every vicissitude: the principle of kingship. He did battle for Henry III wherever and whenever there was need for it; he arrested Jacques Clément, the King's murderer, and conducted the exemplary and penetrating interrogation of the criminal which has been preserved for us. After that, the position became somewhat difficult for Catholic paladins of the defunct monarch; were they to serve the heretic, Henry of Navarre?

Richelieu's father did so; he stuck to the King of France; whether Catholic or Calvinist, no matter, he was the King. And Henry IV rewarded him; he confirmed him in his office and dignities, and made him his companion-in-arms in the subjugation of his kingdom. Together they besieged Paris and fought the Spaniard. Richelieu's reputation and influence went on increasing until on July 10, 1590, a violent fever cut him off from his forceful activities in the thirty-second year of his life.

François de Richelieu had married young, when he was eighteen, the fifteen-year-old bourgeoise daughter of a member of the Paris Parlement, Suzanne de la Porte. His elder brother, who had to uphold the rank of the family, was then still alive, and as the younger brother he could allow himself more freedom in the choice of a wife. He seems to have made his choice out of inclination, but the connection opened a path for him into the influential sphere of the Paris legislature, while the prospect of a rich inheritance must have been tempting. An apparent prospect only—for disappointment soon followed. When François de Richelieu died his family found themselves in such severe though temporary embarrassment that they had to sell the chain of his Order so that he might be given a burial befitting his rank. They were not exactly poor, but the deceased had been speculating, there were many houses to be kept up, some of the estates were mortgaged, and the King had always to intervene with ample gifts of money when affairs grew too complicated. The lot of the young widow was a hard one; winter and summer she had to live with her stern mother-in-law in one of these tense and constricting relationships that are based upon mutual interest, together with her five children, of whom the eldest, a son, was ten, and the youngest a daughter of three. Neglected estates, deep in debt, an uncertain income, perpetual danger, and daily and hourly that haughty old woman with the sharp, contemptuous, inquisitorial eye. A situation that recurs time and again in the works of French writers, who have divined the intense force and toughness of passionate natures constrained by the petty makeshifts of a narrow daily round, a force which often breaks out later to direct great affairs in the outer world. Richelieu's mother has been described for us by contemporaries as a woman of clear understanding and tranquil but iron will, who inflexibly set her whole energies on the reclamation and increase of the family resources and the careers of her children; yet a poet who knew her compared her to a dove, praising her gentleness, kindness, and purity, qualities for which the uncanny Cardinal deeply reverenced her all her life; indeed, his feelings towards her always showed that deep, warm, intimate affection, betraying an inner tenderness, of which Bismarck, born in similar social circumstances, was later to say that only those who had been tenderest in their youth could be fashioned into real hardness by life.

Richelieu was a weakly child; as an infant he was not expected to survive; he nearly cost his mother her life and health; and during his existence he himself was never free from the fits of fever which afflicted him from birth. Mother and son were bound to each other in a strange and secret way by life, sickness, and the peril of death. Illness and the sense of brief mortality were to be driving forces in nerving the Cardinal to effort, while the constant dangers of the time were to steel him. Not a year of his early life was passed in peace; the waves of war and plague broke right against the frowning walls of the family castle, and to the hardships of daily existence was added the strain of the silent, implacable struggle between mother and grandmother. Richelieu was haunted by violent headaches, and nervous disturbances of an epileptic nature appeared after periods in which his faculties were heightened to the utmost pitch. One of his sisters died insane, one of his brothers thought for some time that he was God the Father. Intellectually the young Armand Richelieu was able to grasp whatever was presented to him, with effortless and febrile rapidity. He was educated at home until he was nine; then he was sent to the Collège de Navarre in Paris, that school for princes on whose benches Henry IV had sat; later he attended the Academy under the name of Marquis de Chillon. The first school was neither religious nor military in its system, the second was governed somewhat in the spirit of the present-day English public school, with ideals of self-control and fair play, with a comprehensive curriculum embracing all provinces of knowledge and an emphasis on sport and military science, its aim being to train its pupils for leadership in the King's service. A seminary at which one learned the principles of honour, of style in living, and of elegance. Its director, Monsieur de Pluvinel, Chief Equerry to the King, had very decided views on all forms of address, including the gestures which were proper to a nobleman, the height of his hat, the style of his feathers, the length of his cloak, the manner in which his ruffles should be starched. No doubt the physical courage, the natural daring which distinguished Richelieu were developed during these years.

Henry III had bestowed on Richelieu's father, as a reward for his services, the right to dispose of the Bishopric of Luçon. Jacques du Plessis, a great-uncle of the Cardinal, had been the first member of the family to hold it. A poor diocese, the poorest in France, some people said; still, something could always be made of a bishopric. During his lifetime François du Plessis Richelieu received the small consistorial income; after his death it fell to his widow. Titular representatives, men of straw set up by the family, wore the mitre in the name of M. de Richelieu and his heirs, and for many years the diocese was simply farmed out. The prebendaries of Luçon chafed under this state of affairs. They would rather have done without a bishop, for the diocese had to pay all its taxes regularly without receiving even the most necessary services. So they went to law about it. Suzanne Richelieu, alarmed, set herself hastily to defend her rightful property; she tried to improve the situation, and finally promised that her second son, Alphonse, should hurry through his studies and become Bishop as soon as possible. To clinch the matter, Alphonse was expressly appointed Bishop by the King in 1595. The boy was not yet twelve, but from that date he bore the title. Yet they had reckoned without him; his was a serious, brooding, inwardly tormented, burdened nature, with a painful sense of responsibility; he alternated between periods when he thought himself God the Father and periods of complete self-abnegation. On the day of the investiture he refused to have the mitre set upon his head. He fled where no explanation could be required of him; he became a Carthusian monk.

All Suzanne Richelieu's precautions were nullified; the diocese, it seemed, would be lost to her. Or should she withdraw her third son from the martial career for which his fiery spirit was suited, but not his weakly constitution? Should he be denied worldly ambitions? Would an ecclesiastical career satisfy him? He was adroit, quick, resolute, without sentimentality, ready for anything. In the family council the matter was debated passionately, exhaustively, ruthlessly; Armand Richelieu himself turned the scale by signifying that he was willing to accept.

He was seventeen at the time. At once he flung himself into the study of theology. To attend public courses would mean only a waste of his time, so all by himself he mastered the learning of the Christian Church, working day and night. It was reported that his lamp was to be seen burning into the bright morning hours. This stage of development, the period of acquiring learning with the avid concentration of an eager mind at full stretch, he put behind him at an early age, like so many men of mark. An Englishman, Richard Smith, was his tutor at that time in controversy and apologetics; he had one of the most liberal minds in contemporary theology. Richelieu became an advocate of what was then considered modern philosophy, and demanded an opportunity to conduct an open debate in the Sorbonne. It was refused on the ground that there was no precedent for it. But that was precisely what had attracted him to the idea. Although the Sorbonne refused, the Collège de Navarre permitted the debate, and Richelieu distinguished himself, which was what he was really aiming at. In any case his advancement had to be rapid, for there was no vacillation in his character and the diocese was at stake. In 1603 the family's representative in the episcopal function was ordered by Parlement to devote a third of the income of the diocese to the repair of the cathedral and the bishop's palace. Two of the canons had made a special journey to Paris, and the position of the deputy, the unconsecrated bishop, became untenable. Besides, from October 1604 all episcopal documents were being signed in the Name of N— de Richelieu, as if the family were still hesitating between Alphonse and Armand. Something had to be done. At the end of 1606, without waiting for examination results or acedemic status, the Abbé Armand de Richelieu, five years before attaining the canonical age, was solemnly appointed Bishop of Luçon. Simultaneously Henry IV applied for the necessary dispensation from Rome, without which the young Bishop could not be consecrated. Richelieu had an influential advocate with the King in the person of his elder brother Henri, who was attached to the Court: a lively and generous spirit, who brilliantly squandered resources where Armand, the cool and stubborn calculator with his realization of the perils of life and the long difficult road he had to tread, husbanded them with the utmost care. Armand never ceased to help his family, but always presciently, constructively, in accordance with a clear plan. Later, when he had attained mature powers of judgment, the Cardinal grew faintly contemptuous of Henri's goodness of heart; it was too easy, too cheap to indulge one's kindness in that manner. Meanwhile, Henri Richelieu lived gaily at the gayest Court in Christendom, and he introduced his clever young brother to the great King, who at once took the youth's measure and was amazed at what he perceived. Henry IV wrote to his Ambassador at the Vatican that Armand du Plessis Richelieu had not yet reached the canonical age for the dignity of a bishopric, but he was certain that his gifts and his deserts more than compensated for his youth; indeed that great things were to be expected of him. The monarch had a sure eye for men of quality.

While the Ambassador at Rome was furthering the matter, Richelieu attacked his studies again and brought them to a triumphant conclusion. Then, suddenly impatient of the slowness with which the Vatican was proceeding, the young priest mounted into the saddle and himself set out for Rome.

At that time Spanish was the cosmopolitan language; people of consequence spoke Spanish everywhere just as they spoke French in the eighteenth century and the beginning of the nineteenth century. There was an international ruling class with Spanish manners which maintained its contacts even in the most violent European crises, and could take the real measure of any situation, unlike the bourgeoisie, which, within the confines of its national prejudices, was prone to blind dreams of love and hatred involving cruel illusion.

In Rome Richelieu learned certain crucial things: to take the long view, to be humble, to wait silently for the sudden, belated chance of a great achievement. He learned to contemplate and to read the face of Europe, to understand its laughter, its anger, its thoughtful absorption; the proud countenance of the Spaniard, accustomed to rule, with its own scale of expressiveness, ranging from the most complete indifference and distant coldness to that uncanny contraction of the brows at the unforeseen moment when cruelty, dark and fanatical, breaks out; the Italian, a dramatic contrast between fine proportion of feature and lack of humour, beautiful candour and sudden reserve, a fluctuation between the lordly and the servile, the intimate and the aloof, adroit in everything except a jest; the German, so manifold in appearance, and yet bearing the same fundamental stamp of exaggerated assurance, a swagger arising from utter lack of sureness about one's place in the world, quick to take offence and quick to forgive, incomparably lofty in inspiration as if haloed in music, or else dull and pedantic as if turned out by the dozen, without the grace of manners, of watching silently and protectively over the world of feelings, impelled rather to expose all feelings in the market-place and to believe that distinctions, categories, names are merely empty wind.

Richelieu came into close contact with the great Cardinals of Rome. He learned to master his natural impatience, and saw that the man who could learn from life came off victorious while the man who tried to impose himself upon it lost. To put on a mask became his aim, and behind the mask to reach with iron concentration for whatever was deemed needful. So he learned Spanish, and spoke nothing but that language. He astonished everyone; there was not the slightest danger of his being overlooked. He was on the spot, and he had to be reckoned with. A brilliant theologian, forcible in argument with instances drawn from an inexhaustible memory, and yet hardly more than a child! The Pope himself, Paul V, so difficult of access for others, always kept an open door for the young prelate. This Pontiff went to remarkable lengths in the confidences which he entrusted to the tact and discretion of the young bishop; he spoke to him of his concern about the private life of Henry IV: the man surrendered himself to every temptation of the flesh, though he was newly emerged from the gravest spiritual errors; it was much to be feared that his lax conduct must soon make him indifferent to religion again. Richelieu defended his King so happily that the Holy Father ended the conversation with the playful quip: "Henricus Magnus armandus Armando."

There was no lack of envious enemies. Too much fuss was being made over the young Frenchman. Yet the fact that he repeated word for word to the Pope a sermon he had heard several days previously astonished listeners less than the improvisation which he then delivered upon the same text.

But the result he had hoped to secure from his journey was granted him before his clandestine enemies could undermine his position. "Aequum est ut qui supra aetatem sapis infra aetatem ordinetur." In short, Richelieu received the dispensation. The assertion of his opponents that he produced a false baptismal certificate still remains a subject of controversy. He had not yet reached his twenty-third year.

As bishop he appeared in Paris before the college of examiners, answering their questions with his head covered. His thesis bore as its arrogant motto the words of the Scripture: "Quis erit similis mihi?" Yet he justified them. Both the examiners and the audience stood amazed before the completeness of his knowledge, the precise force of his reasoning.

For the moment he did not leave Paris. But the unceasing strain had overtaxed something within him and drawn too deeply on his reserves; a violent fever, the fever of his childhood, broke out again, and it seemed as if an early death were beginning to announce itself in the frail body that was kept going only by will-power. Severe headaches tortured him almost unceasingly, and medical treatment only worsened his condition; but as soon as a respite set in, Richelieu turned his attention to the outside world again; he preached and filled the church with pious worshippers; he was welcomed at Court, where he attached himself to the influential Cardinal du Perron; the King prophesied a great future for him, and never referred to him except as "My bishop."

Yet from all this the young prelate suddenly fled into the provinces, into the poorest, meanest bishopric of the whole kingdom, as everyone he knew was never tired of telling him. He was at the end of his strength, at the end of his financial means, and what was most important of all, nobody had any idea of it; he held out to the last as if everything were in the best of order. Borrowing a four-in-hand carriage from a friend, he set out in the middle of winter, shaken with fever, guided by an infallible instinct that now was the time to lie low, to disappear, to break off while he was at the zenith of a fresh and unflawed reputation. He reached Luçon in the middle of December.

During his stay at Luçon Richelieu never left out of his calculations the possibility of a political career. It is significant that until recently he was credited with the authorship of a treatise in which a busy man of affairs considers theoretically the art of self-advancement among the great and powerful. "Maxims on the manner in which I should conduct myself at Court" is the title of this memorandum.

In the first year of his episcopal activity Richelieu had little time for idle speculation. His work of reorganization was comprehensive and successful. Besides administering his diocese he occupied himself with theology; he compiled a simplified catechism, of which one passage is worth mentioning. To make clear the omnipotence of God, he wrote: "A sovereign King in France has no peer, and everyone who approaches him is his subject; but God is the sovereign King of the world; there is no one to be compared to Him; He is unique by His nature." A clear and unequivocal creed, opposed to all Jesuitical casuistry, seems to have been Richelieu's aim and belief.

It is worth noting that during these quiet days at Luçon he kept in touch with all the great theologians of his time. The first worth mentioning is the Abbé of Saint-Cyran, Duvergier de Hauranne, the great Jansenist. Richelieu often visited the Bishop of Poitiers, and it is reported that he loved to carry on weighty theological arguments with Saint-Cyran, who was a frequent guest of the Bishop's; the result of these discussions is contained in polemical works of that time directed against the Protestants. By Saint-Cyran, who was a friend of Jansenius, Richelieu was well initiated into the traditions of the anti-Lutheran school. But Jansenism, with its insistence on the inner life which tended to an extreme tension destructive to the equipoise of Catholic Christianity, was not for Richelieu. He felt in it a renunciation of the world; this was a road that led no farther.

It was quite otherwise with the great Bérulle. Not until the later years of his stay at Luçon did Richelieu meet this man, the founder of the Oratorium, who was an impetuous and successful fisher of men as well as a strong, unbending theological personality; we shall hear a great deal more of him.

Already as a young man, Bérulle had had influence at Court and enjoyed the confidence of Marie de' Medici; and probably it was not without other intentions that Richelieu invited him to open a seminary in his diocese. Richelieu's environment was very much in opposition to Bérulle's ideas; these Gallican bishops on the road to Jansenism, these English theologians and Capucin priests were no admirers of the dogmatic, clear-minded, profoundly French priest whose ideas chimed with so much that Richelieu was to accomplish. Nevertheless it was not Bérulle's opponents but Richelieu who prevailed; at the end of his term of office at Luçon, after 1611, the Oratorians were to settle there and found their second establishment in France. Most important of all, Bérulle helped the young bishop in his rise to power; after the death of Henry IV it was he who was to introduce Richelieu into the most intimate circle of Marie de' Medici.

But to another of his acquaintance Richelieu remained faithful, the most curious figure in all his circle and the most mysterious, a man whose silent influence was to help in shaping comprehensive European decisions, a Capucin monk who became known as "Richelieu's grey Eminence," Father Joseph. The name of this monk, born in Paris in 1577, was François Leclerc du Tremblay; he was some eight years older than Richelieu. Like his great master, he had once been destined for a military career, but against the wishes of his family had decided to enter the Church. When Richelieu met him he was a provincial of the Capucins. A powerful imagination was united in him with an ice-cold intellect. He was a man of action, and something of an adventurer. The most remarkable thing in him was his knowledge of mankind; whenever he encountered anyone, even for the first time, he met his man with a smile that was like a sudden glow of recognition and appraisal.

Many of these spiritual friends of Richelieu were genuinely devoted to him. But he remained cautious in returning the feeling; courageous as he was, he was timid in friendship, fearing disappointment. In time he was to forsake these friends of his youth, these men who had early recognized his greatness and his powers and had founded hopes on what they knew of him. In those early days a common religious zeal united them all, yet for Richelieu it was never more than a cloak for other ends. These Gallicans, Jansenists and Catholics—the word "Catholic" had at that time a particular significance—certainly raised Richelieu to power; but once he achieved it he was to turn his back on them and ally himself with the Protestants; whenever he found it expedient he was to deny his old friends, to betray them to exile and imprisonment, to send them even to their deaths at the bidding of political necessity, which meant for him, too, Destiny.

CHAPTER III

DEATH OF HENRY IV

In the years 1607 and 1608 Henry IV began to see the fruits of his leadership. He acted as mediator between Venice and the Pope. He concluded an alliance with the Swiss Confederacy and the Grisons. He gave energetic support to the Dutch, signed treaties with the German Protestants, and negotiated with the Duke of Savoy about the acquisition of Lombardy.

His Finance Minister, Sully, had already paid off two hundred millions of State debt, initiated public works, reduced taxation, and yet increased the State's resources by thirty-five millions (about a hundred millions according to present-day standards). Roads and canals were constructed and great companies founded for the improvement of arable land, while industry was making rapid strides. The manufacture of silks dates from that time, of Gobelin tapestries, of faience, and the making of blown glassware. French influence was increasing overseas; a Consulate was set up in Agadir; Canada was colonized and Quebec founded. It looked as if the time had come for reaping the rewards of great statesmanship.

But on March 25, 1609, an apparently insignificant event occurred which was to prove a disaster for France and for the whole course of European policy: Johann Wilhelm of Cleves and Jülich died. There were many claimants for the succession, first among whom stood the Elector of Brandenburg, Johann Sigismund, son-in-law of Marie Eleonore of Cleves, Duchess of Prussia and elder sister of the deceased. Who was to arbitrate? The Hapsburg Emperor? Was it not to be feared that he would exploit the involved situation on behalf of his friends, or even secure the succession for himself? In any case, Henry IV perceived in this Cleves affair the long-awaited opportunity for strengthening his alliance with the Protestant princes of Germany against the Hapsburg, and proceeded to act as energetically as if his own interests were at stake. Bongars, his chief agent in Germany, he sent to Berlin to further an anti-Hapsburg policy with all the resources he could command. He himself announced that he was going to raise an enormous army, and at the same time threatened to withdraw altogether if Berlin did not stand firm. This sudden sharpening of a policy long and prudently shaped towards that end has been often ascribed by French historians to a private motive well beneath the dignity of these events and of the monarch who directed them, a late-kindled passion of Henry's which Bassompierre, who was intimately concerned in it, described towards the end of his life in his reticent and sober fashion.

This last love-affair of the ageing King happened as follows. Charlotte de Montmorency, daughter of the great Conné-table, made her appearance at Court at the age of fifteen, and among the many admirers of her beauty Bassompierre gained the preference. The King, with the suddenness that character-ized his passions, fell completely in love with the charming young creature, just like David on seeing Bathsheba, and in his obsession begged Bassompierre to retire from the lists, which Bassompierre did. At once the King married the girl to the Prince de Condé, whose mis-shapen figure seemed always to be lurking in waiting behind the throne, and from the day of the wedding attempted to win her for himself. But he had reckoned without Condé's pride. This Prince, so ill-endowed by Nature, tried to keep his wife and took her away to his château at Valéry. An order to return immediately followed him, and now the situation became dangerous; Condé must bend or break; he decided therefore to flee over the border. He crossed into Flanders, where he claimed the protection of the Archduke Albert and of Clara-Isabella-Eugenia, Governor of the Netherlands under Philip III of

Spain. The Archduke behaved with discretion; he offered his services as a mediator, but refused to deliver up the young couple even under the most urgent pressure from Henry, who was beside himself with rage to discover that his authority did not extend to the gratification of his desires. Very soon Condé began to feel that even Brussels was no longer safe for him and fled to Milan, where Fuentes was in command, a declared enemy of France. But it was not Condé the King wanted, it was Condé's wife. He attempted to kidnap her from Brussels and failed. Still he would not give up; he forced the Conné-table Montmorency to summon his daughter back to France by virtue of his paternal authority. Montmorency wrote to the Arch-duke, who answered that he could not take any steps without permission from the lady's husband, unless she were divorced.

That the King now wished to revenge on Spain the agonies he was suffering is a romantic view of the situation, popular in the last century. Yet it is possible that he really had made up his mind to risk everything on a throw against the Spanish Monarchy under pretext of supporting the Brandenburger, and to risk it precipitately, he who was usually so prudent and such a genius at biding his time. It was as if he felt the shadows lengthening and uneasiness growing upon him; he saw Cleves and Jülich, these rich provinces, in the hands of the Hapsburgs and the Hapsburgs of Spain and Austria dominating the lower Rhine, menacing Holland. In face of these possibilities Henry was bound to seek his natural allies among the Germans of the north.

He had had a long time of peace. Except for a brief clash with Savoy in 1602, he had avoided conflict of any kind through a policy of extreme prudence. And now in 1609 there came this sudden and radical change. Sully interpreted the change in one of these fantastic speculations of his that pro-vided the spiritual counterpoise to the sober practicality of his daily life; he wrote that Henry had entered into a secret understanding with various great States of Europe in order to bring about a revolution in world affairs. Nothing less was contemplated than the annihilation of the Hapsburgs, the final expulsion of the Turks from Constantinople and from Europe, the rehabilitation of Christianity in the form of a great League led by France, which was to overshadow and supplant the Holy Roman Empire. Into these words Sully put the day-dreams of France. Yet there had never been any such understanding. Henry was acting entirely alone; England and Holland as well as Venice had expressly declined to take any part in the adventure. The war which was being prepared concerned only Cleves and Jülich, a position of decisive strategic importance for France in her struggle against Spanish encirclement. And in France it was an unpopular war, being waged, people said, for the Protestants and against the Church; there was little understanding of the campaign's vital importance; no one backed up the King, who was haunted by the fear of not being able to finish his task, of having to leave it to other and feebler hands; the fear that waylays ageing men. He was wrought up and bitter, suddenly finding the will of his people set against him. And their blind, unconscious will found an instrument in Ravaillac, a narrow-minded schoolmaster, a cleric of low rank, whose unuttered resentments vented themselves in severe fits of conscience; this gloomy, half-crazy fanatic, in a state of hallucinatory obsession, stole from a tavern the knife which was to murder the King. He carried it about for more than three weeks; he nearly threw it away once, and at another time broke off its point; but then he saw a wayside Calvary with a blood-stained Christ on the Cross and heard soldiers saying that the King was warring against the Pope. Against the Pope, that was to say, against God; so there was nothing for it but to obey his God-given visions and do the deed.

And the queer thing was that the King, as if advancing to meet his fate, was losing his hold on life. He had become terribly restless. He was on the verge of a rash, indeed a hope-less, campaign; he looked suddenly aged, his hair went white, his face was worn, he could not sleep, and while he was awake

HENRY, PRINCE DE CONDÉ

(*From an anonymous portrait*)

[*Cabinet des Estampes, Bibl. Nat., Paris*]

MARIE DE MEDICI

(From the painting by P. P. Rubens)

he was too restless to stay in one spot. To leave the palace, to show himself, put him in a nervous panic. He kept saying that he felt as if there were a dagger at his ribs, he was perpetually shivering as if in a premonition of death; what was to become of his children and of his women? He had fourteen children living, six legitimate and eight bastards. He was now fifty-four, about the age at which so many great men have died. His wife, Marie de' Medici, had burdened his last years with all the weight of an insatiable, quarrelsome and ambitious nature; she was now able to exploit his moments of weakness and to insist on the fulfilment of her selfish wants. After a long resistance, Henry yielded to her urgency and consented to her being crowned, which took place in St. Denis on April 13, 1610. He knew that in case of his death this ceremony would be interpreted as significant, as an indication of his wish to have her made Regent, but he was so exhausted during these days of early spring that he could not fend off irrelevancies to let his real will appear.

On the very next day he pulled himself together and drove out in a carriage with the Duc d'Epernon and other gentlemen to confer with Sully. In a narrow street the way was blocked by several carts, and the runners and footmen scattered to clear a passage for the King. Ravaillac, who had been on the watch at the Louvre gates all morning, was following close behind the wheels of the carriage, pushing his way through the crowd. The King had laid his arm round d'Epernon's shoulder—they were talking together—suddenly Henry broke off in the middle of a sentence; the murderer had leaped into the carriage, glared at him and stabbed him, the second time to the very heart.

It was reserved for the French Revolution to break open and desecrate the tomb of this greatest of the Kings of France. When his peace was disturbed he was found after two hundred years as fresh as if he had just lain down to sleep.

At the time of Henry IV's murder the heir to the throne, his son Louis XIII, was not yet nine years old.

B

33

The first reaction to news of such terrible import was a movement of spontaneous loyalty among the great nobles resident in Paris; it seemed as if in this hour of distress all enemies were to join hands around the young King. The Duc d'Epernon, the general commanding the French infantry, at once ordered out the Guards and the Swiss troops to watch over the Louvre. Bassompierre, the darling of the Parisian populace, rode through the city and harangued the crowds. Sully, on the other hand, shut himself up in the Bastille; he was as if stricken by the news, and surrendered himself to a kind of fatalistic despair.

Among the Princes of the Blood who might be considered for the Regency, Condé, the fair Montmorency's husband, had the first claim; he was still fleeing through Spanish territories but would not now hesitate to return, and it was uncertain what attitude he was likely to adopt to the heir of his dead adversary. Another, the Comte de Soissons, had left the Court in a huff over a question of precedence. The Prince de Conti, who stuttered and was mentally backward, did not count.

There was one body that had enough power and influence to uphold a Regent, the Parlements, that is to say, the members of the justiciary Courts of France, whose office was hereditary and reserved for the upper middle classes. To the Parlement of Paris Marie de' Medici addressed herself with the request that according to usage it should confer the Regency of the Kingdom for the duration of Louis's minority upon her, the Queen-Mother. For form's sake the matter was debated, but d'Epernon pushed into the Chamber, appearing before the President in virtue of his rights as a Duke and Peer of France, to demand respectfully, yet with insistence, that this urgent question be settled immediately. And so the highest Law Court in France, spurred on by the old general of Henry IV, gave its consent to the transference of all power to Marie de' Medici, barely two hours after the death of the great King.

On May 15th Louis XIII, the nine-year-old, held his first

"*lit de justice*," the ceremonial session of the Parlement according to ancient tradition. The Chancellor announced that the appointment of the Queen-Mother as Regent accorded with the will of Henry IV and of the present King, and that the Parlement was merely registering a royal edict. On this argument, Henry's widow owed no debt of gratitude to the gentlemen of the Law; they had done no more than their duty.

The Regent retained for the time being the old Ministers of her husband, Villeroy, Sillery, Jeannin, and the great Sully. She had the officers swear allegiance to her son, and to win over the Protestants, who were deeply troubled by the murder of the King, she confirmed on May 22nd the Edict of Nantes.

But the first important political move was to cancel the warlike preparations against Spain. To think of a campaign in the circumstances, with a precariously unstable régime in charge of a child and a woman, was impossible. Sully strongly advised the immediate dismissal of most of the collected troops. But the promises so solemnly made by Henry had to be kept. Maréchal le Chêtre, the old leader of the League, and Sully's son-in-law, Henry de Rohan, later to be renowned as a leader of the Huguenots, were in command of the army that joined the Dutch in over-running the rich fields of Jülich, which they then handed over, on condition of religious freedom being exercised, to the Elector of Brandenburg and the Count Palatine, who had agreed in 1609 on a joint rule of the province, although they were to part company again as soon as 1613.

Marie de' Medici put an end to Savoy's warlike preparations against Spain by offering to act as mediator while disbanding her own troops on the Italian frontier. Sully circularized the Courts of Europe with a statement of the Regent's intention to refrain from any further action once the Jülich affair was settled.

And so the death of Henry IV ended also his far-reaching political system. Marie de' Medici shed few tears on his grave, and her soft, pampered hands let the reins of State slip almost at once into the grip of favourites. Abuse of power was now the rule. It became only too clear how needful had been the policy of strengthening the royal authority beyond that of the great nobles. For the breath was hardly out of Henry's body before the chief lords of the realm appeared at Court to strike their bargains, offering loyalty or threatening rebellion according to the size of the bribe in sight. The descendant of the Florentine bank magnates paid out money to them, bestowing it wildly and capriciously for the sake of peace. Sully's millions were soon scattered; hardly one of the nobles refrained from netting his share of the spoil.

Condé let fall a few hints of his plans in conversation with the Flemish Comte de Bucquot. He said that together with other malcontents he had formed a League, above all with the Duc de Bouillon, directed towards weakening the royal authority wherever possible. The Queen, he imagined, would put up a resistance, which would provide a pretext for taking to arms. Guyenne, Languedoc, Provence, and Dauphiné would be his for certain; he could count on two harbours and several fortresses. It would be easy enough to let the Spaniards march in. He begged the Flemish Count to inform Spinola of these plans and ask him what he thought of them.

Marie de' Medici paid out money, shut her eyes and paid out more; it was her sole recourse against high treason. Palaces, domains, and rents were lavished away and colossal private debts were squared, while all provincial governors were assured that their offices should be hereditary. From château to château the news went flying that the power of the Kings was over and the time of the great nobles at hand. The divisions among the feudal chiefs themselves afforded the sole prospect of some relief from the danger. The Lorrainers, for instance, the Guises, who had gained more than anyone, set up to be protectors of the Regent. And there was no clear objective, no programme; none of the ideas informing this revolt of the feudal vassals become widely popular. Townsfolk and countryfolk alike desired only peace and security; no united front was organized. Conti, who had allied himself to the Guises by marriage, was opposed to his brother Soissons, and there was nearly a battle in the streets of Paris between Soissons' men and the partisans of the Guises. All these powerful nobles kept their own sturdy and well-armed private troops. Yet whatever their feelings towards each other, in one sentiment they were united, in their hatred of Sully. Sully was the great man of yesterday, a standing reproach to the lesser men of the present; "the best head in France," he was called, but in that head of his were ideas completely opposed to the existing régime; he offered a stubborn resistance to every-thing that was taking shape, and he was as much of a nuisance by virtue of his undeniable prestige as because he desired to do the impossible, namely, to put back the hands of the clock. Besides, he was a danger in practice as well as in theory, for he had great influence with the Huguenots. He was at odds with the half of France, and his autocratic method of adminis-tering the finances out of his head gave occasion for slanderous rumour. In these days of seething disaffection, when the millions he had collected were being squandered, he showed no discretion whatever; he hectored the nobles and pressed them hard, he trod violently on the corns of his colleagues in the Ministry. It was decided to get rid of him.

The course of foreign policy soon provided the opportunity. Sully took it very hard that all his great master's far-reaching plans should be now sacrificed to a feeble policy of connivance and expediency. And when the Duke of Feria arrived in Paris, as an envoy extraordinary of His Catholic Majesty, to bring condolences to Louis XIII and congratulate him on his accession, Sully suffered agonies, old Huguenot as he was, especially when he observed with what deference the Regent treated this representative of the Hapsburgs, with what honours she received him and what negotiations she opened with him. The talk was all of marriage; Henry IV's eldest daughter, Elisabeth of France, was to marry the heir-presump-tive to the Spanish throne, while Louis XIII was to marry the youngest Infanta. Over the question of precedence the

discussion grew warm, for Marie insisted on her son's marrying
the eldest Infanta, and threatened, if her wish were not granted,
to give the Spanish prince merely her youngest daughter in
marriage. But apart from this somewhat baroque idea of self-
importance, her attitude was one of deference to the Spanish
alliance which meant so much to her. Sully threw his whole
authority into the scales against any such policy of friendship
with Spain. For him it meant abandoning the heroic aims of
the old tradition, of his great King, in favour of an easy-going
régime allowing private individuals to enrich themselves
without limit. He had been accustomed to speak his mind
freely and to translate his opinions vigorously into practice,
for Henry had known how to value him, but now Villeroy
and the Duc d'Epernon, the latest addition to the Queen's
Council of Ministers, ignored him completely. It was with
Condé that they allied themselves, and with Soissons, who
had been reconciled to Condé by Bouillon; to rub Bouillon
up the wrong way was inadvisable, since he was as much a
prince of the Empire as a vassal of France, and from his stronghold of Sedan could always call up German assistance. Sully
lost all sense of security and tendered his resignation to the
Regent, doubting even at the last moment whether she would
dare to accept it in view of his distinguished services to France;
but then he withdrew in high dudgeon, a bitter witness to the
greatness of a past age which he felt would never return. The
rising tide of Catholic influence was also against him. Ugobaldi,
the Papal Nuncio, and Father Cotton, the King's confessor,
were doing all they could to ensure a purely Catholic policy,
working against the Reformation and for a close understanding with Spain. Yet still more important in the circumstances
was the influence exercised by two favourites of the Queen-
Mother.

An Italian called Concini and his wife, who had adopted
the great Florentine name of Galigai, had become indispensable
to Marie de' Medici. Eleonora Galigai, a foster-sister of the
Queen, a small, adroit, yellow-skinned, dried-up person,

completely dominated the silly vanity and pampered indolence of her mistress. The Queen-Mother could not do without her, she was always at hand, conversant with the most trivial intrigues, half a lady's maid and half a maid of honour, and as soon as Henry IV died she began to exercise a most pernicious influence upon affairs. In his lifetime Henry had regarded these two creatures of the Queen's with testy impatience. Concini had arrived in France to escape from his creditors in Florence; a good stroke of business for him, since Marie, for his wife's sake, both provided him with money and bought him the Marquisate of Ancre, together with the lordships of Péronne, Roye, and Montdidier. He was soon the centre of an ultramontane coterie, and no one could reach the Queen's favour except through him. Richelieu has left it on record that Concini was not entirely an upstart adventurer. He had a programme, says Richelieu; "of course, office and honours and wealth for himself in the first place, but after that: power to the royal house, downfall of the feudal nobles, and above all the acquisition of Lorraine." In order to get Lorraine, it is true, he was willing to purchase Spain's benevolent neutrality by abandoning the rest of France's ambitions.

From the beginning the Concinis were hated by all classes. The "programme" adduced by Richelieu in their favour was not taken into account by their contemporaries, who bitterly resented, as usual, all appearance of undue favouritism, not to mention external peculiarities such as the Italians' leanings towards astrology and magical arts, their intimacy with Jewish physicians, their free-thinking. A persistent rumour was still going round that if the Jesuits had not murdered Henry IV, the Jewish sects had done it.

It was inevitable that with creatures like these in favour at Court, and the tide of ultramontane influence rising, all the Protestants of France, who were still a powerful force, should feel profoundly uneasy and ally themselves with the rebel nobles. Provincial assemblies of the Protestants were summoned to choose delegates for a general Huguenot congress.

This Congress met at Saumur and was attended by all the great Protestant nobles, including Bouillon, Villeroy, Sully, and the Rohans. Bouillon hoped to be elected President of the Congress, but the delegates appointed Du Plessis-Mornay. There were very definite grievances formulated by the delegates. The Edict of Nantes should be restored to its original form; the Protestant fortresses, which were its guarantee, should be repaired and modernized at the expense of the State; their garrisons should be paid. Sully brought up his own grievance; he said that religious antagonism was solely responsible for his being dropped from the Cabinet and being treated with such ingratitude, a proceeding which violated a fundamental principle in the Edict, that Huguenots should have access to all offices of State. He made an impression on the Congress, but Bouillon at once rose to counter that. Bouillon denounced Sully, saying that his dismissal had nothing to do with religious prejudice but arose simply from the discovery that his hands were far from clean, a fact which could have been established in a public trial. Each of the great nobles, in his fashion, sought to defend the interests of the Court, and, incidentally, his own personal interests, against the claims of the delegates. This split among the Protestant nobles altogether wrecked the Huguenots' attack. Concini knew beforehand what was likely to happen: he got the Regent to return a firm answer to all demands, saying that she reserved her decision. In the end, confused by these intrigues, the majority of those present voted for the dissolution of the Congress and the delegation of all executive action to the provincial assemblies. This meant that every local issue between the Protestants and the Court could be championed directly, without higher intervention, by the Protestant officials of the district, organized in a Provincial Circle. The whole idea of these Provincial Circles was conceived and worked out at that time, chiefly on the initiative of Sully's son-in-law, Henry de Rohan, who for the first time emerged as a national figure. He was then thirty-two, and he was to become the greatest opponent of the centralized Catholic State. Already he was reckoning with the possibility of a long civil war. He embodied the ambitions of the Huguenots and he was to avenge Sully, for he soon over-shadowed Bouillon, that tried old captain. At once he began to exert pressure upon the Court. From the Cevennes to La Rochelle the rumour went round that Bouillon was a traitor to the Protestant cause and that Rohan was the man to get things done. He became the recognized chief of the Party. The Provincial Circles met and announced their demands to the Regent. Marie was alarmed; she began at once to hand out favours and proclaimed an amnesty for all the Protestant revolts that had been breaking out since Henry's death; the whole programme, however, she could not grant, as it ran counter in many respects to various Edicts.

A pro-Spanish foreign policy was Concini's retort to the Protestant threat. During the Huguenot elections for the Saumur congress this radical change in policy had been kept as secret as possible, but when Bouillon's denunciation of Sully made it look as though the first impetus of the Protestants had been checked, Marie de' Medici summoned her Ministers, the Princes, and the chief feudal nobles to a conference in which she confronted them with the fact of a French-Spanish understanding, a defensive alliance between France and Spain, and the betrothal of Louis XIII to the eldest Infanta. The most important and critical of her announcements was that France and Spain were pledged to give each other armed assistance in the event of rebellion breaking out in either country.

The alliance was to extend over ten years, the exact length of time which the Spanish truce with Holland still had to run. In spite of this precaution there was uneasiness in Holland, yet the French could hardly be accused of direct betrayal. Bouillon and Lesdiguières, on hearing of these negotiations, which had been settled between Villeroy and Don Iñigo de Cardenas, could do nothing but accept the situation, yet they emphasized their continued hope that this new policy would not impair the old alliances with the Northern Protestants and Savoy. Condé listened with a gloomy face; the pledge of mutual assistance against rebellion was not very palatable to him. Only the Guises and Montmorency the Connétable welcomed the change as providential. The Regent and Concini were of the same opinion; in fact they felt triumphant. Carnival in that year, 1612, was marked at Court by a profusion of gay and sumptuous festivals to celebrate the success of the new foreign policy, with its guarantee of security at home and its prospect of magnificent connections for the royal house.

But this sense of security was somewhat premature. Rebels pay little attention to considerations of foreign policy; they are fanatical monomaniacs who behave as if nobody existed in the world except themselves.

Concini and the Regent had to spend all their time trying to play off one party of malcontents against another. They made enemies of the Guises in order to placate the more powerful Party of the Princes, as Condé's following was called. Yet Condé was not to be placated; he wanted everything for himself. Besides, the Regent and Concini were not working on parallel lines. Concini had always foreseen the possibility of Condé's coming to power, and he was trying to make sure of a seat in the usurper's future Council. Marie, as soon as she divined Condé's real intentions, fell back at once upon the Guises, smoothing her return with colossal gifts of money, while Concini remained consistently on Condé's side. The Ministers did their best to assure the Italian's final subservience to the Crown. Villeroy, for instance, on behalf of his kinsman, the Marquis de Villeroy, asked for the hand of Concini's daughter. Concini consented to the match, but stuck to Condé all the same. At this point, while Marie was vacillating again and the Guises and d'Epernon felt that they were again being fooled, dissension broke out among the Ministers themselves. The situation now seemed ripe to Condé for issuing an appeal to the people. It was high time, he thought, to sail into power on the tide of popular passions.

With the other members of his conspiracy he quitted Paris and established himself in the fortress of Mézières.

On February 21, 1614, he published a manifesto in which he reproached the Government for allying itself with Catholic Powers while dishonouring the Catholic Church at home. He denounced the religious dissensions in the Sorbonne, lamented the poverty of the country gentry and the overwhelming burdens of taxation upon the people, fulminated against the colossal sums that were being paid for judiciary offices, and suggested that high treason was not unknown among the Ministers of the Crown. The most astonishing thing about him, as Richelieu comments in his Memoirs, was the brazenness with which he castigated the Regent for the bribes she lavished on the great nobles, considering that he himself had pocketed more bribes than anyone. In conclusion, he demanded the postponement of the Spanish marriage projects and the immediate summoning of the Estates General.

Villeroy was the only one of the Regent's counsellors who showed any courage. Like the President of the Paris Parlement, he urged that the rebels, who were assembled in Mézières, should be at once attacked with a strong force, taken into custody and tried before they could find the time to collect their troops. But Concini had other ideas: he persuaded the Queen that it was necessary to negotiate. He did not want the Regent to become too strong, he did not want an army to be established with perhaps the Duc de Guise at the head of it. Guise must not be allowed to come into power.

And so Marie bought the rebels off. Condé himself received 450,000 livres in cash, and was appointed Governor of Amboise. All the other rebels in his camp were also richly rewarded. The postponement of the King's marriage was agreed to, as also the summoning of the Estates General; it was a complete rout all along the line.

CHAPTER IV

THE GENERAL ESTATES

Peace with the rebels—a bad peace—was concluded at St. Ménehoud. "What is now happening," wrote Sully, "is simply a pact guaranteeing that the rebels will get millions and lordships and fortresses whenever they want."

Feeble as the Regency was, it was still living on the savings accumulated by Sully, now under suspicion of embezzlement. And it must be admitted that in spite of the many complaints which were to be raised in the Assembly of the Estates the people in whole tracts of France were at this time better off than they were to be later under the strict régime of Richelieu or Louis XIV. But each generation knows only its distresses and is unaware of its good fortune. The chance of airing grievances, which Condé had suggested, was not to be missed. Yet Condé made a big mistake in assuming that the Estates General would unite all the malcontents of the country behind him. There was no lack of malcontents, but their dissatisfaction was directed against the troublers of their peace, the feudal nobles, who seemed to be heading back towards medievalism. Even the Huguenots, their former allies, had no further use for the nobles after their behaviour at Saumur. Concini had a flair for telling which way the cat would jump; he foretold that the Church, the bourgeoisie, and the petty nobility would carry the day against the great nobles, to the benefit of the Crown.

So the great experiment was tried which was to bring down the Monarchy the next time it was repeated, one hundred and seventy-five years later. In the sixteenth century formal consultation between King and people had proved of great service, but now that the Crown was beginning to identify itself with the State the possibilities of collision were dangerous for the whole social fabric. Everyone wanted an equal voice in State affairs, and there was already something like a feeling that majorities were entitled to prevail.

The conflict that was bound to break out between King and nation was already casting its shadow before it. If the King were to become in the course of this century an absolute symbol of the State, a personification of all its attributes, he could indeed accept advice and hear petitions; but he could not express his wishes save in the form of commands; he could not let anyone dictate to him; the moment he did that a part of the State's authority slipped through his fingers and was lost.

Although Louis had come of age, it was Marie de' Medici who summoned the Estates. This was the last decisive act of her Regency, and it was to make painfully evident the harm that had already been done to the body politic.

In August 1614 she issued the summons. Concini had done everything possible to ensure that only men devoted to the Crown, and above all to the Regent, should be elected as deputies. Loyal country gentlemen, provincial governors, and bishops supervised the voting; and there were more of these loyal subjects than Condé fancied, since Henry's rule had really won the greater part of the nation for the Crown. At first it was considered expedient to hold this assembly somewhere in the provinces, but when no doubt remained that the elections were going in favour of the Court the decision was taken to bring it to Paris.

At the opening ceremony, when the Bishop of Bayonne, the King's Grand Almoner, celebrated high mass, the sermon was preached by Cardinal de Sourdis, Archbishop of Bordeaux, from this text: *Deum timete, regem honorificate*, a text which comprised in one *apte dictum* the whole programme of the next hundred and seventy-five years.

45

So for the first time Louis XIII showed himself to the elected deputies of his realm. Each man saw him, each was able to fix the King's image in his mind and carry it back with him to his distant province. When the figure of the half-grown monarch appeared before the assembly a visible ripple of surprised embarrassment ran along the benches, a sense of disappointment, for all present still had a lively memory of Henry's intrepid freshness in the high, grand style of old Frankish tradition; and now here stood the heir, an awkward, sullen-looking adolescent with a lack-lustre eye and a pallid, prematurely jaded face; the Hapsburg blood, which he had inherited through his mother and which blended so ill with Henry's quick alertness, came out in the heavy thrust of the lower jaw; the mouth had an insolent turn reminiscent of many Medici portraits. It was whispered that the boy was indolent and learned nothing, his peculiarities were almost abnormal, he was solitary and gloomy; nothing enlivened him except wild gallops on horseback through the forest, the hawking of birds and the hunting of deer. There he stood before the assembly, alone under his canopy, and repeated the speech he had learned by rote, a King betrayed from birth, badly reared, improperly fed, already weakened by a course of blood-letting and continuous purging, abandoned to himself and a rabble of lackeys, deliberately kept in the background by his mother and brushed aside by her favourites—still worse, corrupted at an early age by the Italians, out of policy, and initiated into evil habits. Yet he had some kingly qualities, political wisdom, a sense of responsibility, courage in physical danger, an emulous love, not quite free from hatred, for his unattainable father. And all these attributes combined in this heir of France to make a lifelong agony for him, to torment his shy soul, to twist and cripple his nature, to develop that ineradicable mistrustfulness, that gloomy apathy, that weak vindictiveness which characterized him till he died.

Louis is said to have asked what motive lay behind this summoning of the Estates. Was it an idea of his mother's, to create a diversion or to get her policy sanctioned, above all, her foreign policy? It was explained to him that Condé was at the bottom of it. This misshapen prince was to keep cropping up in the life of Louis XIII; there was something insidious about him, and an element of undying malice against the royal house. Behind Condé was ranged all the effective opposition; the feudal chiefs, the Protestants, the opportunists, disappointed careerists and adventurers who are always to be found in any movement that threatens to upset an existing order, and who invariably seek to undermine it again once they have helped it to victory. The pamphleteers who were now defaming the memory of Henry IV were legion.

Condé was firmly convinced that he and his supporters would carry the elections. He was mistaken, and Henry de Rohan, the great Huguenot leader, had warned him of his mistake. "What can you promise the electors, what can you give them?" asked Rohan, "people cast their votes only where there's something to be got!" It was true. The Crown could be munificent with what was left of Sully's accumulations, with benefices, posts, offices, honours, tithes, exemptions, and privileges—what had Condé to offer, he who was himself hungry for more? The Regent's Italian adviser, Concini, must have lent a grateful ear to the clamour for the summoning of the Estates, since he knew what the result would be. The success of the Government's policy roused among the rebels a storm of rage and disappointment which is recorded in the fiery pamphlets of that time. The elections were a swindle, the electors were bribed, the assembly was illegal and its measures null and void; that was what the pamphleteers shouted. But nothing was achieved by such abuse; the thing was to take tactical advantage of the Estates to make as many difficulties for the Crown as possible. The frightful wars of religion were still not far away, and it would not take much to rouse people's passions again. The obvious line for the Opposition was to try for a split on religious issues.

So the Estates General of 1614 were again to bring ecclesiastical questions into the forefront of debate. From all the struggles of the sixteenth century the Church had emerged into the seventeenth century with increased powers. In France it was led by a kind of directing committee composed of the Cardinals Joyeuse, Sourdis, La Rochefoucauld, and Du Perron. Sourdis and Du Perron were forcible personalities, Joyeuse was an invalid, and La Rochefoucauld seemed mediocre beside the others; the really strong man was Du Perron. He was a Swiss-born Norman, a self-made man said to be the son of a Protestant pastor. Ambition had brought him to Paris, within the orbit of the Court; in Paris he became a Catholic convert and entered a religious Order. He was one of those full-blooded, open-minded priests whom the religious wars threw up; he was a poet, and so won the favour of the last of the Valois, which brought him rich rewards; he seems to have been feared in controversy for his frank, often severe and always ready-witted pen; he was no spoil-sport, but a lusty companion who liked good eating and drinking, carried Rabelais around in his pocket, and called Montaigne "the breviary of all right-thinking people." In general, a wary, shrewd, crafty Norman peasant, in many respects like a Swiss. In religious disputation he stood like a rock, giving way not one inch. Henry IV appreciated men of that kidney, men with clear minds and vigorous bodies, and he used Du Perron for his many negotiations in Rome. Du Perron had not an intellect of a high order, but he was trustworthy and solid. In Rome he observed the great power of the Papacy, and attached himself to its service, coming back to France as an ultramontane. He was as if created by Providence to be the spiritual adviser of Henry's widow. And he had many disciples among the younger clergy; one can say that there was a Du Perron school.

This Du Perron group was in evidence from the very first session of the Estates; it was making a strong bid to dominate the conduct of affairs. And as Du Perron had singled out Richelieu, with a sure eye, from among the young bishops, the Bishop of Luçon was one of the first to speak. Every intervention of Richelieu's attracted attention for its acuteness and lucidity, not to mention the skill of its presentation, which made it appear as if he had done nothing but practise parliamentary dialectic. The session had barely started before Richelieu was presiding over a delegation which had to confer with the Third Estate.

Indeed, the ecclesiastical offensive was launched so powerfully that the Court grew uneasy; it had not been intended that the spiritual fathers should have things all their own way and usurp the influence that should have accrued to the Regent and her supporters.

How were the clergy seeking to dominate the Estates? Through a question of procedure, which in all deliberative assemblies is of the first importance and is usually quite overlooked by outsiders. The clergy were proposing that several main questions of theirs should be discussed one by one, the statutes arising from each to be laid then at once before the King, receive his sanction and pass immediately into law. In this manner positive results could be achieved in a very short time, which was hardly the intention of the Court.

Now, in the assembly the clergy had 140 representatives, the nobles 132, and the Third Estate 192. What became clearer from day to day was the sharp conflict of interests between class and class, a conflict which gradually overrode religious differences and relegated them to the second place, in this respect completely reversing the prevailing attitude in the assembly of 1484. Much that seemed crucial to the clergy, requiring special facilities, seemed to the other estates either of secondary importance or inopportune.

The clergy desired first and foremost to have the Council of Trent's resolutions promulgated, which was all the more important to them as France was in any case belated in subscribing to this great alliance of counter-reformation forces. The clergy's line in general was to secure the greatest possible independence of action for the Church. But the nobles were chiefly interested in their pensions and tax-exemptions, as well as in keeping down the new class of nobles by letters-patent, who came from the upper bourgeoisie. The Third Estate was divided against itself, for although it was willing to increase its prestige as a whole, the petty bourgeoisie and the farmers were inclined to side with the nobles in keeping down the upper bourgeoisie, which was fighting for a hereditary right to its titles of office.

Each estate had to present its programme in the form of a memorial, called a "cahier," in contradistinction to the postulates of the Crown, which had the right of priority and were on occasion despatched with speed, unlike the memorials. As for the memorials, whatever their fate in discussion, they might simply be annulled at any time by the dissolution of the assembly. And what the ecclesiastics were aiming at was nothing less than to have their memorial placed almost on an equal footing with the royal postulates, well before those of the other estates.

The most remarkable thing about this assembly of 1614 was its complete lack of any community sense. Richelieu's almost fanatical obsession with the need for a centralized State authority received a great impetus at that time from his observation of these self-seeking intrigues.

It was the Third Estate that, willy-nilly, had to suffer most attacks from all quarters because of the ambitions of its bourgeoisie. On the very first day of getting down to business, an orator from among the nobility exhorted the King to take cognizance of the difference between true nobles who bore arms and those others of inferior birth who had the arrogance to claim superior rank merely by virtue of their offices. The representatives of the old nobility were of the opinion that the impropriety of such a class rising to power could be checked only by the abolition of the so-called "Paulette," that is to say, the right of the higher civil servants to secure the hereditary transmission of their offices by paying a yearly tax to the State. The Third Estate at once retorted to this class-conscious attack by demanding the suppression of the enormous pensions paid out to the nobles, especially the great nobles.

"Sire," said the speaker for the Tiers-Etat, "the lily is a lovely flower, tall, straight, and white like a stainless conscience: Your Majesty's actions must have the same purity, being kingly, righteous, and merciful. In Your Majesty's childhood you reproved a nobleman for treading on small insects and worms before your eyes; to-day it is not insects who beseech your mercy, but Your Majesty's own people, who belong to you, whose father you are. If you had seen as I have seen in the Auvergne men eating the grass of the field like beasts, Your Majesty's heart would overflow with sorrow. . . . The nobles are asking you, Sire, to abolish the Paulette, to deprive your treasury of the 160,000 livres which your officials contribute to it every year. How frightful to think that in the prevailing misery of the country Your Majesty should pay out during the same length of time five million 660,000 livres in pensions to the nobility!"

Words such as these were unprecedented. The nobles announced that their honour was impugned and that until they obtained satisfaction they would absent themselves in a body from further proceedings.

The clergy now came forward as mediators. Richelieu was entrusted with the mission of persuading the speaker of the Third Estate, Savaron, to resolve the conflict by uttering a formula of apology framed by the young prelate in his own brief style. There is food for meditation in this meeting between the cool and elegant young bishop and the sturdy orator of the Third Estate, the last defender of those medieval rights of the populace which Richelieu was to wipe out of existence.

But these were only preliminary skirmishes. There was an obvious split in the ranks of the Third Estate itself, in which a left wing was forming which sided with the nobles in their attack on the ambitious upper bourgeoisie; a straw showing how the wind would blow later on in the prologue to the great French Revolution.

This dispute over the Paulette is a symptom of many later developments. It stood, as it were, at the turning-point between the theocentric hierarchy of the Middle Ages and the anthropocentric mass domination of the future. The classes that were rooted in the medieval system were fighting for their lives against the still formless masses which were to be their masters, while the clergy were seeking to affirm their position as the custodians of eternal values unaffected by Time. What a catastrophe it would be if all these forces were to clash with one another before the State had been made strong enough to withstand the shock!

Yet the strife between class and class, the social evil that was to prove incurable in the course of centuries, was overshadowed in its turn by the great European problem of the One or the Many, the unity of the oecumenical Catholic Church or the division of national feeling. The bourgeoisie, that new class, already ground between the nether and upper millstones, was shaping Nationalism as a bulwark round the monarchy and proclaiming Nationalism as a basis for its own self-assurance, as a value transcending all others. The still amorphous mass of the populace, which in this assembly, for the last time in many years, crept like something blind and formless into the light of the King's mercy, and on the other hand the feudal chiefs, were alike partakers of a heritage reaching beyond the bounds of the nation, the nobles by virtue of their arrogant assurance which made them fancy themselves the peers of anyone in the world, the others as the burdened classes whose burden was everywhere the same, a common bond uniting them to each other.

At first the cleavage between the desire for European unity and the exclusiveness of Nationalism expressed itself in the old form of a quarrel between spiritual and temporal power. This was where the clergy entered the lists against the Third Estate.

Since the Middle Ages the Third Estate, especially the representatives of the law, had propounded the theory that the King held his crown from God alone, and that no power, not even a spiritual power, had the right to interfere with his subjects' allegiance. This doctrine, which contradicted both the teachings of Rome and the beliefs of the Huguenots, the Third Estate now wished to raise to the dignity of a legal statute. All officers of the State, including ecclesiastics, were to subscribe to it on oath before taking office; anyone who opposed it was to be sentenced to death for *lèse-majesté*. The bourgeoisie wished to establish the supreme autonomy of the Monarchy so that they might be on the same footing before the Crown as the other Estates, while avoiding the burden of responsibility by binding everyone alike to complete obedience. In this way, all would be equal before the King, as before God, while each could pride himself on being a member of a powerful nation. It was the beginning of State-mysticism as the expression of Nationalism.

Against this stood the uncompromising Curial teaching of Rome, the supremacy of the Pope. But while in other countries the national revolt against the claims of the Catholic Church had found a vent for itself in the Reformation, in France the workings of the Reformation were incalculably weakened by the existence of Gallicanism, an earlier movement. So the Catholic Church in France was still divided against itself, just as the Third Estate had been divided in the matter of the Paulette. Gallicans and Ultramontanes now split the French clergy into two camps.

The leader of the Ultramontanes was Du Perron, representing an international principle opposed to any assertion of the Crown's sole supremacy. And with this principle the feudal nobility now associated itself—a most enlightening development. Not only for tactical reasons, not only because the clergy had previously backed up the nobles in the matter of the Paulette, but for reasons of simple self-preservation. The feudal nobility, as a class, sprang from the whole Christian system of the Middle Ages, and without that international system would be reduced to a narrow local or a precarious biological significance.

Du Perron insisted that nothing could be more destructive to the Church than this schismatic doctrine of the Third Estate. The priests, he said, would be dragged at a rope's end to execution as martyrs rather than let the supremacy of the Holy Father in Rome be called in question.

But the supremacy of the Pope over the King seemed to the whole of the Third Estate and to the Gallican clergy a dangerous principle which might lead to the darkest deeds; the thought of Ravaillac was in their minds. The death of Henry IV was still too near. A conspiracy to murder him had always been suspected and now was hinted at in open rumour. The real instigators, it was said, were all at large, unpunished. And the monarchy itself, for which defence was needed, was not to be trusted at the moment; there were too many doubtful figures at Court; D'Epernon, the Governor of Metz, might change over any day to the side of the rebel nobles; Concini was a sinister adventurer who had brazenly overturned the foreign policy that guaranteed the future of France. There were Spanish alliances, Spanish marriages, only four years after the death of the greatest of French kings, who had been made away with just when he was going to deal Spain a crowning blow. And the opposition between the Houses of Bourbon and Hapsburg, which the French patriots saw as an inevitable necessity, was now meeting cross-currents from the opposition between Reformation and Counter-reformation; yet the Counter-reformation was entirely a Hapsburg affair in which France could play none but a subservient part.

The question arose now: What did the Regent intend? One could hardly say that the Regent intended anything. She had never understood her husband's plans; she had opposed them obstinately wherever she became at all aware of them. Her mother had been a Hapsburg and she reverenced the Hapsburg blood in her veins. By heredity and inclination she was a bigot, devoted to the Church. All her decisions on foreign policy were influenced by clerical arguments of the following nature: the ancient Church Law of France excluded the children of heretics from succession to the Crown, so that she herself, ruling in the name of a former heretic's son, would get but short shrift from a National church and could depend solely on the Pope's supreme authority, which was alone able to grant the necessary dispensation to legalize her marriage and the succession of her children to the throne. One did not need to be too particular in the choice of arguments to impress her. Besides, in any case, the Ultramontane party was in the majority among the French clergy. The Regent was completely in their power.

In the beginning of January 1615 this Ultramontane majority attempted to get the King in person on their side in the question of Papal supremacy. Condé was in Paris, much disappointed by the course of events in the Assembly but inclined to think that the moment had come for him to fish with advantage in troubled waters. The Gallican clergy and the Parlements regarded him as a danger to the nation; now, he thought, was the chance to win them over. Perhaps he even hoped that they would offer him the Crown. At any rate, before a full assembly of the Estates he announced, in the King's presence, that while the Pope might be spiritually the King's superior, he could not claim superior temporal power. The King must be absolute in his kingdom, entitled to tribute and obedience even if he were no true son of the Church. With indignation in his voice Condé denounced the ultramontane doctrine; it could lead, he said, to the dethronement, even to the murder of a king, to usurpation and the worst of all horrors, foreign domination. A most patriotic speech, yet the patriots gave him no reward for it. Having put on the sheep's clothing of loyalty, Condé was left to swelter in it.

The Ultramontane clergy now tried to get the question expunged from the memorial, to prevent the Assembly from discussing the Church's teaching at all. Abetted by the nobles, they sent deputation after deputation to the King. There were high words between Condé and the sickly Cardinal de Sourdis. The clergy sat in session from the eighth to the fourteenth of

January; during all that time nothing else was debated. The Ultramontane majority was so united, the nobles so resolute, that the Regent grew fearful and herself urged submission to the Church.

The Third Estate was seething with anti-clerical feeling. The desire to have the King's absolute sovereignty legally established, as a foundation-stone for the National State, had taken deep hold of all French patriots. And in its fight for the rights of the monarchy the Third Estate had the Parlements behind it. Later on, under Louis XIV, this loyalty of theirs was to be but ill-requited, for the French Monarchy, having once become a symbol of the State, made the mistake of deriving its authority from the dynasty, from the House of Bourbon, rather than the nation. The prime causes of the French Revolution are to be found wherever one turns in tracing these developments. Yet at this time, in the years 1614–1615, the only consolidated power in the State was that of the Ultramontane clergy. It could not achieve all that Du Perron wanted, but it could be obstructive enough. The Court had to give way in the matter of the King's divine right to absolute rule. On January 19th the President of the Third Estate—it was at once rumoured that he had been bribed— was summoned, together with the Presidents of the twelve District Governments, to the Louvre, where the Regent announced in the King's name that it was no longer needful to pass such a statute, since His Majesty was content to rest the security of his kingdom on the loyal principles expressed by the Third Estate. What should have been forged into an institution was thus reduced to a mere profession of loyalty tendered and accepted.

The Pope, whose Nuncio, Ugobaldi, had done much to achieve this compromise, issued his thanks to the nobles and the clergy, while the greater part of the Third Estate was deeply resentful and full of protest.

But now the clergy seemed in a position to take everything by storm. The Court was resisting the Third Estate's demand that a budget and an account of fiscal revenues should be laid before the Assembly, and here the clergy intervened decisively. One of the speakers made this famous comparison: "The finances are the nerves of the State. As the nervous system lies hidden beneath the skin, even so must the strength or weakness of financial resources lie hidden." With regard to the finances the clergy were not prepared to allow any compromise, and the service they rendered the Court was a fair requital for their victory in the matter of the Papal supremacy. Yet the Court was even more grateful for the solid opposition they offered to Condé in his attempt to suborn the patriots and Gallicans. The clergy were now strong enough to make threats that Henry IV would never have permitted; Cardinal du Perron was already referring to the Protestants as a doomed sect that gained merely a respite from destruction. He was to be proved right.

Only one thing the clergy could not achieve: the promulgation of the Council of Trent's decrees. All over France there was a sullen feeling of resistance to that. The Speaker of the Third Estate said that no decrees of any Council had ever been promulgated by the Assembly, and why should the Council of Trent receive special treatment? Let the clergy themselves begin to order their lives according to the Council's prescriptions.

Tension in the Assembly was daily increasing; there were violent outbursts against the Court; all three Estates were now divided among themselves, for through the machinations of Condé the nobles had lost their first solidarity. Violent words led to deeds of violence, even to murder; a noble in the Regent's service, Marsillac, was stabbed by Condé's men. It was high time to make an end. The closing session was fixed for February 23rd.

Each Estate had now to be represented for the last time by a Speaker, who should summarize the proceedings. The Speaker for the clergy was Richelieu. Presumably the Queen-Mother had suggested him for this honour, since in the course of the debate he had seized many opportunities of parrying attacks on her. Richelieu was the first to take the floor, and his address to the King lasted for an hour. Later he made his secretaries transcribe this speech into his Memoirs, but it contained little save compliments and had no importance except for the fact that it was his first political oration and decisively influenced his career.

What he had to say was prescribed for him. Yet the way in which he said it was entirely his own; his style already had all the trenchant precision of his prime, a precision which was never abrupt but rounded itself in suave and eloquent periods.

"Among all peoples in the world," he began, "from time immemorial, even in the days of false gods, the priests of religion have occupied a leading place in the counsels of sovereign rulers, not only in spiritual but also in worldly affairs." He went on to cite examples, including even the Druids, and then continued: "Yet to-day it may be averred that the Church has been as it were stripped of her honours, her possessions, her authority, that she has been profaned and so profoundly humiliated as to have scarcely the strength to raise her voice in lamentation." This, when the clergy had just given a convincing manifestation of their political power!

But his next argument struck a more positive note: "By their vocation the clergy are peculiarly fitted to hold offices of State. As clergy they are called to be men of a certain quality and to show a certain ability; their office is a warrant for their integrity and discretion, the most necessary attributes for a servant of the State. A churchman is divested of all self-seeking; he has no children to provide for; nothing survives him but his soul, which cannot lay up treasures on earth, and strives only to merit salvation in Heaven." For all these platitudes, which even sixty years later could hardly have been palmed off on any assembly of Frenchmen, Richelieu was merely the mouthpiece; yet he fascinated his audience by the manner of their delivery. On all sides we find evidence that his personality made a strong impression. The way in which he pointed the conventional phrases with irony, the lightness with which he launched his assertions, suggested reserves of force in the speaker.

Still, these rhetorical flourishes—a concession to contemporary taste—were less remarkable than the concise reasoning of the synopsis that followed them, with its undertone of assured mastery. Even in small things there were indications revealing the speaker's character. In his impeachment of the Huguenots, who had broken into a church and profaned the Host, he said: "Huguenots have been guilty of violating a Catholic church, and the actual offenders must be punished, yet there are thousands of Huguenots who are loyal subjects of Your Majesty and not to be held responsible for the deed." Richelieu never indulged in generalizations.

He also touched again upon the question of inheriting judicial office, which was to be handled, he said, firmly yet with discretion. And then he outlined a policy which was like a prophetic forecast of centuries to come. "We must inaugurate the rule of reason," said this Catholic bishop in the year 1615. "Justice has only one native element, that of clarity and integrity. The dictatorial authority of high administrative office must not become a hereditary family possession; all officials become venal when office is bought and sold; and that is a disease which has already brought great empires low. Unnecessary and uneconomic posts are to be abolished; when advancement falls only to the deserving and the idle are punished, good service will never fail to get its reward. The level of general culture will rise again, the finances will be sparingly administered, bonuses cut down, and pensions diminished." (This was a small concession to the Third Estate and a dig at the nobles, especially Condé.) "Here, too, we must be able to call a halt where Henri Quatre would have done so. The arts will flourish again; religion find new life; nobility will once more enjoy rights which it has earned. All the noble blood of the land will be again enlisted in the King's service when the vice of duelling is once firmly put down."

59

(To what extremities of severity was Richelieu to proceed in this very matter!) "The populace will be set free from the oppression of corrupt officials, from the humiliation of suffering injustice, and will be relieved from the frightful burden of taxation that weighs upon it."

And then, unexpectedly, the young bishop turned directly to the Regent, who was listening with pleasure and some astonishment to the comforting optimism of this address.

"The whole of France," the words rang out, "regards itself as pledged to give Your Majesty all the honour which in every age has been accorded to the guardians of peace and order and public security. Your Majesty has already accomplished great things, yet there is no standing still on the path of honour; not to advance, not to surpass oneself is to slip backward."

And so the smooth phrases went on, like music in the ears of the listening Regent. The King was of age, and yet it was to the Queen that the Bishop had addressed himself! And so his career, for the next few years, was decided. The Court rang with his praises. That was the kind of speech one wanted to hear! Especially after having to listen to shocking outbursts from men like Miron, President of the Third Estate, who told the nobles: "Your lives, gentlemen, are passed in reckless gaming, in luxury, in dissipation, in public and private brawling; the ancient glamour of your estate has faded. The mass of the people are groaning drudges who have to labour for everyone, for Throne and Nobles and Church. Even tigers and lions and other wild beasts are not in the habit of ill-treating those who nourish them—how different from our armed nobles! If Your Majesty does not come to the rescue, it may well happen that the scales will fall from the eyes of the poor drudges, and they will see that a soldier is merely a peasant with a weapon in his hand, and" (raising his voice) "it may well happen that a vine-dresser with an arquebuse over his shoulder will suddenly realize that it is his turn to be the hammer instead of the anvil." That was the kind of language heard in Paris, eight years before Richelieu seized the reins of power and postponed for a century the day of realization prophesied by Miron.

How smooth and eloquent were Richelieu's periods by comparison! They fell like balm on spirits troubled by such nightmare threats. Not that Richelieu was unaware of the facts stated by Miron; it was simply that he shrank, his whole life long, from stirring up forces that could not be organized and controlled. He might have said with Goethe: "My nature is such that I find it easier to suffer injustice than disorder."

Whenever he discovered deep-seated evils in the social system he came always to the same conclusion, ultimately an obsession with him, that the sole remedy was the existence of a State strong enough to withstand the perils and shocks of human imperfections when these were no longer controlled by a metaphysical unity. To the achievement of this end it was not permissible to use any and every means, but it was necessary to seize on what was most expedient at the moment. And so in this explosive assembly, which threatened to expose all the miseries that were a legacy from the sixteenth century, Richelieu's one idea was to prevent an unleashing of destructive forces, to preserve the framework of authority, to make possible, even at the cost of human suffering, the creation of a new order. It was a desire for order that obsessed this young bishop who spoke a language so pleasing to the Court.

But the Court had had more than enough of menaces and wished only to see Paris rid of the Third Estate's scowling and sinister faces. On March 24th the King summoned the deputies to the Louvre and informed them that he would abolish the sale of judicial offices, that he would appoint a Supreme Court of Justice, and that he would reduce the list of pensions. That was all, except for some baleful reflections on the Protestants, the majority of whom had allied themselves with the most dubious party in the State, that of Condé.

A melancholy ending to that Assembly which was not to meet again until one hundred and seventy-five years later—

although when it did meet it was to smash up the order of things before which it now had to capitulate. Bitter and disappointed, the deputies trailed back to their provinces, and bitter was the seed they were to sow there.

But the Court breathed freely at last. It was carnival time and a round of festivities began. The *Mercure de France* reported that "to celebrate the happy ending of the Estates-General, it has been decided to stage a ballet which is to surpass in magnificence all that the past has ever beheld, and all that the future may strive to achieve."

CHAPTER V

RICHELIEU'S FIRST TERM OF OFFICE

In no period of Richelieu's life can there be found utterances more shameful and less in accordance with his greatness than in the years after Henry IV's death, when the young bishop seems to have pursued his ambitions with every means, including a self-humiliation which verges on the ludicrous. We must be cautious here; it will not do to accept things at their face value and tell ourselves that genius has to overcome circumstances by any means it can, including the most despicable, and that conscience and honour have to fall silent before the greatness of the ultimate aim. It is certain that Richelieu applied great subtlety to achieve power, including a keen and sure knowledge of men; there was also in his policy a certain contempt for the people of whom he made use; he flung to them on occasion whatever they wanted; he operated by psychological means which he scarcely tried to conceal. His very first encounter with Marie de' Medici was sufficient to inform him that with her he would have to over-simplify and over-emphasize everything. He did so without scruple during her Regency, and also during the Assembly, the months when people first began to talk about him. But his flattery was so open, made almost with an ironical side-glance to the public, that everyone could see what he was at; so that it can hardly be called double-dealing.

Nor must we take him too seriously when he writes to Marie de' Medici in this vein: "I pray to God that He may shorten my life if I may only devote what time I have to Your Majesty, and that He may punish me with every evil except the loss of Your Majesty's favour, if only my sufferings may bring joy to Your Majesty." This is merely an example of the theological rhetoric fashionable at the time, an act of homage coloured by the Catholic assumption that another's sufferings can be redeemed by one's own. By adducing such passages little is achieved; on the contrary they show how questionable the value of such evidence is, and how excessively the written word is sometimes overestimated as historical evidence. Letters are often written to disguise the writer's thoughts, and to reconstruct a character from some fortuitous passage in them is the most senseless undertaking. A historical character can be grasped as a whole only by taking into account the assumptions of the age and the achievement of the man involved; whether that achievement is worked out in deeds or in the precipitation of ideas is immaterial; where some laboriously discovered chance trait is seized upon as if it were a generic one, the vicious analytical method begins its work, and ubiquity of view, the only thing which makes historical vision possible, is lost.

The circumstances which led Richelieu to the immediate circle of the Regent were of a very mixed kind. His political career was to a great extent a natural development. He was the son of a captain of the Guard under Henry III, a "Prévôt de L'Hôtel" and Grand Prévôt of France who enjoyed the special confidence of Henry IV, served him daily and lost his life in his service. His brother Henri had been a privileged friend of the dead monarch; he had occupied a place of special favour at the Court and could count on the particular favour of the Queen; also the fame of the Bishop of Luçon had been spread in Paris by his sermons, and Cardinal Du Perron, out of entirely practical grounds, had supported it with his full authority, favouring and distinguishing the young priest in all sorts of ways. His relations on his mother's side, including Pont-de-Courlay, his brother-in-law, who was at home in the most intimate circles of the Queen, had worked for him. He had owed much, too, he said later, to a distant relation,

LOUIS XIII

(*From the painting by Ph. de Champaigne*)

CHARLES D'ALBERT, DUC DE LUYNES

(*From the bronze bust by F. Rude*)

[*Musée des Augustins, Toulouse*]

Antoinette de Guercheville. But the high clergy in particular were for him: Du Perron, Sourdis, Chasteignier, Gabriel d'Aubespine, the Bishop of Langres, Zamet, Bérulle, and, although he had about this time drawn close to the princes' party, Father Joseph, who worked for him on all sides. The Capucin priest had been the first to recognize his real greatness; later he was to say of him: "I saw that young eagle before he had yet left the eyrie, as he gazed without winking into the sun."

After the rising of the Estates General, Richelieu returned to his bishopric; he resided by choice in his priory at Coussay, where the air was healthier than at Luçon and where there were gardens. He was ostensibly occupied now solely with his ecclesiastical duties, but it was already clear to him that Henry IV's ministers had outlived their hour, including Villeroy, whom he was fond of calling the "petrified colossus," and who had for decades conducted the foreign policy of France as if he were the head of an institution; Sillery, Villeroy's disciple, later to become his rival; Jeannin, whom Henry IV had detached from the League to make one of his councillors; and finally Sully: men who had grown grey, important, and experienced in office, and who in collaboration with Henry IV and in complete subordination to him had been great servants and executives of a great master. But now the reversal of all policy, the complete change in their position, came as a painful surprise to them; what could be done once by raising a finger now required the expenditure of all their energy; where, in Henry's time, they had worked in the fullness of authority, they could do nothing now without risking their freedom or their heads. Jeannin with his dignified, coloured, ample periods, Jeannin who, secure in his office, seemed to radiate contentment and conviction, and, people were fond of saying, was as solid and as full of comforting warmth as the precious furs of office which he always wore, was sadly changed; now every word he spoke rang false, and people laughed as soon as he began his grave and weighty utterances. All these ministers appeared to have suddenly become their own masks; their power had died with the master they had served. Alone among them, Sully suffered from both rage and fear, for he was keenly conscious of the change; he could not bear to see the State treasures he had accumulated being squandered, and he feared the possible consequences of his having enriched himself very greatly in the process; he therefore retired voluntarily while there was still time, and using his son-in-law Rohan as a spear-point took up the fight again in his own way. But his colleagues noticed nothing for a long time; they were abused in all the pamphlets and called "the grey beards"; yet they stuck to office, trying all sorts of abortive innovations—new measures, they called them; but the new style did not suit them; as the months went on they became quite impotent. All this was a sure sign that the times had radically changed, for in ages which go on surviving the old become the most powerful of all.

Already in May 1615 protests made by the Parlement to the Queen-Mother had shown how far the general embitterment went against the illegal power of the Concinis. The Parlement could not have risked so much if it had not known the deep indignation of the people, above all of the Parisians, against these foreigners. Concini was not mentioned by name, but a great deal was said of undeserving persons who had insinuated themselves into the counsels of the Queen, and it was demanded that provincial governorships and high military charges should be given only to Frenchmen and not to foreigners; also reference was made to the too intimate relations between certain influential personages and the representatives of foreign powers. The Parlement gave a warning that, if this were not remedied, the persons to whom these charges applied would be more definitely designated at the first opportunity.

The rich burghers, economically and nationally inclined, thus turned unequivocally against the internationalism of the aristocracy, which already in its extreme manifestations was indistinguishable from a policy of mere adventure; the burghers condemned it as they condemned the squandering of money, the expense of pensions, the craven extrication of the Crown from all its difficulties by money presents, the criminal compliance of the old ministers, and the ruinous powers of Concini; just as they supported on the other hand the Paulette, which benefited their own class.

Up to the beginning of 1615 Concini had worked chiefly for personal enrichment. It was the enormous extent of his riches that now forced him to exploit the State's resources of power for his own protection. How foolhardy he had grown may be judged from his saying that he would essay how far luck could carry a man. What he needed was a province on the French frontier, from which in case of danger he could keep in touch with the outer world. He already possessed several fortified places between Paris and Spanish Flanders; now he demanded the governorship of Picardy, from where it would be easy for him to threaten Paris. The young Duc de Longueville ruled in that province; Concini sent Villeroy to negotiate for his withdrawal. When the old man returned without having succeeded, Concini used the dissensions among the leaderless ministers to drive him from office. In the Queen's presence he called hima traitor. Henry's Foreign Minister proffered his resignation, and retired to his estates; then he repented and returned again, tried to justify himself, to excuse himself, and lost all authority. Concini had gained more than if he had forced him, like Sully, to retire for good.

Meanwhile Concini had acquired a new enemy in Longueville, who began to hatch a conspiracy against him, with the assistance of Bouillon and Mayenne. Condé at once perceived the advantages of the situation: Concini's unpopularity must win for any conspirator the support of the burghers and the people. So in spite of the great services which Concini had rendered the princes' party, every hold against him was now used; besides, Condé saw that he could be exploited to further his own dearest aim: the prevention of the Spanish marriage.

There could now be no more doubt of it; Condé was aiming at the throne, and Richelieu was already reckoning with the possibility that the plot might succeed. There is a letter from the Bishop of Luçon at about this time which can be read as an attempt to approach the princes. For the moment Richelieu seemed to be vacillating between the possibility of joining in the *coup d'état* and the prospect of a swift rise to power in the service of the Regent and her favourite. Concini's plan of action was obvious enough to the young bishop: first to expose the "old gang," the "barboni," as he called them, and set them against one another; then to dismiss them and put new and fresher men in their places, and surround himself with a young guard who would serve and protect him for the sake of their own future. Richelieu watched the situation and lay low.

In the autumn of 1615 Marie de' Medici set out with her Court for Guyenne to meet the Spanish embassy approaching by the Bidassoa to solemnize the two marriages. Condé once more addressed a manifesto to the people, more bitter, violent, and urgent than the first, summarizing in malicious and trenchant terms the complaints of all the estates; the operative clause in the manifesto was the denunciation of the Italian favourites, who were now hated by the very street porters. Condé's idea was: no Spanish marriage until the reforms demanded were fulfilled; but as these reforms were countless and unfulfillable, that meant no marriage and no succession to the feeble heir of Henry IV. It was a last desperate attempt to put an end to the great European connections of the dynasty and the final establishment of the King's position.

Concini no longer felt himself safe in Paris. Had he been a brave man he would have taken command of the army and assured the safety of the royal party against the rebels during their journey. But he found excuses. The Duc de Guise, his personal enemy, commanded the escort, and Concini betook himself to the North behind his fortified walls. Yet not even that lost him the favour of the Queen-Mother. Habit ruled most of her feelings; the mere fact that he brought a Florentine atmosphere into her councils and her daily life made him indispensable to one who never felt quite at home in the French language.

On October 17, 1615, the Court reached Bordeaux and remained there until December 14th. The marriage of Louis XIII and the Infanta, who was the same age as he, that is fifteen, was there celebrated. During the journey there had been no serious attack by the rebels; such skirmishes as occurred are scarcely worth the name; but Condé's bands, who lived on plunder, ravaged the land dreadfully; they despoiled the inhabitants of the plains who were attached to the monarchy as the guarantee of order, shocked them out of all indifference, and laid the foundations of that hatred which was to follow the French nobles from now until their final overthrow.

The journey of the young Queen to Paris was scarcely a triumphal procession. The escort had been decimated by sickness; that December was bitterly cold; the roads were almost impassable, the land laid waste yet once more, the people dazed or despairing.

But Condé's position was still worse than that of the Regent. His method of waging war had lost him the popularity with the fickle populace which he had possessed a month before. His behaviour almost seemed to justify Concini. Concini, people said now, had shown sense in not accompanying the gloomy and ostentatious marriage procession through France, in keeping quietly in the background, for now, amid the universal indignation at Condé's misdemeanours, he was almost forgotten. Once more Condé had done the wrong thing; for the present—as many people began to realize with astonishment—the monarchy was far more firmly established than it had appeared to be since Henry IV's death.

Richelieu from his retreat gathered all the news he could. In spite of the ease and skill he had shown at the assembly of the Estates-General, that effort had exhausted his reserves of strength, and he had once more broken down; he was tormented by fever, melancholy, fears, and doubts; but in his sickness, as behind the bars of a prison, he lay and watched. If he were summoned, if he had to appear, he was prepared, equipped to make the right response whatever the fluctuation of events.

Among those who kept urging him at intervals to appear and take his part in public life was Louis XIII's confessor, the Bishop of Bayonne, Bertrand d'Echaux, a high-born Béarnese. The two prelates had been acquainted since the first years of Richelieu's stay at Luçon. Duvergier de Hauranne and Jansenius were d'Echaux's friends, and Duvergier, too, kept up a constant correspondence with Richelieu. "I submit my mind to yours," he wrote one day, and that curious expression was more than an act of politeness; it gave utterance to something which all churchmen who came in touch with the Bishop of Luçon at that time felt, none more strongly than Father Joseph: a sense of the extraordinary power which goes out from a man before the emergence of his destiny.

In August 1615 d'Echaux wrote to Richelieu that the Bishop of Orléans, Gabriel d'Aubespine, was the prospective candidate for the post of almoner to the young Queen, Anne of Austria, whose suite was now being formed. Villeroy supported the candidature (which in the circumstances was bound to have only a negative effect). The formal nomination had already been drawn up, but the Queen-Mother, when it was put before her, had changed colour, crumpled the parchment into a ball, and stuck it into her hand-bag in a towering rage. Then d'Echaux went on: "The Marquis de Richelieu and myself are resolved to help you in spite of your too stoical resolve to remain in retirement. . . . Do not plead the duties of your bishopric; even if you disapprove of our measures, we know better than you at the moment where your immediate interests lie." But Richelieu had to be implored; he made difficulties; he succeeded in conveying the impression that he had no wish to make a career at Court. All his energies seemed to be absorbed in theological labours; he was reading Paroeus against Bellarmin: *"De amissione gratiae et statu peccati"* or *"De libero arbitrio."* He kept sending to his book-seller for learned works. When he wrote to Zamet, the Bishop of Langres, it was in the tone of an aged prince of the Church, humorously resigned to the limits of his diocese. Only in disciplining his subordinates did he sometimes betray the unendurable tension within him; a cutting irony, an intentional desire to wound sometimes flashed out.

But the tension was soon to break; while he bent all his energies to keep up the pretence of being unconcerned, the Court itself was coming more than half-way to meet him. The Royal party was in Poitiers, so near to his diocese that the young bishop had naturally to pay his homage to the Regent. Marie de' Medici, who had a gift for forgetting people quickly when they were absent and recognizing them royally when they were present, was reminded by the sight of the young bishop of his eloquent phrases at the assembly of the Estates-General; they had been like balm to her then; all the flattering things which she had heard about him with half an ear, the appreciative words of weighty theologians, now returned to her mind; this keen, quick, energetic young priest and noble interested her; she kept enquiring about him, she wished to know more of him, to see him again. The post of almoner to Louis XIII's bride was now assured to him, and the appointment was fixed for November in Bordeaux; the step was taken; Richelieu was now in contact with the wielders of power.

That meeting at Poitiers began a correspondence which was to continue for many years, far beyond the point when Richelieu's relations with the Queen-Mother had ceased to be amicable. While the Court journeyed towards the Spanish frontier, the young Princess had to remain behind in Poitiers with a slight fever. Richelieu regularly informed the Queen-Mother of the invalid's condition, but, curiously enough, he did not accompany the Court to Bordeaux. He returned to

Coussay instead, where he went on waiting and watching, with reports coming in to him from every quarter. Nowhere in the kingdom was anyone better informed than at Coussay. The movements of the Protestants, the designs of Sully and Rohan, above all of Condé, occupied the Bishop intensely. Before a definite decision emerged Richelieu would never subscribe to any policy, would never commit himself. The immediate problem for him was whether the royal marriages would take place, whether the great international consolidation of the royal house would succeed, or whether a sudden stroke by the rebels would give everything another direction. The reports were uncertain. In all the provinces there were rumours of martial preparations. Rohan held the South with his rebellious Huguenots; Condé had crossed the Loire, Boisdauphin having failed to stop him; presently he might join forces with the Protestants; if he succeeded, the royal army might be advancing towards disaster. Henri Richelieu wrote to his brother that he was ashamed to look on and see nothing being done; every good counsel was brought to nought by an invisible power. This was a reference to Concini, for at any cost Concini wished to avoid a sharp collision, a victory by arms, an unequivocal solution. The old ministers of Silleroy's school were like puppets to him; he pulled the strings and they bore the ostensible responsibility. Pontchartrain, Vic, and Thou were sent to negotiate with the princes. Thou was a man towards whom Richelieu found himself in a curiously anomalous position; that statesman, from whose sense of actualities and sober judgment he was to learn so much, had confronted him too often at every turn during his youth; a strange repulsion had grown in him against a man whom he admired, a man famous for his knowledge of men, who yet completely overlooked the coming man. Thou, who held in his prodigious memory almost the whole of the previous century, had been a witness of St. Bartholomew's Night; he had been a spiritual councillor in the Parlements under Henry III before he became a secular power; he had been a councillor of State in 1588, and had then become the adviser and friend of Henry IV; and he was famous as the incomparable chronicler of his term of office, a new Livy who had written the history of France from the death of Francis I to the assassination of Henry. Thou was a judge of men feared and hated by many of his contemporaries; he had vexed Richelieu in particular by his trenchant character sketch of his uncle, the first bishop of Luçon. Now the old man again managed to bring off a *coup*; in the negotiations he broke the spearhead of the princes' revolt and consolidated the position of the old ministers, his friends; and that itself was the worst of news for the young, who were wasting their energies in waiting. Measured judgments on everything and everyone emanated from that old man; Richelieu smelt the danger of a return to sobriety. That of all things must not happen now, for it meant the confirmation of the existing state of affairs. In his inactivity Richelieu was torn by contradictory feelings. At moments he almost hoped for a victory for the princes; yet now his own domains were being damaged by their sporadic ravages, his aged mother was being threatened. "For forty years," she wrote, "I have lived in my house; I have seen all the armies passing by, but such murderous bands, such desecration of the country I have never known before." Richelieu sent a protest to the Government, demanded compensation, wrote humbly to Condé himself; but by the way in which his complaints were treated it could be seen that he had enemies in the Ministry, and that the old gang did not trust him; he had dallied too long with Condé, though now he was complaining about him. Knowing all this and imagining more, he suddenly abandoned his reserve and turned to the Queen-Mother; he thanked her for her pledge to make him almoner "in spite of the machinations of my enemies." In this respect his character did not change. He held the powerful to a lightly given word, and simultaneously showed a morbid touchiness, which it is almost impossible to reconcile with his unbending resolution; only a knowledge of his later years gives an explanation of his deep inner antitheses.

The manner in which Marie de' Medici concluded peace with the princes showed a weary obliviousness to honour; behind Villeroy and Jeannin, who advised an accommodation, Concini was at work. She negotiated with the rebels as with foreign powers. A peace congress met at Loudun on February 21, 1616. The Marshal de Brissac, Villeroy, Thou, Pontchartrain, and Vic represented the King; the princes appeared along with their wives, who took the liveliest part in the deliberations; the Comtesse de Soissons and the Duchesse de Longueville showed themselves particularly insatiable in their demands. The Protestants, too, had sent their delegates. That the Council of Trent's decrees should not be promulgated was the chief demand of the princes; in their opinion it strengthened the clerical party too much. They demanded a renewal of the alliances with the General States, Savoy and Venice. To win over the Third Estate and produce a national-Gallican impression, they moved for the acceptance of the famous article touching the King's sovereignty; and that itself was proof that Condé still aimed at the throne; he wanted these full powers for himself. They also unequivocally demanded an anti-Spanish policy. Finally, they insisted that the Marshal d'Ancre should be deprived of the citadel of Amiens, which gave him too much power, and that Condé should preside over the Royal Council and sign all ordinances. The Queen-Mother gave way in everything, though Villeroy warned her of the disastrous results if Condé were admitted to the Royal Council. Concerning the article of the Third Estate alone Marie remained inexorable; here she was supported by her ultramontane friends. Condé for his part refused to retreat an inch; but in the midst of the negotiations he fell gravely ill; that and the influence of his confessor suddenly changed his mind. He feared excommunication, and at last yielded on that one point—absolute monarchy, in which the Regent represented the opposition party, the Church and the rebels.

Now the Huguenots had to carry on their fight alone. In La Rochelle, the rich port on the Atlantic Ocean which was then generally regarded as impregnable, they concentrated their forces. They, too, had to be given concessions, in what measure the sequel will show.

The peace treaty signed at Loudun on May 3, 1616, signified a victory of the great nobles over the Queen-Mother, whose sole aim was her own peace, and who employed every means to secure it, who desired power merely that she might enjoy comfort in all that she did.

Besides the governorship of Berry, Condé received the sum of 1,500,000 livres, to liquidate his war expenses, it was said. Over 6,000,000 livres was distributed among his confederates.

But the cup of the old ministers, all of them over seventy, was now full, for when all was over and every humiliation drunk to the lees and Condé the rebel sat in the Council. Concini emerged again, pushed all the blame for the scandalous situation on the aged councillors, and dismissed them in rapid succession.

In the early summer of 1616 the Court was once more back in Paris. Marie de' Medici had quietly returned by night; but Louis XIII and his young wife made one of those pompous allegorical entries, rather like a triumph, which, under Italian influence, had developed from the strict symbolism of medieval Church ceremonial. No one yet believed in any future for their morose sovereign. Richelieu, who arrived in Paris on June 6th to assume his post, could make nothing of the apathetic young King; then and for a long time afterwards he regarded him as negligible, and accustomed himself to reckon without him. That one could be so destitute of all will, all interest in things, all power of resistance, that this young man did not rebel and seize what was his, and his alone, his task and the meaning of his life, was incomprehensible to Richelieu. The young King was less than nothing to him; he looked through him during these early days into a future which was another's.

Sometimes he set his hopes on Gaston, Louis's younger

brother, who was still a child. Sometimes, as we have seen, he actually entertained the possibility that Condé might reach the throne; but Condé, the husband of the beautiful Mont-morency, was ruining himself by a way of life that was lampooned in the lowest streets of Paris; and he was always needing more money, always embarking on some treasonable adventure likely to ruin the State merely to satisfy some whim of his, or appease his shortsighted greed. Power apparently lay only with Concini, to whom the young bishop therefore sought to attach himself. Ever since coming to Paris and taking up quarters in the Rue des Mauvaises Paroles, Richelieu had been regarded as a supporter of the Italian. In the circles he frequented the King was scarcely mentioned.

Saint-Simon has set down what his father told him concern-ing the education or rather the complete neglect of Louis XIII by Marie de' Medici. "The Regent required," he writes, "a son who was King only in name and who did not disturb in anything the doings of her favourites. He was educated for this end, and consequently in a manner as deleterious as possible to his nature. He was left in complete idleness, and provided with no instruction whatever. He often complained of this to my father, and later in life frequently referred to the fact that he had not been taught even to read. A scrupulous watch was kept that no courtiers should gather round him. It was counted an offence for anyone even to linger near his apartments; the young King saw no one but his attendants, creatures chosen by his mother and at once dismissed as soon as the slightest sign of intimacy with Louis became apparent."

A report of the Venetian Ambassador at the end of 1615 is to the same effect. "The King is kept as much as possible out of affairs," he wrote. "He is made to spend his time in puerilities, to devote himself to dogs, birds, and other dis-tractions, and he can follow the hunt, his favourite sport, to his heart's content. He prefers to associate with people of the lower classes. . . . The Queen-Mother completely governs his suite, and chooses them for their dullness and stupidity, so that there may be no one to rouse a manly temper in the King. The young monarch lives in entire obedience and dependence; the authority of the Queen-Mother is still increasing. Yet the King is not without virtue; he is lively and quick in apprehension; he might promise much if his education were a better one."

The hunting of the stag, the most ambitious sport permitted to Louis, at last brought a comrade into the circle of his solitude. The King hunted regularly every Monday, Wednesday, and Saturday, and when possible on the other week-days as well. On the way to his wedding at Bordeaux and on the way back people had noticed that he was always racing at full gallop on a fast horse round the slow procession of carriages, flying falcons at herons in the company of his falconer Luynes, a Provençal without background or pedigree, who had come to Paris with his two younger brothers, Brantes and Cadenet, in Henry IV's service, had pleased by his good looks and modest ways, and had received a small post at Court and a modest pension. Luynes was already approaching his fortieth year when, to his surprise, he was chosen by the Controller of the King's Household, the inefficient Souvré, to organize the King's hunting expeditions. The commander of the Royal Bodyguard, Vitry, had had in mind a creature of his own for this post; one of his soldiers had already become indispensable to the lonely Prince; he caught sparrows for him, and in rainy weather the King would hunt these little birds all day with falcons, while they dashed themselves against the walls in despair. Gruesome amusements were the sole resource of his existence; when he was not hunting, dogs drew his cannons at a gallop through the long corridors of the palace for him, and he fired the pieces from the balconies. When he was fifteen Marie de' Medici still thrashed him with her own hands in the presence of his tittering subjects.

But now the quiet, mature Luynes entered the King's life. It was assumed that the great disparity in age would prevent the formation of any dangerous intimacy which might enlighten Louis about his position and his rights.

Louis XIII stuttered in talking, and as he had often been punished and ridiculed for his failing, he was awkward and silent in the presence of strangers, especially if they were women. The almost hostile shyness and apprehension with which he regarded his young Queen was a result of this awkwardness, and also of his conviction that the beautiful, reserved creature was completely influenced by Marie de' Medici. But the quiet assurance of Luynes and his expertness in Louis's favourite sport set free something in the tormented nature of his pupil. After their long and rapid gallops they would find themselves in the great silence of the woods; at the edge of a clearing, when the light was failing and their followers had been shaken off, they would fall into conversation. Laboriously, in stammering words, the King confided in his falconer, and the falconer gave him the best that such weak and tormented natures can receive, understanding and an active sympathy, which changes hopeless resignation into resentment and raises the victim in his own esteem. Luynes aroused much more in the young King than he himself was capable of divining: an abysmal wrath, which was still so painfully stifled by fear and his deep dependence on his mother that it could only shake him and collapse again, to be buried, along with the dark deeds of vengeance acted in his imagination, under the debris of his feelings, from which it was to burst later like a flame. But something very different was also awakened in the forlorn boy: a love, almost a passion for the friend who had first given him the ineffable comfort of a confidant. "Luynes!" he cried out in his sleep, and his attendants began to remark it; they whispered of this attachment and watched its progress. For once in his life Louis XIII was troubled by no shadow of suspicion in his affections; he did not guess that his friend, like everyone else, was actuated at bottom in all he did by a concealed lust for power.

But it was not the King only; everyone misjudged Luynes

and regarded him as handsome and amiable enough, yet insignificant, with the placid equability of a pleasant but somewhat hollow personality. The Queen-Mother wondered at first whether he should be removed, should be made to disappear; but then she fell back on her favourite remedy, purchase; and so in future Luynes, too, was subsidized; he was given for a start the governorship of Amboise, and from that moment his greed was awakened.

Among those in Paris who observed the connection between the King and his falconer with a certain disapproval was Richelieu. The nobles had pocketed all they wanted for the time being; the star of the Concinis seemed in the ascendant again; a new Government might now be formed to protect the Queen-Mother and establish her for a long time to come. The old men, the shadows of the past, had vanished, following Sully in his fall, and it was disturbing to feel that something was emerging which, even if it could not be taken very seriously, might yet serve as a rallying point for discontent.

Urged by the Concinis, Marie de' Medici resolved to have an explanation with the King. She had a fondness for exploiting sentimental scenes. She enumerated all that she had done for Louis, all the cares she had taken on herself for him: the burden of Regency, the anxieties of office, the personal danger; she told him how she had preserved his inheritance and arranged a brilliant marriage for him; and now, she averred, she was prepared to renounce everything; all he had to do was to acknowledge her good administration and bid her relinquish her cares, so that she might realize her dearest wish and withdraw into retirement far from France: she was already negotiating for the acquisition of the principality of Mirandola. It was as if she were indicating that her trunks were already packed. But Luynes was present; he gave the King the necessary confidence, and had schooled him in all the right answers. Louis had already begun to acquire the art of dissimulation which he was later to master so brilliantly; he seemed amazed and respectful; no one, he said, had ever dared in his presence

79

to refer to the Government or to the person of his mother without the greatest respect and the deepest appreciation; he declared that he was fully at one with her policy and made no reflection on Concini's activities. Marie de' Medici ended the interview with tears, laments, and assurances, thus successfully confusing the issue; but when she left the King she was completely reassured. She thought that she had won the day.

So it appeared that there was no longer any obstacle to the reconstructive work of Concini. In May Du Vair was given the State seals in place of Silleroy. Eight days later Jeannin had to go; he retained a seat in the Ministerial Council, but the real functions of the Finance Minister were allotted to a man who was to have a decisive influence on Richelieu's career.

Barbin, a bourgeois official unearthed by Concini, was like a rough sketch of what Colbert later became, and Richelieu was even to show a sort of gratitude towards him—no small tribute from Richelieu. The Apostolic Nuncio described Barbin as follows: "A man of humble ancestry, alert and keen of mind. His knowledge of financial matters is profound; his inventive resource in finance first gained him Concini's good graces, and the Florentine created for him the special post of General Controller. Now through his position and the esteem in which he is held he controls the whole financial system of the kingdom; he is incorruptibly firm and sober in business; he is hated because of his absolute powers, and also because of the patron who bestowed them on him. He is accounted to be perfectly honest, and he is a good Catholic. He has judgment and resolution, authority, and great firmness as a speaker."

Through an acquaintance of his mother's relatives, Denis Bouthillier, Richelieu came to know Barbin, and from the first meeting regarded him with respect; the man's firmness and directness attracted him. Under Henry IV Barbin had been royal procurator in Melun. He had called on Eleonora Concini each time that she came to stay in Fontainebleau, seeing to her comfort and paying her attentions. For his impatience the path of official promotion was too slow; he insinuated himself among the partisans of the great, and Eleonora, his patroness, conducted him to the Queen-Mother. By 1611 he was Marie's Intendant, the steward of her finances. Many of his plans Richelieu was to carry out later. He wanted to create order in the kingdom, confine the Protestants within their bounds, and break the power of the nobles; with that end in view he courted the support of the Concinis. There was constant communication between Barbin and the Bishop of Luçon. Indeed, Richelieu lived for a long time in Barbin's world of thought. It was Barbin who first introduced him to Eleonora Concini Galigai. A letter from the young priest to her shows that in a short time his intimacy with that dark and brilliant creature, whom the people of Paris held to be a witch, had gone very far. Richelieu had no fear of her witchcraft, but on the other hand she is known to have said that she could not bear the penetrating eye of the bishop, and always turned her head away when he looked at her. She played a large part in recommending Richelieu's talents to the Regent.

During the peace negotiations with the princes Richelieu had had several meetings with Father Joseph; often he rode out within a few miles of Loudun to meet him. The Father was in close contact with the rebels; Richelieu, on the other hand, had been drawing closer to the Concini coterie after the plundering campaign of the nobles, chiefly under Barbin's influence. His estimation of Condé and his prospects was dwindling day by day. About this time he agreed with Joseph that Condé must be allowed to take part in the government, so that his power might be neutralized. The thing which had drawn Father Joseph the Franciscan to the discontented nobles was the great dream which pursued him like an obsession all his life: the dream of a crusade against the infidel, and the conquest of Constantinople and the Holy Land. Among the nobles, the Duc de Nevers, a Gonzaga of the junior line, descended on his mother's side from the family of Paleologos, was prepared to back the crusade. With the help of various religious orders, Joseph had been acting as an agent for the

Duke, who aimed at the throne of Byzantium: the threads of his intrigues ran through the Balkans to Constantinople; two hundred and sixty-three years after the conquest of Eastern Rome by Mahomet II sympathy in Europe for the Greeks was still warm. It is notable that among those in favour of European intervention in the East at the beginning of the seventeenth century so many Greeks are to be found. The baroque chivalry of the Counter-Reformation roused hopes of freedom in the Hellenes. Again and again they sought to secure the support of France; again and again, in spite of many promises, they were disappointed, for France needed the Turks as allies against the house of Hapsburg. In 1607 several noble Macedonians had approached Charles Emmanuel of Savoy and asked him to restore their nation; and about the same time Giovanni Fantin Minotto founded the first secret nationalist associations in the Greek islands, chiefly in Chios and Morea. But both Giovanni Fantin and the Macedonians appealed to Henry IV in vain.

There existed then a quite unromantic, immediate connection in people's minds between the old Greek tradition revived by the Humanists and the living Greeks suffering under Turkish oppression. Nevers, the grandson of Margareta Paleologos of Montferrat, stood in direct blood relation with Byzantium, and so with the Humanist idea. At once a great noble of France and a member of an Italian ruling family, this chivalrous, dreamy prince was admirably fitted to negotiate between the royal house and the rebellious nobles. He was not easy to handle; he had to be manipulated with the utmost care, according to Father Joseph. He was impulsive and easily discouraged, mystically pious, yet not at all steadfast even in matters of his faith. In company of Father Joseph, Richelieu went to visit him, and actually persuaded him to become a mediator. In this way Richelieu had a hand in the peace of Loudun. Father Joseph was filled with admiration for his friend's diplomatic gifts, so brilliantly shown in his handling of Nevers. Later on, the all-powerful Cardinal was to show something approaching gratitude to the Duke for assisting him to win his first diplomatic triumph. More, Nevers exerted an attraction on him; it was as if the Duke's chimerical plans enchanted his severely practical mind.

The success of his conversations with Nevers led to his employment on his first official diplomatic mission. After old Villeroy, still wretchedly clinging to office, had been thrust from it, and Du Vair, summoned from Provence, had been put in his place, and the Du Vair-Barbin Ministry had initiated its new policy under Concini's guidance, Richelieu was sent to Condé, who had begun to cause further trouble on the signing of peace, not going to Paris to take up his new office as councillor to the King, but making mischief in his newly-acquired governorship of Berry.

While Condé was ravaging the country Richelieu had written to him in a tone that must have made him seem very harmless. "Those who have no weapons but their prayers, the weapons of peace," he had written in reference to himself and his mother. Now he appeared in his bishop's robes as the Regent's emissary, with a slight trace of irony to indicate the strong will couched behind his humbly courteous manner. A brother of Father Joseph, Du Tremblay, had already represented Richelieu to the Prince as a reliable negotiator, a coming personality, to whom it would be well to listen carefully. And Richelieu's mission to Condé was completely successful. Condé let himself be persuaded; on July 17th, without even having consulted his colleagues Bouillon and Mayenne, he appeared at Court.

He was cheered by the Parisians on his entry to the city; if he now remained on the Queen's side, his friendship and collaboration would mean a strengthening of the royal power, above all a guarantee against the mounting hatred of the masses for Concini. But he began to swagger childishly, complicating all relationships and flaunting the armed forces at his back. He no longer minced his words; in his cups he boasted of what he would do, and finally shouted in Barbin's hearing that he had only the last step to take now: push the King from the throne and set himself upon it. He might actually have done so if he had been a better man, and if his followers had not been torn with jealousies; nevertheless, in spite of his weaknesses, he was a danger to the monarchy. Nevers, too, urged the fulfilment of the promises which he asserted had been given in exchange for his mediation, promises to help him in his crusade. And Bouillon, Mayenne, and Longueville were now all demanding immediate action against Concini; a rallying cry which could always rouse the populace. This time Concini was really afraid; to his undoing he unlearnt that fear later; but in August 1616 he and his wife spoke to Barbin of their desperate situation; they thought that both they and the King were lost; they wanted to flee in disguise to Caen, and from there take ship with their treasures for Italy. Yet as Richelieu wrote in his Memoirs: "The Ministerial Council now consisted of people who were passionately resolved to strengthen the authority of the State."

One day while the Queen was in her room listening to the lute, an old man in the obsolete dress of Henry IV's time entered: Sully, the long-vanished and forgotten statesman. The young King was summoned. "Sire, and you, Madame," said the old Huguenot, "I must unburden my conscience. Would to God that Your Majesties were far from here in the middle of twelve thousand horsemen!" No doubt he fancied that only he could rescue the royal house and the kingdom from their desperate situation.

There was much talk among the nobles, but little action. Marie lamented to everyone she saw, protesting and explaining and persuading; Condé wasted his precious time in making empty and insolent threats; but the Ministry was there, and it acted. Richelieu is supposed to have had a strong influence on Barbin's decision.

There was a noble from Gascony of whom Henry IV had once said to Marie de' Medici that he would never recognize anything but the monarchy, and that he could be relied upon.

This man, the Maréchal de Thémines, was given his orders; soldiers hidden in bales of Italian silk were conveyed to Barbin, on September 1st Thémines stepped up to Condé as he was proceeding to the Royal Council, put his hand on his shoulder and arrested him. Condé was kept in the Louvre for a few days, then taken by night to the Bastille. None of the other nobles made any resistance; Mayenne, Bouillon, Guise, and Henry's bastard son Vendôme fled by every gate from Paris. Only Condé's old mother rushed into the street crying: "To arms!" Yet the mob which gathered in the course of the day contented itself with storming and plundering for two days the palace of the hated Concini. The fact that two dresses belonging to the Queen-Mother, one of them worth more than 150,000 francs, were found in the Marshal's room gave new matter to the pamphleteers; never before had such scurrilous songs been sung about the Regent. But nothing more happened. The nobles still went on blustering, but without effect. Then the sole territorial magnate who had remained aloof from events in Paris, Nevers, now on the point of leaving for Germany to enlist men for his crusade, suddenly announced that he had been cheated, espoused Condé's cause, constituted himself the leader of the opposition party, and got in touch with the Protestants. So once more he was interviewed by the Bishop whose negotiations had twice already proved so successful. When after prolonged and urgent argument Richelieu left, he felt that he was sure of the Duke. Yet as soon as Richelieu's back was turned the vacillating Nevers went on with his war preparations. He had unexpectedly received help and support from the Ministry itself. Du Vair, who was deeply disgusted by the influence of the Concinis, was encouraging him. Back in Paris, Richelieu advised that immediate armed measures should be taken against Nevers, but Du Vair, turning violently against Barbin in the council chamber, opposed it. He was dismissed and replaced by the State Secretary Mangot; accordingly the important position of Secretary for Foreign Affairs fell vacant. Du Vair withdrew into the semi-shadow of the growing Opposition.

It is beyond doubt that Barbin had the qualities of a strong statesman: resolution, great powers of work, knowledge of affairs, and complete integrity. But his Government was doomed from the start; it was founded on the fluctuating fortunes of Concini, on the insecure favour which he granted, and on the not less insecure favour he enjoyed.

Richelieu stuck to Barbin. This has been counted against him as a political error, as an amazing instance of lack of fore-sight. There is no evidence that Richelieu did not foresee everything. The contrary is the case. He wished to attain the function for which he was born, the conduct of the foreign policy of France; for that end he availed himself of the existent situation; but scarcely was he in office when he tried to free the Queen-Mother from her morbid dependency on the Concinis. He also imperceptibly drew closer to a man whom he had begun to observe, and who was taken seriously by no one else: Luynes.

A few days before the scene with Du Vair made a vacant post in the Ministry, Richelieu had been chosen as extraordinary ambassador to Spain. He said later that he would have pre-ferred that temporary function to the more permanent office, but the Queen-Mother's, or rather Concini's, wish had been unequivocal, also the foreign secretaryship comprised public esteem, favour, and the conduct of important affairs in one, strong temptations to a young man, and he concluded: "I therefore accepted the post which the Maréchal d'Ancre and the Queen-Mother urged upon me, all the more as Barbin, who was my close friend, pressed me earnestly to take it."

The general approval of his friends, relatives, and ecclesi-astical superiors upbore him. "Everywhere one heard only good of him," said a contemporary. "The man who was later to be overwhelmed with curses and execrations and admiring hatred began his career under the most brilliant auspices; Zamet, the Bishop of Langres, praised him highly to the

Queen; Du Perron and Sourdis exerted their influence for him." Father Joseph damped the opposition of the nobles to the appointment; from Eleonora Concini to the pious ladies of the rich bourgeoisie there was no social class which was not favourable to him. He had gone a long way since those weeks in which he had worked so hard to be appointed representative of the clergy at the Estates-General, since those first visits to Paris after the murder of Henry IV, when his friends had advised him not to show too much zeal and ambition; at that time he had been tormented by the thought that everything depended upon his being able to make a show, to take the public eye, and thus secure a niche for himself. He had allied himself completely with the Ultramontanes; more, he, the future ally of Gustavus Adolphus, had risen first by the help of the Catholic League; he had written to Concini and offered his services with a devotion which might soon prove extremely compromising.

Richelieu's term of office was to be of brief duration; heavy reverses were in store for him. Yet this first period of active participation in affairs of State, with its grave results to himself, must be counted among his years of apprenticeship; he learned essential things in these few months.

The definitive appointment was made on November 25th. On the 14th Richelieu's mother had died in her sixtieth year. The eldest son, the Marquis, had written to his sister Nicole saying that the body was to be laid in the castle chapel until the Bishop of Luçon and the other members of the family could take part in the funeral.

They waited for three weeks, but Richelieu could not get away from Paris. "Torn with grief," he wrote that he would have to refrain from coming, and he said in a letter to his other brother Alphonse, the Carthusian: "In her death God has shown her as much grace and comfort as He laid upon her heavy and bitter sorrow during her life."

On December 2nd Bentivoglio, the new apostolic Nuncio, wrote to the Curia from Lyons: "Mangot's post has been given to the Bishop of Luçon, a prelate who, despite his youth, is, as your Holiness knows, one of the most richly endowed in France in capacity, oratorical powers, sense of duty and spiritual zeal. We may assume that this change will be to our benefit." The Duke of Monteleone, the Spanish Ambassador, wrote to the same effect to Philip III; Richelieu, he said, was his personal friend, and there was not another man in France who showed more zeal for the service of God, the Spanish crown, and the common cause. In complete agreement with this judgment was the report of the Venetian Ambassador, who described Richelieu as completely devoted to the Spanish party, even implying that he was drawing a Spanish pension, but could see in this only evil prospects for the Republic of Venice.

The fundamental nature of the international situation with which Richelieu was confronted on assuming office is well described by Sully's son-in-law Henri de Rohan, who had a sure and sober judgment of European questions, and would have been a great tactician not only in the field but also at the council table had not all his later actions been dominated by the desperate situation of the Huguenots. He wrote: "There are in Christendom two powers like opposite poles, on whom peace and war between other states depend: the houses of France and Spain. Spain, with her sudden vast increase of strength, can conceal from no one that her aim is supreme power in Europe and the erection of a new world monarchy in the occident. The house of France must provide the equipoise. The other powers ally themselves with one or the other of these two great states, each in accordance with its own interests." This was, quite briefly and simply, the international framework which Richelieu had to face as soon as he found himself in the Ministry. All parleying with Spain could mean only a temporary accommodation during a time of internal weakness, of threatening revolt and the uncertainties of a minority. To let France be involved in a foreign policy oriented towards Spain would be equivalent to making foreign

policy dependent on domestic policy, which is always a mark
of weakness. Since foreign policy as the general expression of
the power of the State must take precedence in the end over
domestic policy as the particular, France in the seventeenth
century necessarily had to return, by the unavoidable workings
of international realities themselves, to Henry IV's fundamental
attitude towards the other Christian states.

Already before Richelieu assumed office the Duke of
Savoy, who found his country vitally threatened by the expansion of Spain in North Italy, had taken arms against the
menace of Hapsburg world-power. France, which a little
before Henry's death had encouraged him in this policy, at the
beginning of the Regency had withdrawn its encouragement
and left him in the lurch. But now that the wavering balance
of power had again been upset by a change in the Mantuan
succession, war broke out between Spain and Savoy. Don
Pedro of Toledo, the Governor of Milan, invaded Savoy
territory in force. The Duke struck back and flung himself
on Mantua, whose ruler was a vassal of the Empire, and also,
for greater security, an ally of both Spain and France. The
Duke went further: for assistance against the superior forces
of Spain he did not turn to the French Government but to
the old Huguenot leader and comrade-in-arms of Henry IV,
Lesdiguières, the sworn enemy of Concini's Spanish policy,
who was Governor of Dauphiné and resided at Grenoble. It
is one of the clearest symptoms of the disintegration of France
during Concini's rule that Lesdiguières could simply march
off on December 19th with 7,500 men without even asking
permission from Paris. For the moment the French Government contented itself with condemning this arbitrary proceeding. To judge from the available papers, Richelieu was strictly
governmental in his attitude to this violation of discipline;
but Avenal, who holds that he secretly supported Lesdiguières,
has a great deal of *inner* probability on his side, the more so
as such a policy, running counter to the official policy of the
Government, would certainly not be preserved too scrupu-

lously in documents. It is clear that even at this time Richelieu was already imperceptibly approaching his later policy. Besides, the rebukes which Lesdiguières received from Paris were entirely platonic, for even the bold Barbin feared that if Lesdiguières were recalled, he might turn back, unite with the nobles, and draw the Huguenots to his side. As a consequence nothing could be done except to call the Governor a rebel in Madrid, while taking no decisive steps against him.

At the time when the Savoy-Spanish conflict broke out the Republic of Venice was at war with the Archduke Ferdinand of Steiermark, who was later to become the Emperor Ferdinand II; the cause of the dispute was piracy in the Adriatic carried out from the mountains of Istria by the Uskoks, who were supported by Ferdinand.

Richelieu's embassy to Madrid, which had lapsed on his appointment as Foreign Secretary, had been connected with the Savoy conflict. In his place the Comte de La Rochefoucauld was chosen, but encouraged by the boundless laxity which had become customary during the Regency, the Count kept postponing his departure for private reasons, and the pretext provided by the renewed outbreak among the nobles put a definite end to it.

As both pairs of warring powers—Spain and Savoy, Venice and Austria—appealed to France for mediation, Richelieu drew up a plan and sent it to Béthune, the Ambassador in Rome: his idea was to invite the four conflicting powers as well as the Duke of Mantua to a congress in Paris. He hoped in this way to preserve peace for France and bring it to Europe at the same time.

In this his whole character is displayed: for a France which during six years had been apprehensively accommodating and yielding and trying to avoid the limelight, he now suddenly demanded the first place and the right to decide the affairs of Europe. He was to have a sharp disappointment. For while the Venetians had turned to France, they had appealed for Spanish mediation as well, and Savoy summoned the help of the Curia. France was passed over; the Venetian conflict was settled in Madrid, the Savoy conflict in Rome. The peace negotiations in both instances were outside Richelieu's sphere.

From this affair the Bishop of Luçon learned to subordinate his prescient imagination to the course of events and to do nothing until the time was ripe. But he gave expression to his disappointment. "Louis XIII," he wrote, "has not forfeited the claim of his father to be arbitrator of Europe." And in a letter to Béthune he said: "Between ourselves, I may tell you that the conclusion of this business has made me see that in spite of our present weaknesses there is no prince in Christendom who is really more powerful than ours; the others who talk so loudly are incapable of action." In realizing this he had won decisive insight for his future labours, and he owed it to the first few months of his authority.

Simultaneously with these negotiations Richelieu took another step rich in future consequences, which clearly showed that he pretended to pursue a Spanish policy only so long as his career demanded it, and that once confronted with the grave tasks of his office he followed a clear and unequivocal line. He sent to the allies of France in Germany, the Protestants, a man of peculiarly steadfast and pure character, Schomberg, the son of a German cavalry captain. In the instructions which he gave him he said: "It is pure slander to make us out Roman and Spanish in our policy, to assert that we serve Roman and Spanish interests to the detriment of our old alliances or our own people, that is to say, our Huguenots." But this text was preached to the converted; for the Protestant Electors, above all the Elector of the Palatinate, had every interest in keeping France's friendship in their resistance to Spain. Indeed, any attempt to prevent the Germans from supporting the rebellious nobles seemed superfluous; looked at from abroad, the perpetually confused and contradictory policy of these feudal barons seemed to have little prospects of success. It is characteristic of Richelieu in his youth, before he had learned to conceal weaknesses as successfully as in later life, it also shows his curious tendency to premature apologetics, that he instructed Schomberg to insist that it was unjust to charge their Majesties with the squandering of the State treasures; they had had to buy off the great nobles with seventeen millions, and spend about twenty millions in crushing revolt. The real cause of the present financial stringency was to be found here, not in the much-talked-of influence of certain foreigners. The man of whom people spoke so much was far from having achieved such power as other foreigners had possessed before him, he was also the only foreigner at present in office, and one who had become virtually French, since he shared his influence only with Frenchmen. What Richelieu intended was clear; the propaganda and the recruiting by the rebels in Germany, above all by Bouillon, must be combated. But the technique was wretchedly inefficient; it might have done actual harm save for the fact that the German Protestants had no interest in weakening France by encouraging the rebels, and thus increasing the power of Spain.

This defence of the favourite before foreigners, this acknowledgment of trouble with the nobles, reads very strangely; the reason for it was, as already said, that here we touch a specific weakness of Richelieu which lasted in a modified form to his later years, and which consisted in the need to forestall the adverse judgments of others, a policy which often achieved the opposite of what it intended. Generally it was only after such errors, known very well to Richelieu himself, that he regained his unimpaired capacity for action, and then he was faultless in his choice of means and adopted a diametrically contrary policy, sometimes with ruthlessness.

Other traits showing the beginner can also be found in the period of his first authority.

These may be seen, for instance, in the way in which the young Foreign Secretary initiated his official relations with the King's diplomatic agents abroad. He began by sending a circular to all the embassies requesting them to forward a copy of their existing instructions and the kind of report which would enable him to intervene at the right moment where necessary; mere opinions, however, and advice on points which he could judge for himself he did not desire. The ambassadors seem to have taken this rather badly. One replied by pointing out faults in Richelieu's own conduct of affairs, his failure properly to acknowledge correspondence received, and the absence of regular reports from Paris; another fulminated over the omission of certain forms of courtesy: a kind of passive resistance was perceptible. Richelieu thereupon appointed new men, whom he sent as ambassadors to Holland, Switzerland, and Germany. But his relations with the accredited foreign diplomatists at the Court of Louis XIII were no better. The Nuncio reported that the Spanish Ambassador was complaining of the new Foreign Secretary that he was distrait and absent in conversation; hardly surprising when one reflects in what a difficult position the inexperienced minister found himself.

At moments he was on the point of another breakdown. "I cannot stand it any longer," he wrote. It was not the burden of his circumscribed office that oppressed him, but the events happening round him which threatened the existence of the monarchy. The Ministers worked hard, but already they had reached a point where they saw they could survive only by stern and summary measures.

Richelieu secretly began to serve the King more and more directly. He knew now that Concini's position was untenable. The adventurer was taking ostentatious defensive measures against the enemies whom he saw springing up over all France. He had the citadel of Caen in his possession; he occupied bridge-heads, he fortified towns. He negotiated for the acquisition of various governorships. It was said that he wanted to become Constable of France and aimed at dictatorship. At every turn he bullied and made his power felt; since Condé's arrest he had completely reversed his former cautious tactics; his display of pomp and power betrayed a desperate arrogance, a pathological over-estimation of himself. He treated Ministers like lackeys, and when they showed any resistance threatened to dismiss them. Marie de' Medici herself began at last to recognize the danger she would run if she identified herself too completely with this fortune-hunter who seemed struck with blindness. The Bishop of Luçon did everything he could to strengthen her in this attitude. Eleonora had violent scenes with her benefactress; once more there were rumours of poison, of black magic and Jewish conspiracy. The Queen-Mother at last advised the favourites to flee. Eleonora would have gladly departed with her accumulated riches, but the Marshal seemed to be drunk with power; he would not hear of it.

Richelieu quietly continued to draw closer to the King and Luynes. Luynes now and then asked him for advice, and through him Richelieu sent a message to the King, saying that there was nothing either in his own sphere or anywhere else in the State, of which he would not faithfully inform him at any time.

On the other hand, Concini humiliated the King at every opportunity. Louis once asked the Finance Minister for 2,000 thalers; it was refused; and to crown the insult Concini thereupon offered him the sum as a present; more, he had the insolence to write to the King not to worry about the great expenses to which he, Concini, was put by supporting his bodyguard of six thousand men. Yet every copper coin he had acquired since he came to France a beggar had been extorted from the State treasury and the royal estates and the taxpayers of France. While the King stood at a window with Luynes, and no one else to attend him, he would see Concini parading in the courtyard of the Louvre with an escort of several hundred nobles.

In his consultations with Luynes, Louis had thought of the desperate plan of taking refuge with the rebellious nobles and seeking their protection; but then another design matured. Few were let into the secret, not more than seven persons all told, among them a secretary of Barbin and spy of Luynes, a certain Déageant. After Condé's arrest the nobles, as if stunned, had quickly withdrawn to their provinces. On January 17, 1617, the Parlement of Paris ratified a royal decree by which the Duc de Nevers, who was now the centre of discontent, was declared guilty of *lèse majesté* if he did not appear in person within fourteen days to beg the King's pardon on his knees. The Duke's answer was proud and unconciliating; it had been drawn up in collaboration with Mayenne, Bouillon, Vendôme, and the President Le Jay, and it justified his disobedience and his absence by the "measureless power of the Maréchal d'Ancre, who has driven away all the former advisers of the Crown."

The energetic and resolute Ministry refused to negotiate. Three armies, strongly equipped and well paid, marched against the rebels and attacked at once with success. But the Duc de Guise, who was in supreme command, saw the general situation in dark colours in spite of this military advantage, for now the people everywhere, even in the provinces, were transported with hatred of Concini.

An unbearable weight lay on Paris; every day something was expected to happen, but none knew what it would be. Only the seventeen-year-old King, his one confidant, a resolute soldier, and a few questionable figures who might betray the plan at the last moment, saw clearly before them the event which was to change everything.

CHAPTER VI

ANCRE'S END

On April 24th it was rumoured that the King would hunt; he had got up very early, which was unusual, and everyone was surprised to see him still in the palace at ten o'clock in the morning. There was an unusual coming and going; something uncanny was in the air. The King was closeted with Luynes and a few officers; they spoke together in low voices, and if anyone came in they fell silent. Vitry, the commander of the guard, had posted twenty stout and resolute men in the inner courtyard of the Louvre; he himself sat in the anteroom on a chest, peering through the open door and making patterns with a long stick on the floor in assumed composure.

Then a stir went through the waiting men; only for an instant; their tension relapsed again into apparent indifference. The Italian adventurer was approaching, followed by countless petitioners and courtiers; he was as usual both unsure and too sure, challenging, graciously granting favours and ungraciously refusing them. As he entered the inner courtyard Vitry quickly tried to intercept him but was held up by an acquaintance, and so lost sight of him in the crowd. He asked: "Where is the Maréchal?" Concini was standing among a cluster of nobles reading a letter. Vitry forced his way through the gossiping groups, seized the hated Italian by the arm, and said: "In the King's name." Concini whirled round and with great presence of mind shouted in Italian: "A mè!" But Vitry thought that the words had a very different meaning, that is: "You dare to do this to *me*!" and he cried: "Oui, à vous!" "Yes, to you!" With that he seized him more firmly,

96

ANNE OF AUSTRIA

(*From the painting by P. P. Rubens*)

[*Prado Museum, Madrid*]

QUEEN HENRIETTA MARIA

(From the portrait by Van Dyck in Windsor Castle)

and gave the appointed signal to his confederates; they raised their heavy cavalry pistols from under their cloaks and fired into Concini's face, shattering his forehead, cheekbones and throat; then they drew their swords and struck at the dead man, who had sunk to his knees. With a kick Vitry sent his body flying along the pavement and cried: "Long live the King!" No one had made the slightest resistance. The adventurer who had climbed to such dizzy heights was dead; now it was the turn of his favourites and partisans.

First, they robbed the corpse and dragged it behind a staircase; then when night came they buried it secretly in the church of St. Germain-l'Auxerrois under the organ. But the mob had got wind of the deed; they broke down the church doors, dragged the body through the city and hung it by the feet from the Pont Neuf, where for hours they vented their bestial rage upon it.

The Queen-Mother's reaction to the news was remarkable. "What has happened?" she asked a lady-in-waiting when she heard the tumult in the courtyard. The lady slipped out through the french window and applied to Vitry himself who was walking up and down seeing to everything. "The Maréchal d'Ancre has just been killed by order of the King," he answered the terrified woman, adding: "It was I who did it." The woman slipped away as she had come, softly closed the window, and in a whisper told Marie de' Medici what had happened. "This is the end," the Queen-Mother cried, "for seven years I have been a ruler; now all I can hope for is a crown in heaven!" Then she completely lost control of herself and rushed up and down the room, tearing her hair, and burying her face in her hands. Someone asked: "How are we to tell the Maréchal's wife?" " I have other things to think about; leave me in peace!" cried Marie. "If you can't say it to her, then sing it! Don't talk to me about these people; I have warned them; they should have fled to Italy long ago; I can't bother about such things now; I have enough to do thinking about myself!"

Eleonora was made of different stuff; at first she too was paltry, but after that she seemed to grow in stature under the torments which were inflicted upon her. A few men of the bodyguard forced their way into her room. She shouted at them: "I know. You don't need to tell me. He is dead, the King has had him killed; it was bound to come; he was a conceited fool, yes, a fool; I told him long ago that this would happen." As soon as the soldiers had left the room she acted quickly and resolutely. She cut up her mattress, concealed her money and jewellery in it, and lay down on top of it. But then Vitry's soldiers arrived to search the house; they pulled her out of bed; her treasure was soon found, every drawer in the room was wrenched open and everything left in confusion. The ambitious little brunette was next put through the full horror of a political trial, and driven by way of the dungeon, hunger, cold, and torture to her death at the stake as a witch. But as if she were passing through a process of purification, she grew to true greatness. She justified herself before the court of history when at the very end, in reply to the charge that she had charmed the Queen with black arts, she answered with the brave words: "I have never summoned any power to my help except that power which is given to strong natures over the weak."

During these events Richelieu was in the house of one of his friends: the Rector of the Sorbonne. A student brought the news. As was only to be expected, the Bishop of Luçon did not lose his composure. He had miscalculated, he told himself; he had not credited the King's friends with such powers of decision. He at once returned to the palace, where he found his colleagues Barbin and Mangot hiding in the Regent's stables in great fear. They sent him to the King. The King was in the gallery of the Louvre surrounded by a crowd of excited nobles outdoing one another in protestations of loyalty. In his clerical garb Richelieu calmly approached; his appearance caused a silence; a path was made for him; the King saw him and cried: "So there he is! I'm free of his tyranny at last!

Get away from here, I say!" But the prudent Luynes spoke to him and tried to soothe him; Richelieu had always advised the Queen and Concini well, he said. For a moment fate had touched the young bishop as with an icy pinion; now it was over and he knew that he was saved for the time being. He tried to get a hearing, and actually put in a word for Barbin and Mangot. But the King cut him short: "You will put yourself at the disposal of the Ministerial Council." The old Ministers were back again, Villeroy among them; shortly before the assassination of Concini they had returned to Paris. Villeroy had had to stomach much bitterness to reach this triumph. "In what capacity are you here?" he shouted at Richelieu. For a moment the bishop stood silently in the doorway; then he softly withdrew without answering. When he reached home he learned that Mangot had been arrested, and that sentries were posted in Barbin's house.

Richelieu never knew what personal fear was. Next day he drove out. He came to the Pont Neuf, where mobs from the suburbs were still gathering. The coachman refused to stop, and whipped his horses into the crowd: then Richelieu saw the naked, mutilated body of Concini. He has related what followed: "My coachman had begun to shout at them because they would not let him through; the crowd became hostile; I saw the danger at once; if anyone had recognized me as a supporter of the Maréchal all would have been lost. I shouted at the coachman: 'Be silent!' Then I asked the people nearest to me what they were doing, what had happened; they yelled out their hatred of the Maréchal; I replied: 'I am sure you are people who would gladly die for the King!' and then I shouted them down with the cry: 'Long live the King!' Everyone joined in enthusiastically and let my carriage through."

For five days Marie de' Medici remained uncertain of her fate. At last she could no longer endure her situation; she sent her equerry to her son to ask him what was to happen to her. Nothing would happen to her, was the answer, if she kept quiet; the King would treat her as his mother, but thenceforth he intended to rule by himself. The Queen's bodyguard was replaced by Vitry's men.

On May 10th Richelieu wrote to Luynes: "I thank you a thousand times for the good offices which you have shown me day after day, above all I wish to thank you for the confidence which the King has shown in me, a confidence for which I am obliged to your mediation."

Luynes took pains to spare Richelieu; he knew his gifts and felt that he might yet need him; he recognized the clear, deliberate, and yet natural-seeming chivalry which Richelieu was showing in remaining faithful to his mistress, now fallen into misfortune. Richelieu's new role, which he was to play for some years, began now: he became the Queen-Mother's adviser. If he entered the King's service at once, his presence would have become banal; the others would have grown accustomed to him, and he would have lost his hold on their imaginations. Luynes, the favourite, must first run his course and exhaust his master's favour; he must feel himself in need of help; then and only then, when he was summoned, would Richelieu return. Until then his task was to mediate and serve both parties. His colleagues in the Ministry were in prison; the supporters of Concini were banished; the partisans of the Queen-Mother had lost their places. He, Richelieu, alone remained; more, Luynes had gone the length of suggesting that he should remain in the Ministerial Council.

A decisive part was played, too, by Richelieu's family connections among the Parlement lawyers and the support given him by the Curia. He was in a favourable position to conduct negotiations regarding the further fate of the Queen-Mother. It was decided that she should reside in her castle at Blois. While that huge building was being prepared for her reception she should stay in Moulins. She was permitted to form her suite according to her own wishes; in her place of residence and the province of which it was the head her power should be absolute; and she would enjoy the full benefit of appanages and civil list pension. She set out on May 3rd. The King paid her a parting visit; their encounter was cold and correct; in her offended pride the Queen had to struggle to restrain her tears.

Richelieu compared the departure to a pompous funeral cortège. In full daylight the Queen and mother, ejected by her son, was forced to drive through the streets of Paris past the gaping populace. The general indignation over the rule of her favourites was still so great that her progress was greeted with hoots and curses. Has there ever been a mob which has treated with dignity the spectacle of fallen power? Perhaps the crowd which was later to be present at the execution of Charles I of England.

In Paris all were now completely won over to the King, of whom they had known nothing the day before, and all classes in most of the provinces were soon to follow. A feeling of reassurance came from the apparent lack of any intermediary between the King and the nation; the King was quite new to everyone; people began to recognize in him traits of greatness deriving from his ancestors, to weave a legend round him, and to see in their young monarch what they wished to see.

CHAPTER VII

RICHELIEU IN BLOIS

In Richelieu's life the period during which he exercised power is comparatively short. It lasted from 1624 to his death in 1642; eighteen years of rule for this born ruler. But the previous nineteen years from 1605 to 1624 saw the development of all the elements that determined his political genius and solid achievement; in fact, this period of apparent waiting laid the foundations for all his later work. His objective, which, apart from his own ambition, remained a purely ideal aim, he never lost sight of for a single moment; on the other hand, the possibility of realizing it seemed again and again to escape him, and at such crises he reached more than once the verge of despair. His banishment to Blois in the suite of the Queen was one of these crises, yet not by any means the worst. At first he had been hopeful; he had acted with cool deliberation; he had risen through the favour of Henry IV, and had done all that was possible to retain the favour of the Regent. On his assumption of office circumstances were all against him; only with great caution had he dared to attempt a gradual alienation of the Queen from Concini. After all, Concini was his benefactor; he could never openly oppose his influence, for he was too close to him; and though in spite of this he had succeeded in persuading the Queen, by an almost imperceptible pressure of the will, that the Italian was dangerous, his work had not nearly reached its fulfilment when the assassination forestalled his schemes. Now the situation had changed completely; the ambitious, gifted young statesman in full career had turned into the adherent of a banished Court torn with impotent rage and worm-eaten by intrigue. In power was a new favourite, who had grown great in a single day, and whom no force in the world at the moment could part from the strangely reserved, shy, crafty, stuttering young King. For the first time the King had shown some sign of affection. What he felt for Luynes, his falconer, was more than mere gratitude to the man who had freed him from the burdensome guardianship of his mother.

Luynes at the time of his sudden rise was considerably older than Richelieu. He struck people as elegant and amiable, entirely likeable, with a background of apparently serious reserve. He possessed the great gift of being well informed; for years he had known of the slightest fluctuations in the life of the Court through his two brothers and through trusted friends. Himself a courtier, he watched everything closely, and he moved lightly and noiselessly through the confusion of cross-currents. At first glance he seemed a resolute and even a far-sighted man; he had made, for instance, an excellent falconer. Now he was the King's Minister, and it remained to be seen what reserves were concealed behind his surface brilliance. The weak point in Luynes's intellectual constitution was his sad lack of belief in himself, which made him incapable of enduring setbacks and rendered him insatiable in his lust for favour and success, as if by some obsession. He had to possess, and like everyone who is incapable of gambling boldly to win, he was at bottom apprehensive. He used flattery to gain his ends. With a kind of sickly sweet gentleness which disgusted many people he set himself to be charming at all costs; if he were repulsed or disappointed, his sweetness could easily turn to bitterness and hatred. Borne up on the love of a young prince reared in lovelessness, he rose to a height for which he was in no way fitted. Richelieu and Luynes distrusted each other utterly, and wherever possible tried to do each other an ill turn. Between the Bishop who had lost what power he had, and who now resolved to save for the Queen all that could be saved, and the favourite, the

Queen's deadly enemy, there was conducted both in words and in correspondence "a duel of keen and scrupulous politeness." When they lowered their rapiers for the first time they were almost friends, and yet final and lifelong enemies.

While Richelieu departed into precarious banishment, Luynes as was the usual custom filled the influential posts at Court and in the State with men of his own choosing and his own party. Sillery, Villeroy, Jeannin, and Du Vair formed the Ministry. Excellent, experienced men, indeed too experienced and not very convincing. Among his confidants were his two insignificant brothers, garrulous Southerners, who presently became dukes of Chaulnes and Luxembourg. A certain Modène was also among his friends, a capable man, but dangerous and an intriguer; and finally there was Déageant, Mangot's former secretary, who had all the gifts of a statesman but courage. All these men were fairly well known to Richelieu, and he could reckon with them. But the mob of transient busybodies who emerged for a moment to vanish again in the darkness were more confusing. Italians, Machiavellian figures out of a Goldoni comedy, who now began to intrigue between the Court and the banished Queen, talented improvisers and wretched swindlers; clerics like the Florentine Abbé Ruccellai, who through the favour of Pope Paul V had once almost reached the purple but soon had to disappear from Rome and continue his will-o'-the-wisp career elsewhere. Concini encouraged Ruccellai; he is even said to have thought of putting him in Richelieu's place; but Ruccellai, cunning and revengeful rogue though he was, had a little too much guile, and always turned up a quarter of an hour too late. From Ruccellai there descended a whole hierarchy of intriguers, down to the all-knowing indispensable Tantucci, who was always being kicked from one lie to another. Creatures of this kind wove and unwove, confused and disentangled the network which stretched between the Court in the fine castle of Blois and the royal Court in Paris.

At first Richelieu and the Queen were inseparable; he had

her completely in hand; she did nothing without his counsel; and he was backed up by her first lady-in-waiting, Madame de Guercheville, who was always to support his policy with the greatest wisdom and prudence. Otherwise there was no one of any real worth; fluttering figures, equerries, chamberlains, Italian barbers and apothecaries, and countless transitory apparitions like Ruccellai and Tantucci, who were kept busy coming and going as treacherous agents of the weak and unprincipled Queen.

On arriving at Blois on May 7th, Richelieu at once began a direct correspondence with Luynes. He wrote to him and to Déageant, in whom he seems to have had a certain trust. He informed Luynes that the Queen had learned a lesson from recent events, and that her intentions were good. To Déageant he complained that there was much intriguing against him in the Queen's circle, but thus far without success. One can divine the atmosphere; a crowd of isolated, discontented careerists filled with reciprocal suspicion forced to live together at close quarters in a stifling cloud of malice.

Richelieu's letters received correct but cool responses from Paris; the more he tried to clear himself, to lessen the tension, to achieve closer relations, the more his correspondents in Paris drew back. With Déageant he corresponded in cipher, sending him curious reports on the doings of the Queen and her friends, as if he were an actual agent of Luynes; on the other hand it was he who constantly encouraged the Queen in any move or utterance which was likely to strengthen her position with the King and take the sting out of Luynes's charges against her. Finally it all grew too intricate even for Richelieu; while he laboured in the interests of his career, of the royal house and of the State to loosen the tension between mother and son, at the same time trying to damage Luynes as much as possible, he got himself so entangled that no one believed anything he said.

The Queen herself, informed of his double game, reproached him. That these reproaches were not more severe may be put down to the passionate interest she felt in Richelieu, of which so much was made by their contemporaries and has been made since by historians, an interest of whose nature it is impossible to say anything definite. In any case, Richelieu was in no way bound to Blois; irritated at every turn, he tried almost with desperation to join the King's side and leave the sinking ship; but it was both too late and too soon for that. On June 10th he wrote to Déageant that no one interpreted him rightly, all that he did had been done—had always been done—to serve the King; no turn of fate could alter that loyalty. Simultaneously he begged a Jesuit priest, a friend of the Queen, to come at once to Blois to look after her. A few days later, possibly the very day after the despatch of the letter, the Court awaited the Queen and the Bishop in vain for supper. After some time word was sent that the Queen would not sup, and somewhat later came the astonishing news that Richelieu thought of leaving next morning. And indeed, in the early morning, before anyone could question him, he disappeared.

From Richelieu's and from Déageant's memoirs we know that on the day of his decision the Bishop had received a letter from his brother, the Marquis de Richelieu, who warned him that the King would no longer suffer him to remain in the Queen-Mother's suite and intended immediately to order him to return to his bishopric. This letter was founded on false information; the King had never had any such intention.

Richelieu included in his notes a second letter from his brother, in which the Marquis apologized for sending wrong information. In spite of this document, the question remains open whether this correspondence had not been deliberately planned beforehand.

His departure plunged the Queen into deep despair, to which she gave reckless utterance. To the King she wrote: "If the fact that I am your mother has the slightest influence on you, my son, I implore you from my heart not to withdraw from me the favour of letting the Bishop of Luçon remain in my service. Do not insult me! I would rather die than swallow such insults. There is no desire of my heart, except for the desire to serve you, which touches me so nearly."

And she wrote to Luynes: "After having brought the King into the world, and educated him, and worked seven years to establish his kingdom, I am now reduced to the shameful state of having to swallow insults from my enemies, even from my own servants; I have become the laughing-stock of the nation. To take the Bishop of Luçon away is to treat me no longer as a mother but as a slave; apparently I am to be forced out of the country."

Is not that the language of passion? And does not the tone in which Richelieu wrote the Queen, after an interval, show his awareness of it? "Madame, every day on which I have not the honour to see Your Majesty is a century to me. The passion with which I serve you will not suffer me to wait any longer. I end with the assurance that even when you are absent all my thoughts are constantly concerned with your person, as is but fitting in consideration of your kindness to me."

But Richelieu did not write that letter until the Queen had repeatedly begged, almost implored him for news.

After all these excitements and the agitation of trying to shift his allegiance from Blois to Paris, Richelieu returned to his diocese much as he had made his first sudden departure for Luçon at the end of his studies. Again he was seeking peace and recuperation for himself, and a slackening of tension in his public relations. Henceforth all his letters tell of quiet occupations, of cheerful intercourse with his neighbours and with books. What could be more harmless? All that he wrote breathed reassurance, his very letters grew more infrequent; it was as if he wished to make himself invisible. He did not succeed entirely in avoiding trouble; the General Procurator, being violently anti-clerical, had managed to involve the Bishop in the process against Eleonora Concini, which was of course in essence a process against the Queen. Richelieu had Déageant to thank for the fact that the charges against him were ultimately withdrawn. But still he did not abandon his retreat and his silence. He scarcely even answered letters, as if he were no longer concerned with this world. It transpired that Tantucci had been making all sorts of false allegations against him. Ruccellai was now the Queen's man, and Richelieu had no intention of restraining him if he incited the Queen to break with the Court and fling herself on the mercy of the nobles. Richelieu knew quite well that such a course, which he had already condemned, must lead to disaster and show up in a clear light his own contrasting policy of loyalty to the King.

Even when Déageant informed him that Luynes thought of recalling him to Court, Richelieu made no response. He knew *how* he wished to return to the Court: as the man who had been proved right when the insinuating Southerner was at last exposed in all his emptiness and renewed disaster and confusion demanded a strong hand. It is remarkable that Luynes, who never thought so far ahead as the Bishop, had come to the same conclusions regarding the Queen, but for different reasons. If Richelieu calmly permitted the mother of his sovereign to involve herself in errors it was because he had been right, and at the proper moment was resolved to demonstrate what was right. Whereas when Luynes began sending emissaries to Blois with the object of furthering Ruccellai's designs, it was from the compulsion of weak natures to provide a justification for their policy, in this case to strengthen the force of his slanders against the Queen-Mother by showing fresh evidence to the King. Yet Richelieu, too, had moments of weakness, above all when he felt that he was born to do great work and that his days were being wasted; then he sometimes wrote to his sister complaining that he was lonely and forsaken; more, he suddenly wrote to Luynes himself in a tone of genuine diffidence, imploring him to put in a word to the King for him. He even assailed the King directly with petitions and explanations. But as soon as he showed any such weakness, the Court turned a cold shoulder to him: he became at once a less important figure, and with that the danger of his situation obviously grew greater.

At the end of September 1617 Richelieu thought of the mysterious man whom he almost regarded now as a friend: Father Joseph. "My father," he wrote, "I hope to show you by this letter that I put complete trust in you. . . . I suffer so deeply that I wish to open my heart to you." And Richelieu described all that he had endured for four months, adding that he had borne everything with Christian patience; he begged the Father to ask Déageant to explain his complicated case in a favourable light. Then followed a sentence which Richelieu knew would go home to the heart of the monk; all his energy in his diocese, he wrote, was devoted to fighting heresy. He reminded Joseph of their common missionary efforts in the past, and emphasized that his battle was made very difficult by the attitude of the Court, which lowered his prestige throughout the country.

It is certain that this letter moved Father Joseph, and that he tried to fulfil his friend's wishes. Slowly and persistently from now on he worked for the rise of Richelieu, but many obstacles had to be overcome, and for the time being Joseph was a better judge of these than the Bishop isolated in his diocese.

Richelieu's leisure now enabled him to demonstrate in practice that his energies were indeed engaged in the fight against the heretics. He seized his pen again and composed a brilliant polemic against four priests of Charenton who had dedicated to the King himself a treatise against the Jesuits. "A Defence of the Cardinal Points of the Catholic Faith against the letter of the Four Priests of Charenton" was the title of this powerful, lucid, and terse treatise. It dealt with the eternal antithesis. The Protestants, he said, all insisted on the same thing, the suppression of any mediator. According to them, God spoke direct to men, and had spoken only once, in the Book which He Himself had dictated. What need, then, was there for priests and priestly consecration, for the Mass, the cult of Mary and the saints, the images? A clear conscience sufficed in the soul which God had chosen by His inscrutable decree. Faith alone was effectual, and works could at most support it. The Catholic, on the other hand, was concerned with the universal, not the individual, with mankind, not the single person, with the Church, not the separate believer. Hierarchy and authority were necessary in order to avoid the worst of all evils: disorder and anarchy, the consequences of individualism and freedom of judgment. Religion had rescued men from anarchy, and anarchy took them back to itself again once the bonds of religion were loosed. The pedantic, pharisaical character of Protestantism, which sought to derive everything from the written word, and its dialectical methods Richelieu condemned as sheer intellectual arrogance. He referred to those who were Christians before there was a written Evangel, those who believed in Christ in the time of the holy Irene without prayer and without ink, as was testified.

But the undertone of this great work is political: the principle set up by the Protestants, said Richelieu, was that of a State representing the people's will; it delivered the State into the hands of the people, and the people was a many-headed monster which did not know its own desires, and nothing could be more ruinous than to exchange a paternal authority for the rule of that blind and deaf mob. After a century of reformation the Roman Empire of German Nations and the kingdom of France were in a state of turmoil, weakness, and division. Unity was as sacred as the seamless garment of Christ; division was ruin.

The demoniac element, the unconscious guidance, in all human struggle becomes clear when such a man as Richelieu speaks out. The predominating idea in his thesis was the autonomous existence of the State, for whose sake he demanded law, order, unity. At this point the two antithetic views met without knowing it, for nothing in the new times had done more to strengthen the idea of the State than Protestantism in its own way. Richelieu perhaps divined this, for he excused the sharpness of his polemic in the introduction, in which he appealed for common collaboration for the good of the State, and like his great teacher Henry IV advised toleration.

The composition and publication of this work occupied Richelieu all the summer of 1617; the success of the book was such that his personal enemies became uneasy and were also fortified in their resolve to keep him out of the political world.

The star of the favourite was still rising; power and success, wealth and glory were added to him in that parasitic fashion which to a cool observer seems thoroughly unsound. Luynes was already quartered in the Louvre; he was chief chamberlain, and Lieutenant-General of Normandy; he had acquired the confiscated properties of d'Ancre; and he designed to marry the natural sister of the King, so that Bourbon blood might flow in the veins of his descendants. Here for the first time he encountered resistance and became aware of the disapproval growing around him. He took alarm and yielded; but after this setback he made a great marriage with the lovely Montbazon of the house of Rohan, who was later, as Duchesse de Chevreuse, to have so much varied influence on the history of France. The dowry was enormous, and he was now allied with the first families in the kingdom. Already he found himself in a situation which had much resemblance to that of the deceased Concini.

It was now necessary to provide a firm foundation for all the wealth he had gathered. His policy against the Queen-Mother must be given a legal aspect. Accordingly Luynes summoned at Rouen, the capital of his lieutenancy, an assembly of notables, which was opened on September 10th in the presence of the King by a speech from the Chancellor, Sillery. The assembly did excellent work; it dealt with justified and long-standing complaints; a regrouping of the Ministerial Council was outlined; the Paulette, which the Estates-General had failed to deal with, was abolished; and it was decided to restrict drastically the money spent in pensions. A Government which could effect such important changes with the consent of an assembly of notables seemed to be firmly fixed in the saddle and to have general sanction for its policy. But none of its decisions, none of the promises given by the King were carried out, and, like every other parliamentary experiment in France during the seventeenth century, this came to nothing.

Luynes kept an apprehensive eye on Blois. What disturbed him most was the political inactivity of the Bishop of Luçon, who seemed recently to have strengthened his influence by his literary success; that from time to time he still kept on sending petitions and explanations was merely a cloak for his evil designs.

To give his rule a legal complexion Luynes had summoned the asembly of notables; but he was not in a position to execute its decisions. He noticed that people were beginning to murmur against him; he feared that the discontent might find a focus in the person of the Queen-Mother, and a leader in the Bishop. Richelieu was still too near at hand, so he was forbidden to leave his diocese, whose swamps and fevers were bad for his health. His brother, the Marquis, and his brother-in-law Pont-de-Courlay were exiled from the Court to their castles. Richelieu felt that a storm was brewing; but at this very moment the Queen-Mother, still at the mercy of intriguers and anxious for his counsel, renewed her attempts to get him back to Blois. Richelieu wrote immediately to his brother, asking him torestrain her by every argument in his power.

As a means of prying into all these secrets, Luynes permitted Barbin, who was still in the Bastille, to correspond with the Queen, and relaxed the severity of his confinement. The letters came and went; the Queen, as usual, wrote quite without caution. Certain nobles, with the best intention of effecting a general reconciliation, joined their entreaties to the Queen's; Henri de Rohan was among them, also his cousin Montbazon, the favourite's father-in-law. Luynes had all the letters secretly intercepted, noted their contents, gave away everyone involved, and by doing so was later to earn their enmity; but now he had in his hands what he wanted; he had evidence of imprudent or dangerous utterances. Suddenly he struck; he put before the King copies of the incriminating passages, and loudly declared that a grave plot had been unmasked. The Governor of the Bastille, who had permitted the correspondence, was arrested. His protestations that he had acted on Luynes's instructions did not avail him. A few pamphleteers who had supported the Queen were publicly burned on the Place de Grève. Then—and this was the chief aim of the manœuvre—Richelieu, who had not been implicated at all, was given orders at once to quit his bishopric and the country: he had reached the nadir of his fortunes.

✶✶✶

CHAPTER VIII

EXILE

It is the mark of a genuine passion that it destroys its possessor when its object becomes unattainable. At the time of Concini's assassination Richelieu was thirty-two. For seven years circumstances forced him from his true course. For seven years he was to remain exiled from affairs. Yet as long as he was in France he could still hope; he might suffer and fear and be torn by impatience, but like Antaeus his strength was renewed by contact with the soil. Now, however, he had to cross the frontier, to become an outcast from the kingdom of France. At the end of winter, by wretched roads, he started on his journey to the Papal stronghold of Avignon. By May 12th, a month later, his secretary Le Masle was arranging with the authorities of the collegial church for the renting of a palace in the town, where, to judge from the inventory, Richelieu could live with his accustomed pomp and in accordance with that beauty and dignity of style which he always maintained. For a man of different character one might have predicted a period of serene waiting during that Provençal spring in one of the most beautiful towns of southern France. Richelieu was not alone: the Marquis and his brother-in-law accompanied him. He himself expressed his relief that his enemies had not sent him into exile without his relatives: though they had done so merely to keep them the better under observation. Avignon itself was a rich town, which then reminded travellers of Bologna, what with its flourishing trade, the beauty of its churches, palaces, and squares, and the prosperity of its people.

A modern man, accustomed to uproot himself easily and to draw refreshment from many sources, might have found in these surroundings recuperation and security; not so a Richelieu, whose powers, nourished for centuries on the same soil, grew in one direction only. He was a man genuinely banned, separated from all that he loved and desired, divining that the object of his love as well as himself must come to grief through that separation. There is a document which he dictated at Avignon at his moment of deepest despair; he called it "Caput apologeticum." All that had happened, his relations with Concini, with the Queen, with Luynes, his faith in the kingdom, his labours, his self-renunciation, his decisions, can be read there, feverishly poured out in sharp, striking, pregnant sentences. Never had he had any other wish, he could say it before the throne of God, than the one wish to serve the King, or rather the man, Louis XIII. It had been charged against him that he lived wastefully, that, like Concini, he played the great man. On that point he defended himself; he had lived in honourable dignity, he said, as beseemed one who served the King; but now every virtue he possessed was turned into an offence, a crime; everything evil was imputed to a man in misfortune. The son of a father who had died in Henry IV's service, himself enlisted by the King in that service, a loyal servant of the Queen after the King's death, advanced by the King, recognized in Rome, praised by the Sorbonne, thorough in the administration of his diocese as a bishop: such had been his record—and now such a downfall. With almost painful lucidity, and in full possession of that far-sighted vision which he always showed in political matters, whatever his situation, he reviewed the work of his successor with keen criticism, and as if he were on the point of death and had to justify himself for the last time in a matter of such grave import, he commended Barbin, whom he called a courageous and honest statesman.

But the will to live and the desire for action are stronger than such melodramatic broodings over oneself and one's fate. He laid the document aside; he did not fling it as a polemic into the fray; it was to be kept as a great impeachment should he ever have to leave the stage. It was both a contribution to history and a relief to his proud, deeply wounded spirit; but he slipped it among the other papers in his desk, and did not give it to the unsettled world.

Again he plunged into work, reading more books than ever before or after. He continued his theological dispute with the Protestant pastors, living in pious retirement as his spiritual office demanded. With Jean Marie, a Carmelite priest from Fribourg, he united in prayer and work; and the bare-foot monk prophesied for him a return of fortune and a career of dizzy elevation. His great political conceptions grew clearer during this time of solitude. Like a vision there appeared to him the world which he was to shape for the coming generations of Europe: the world of national autonomous States. He knew now that it was necessary to subordinate a Catholic policy to one which would finally break the predominance of Spain in Europe. This idea perpetually haunted him; as a young man he had sometimes subordinated it to the idea of serving the Catholic Church; but now that his love for France had been so deeply wounded, now that he thought he saw in his misfortunes the clandestine influence of Spanish diplomacy, his decision crystallized and became indestructible for the rest of his life. His enemies had reproached him with working in Spain's interest. He would show them what his intentions were, and why he had for the time being spared that great power. And now, at the moment when Rome was his sole and last support, when the Pope was intervening for him, the courage required to declare his political views even in his letters was very great. The Pope had spoken to the French Ambassador on Richelieu's behalf; the King was enraged at such a step and answered: "If this bishop had minded his own business instead of grossly intriguing in provinces outside his competence, nothing would have happened to him." Richelieu set his heart on convincing the

King that France, and not the Holy Father, had the first claim on his allegiance.

The autumn of 1618 found Richelieu at the end of his strength. What irked him most was the inactivity and the equivocal appearance of his position, which nobody but himself could construe. To everyone he appeared double-tongued, dissimulating, false. He alone knew the deep consistency of his aims and actions; he knew it, but he could no longer explain it, and there was no one to listen to him. On top of this he had material cares, and personal misfortune came to darken his exile still further. In the haste of departure the Marquis de Richelieu had had to leave his wife, who was pregnant, in the family castle. She died, quite alone, while giving birth to a son on October 15th. The Marquis implored the King for permission to return and look after his newly born child. Permission arrived along with the news that the child was already dead. The Marquis and his brother-in-law left, and Richelieu remained alone in Avignon; his thoughts grew more and more gloomy.

His family was passing through a phase of misfortune, and he could see no end to it. The severe fever of his childhood broke out again. He could feel his powers deserting him, and prepared for death. He drew up his will in the form of a letter to the chapter in Luçon. "No one," he wrote, "can foretell the course of his life, and as for me, I do not know how it will please God to decide upon mine." He determined the place in the cathedral in which he was to be interred, and enumerated his legacies. His silver, vestments, and his three pavilions of Flemish tapestry he left to his bishopric, and regretted that there was not more. To the seminary which he had founded he left the sum of 1,000 livres and his whole library. On February 13, 1619, he instructed his secretary to terminate the lease of his house. Still without any news from his brothers, he wrote to them asking them to distribute a few trifling mementoes, if he should die.

Did he really believe that his death was so near? Had he

the intention of withdrawing completely into the Minorite monastery where he spent so much of his time every day? That he, who had daily to wrest from death his existence and his work, ever thought of suicide is unthinkable. Considering the high conception which he had of the place he occupied and would yet occupy in the world, such thoughts could only have appeared to him as temptations of Satan. No, he did not seek death; he felt it approaching.

But now that he had reached the deepest point of despondency, help was already near. On March 7th there appeared at Avignon a mounted courier from Paris. It was Du Tremblay, Father Joseph's brother. He brought a letter to Richelieu written in the King's hand. Louis ordered the Bishop of Luçon to proceed to Angoulême by the shortest route and at once to resume his service with the Queen-Mother.

CHAPTER IX

RICHELIEU AND THE REBELS

The sudden turn which brought Richelieu back to France was to be explained by the new resistance of the nobles to Luynes, the intervention of the Church on behalf of Marie de' Medici, and the natural feeling of the French people, a feeling drawn from a sense of Christian and antique piety which was still strong and which regarded with mounting indignation the King's treatment of his mother.

After Luynes's exploitation of the correspondence between Barbin and the Queen, a correspondence instigated by himself, Marie, torn between impotent rage and fear, had no support left. She suffered deeply from her isolation, and in her despair did everything she could to induce the King to recall Richelieu. How quickly, almost apprehensively, Richelieu had intervened to prevent her efforts has already been seen. There was nowhere that the ageing woman could turn, and so the hour of the intriguing Ruccellai inevitably arrived. All Richelieu's enemies were backing him and he was not content with having the Queen returned to favour; rejecting Richelieu's prudent, waiting policy he advocated one of violence. He could count on a certain support from public opinion; Luynes's insults to the Queen had gone too far. His action in the Barbin case was regarded as scandalous; even according to the ideas of that time there was something contemptible in such double-dealing. His measures against the Queen overshot their mark; he actually carried them into the sphere of foreign policy. Against all diplomatic usage he deported the ambassador of the Duke of Tuscany, with the excuse that he was carrying on secret intrigues with the Queen. At every opportunity he sought to humiliate or cast suspicion on the mother of his King. Even the betrothal of her daughter to the Prince of Piedmont had taken place virtually without her knowledge and assent.

The nobles had long since deserted the favourite as in Concini's time; they banded together and sought an excuse, a pretext for resisting the power of Luynes; they found it in his treatment of Marie de' Medici.

To exploit such a situation was a heaven-sent task for a man like Ruccellai; his business was to nurture and exacerbate the mounting discontent, the desires and secret designs of the widely dispersed nobles, many of whom were at odds, and play them off against each other, so that one by one they might be forced to come over to his side. Those who had been involved in the Barbin affair would form a nucleus for the attack on Luynes.

Among Henry III's "mignons" one of the most elegant and overbearing had been Louis de Nogaret-La-Valette. He, too, had scrambled his way to power; he was now old, and with age had become a surly, unbending figure, much looked up to and a prime favourite of the army; he was also the Duc d'Epernon, Governor of Metz, the strongest frontier stronghold in the country, Commander of the French infantry, and Governor of Saintonge and Angoumois. His two sons were the Archbishop of Toulouse, later to become Cardinal, and the Marquis de La Valette. Proud and irascible, he regarded himself as the first man in the kingdom after the King, and showed it at every opportunity. He had once induced the Parlement to confirm Marie's position as Regent, but Concini's hangers-on had shown him little gratitude; they had no love for the former paladins of Henry IV. D'Epernon disdained to put up a fight; he punished the Court by absenting himself in complete indifference. Only once did he deign to pay his respects to the King, shortly after Concini's death. When he entered Paris all the officers from the capital and the provinces came streaming to greet him, so great was the respect he enjoyed in the army. He, too, had been a favourite; he, too, had risen very high, and a man like Luynes could not impress him; the very fact that their careers had so many points of resemblance doomed them to become enemies. Luynes had often tried to humiliate him; he had refused support to his family; he had tried to cross the careers of his two sons. One day the favourite and d'Epernon met on the steps of the Louvre. The old soldier was leaving the palace; Luynes was entering. "You gentlemen are on the up grade, it seems, but we are going downhill," said d'Epernon in passing. The Duke's presence was feared; his following was so great that there was actually some apprehension of a *coup*. His arrest was already being considered when he got wind of it and left the city. He made his farewell visit to the King at the head of three hundred horsemen, and then set out posthaste for his fortress of Metz, where he shut himself in.

When Ruccellai was weaving the first threads of his plot he turned to the Duc de Bouillon, a man whose international standing, whose relations to the General States and the German Calvinist princes, whose influence in the frontier provinces of France must always be regarded as dangerous. But Bouillon gave Ruccellai the cold shoulder; he himself had greater plans. He was dreaming of a mighty Calvinist republic; the family affairs of the Bourbons did not concern him. Still he advised Ruccellai to try d'Epernon. But unfortunately Ruccellai did not stand well with d'Epernon; he had once, to ingratiate himself with Luynes, crossed the Duke's path. So he had to work under cover, and first involve the Duke unwittingly, until he could no longer retreat. The Queen must appeal to the old man's chivalry; from every side he must be assured that his former sovereign lady, the widow of Henry IV, was in need of him. Plans were unfolded to him. A reliable courier was to make contact with Marie; meanwhile d'Epernon was to leave Metz secretly and proceed to his residence in Angoumois, where the Queen-Mother, having quitted Blois by stealth, was to join him. Although more than a hundred men were in the secret, Luynes learned nothing, and hints that were dropped he airily dismissed. He thought that Ruccellai was in Germany, though that dexterous gentleman had been tirelessly posting on horseback backwards and forwards across France from one conspirator to another, without even an escort. And his dexterity and perseverance were no greater than the Duke's decision and resolution, though he was now sixty-five.

D'Epernon's younger son, the Marquis de La Valette, assumed command in Metz; the other, the Archbishop, preceded his father eight days in advance; the Duke set out on January 22nd. The weather was warm and bright for the time of the year. He passed Dijon. Not till he had crossed the river Allié by the bridge of Vichy did he write to the King, saying that he was visiting his governments, and that he had no wish except to live as an obedient subject of his sovereign. Luynes was deeply alarmed; he was now certain that something was afoot, but he did not yet know that the Queen-Mother was involved in it. Now that the decisive hour had come, Marie de' Medici was remarkably calm; she showed composure and fortitude. Ruccellai's courier, sent to inform her of the Duke's departure, proceeded to Paris instead, hoping to be well paid for his treachery. A friend of the Queen, a member of Parlement, not knowing quite what was happening, intercepted and held him, but owing to the non-arrival of the messenger the Queen was now without information from outside. Equally uncomfortable was the situation of d'Epernon and his son, who after arriving in Angoumois found no word awaiting them from the Queen. They formed the foolhardy plan of getting in touch with Blois. They sent a certain Du Plessis there, preceded a few hours earlier by a chamberlain to announce his arrival. Du Plessis halted at Loches, where soon afterwards the Archbishop joined him. The advance courier Cadillac arrived in Blois to disentangle the difficulties of the situation by himself. He asked to be admitted to the Queen;

she received him at once. He acquainted her fully with the situation. A grave problem for her. Without any reliable confidant, simply on the spoken word of this lackey, was she to entrust herself to such an undertaking? She would scarcely have acted had not Du Plessis now appeared. It was he who persuaded her to let a young gentleman of her Court, the Comte de Brenne, into the secret. Cadillac returned to the Archbishop to inform him of the Queen's decision; at once the Archbishop set out, and that same night, February 22nd, halted six miles from the castle of Blois. The Duke himself was still at Loches. Cadillac went on to him; he had to repeat several times to him what the Queen had said. For a moment d'Epernon shrank from the whole foolhardy enterprise; but then he made his final preparations. He sent off Cadillac again, who rode to Blois at a gallop and arrived at half-past twelve o'clock at night. Brenne admitted him into the town. The carriage for the Queen was already waiting. Lights could be seen in the Queen's apartments. By two ladders which Brenne had procured Cadillac climbed up to the room and in through the window where Marie was waiting. Her whole suite, when informed of the plan, implored her to abandon it. But Marie was resolved; she ordered them to open the window. Cadillac jumped into the room and flung himself at the feet of his sovereign. As soon as he mentioned the name of d'Epernon, all the courtiers suddenly understood what was afoot and gave up their resistance. The heavy, ageing woman had packed her treasures. She tucked up her dress with her own hands, and without showing any fear stepped from the window ledge on to the rungs of the ladder. Brenne had preceded her; Du Plessis, Cadillac, two bodyguards, and her lady-in-waiting followed. The window was over a hundred feet from the ground. The Queen was so completely exhausted by the time she reached a terrace that she refused to go further. There chanced to be a fall of rubble running over the walls from the terrace to the ground. Ropes were fastened round the Queen, a cloak was flung over her, and she was lowered over the rubble. Scarcely had she arrived in safety when Brenne and Du Plessis supported her on either side. Some soldiers who saw her took her for a whore. She said laughing: "They think I'm a light-of-love." She arrived safely at the carriage. The chests, filled with gold and jewellery, were packed in. No sooner were they clear of the town than they lit the carriage lamps and drove at full speed to Montrichard, where they were met first by Ruccellai, and then by the Archbishop. Then they changed horses and drove on to Loches, where the Duke offered his services to his deeply grateful Queen.

On the 26th Louis XIII received by courier a letter from his mother written in Loches. She informed him that she had set herself free in order to be in a better position to exchange counsel with him concerning the matters he held most at heart, above all her anxieties concerning the State, whose downfall she foresaw if it remained any longer in the hands at present directing it. She had withdrawn to the government of d'Epernon, since no one had ever dared to question the loyalty of that old friend of her husband.

Louis's immediate impulse was to take to horse and set things right by armed force. But Luynes succeeded in calming him. The first thing was to gain time, and when the reply was sent, it was d'Epernon who was attacked, and not Marie. This manifesto against the Duke and the letter from the Queen were then made public. The tables were turned on d'Epernon, who was accused of having made an attempt on the liberty of the Queen at a moment when the King was taking steps to draw closer to her. The Duke was deprived of his post as Commander of the Infantry, and was informed that he would be treated as a rebel. The Marquis de Béthune and Bérulle, the founder of the Oratorium, were ordered to proceed to Angoulême at once. Exactly what the Bishop of Luçon had foreseen and hoped for had now happened. It was at last recognized what a great mistake had been made in separating the Queen from Richelieu, who "counselled moderation, and worked in the interests of the Court." The moment had come when all his friends could freely plead for him. They saw it at once; they came loyally up to scratch, and achieved the utmost he could have hoped for; a situation in deep and gratifying contrast to that in which he had previously found himself. The King wrote him a cordial letter with his own hand; the letter which Father Joseph's brother brought to Avignon. One cannot help asking whether Richelieu had really thought he was dying. Or had he terminated the lease of his house because he had a premonition that his real life was now about to begin? In all probability reports had been reaching him; he may have hoped even while he despaired, and perhaps had given his despair free vent, as a man gives way to tears when a crisis is over. He wrote: "As soon as I received His Majesty's despatch, I left Avignon at once by carriage, in spite of the bad weather, the deep snow, and bitter cold, in order to obey his command and proceed where my wishes and my duty led me." The journey was not without incident. Richelieu avoided with difficulty being arrested by ignorant provincial officials. On March 27, 1619, a year to a day since his departure into exile, he appeared to put his services at the disposal of Marie de' Medici, who, moved at this proof of the King's indulgence of her deepest wishes, once more completely entrusted herself to his guidance, and turned from Ruccellai and d'Epernon. Nothing could have been more unfortunate for Ruccellai than the return of this man, whom he had the impudence to regard as his rival.

Political capacity, especially capacity for foreign affairs, is closely related to a man's practical knowledge of society. What a sure knowledge of human nature can be seen in Richelieu's decision to abandon everything and go away after the death of Concini! Blunder after blunder would meanwhile be made at Blois; it would become obvious to everyone how good his influence on the Queen had been, and his enemies, that crowd of intriguers, must expose themselves completely. His calculations had been just: and after months of slow pining away in Avignon he was suddenly to the fore again, more keen and efficient than ever. On his arrival in Angoulême on March 27th he behaved with faultless tact. His first visit was not to the Queen, but to the Governor, the Duc d'Epernon. The Duke received him courteously and conducted him to the Queen. She let him wait for a little, but once she was alone with him the long-shut sluices of her intimacy were opened at once. She wanted to know everything about his own state, his health; she described her own situation passionately, in a torrent of words.

Richelieu let her speak and remained quite cool and unimpressed. He had no intention, he indicated calmly but unmistakably, of involving himself in difficulties for which others were responsible. He would not take part in the Queen's council on these terms. After being sufficiently implored from every side, he at last consented to be present at the deliberations, but said nothing; modesty forbade him, he said. Ultimately, on being urged to speak, he uttered one sentence, but that sentence was both decisive and the last thing anyone had expected. They must at once come to terms with the King, he said; they had not the power necessary for resistance. Through d'Epernon, Ruccellai threatened to resign; the Queen accepted his resignation in silence. It had taken Richelieu twenty-four hours to defeat his Tuscan rival. Ruccellai lost his head and became violent and abusive. The Duke still hesitated: a strange idea had occurred to him: he thought for a moment of playing against Richelieu a remarkable man living in Angoulême, no other than the great letter-writer, the stylist Guez de Balzac. While all this was happening the royal army set out against the rebels under the command of the inflexible Schomberg.

It was now a question which would be quicker: the negotiating priests, Bérulle and Richelieu, or the marching soldiers. The priests won. Richelieu soon got the Queen to the point of definite decision; and Louis XIII, to give the negotiations with his mother the requisite solemnity, sent to her one of the most highly placed personages in the country, Cardinal de La Rochefoucauld. She accepted all the King's conditions.

The internal peace of the land was saved; Te Deums were raised and all the bells were set ringing. It was all Richelieu's work. He was saluted with admiration and gratitude from every side; everyone suddenly turned to him; he was the man of the hour. His daily correspondence was multiplied; and he had to keep at a distance former enemies of his who now sought the favour of the man who had been proved right.

The danger now lay where the sphere of Luynes's influence began. Once more Richelieu and Luynes were on opposite sides; it would be disastrous if the situation were to become static and Luynes remain the King's man and Richelieu the mere confidant of the Queen, just as they had been before. For now that the immediate danger was past, the saviour too would be forgotten in a few weeks or months. The Queen could not be counted on; she had inspirations; but at bottom she was foolish to the verge of insensibility, without self-control or purpose, obstinate and violent, ambitious, pampered, sentimental and fond of her comfort, yet on occasion surprisingly hard with herself and equal to danger. It was impossible to count with any assurance on her, for when she was tired of thinking she claimed that she was following her instincts; and her mind could be changed from hour to hour.

There was much to be done. A party must be founded, a group which could be relied upon; some people belonging to the Court and the nobility and a few priests. There was Richelieu's brother on the one side, and Father Joseph on the other to build on. Three questions had to be answered. Would the Queen-Mother return to the Court? Would the Prince of Condé be released from captivity? And the third—a burning question for Richelieu, for the right answer to it would protect him for the future against the vicissitudes of outward fortune, and be his reward for his labours in saving the peace—would Richelieu become a cardinal? The King must propose his name to the Pope.

As for Marie de' Medici's relations with her son, Richelieu

set everything in motion to reach an understanding as quickly as possible. That is, in principle: for in practice he let the Queen propound her own conditions, among which a guarantee of her security kept recurring in the conversations she had with the King's two emissaries. Cardinal de La Rochefoucauld and Béthune tried in vain to discover what she meant by security, but it could not be got out of her. She held to her formula and gave no explanation. From the letter containing La Rochefoucauld's instructions, it is clear that the Court, on whom public opinion had begun to lay the odium of inhumanity to the Queen-Mother, was this time prepared to make the widest concessions. The instructions ran: "In view of the fact that the Queen-Mother's office as Governor of Normandy has till now existed more in name than in reality, His Majesty proposes to grant her the real administration of a province, whereby she shall have full authority and the disposal of several fortified places, into which if necessary she may withdraw herself. To this end Monsieur the Cardinal shall propose to her that, if she will remit her office as Governor of Normandy into the hands of His Majesty, the King will invest her with the government of the province of Anjou with the castle of Angers, whereupon she shall be at liberty to occupy this castle with such persons as she may please to name. Also His Majesty gives Monsieur the Cardinal full powers to offer the Queen the bridgehead of Pont-de-Cé on the Loire, or if she has no desire for it, he may offer her the protection of the town and castle of Chinon, where she may make similar arrangements to those proposed in the case of Angers. But if she should not be satisfied even with the two strongholds of Angers and Chinon, the King will add the already named bridgehead. In the circumstances, more can hardly be promised." And indeed this was how the negotiations were concluded.

Richelieu supported Béthune in every way he could. Béthune knew this, appreciated it, and acknowledged it. Much had been achieved; Richelieu had once more done a service to the Court, and a great one to the Queen, and Marie now actually possessed a strong and excellently placed strategic base, if another break with her son should ever come. As for the grounds which made the Court willing to grant such comprehensive concessions, they may be found in the perpetual threat of the Huguenots, and the fact that the Queen, the ever-lastingly discontented nobles, and the powerful d'Epernon, might join forces with Henri de Rohan and the Protestants of all France; in which case no one could foresee what might happen, and foreign intervention would be unavoidable. How strongly Richelieu emphasized the value of strategic advantages for the Queen-Mother is shown by the fact that in a memorial to her which he drew up along with his brother he praised the climate of Anjou and the strength of the chief fortress there, yet insisted that Nantes as a seaport and Amboise with its command of the Loire would be far preferable. Through Nantes their connection with other countries would have been secured. This last ground, which Marie calmly advanced during the negotiations, almost put an end to the goodwill shown by the Court. Schomberg moved his men a little nearer; this at once curtailed the Queen's demands; and so on May 12th she came to an agreement, which however was only verbal, with La Rochefoucauld. The actual treaty merely said that the King permitted his mother to dispose of her Court as she pleased, and to engage in her service or dismiss from it whom she liked. Under Schomberg's pressure she had hastily pronounced herself satisfied; and naturally, as soon as Luynes felt that he had the whip-hand again he tried to get round La Rochefoucauld's verbal assurances. Richelieu was accordingly provided with further work to do. He wanted a reconciliation, but not a complete reconciliation; for if the Queen were to return to her son's Court and live there in peace, his post would at once lose any importance. But if she were merely to visit it to receive final possession of her provinces and fortresses, he would remain at the head of a sort of alternative government, and great possibilities would lie

E

in his hands. He adroitly fanned the rumours of unrest among the Protestants, and it was Luynes who now gave way. On June 11th Marie de' Medici was granted by royal decree the governments of Angers, Chinon, and Pont-de-Cé. She at once appointed the Marquis de Richelieu as governor of Angers; the Bishop of Luçon remained her closest adviser.

In the course of his astonishing career Richelieu was to influence the fate of Europe for centuries, but perhaps never did he find a more perfect solution for a problem than this one. Yet at this point he was also to suffer one of the heaviest blows of his life.

Richelieu had loved his mother sincerely and from his heart; his tenderness for her was above his ambitions and his animosities. The friendship which bound him to his brother, the Marquis, was of a different order. It was genuine, but also completely involved with cares and hopes, memories of the dangers they had faced together, the troubles they had borne, the fortunes of the family, in which Richelieu always had an eye on the future, which he hoped to see realized in his brother. There was much for which he had to thank his brother; he admired in him the excellent soldier, the man of clear judgment, also the bold, handsome man expert at all physical feats. A deep community of interest bound him to this sound member of the family which seemed otherwise to be threatened with destruction on every side. The qualities of the two brothers were complementary. They both stood high in the favour and the service of the Queen. They were surrounded by envy, yet it seemed no longer capable of touching them. But there was a certain Thémines, a son of the Thémines who had once arrested the Prince of Condé, who felt that he had been passed over; he had hoped to be made governor of Angers. He expressed himself in the most abusive terms concerning certain fortune-hunters. His words were brought to the Marquis de Richelieu, who, insulted in his honour, sent a message to Thémines signifying his readiness to meet him. The Queen intervened, but the two men hated each other and looked for opportunities. By chance they met on June 8th outside the citadel, and sprang from their saddles at once. In the first round of the duel Richelieu wounded his opponent. But Thémines had a short dagger, and darting under Richelieu's sword stabbed him to the heart. The Marquis could only cry: "God forgive my sins!" before he died.

Shortly afterwards the Bishop wrote to one of his friends: "My sorrow at this loss bows me down, so that I can neither speak nor write." And much later he was to say in his memoirs: "It is impossible for me to describe the state into which I was cast by this calamity. The complete despair which seized me then was so great that I felt prepared to renounce everything," and he continues: "My personal life was over; only my sense of duty supported me." He kept a sort of diary in which he occasionally jotted brief observations intended only for himself. It contains the following entry: "The separation of soul and body can take place only through a great convulsion of nature, and the separation of two souls who have always lived together in the closest friendship and understanding is attended by almost equal torture." Or this: "I have never suffered a deeper loss, and the certainty of my own approaching destruction would have oppressed me less."

This sorrow accompanied Richelieu like a shadow all through his life.

Nevertheless, as was bound to happen, after the first violent shock of grief, he acted as his nature fitted him to act: he worked, pulled himself together and struggled on, exerting all his powers. He filled the place of his dead brother and of the fleeing Thémines with relations and men he could trust. He appointed as Governor of Angers his uncle on the mother's side, La Porte, a rude frank man, independent even in his dealings with his nephew. Richelieu now sent him to the Court to report faithfully on the first meeting between the Queen-Mother and the King. He instructed him to represent the visit of the Queen to Paris as the wish of all well-disposed men, and in particular of the Bishop of Luçon, and to reply to all questions not at all or only in the most general terms, so that nothing could be taken out of his words. What Richelieu was chiefly resolved on was that this meeting, which meant reconciliation for all France, and for the Queen forgiveness for much folly, should bring about a new consolidation of his own position, one might almost say of his party.

The further the reconciliation went, the more the power and influence of the Queen grew. Those Protestants and nobles who had bargained with her for their help when she was most in need of it, now offered it freely and without conditions. Richelieu gathered them in and encouraged their zeal. He formed a group round the Queen, with the intention of using it not against the King, only against Luynes. And Luynes guessed it and grew alarmed. He did all he could to placate Richelieu. The letters they exchanged were scrupulously polite on both sides, but the Bishop made the conditions. Luynes, on the other hand, merely tried to save what he could; he actually consented to refuse the offices of Ruccellai, the turncoat, who wished to enter his service.

Richelieu wanted the cardinal's hat, and many more things as well; and to secure them he required pledges and means of applying pressure. Accordingly he did not let mother and son reach the length of full reconciliation. He would not a second time ally himself with a Court which alienated the country for the sake of a favourite.

There were many things to be done simultaneously. The death of his elder brother left Richelieu in acute money difficulties. He first annulled the will, and then drove a hard bargain with the creditors; his enemies have dragged many secrets to light regarding his behaviour at this time. He ruthlessly broke with the obligations which for so long had impeded his house and had once made his mother's life wretched; he was not scrupulous in doing so, and began now to build up the enormous fortune which he left behind him at his death.

In place of his brother, Richelieu began to initiate his uncle La Porte into all his plans. He had secured much for the

Queen, but he was not by any means satisfied, although after Ruccellai's fall he was complete master of the situation. When Luynes urged that a public meeting between the King and his mother would have a good effect on public opinion, Richelieu delayed the execution of the plan as long as he could. He tried to achieve the utmost from both sides. He hinted to the Protestants and the nobles that the widow of Henry IV, overborne by the Court, was on the point of a complete reconciliation with her son. To Luynes, on the other hand, he hinted at the daily increasing rebel reinforcements, the love of the people for the ill-used Queen. The result was that Mayenne, Soissons and the Huguenots pressed their support on the Queen, and that Luynes, who no longer knew where he was, yielded one concession after another.

For three years Condé had been in prison. From the Bastille he had been removed to Vincennes. There he was treated more mildly; his wife Charlotte de Montmorency, who had had to endure so much shameful treatment from him, voluntarily shared his captivity. Condé promised anything the favourite asked in the hope of being released. Luynes hesitated. If he really succeeded in winning Condé as an ally it would completely take the wind out of the sails of his enemies, Condé's former comrades-in-arms, and of the Queen-Mother. But Richelieu had long foreseen this possibility, and forestalled it. In a manifesto dictated by him, the Queen pushed all the blame for Condé's arrest on Concini, and deplored his long captivity. Popular feeling, fickle as ever, agreed with her. Above all in Paris, where Condé had always given the craftsmen work to do, and where his extravagance had made money circulate, there were loud murmurings against Luynes, who had dared to treat the first prince of the blood as if he were a common criminal. This point of view spread. Now began a silent duel between Luynes and Richelieu; it was a matter of who was to set Condé free and have him on his side.

At this point Richelieu, as so often in his early years, lost his patience and acted hastily.

Until now he had kept postponing the meeting between mother and son. People began at last to ask what his ulterior aim could be. Only his closest friends knew that he was resolved not to let his pledge out of his hands until what had been a casually dropped hint became a definite promise, and he was made cardinal.

Yet he lost his nerve and set out one day for the Court on the pretext that as steward of the Queen-Mother he must see to the preparations for the royal meeting. He appeared among his enemies in the Court at Tours, confessed his desire for the purple, and in exchange promised Marie's imminent arrival, thus losing his advantage.

Luynes smiled when he was alone or with his friends; he felt strong after his victory over such an opponent; but outwardly he gave no sign of it. While taking no notice of Richelieu's burning wish, he treated him with the greatest consideration, and let it be understood that if the meeting took place Richelieu as the intermediary would receive ample recognition, since it was well known how decisive had been his share in the reconciliation. The place and the hour were at once decided upon. In a castle belonging to Luynes's father-in-law Montbazon, on September 5th, the interview between the Queen-Mother and her son was fixed to take place.

And so it happened; on a fine autumn day mother and son met in the castle garden; they wept and vowed to forget and to be friends, but in a little while they fell into deep embarrassment which betrayed a painful, insoluble tension. Mother and son could not do without each other, but whenever they were together there began a cruel wordless struggle whose cause Louis was to understand only many years later, when he was to end it ruthlessly.

All the Queen-Mother's wounds opened again. Vitry, the assassin of Concini, was now Maréchal of France. Turncoats and detractors from her days of captivity in Blois encountered her at every step. She followed the Court to Tours. On the evening of September 6th a messenger was hastily despatched to Paris. Marie asked why he had been sent, and received the reply that he carried an order to release the Prince de Condé. So for this Condé had to thank the King, and the King alone; she wondered if it had been also hinted that she had tried to prevent the step, and Richelieu asked himself the same question. There were painful incidents. The old princess once turned to Luynes, looked him in the eyes, and said: "What happened when Concini was murdered?" She was spared no humiliation; everywhere the young Queen, Anne of Austria, took precedence over her. The holy Francis of Sales, who was present at the Court at this time, said that the venomous, greedy ambitions and intrigues there were like the hissing fury of a swarm of wasps devouring a dead body.

Richelieu longed to be a cardinal, but after the royal meeting Luynes mentioned casually that the King would have to ask the cardinal's hat for La Valette, the Duc d'Epernon's son; more, he went so far as to beg Richelieu to draw up the Latin epistle or recommendation to the Holy Father. Old d'Epernon knew who was his son's rival. "Watch out for the Bishop of Luçon!" he wrote to La Valette. Meanwhile Richelieu corresponded with La Valette over the appointment, and his letters, swollen with elaborate pathos, are filled with a pulsing, raging lust for power.

One day the holy Francis of Sales touched Richelieu's shoulder with his finger-tips, and it was as if a strange power flowed into the tumultuous heart of the Bishop. The great mystic said: "Return to your bishopric; turn your back on all this!" And strange to say, Richelieu obeyed.

He departed, but Marie de' Medici was by now completely under his influence. When she in turn left the Court, and the Court went to Paris, she took the road to Angers. The Huguenots were assembled in Loudun; they were once more on the verge of revolt. Marie did not exactly enter into negotiations with them; nothing was actually done, but there were talks. Her return to Angers was like a triumphal procession; all who were against the favourite and his countless hangers-on were there; over a thousand noblemen rode out to meet the insulted princess as she made her entry by the great bridge of Pont-de-Cé. The freshly renovated palace which the town put at her disposal was during the whole winter the centre of the discontented elements in France.

But Paris seemed resolved to think out fresh insults. Gaston, her younger son, on whom she set all her hopes, was given by Luynes a new Controller of the Household, a Corsican, Colonel Ornano, without her advice even being asked. Sixty new knights of the Order of the Holy Ghost were created, and the list was not submitted to her; all those whom she had recommended were passed over; a great host of Luynes's relations were among those who were elevated. But worst of all, the King at Luynes's instigation followed Condé's order of release with a rider, ratified by the Parlement, to the effect that the ruinous error of the arrest was attributable to the Regency; it had abused the royal authority on this occasion, as in so much else.

At this time Richelieu hated the favourite from the bottom of his heart; if hatred could have killed, Luynes must have died before that storm of enmity. Nevertheless the black passions which tormented Richelieu in the peace of Luçon were nourished on the idea of the unified State which now wholly possessed him. His manifold shameful shifts, his cold calculations interrupted again and again by bursts of impatience are, compared with that positive fact, quite immaterial; that genuine devotion purified everything else. Now that Luynes, leaving Concini far behind, was apparently exploiting France simply as a means to secure his own possessions and his own position, something elemental broke out in Richelieu.

Years before, when Marie de' Medici had given her son's falconer money and fortresses, she had started him on the road to ruin; now he had become insatiable. After having raised himself and his brothers to ducal rank, after whole shiploads of poor relations from Avignon had appeared, and their claims, along with those of their relations, friends, and hangers-on, had been provided for, after a whole new class of country gentry, high officials, and officers had been scattered over the country by him, the nobles at last lost patience, as in the time of Concini, and decided to bring down this new parasite, whom they suspected of aiming at the position of Constable, the highest in France. Richelieu wrote bitterly: "There is not a fortress in France which Luynes and his supporters do not hope to buy, and if it cannot be had for money, they seize it with violence. They have secured in this way some eighteen of the most important strongholds; they consolidate their position by distributing armed men everywhere; they maintain regiments in the provinces, troops in the woods of Vincennes; they have raised company after company of guards; the King's light cavalry are already in their pocket. If all France were for sale, they would give away all France for it." But this burst of anger was nothing compared to the bitter despair which seized him when he saw Luynes strengthening the house of Austria against the Bohemian and North German Protestants; a successful Counter-Reformation in Germany, a Spanish-German union meant certain ruin for France. It maddened him to think that this puffed-up amateur should persistently overlook the simple and fundamental facts. At moments Richelieu lost control over himself, but he pulled himself together again, and with coolness and concentration continued the fight. He assembled all the enemies of Luynes and hastened to the Queen; the mild and purifying influence of the saint of Sales, which for a moment had seemed about to lead him—and with him almost the whole world—into other paths, was now exhausted, its effect over. All he thought of was how to gather to the standard of the Queen-Mother Soissons, Mayenne, the Vendômes, d'Epernon, Lesdiguières, with Henri de Rohan as a last resort: the figures whom we shall find again in the later Frondes. Luynes played into his hands in spite of himself, for he was a friend of the Jesuits; he had granted the Company of Jesus the right to found a college in Paris, and by a single stroke of the pen he found now against him, in addition to the others, the Protestants, the Parlements, and the universities.

But Condé was at liberty, and his partisans meant for the time being a great accession to the King's cause. Another man whose name was already almost forgotten, Barbin, was living in exile abroad, Marie de' Medici having secured his release during the deliberations in Angoulême. She now thought of using this man who had served her and Concini so well. The correspondence which Barbin carried on with her at Luynes's instigation is only a brief excerpt from a larger correspondence which he continued to send her, wherever he might be, and in the face of no matter what difficulty.

Shortly before his banishment to Avignon, Richelieu had done what he could to help Barbin, that honourable, adroit, resolute, and courageous man, to whom he owed so much, and for whom he expressed his admiration in several letters. But now Barbin was not only in exile, he was destitute. It appears that Richelieu did nothing to prevent his banishment, and when Barbin appealed to him for financial help, merely complained of his own difficulties; the little that he had, he said, he would gladly share with his friend; but he did not share it, and his letters grew colder and more infrequent. Barbin vanished, and Richelieu, having achieved power, never sought him out, never brought him back. It was one of the many dark qualities in his character that he buried as dead all that lay behind him; clearly he wished no recurrence of the position of 1616; he had no desire to see his old mentor taking office again under the Queen; he refused to be pushed again out of the first place. So Barbin did not come back.

Richelieu now set himself to prepare the revolt against the King; but at the same time he provided himself with an alibi, and kept a door open by which he could escape The clergy were labouring to find an accommodation between mother and son. Richelieu seemed to work with them as a modest collaborator. There are many letters in his hand from which it would be easy to assume that he was honestly seeking a reconciliation. But with the nobles and the Protestants he spoke a different language; he talked more and wrote less. To Luynes himself he was quite frank; if in the beginning of his correspondence with the favourite finesse and assumed politeness still predominate, one can read in the hatred nakedly breaking through the later letters the growing strength of the resistance to Luynes and his increasing isolation at the Court, the chief cause of which was the Comtesse de Soissons.

It was Richelieu who took the necessary military preparations against the King. Without divulging the fact, he gathered all the threads in his hands. Rohan had advised the Queen-Mother to give up her bridgehead over the Loire, and for greater security withdraw to the south of France; Richelieu dissuaded her. For the moment he did not want her to have too much security; he merely wished the approaching troubles to fall on the head of the favourite and crush him. The South and security meant the emergence of an alternative kingdom in which Marie, surrounded by little potentates, would once more escape him and fall under the influence of her protectors; and withdrawal to the Protestant South also meant actual rebellion against the King in league with the Huguenots. But if she were to remain at Angers and from there issue protests against Luynes, it would be possible to pose as the injured party, submit to the superior forces of the King, and push the blame for the misunderstanding on Luynes.

Marillac was the name of the inexperienced soldier to whom Richelieu gave command of the forces assembled at Angers.

The resistance to Luynes was being organized all over the country. In Normandy, in Rouen, in the fortress of Caen Longueville was master; he kept the way to the sea open. Villars, stationed at Havre, controlled the estuary of the Seine; the Vendômes regarded Brittany as their domain. A violent enemy of Luynes, Maréchal de Boisdauphin, held all the positions in the region of the river Sarthe, and the Queen-

Mother with her daily growing army defended the bridges crossing the Loire.

The other semicircle on the left bank of the Loire, formed by Vienne, Saintonge, Poitou, the environs of Bordeaux, the mouth of the Gironde, Dordogne, were all in the hands of great nobles faithful to the Queen, and behind them was the threat of the assembled Huguenots of France. From Metz, where d'Epernon's son was in command, the doors could be kept open for help from Germany. In Belgium there was Barbin. The Duc de Nemours was raising troops in the Swiss cantons, Savoy and Geneva. Marie de' Medici was simultaneously in touch with the King of Spain and the German Protestants. Madrid promised any assistance that was needed, for Spain thought that the days of the League had returned, and that it would soon have a Spanish garrison in Paris; in Germany help was demanded against the friend of the Jesuits and his Spanish policy. Richelieu conducted the whole conspiracy.

As always during the seventeenth century, when the feudal nobles rose against the monarchy the towns and the great bulk of the bourgeoisie withstood them. Also Condé was standing up for the Crown. This first noble of France had only one thought, as he was to confess to the Venetian Ambassador: to revenge himself on the Queen-Mother. "To be Protestant if she is Catholic, royalist if she is on the side of the rebels, for Luynes if she is against him." Luynes was alarmed; the Nuncio Bentivoglio considered that he was prepared to do anything to preserve peace, but of Condé he said that he was like Mars in person, and dreamt only of the tumult of battles. Luynes tried again and again to get in touch with the Bishop of Luçon, for he, too, it seemed to him, could have no interest in provoking the uncertain arbitrament of arms. Condé and Bassompierre laughed over the constant messengers who passed between Luynes and Richelieu. Richelieu received these messengers, but did nothing; he wanted at all cost to be the non-aggressor, and so he let things take their course.

On July 7th the King set out in rain and wind on his campaign against his subjects. He was accompanied by Condé and his young brother Gaston; his small army was commanded by Schomberg. First, he was resolved to obtain possession of Normandy. He marched on Rouen, and at once, in spite of all prophecies, the irresistible prestige of the Crown was manifest: the city opened its gates to the King of France without a single blow. From Rouen he advanced on the fortress of Caen, whose commander would have fought any army, no matter how numerous, led by Luynes; but before his King he at once capitulated. Meanwhile Maréchal de Créqui marched with a strong force against the Loire and the centre of revolt. Marillac and Vendôme, who were posted with their men on the right bank of the river, had hastily to withdraw to the bridgehead of Pont-de-Cé, which formed the line of communication between d'Epernon and Mayenne. Between Nantes and Amboise there existed no other crossing of the Loire in the seventeenth century. Angers, the residence of the Queen-Mother, lay somewhat above the junction of the Mayenne and the Sarthe, at a distance of some three miles from the Loire. The bridge could be raised at two places, and thus made unusable.

After their peaceful occupation of Normandy the King and Condé joined up with Créqui's army, and they now advanced from the north. They chose the corner formed by the junction of the Mayenne, the Loire, and a small stream, the Anthion; Angers was on their right, the bridge on their left, and in front was a level road connecting Angers with the bridge. Marillac had strengthened this road with earth fortifications which were not yet complete; these inadequate walls stretched only for a mile along the road, and they had to be defended by an undisciplined force of 4,000 men against the royal army of 14,000. The issue of the fight was soon decided. The battle has been called "the Folly of the Loire Bridge," so little seriousness was attached to it. The rebels were driven in wild flight on to the narrow bridge. Scarcely had the battle begun when one of the Queen's supporters, the Duc de Retz, marched from the field with pipes playing and banners flying; a panic broke out among the others; the King's forces pressed after them into the narrow defile; in an hour seven hundred had been slain. At seven o'clock in the evening the bridge was taken. During the whole battle the King had been in the forefront and in his saddle. He was wildly cheered; it seemed that after all he was the true son of his father; for everyone he had a jocular encouragement; and he had exposed himself unshrinkingly to the musket fire.

His half-brother Vendôme behaved very differently. He rushed into the Queen-Mother's apartment in Angers, crying: "All is lost. I wish I were dead!" A Court lady retorted: "You had a better chance of death outside!"

Everyone on the rebels' side demanded the immediate cessation of hostilities, immediate negotiation. But would Luynes negotiate now? they asked themselves.

Richelieu alone remained calm; he was convinced that Luynes would be very willing to negotiate, and liberally too. He advised the Queen to retire for a few miles towards the south, assemble the troops there and wait; the rest could be left to him and the clergy; Luynes was certainly prepared to do anything for a settlement, for now the victor Condé was in the saddle, and the young King was slipping from his hands. And indeed a more exciting hunt had begun; the King had smelt powder; the falconer, the friend and helper of his youth, might easily be forgotten. For his own sake Richelieu must maintain the strained relations between mother and son.

The very next day he was with the King. He was received by Luynes with great consideration: he was informed that regard must be shown for public opinion; the struggle between son and mother must not be carried too far. As ever, they were afraid of one thing above all: that the Huguenots would unite. The battle of the Loire Bridge was only a vanguard fight. On August 10th Richelieu had already come to an agreement. The treaty of Angers was confirmed on every point; Marie de' Medici was granted a full amnesty for herself and her supporters; Richelieu had managed to represent her as the prisoner rather than leader of the rebels; the agreement was one-sidedly in her favour. For her part she promised little more than that she would thenceforth live on good terms with the Court. Mother and son met on August 13th. Louis, encouraged and liberated by his victory, inwardly more unconstrained than usual before his mother, was gay and generous.

Marie regarded the whole result as a miracle, and the miracle as the work of Richelieu, who seemed a wizard to her. Luynes visited Richelieu and informed him that the King had now begged the Pope to grant him the cardinal's hat as quickly as possible. The royal ambassador in Rome had been instructed to the same effect. Luynes went even further; he made the suggestion that Richelieu's niece Vignerod should be married to his own nephew Combalet. Richelieu did not consent until he had received the Queen-Mother's approval.

Once more he had the whole clergy behind him, as well as all Luynes's enemies, but above all the total opposition to Condé, which meant the country at large, for Condé's former comrades-in-arms now regarded him as a traitor; and at the head of his enemies stood Luynes himself, who feared him more even than the Huguenots. Richelieu rose steadily; everyone saw in him the sole possible saviour, the pacifier, and only in the most intimate circles of Louis XIII did the suspicion still exist that he betrayed every cause he served.

On his experiences in the camp of the rebels Richelieu later wrote as follows: "I recognized in the course of this conflict the weakness of any party drawn from separate camps, which has no internal bond except the light-minded resolve to overturn the Government; I saw that those who fight against the power of the State will always be defeated by their own imagination, since behind the enemy they cannot help seeing the executioner."

The power of the State had triumphed over all the obstacles put in its way, and Louis was resolved not to give up the struggle. Even Luynes, who wanted to return to Paris, could no longer restrain him; the two Bourbons, the King and Condé, who still nursed hopes of being King, were resolved to go on. After the reduction of Normandy and the main army of the Queen-Mother, they insisted on attacking the Protestants. Luynes could not get out of this new and difficult task.

In his surprising diplomatic victory over the King and Luynes, Richelieu had made use of a decisive argument; he had suggested that if they made peace and put up their swords, they might use them again together against the Protestants. The hint had worked wonders. The royal army from now on was daily swelled by recruits from the ranks of the Catholic rebels. By suggesting this possibility Richelieu had simultaneously strengthened his position with the clergy, and opened a way for men such as Mayenne and d'Epernon to return to the Court. As in the old days, d'Epernon could once more be seen exercising his authority at Court as commander of infantry. The Nuncio Bentivoglio also urged that the scattered Protestants should be attacked at once. Luynes protested in vain that the treasury was empty; he would gladly have waited until Condé had time to ruin his position at the Court again. But the Nuncio had a strong ally in the King's zeal. Luynes suggested the spring, but Bentivoglio replied that if it was not done now, in the autumn, it would never be done. The restoration of the Catholic faith in Béarn, the native place of Henry IV, had been one of the conditions on which Clement VIII had consented to absolve that great King. Here, too, Henry had tried to effect a real settlement; he had inducted bishops and paid them out of his own pocket; in many places he had re-introduced the Mass and opened official posts to Catholics, with the proviso that their numbers should not exceed those of the Protestants. During the whole rule of Henry and the Regency, these new bishops had appealed in vain for the restitution of their confiscated Church properties. Now their wishes seemed about to be fulfilled. As he saw there was no choice, Luynes decided to proceed as severely as possible against the Protestants.

On June 2, 1617, at the opening of the general assembly of the French clergy, the Bishop of Maçon had demanded in the name of his order the old Church properties in Béarn. By a decree in Council Louis XIII ordered that they should be restituted. The Protestants, represented by their titulary king La Force, objected violently, but on September 7th the King confirmed his order, and after the quarrel had lingered on for several years, he now seized the opportunity of crushing the resistance by armed force. Béarn lived in provincial hope; the people flattered themselves that the King would do nothing, since he was threatened by England and Spain. Anyone who maintained that the King's army would soon be in the country was regarded as a traitor and a Papist.

The province was prepared for defence. It possessed an efficient military organization. But nothing was done; behind the closed horizon of that secluded neighbourhood everyone maintained to the very last that the King was not coming; all contrary reports were fables to frighten children. And then he was suddenly there with his army. He crossed the frontier of the province without encountering resistance; Navarrenx was captured, the Huguenot militia disbanded, and the royal edicts everywhere proclaimed. The provincial-Protestant character of the Government was destroyed; a Catholic regent was appointed, and in the law courts as in the administration the French language was made obligatory. Béarn was completely incorporated into the kingdom of France. The Edict of Nantes was now law, though it had not hitherto applied to Béarn. Scarcely was the central power of France established there before it began in accordance with its Roman spirit to strangle the life of the province.

The question now rose whether French Protestantism would accept this action docilely.

The two strongest bulwarks of the Huguenots were the city of Montauban in the south and of La Rochelle on the Atlantic Ocean. In La Rochelle a Protestant assembly was summoned which demanded that the state of things which had ruled in Béarn in 1616 should be restored, the new garrisons withdrawn, the wrongs of the Huguenots redressed. Threats were uttered. The Huguenots still felt strong, and threatened to call all the Protestant provinces to arms.

And in fact the Huguenots began to arm everywhere; they divided France into seven provinces, each province with a regent of its own; a council consisting of the military leaders and the members of the provincial councils were to consult with each of the generals; the whole army, however, was to have a single supreme commander with powers to declare war and conclude peace. The man chosen was Lesdiguières, whom people called the King of Dauphiné. That the Protestants thought they were in deadly peril is clear from the daring of their plans; in extreme groups there was talk of separatism and of organizing themselves on the model of the General States of the Netherlands.

But their very choice of a leader showed a certain lack of knowledge. Lesdiguières, impelled partly by his love of all forms of art, partly by scepticism, ambition, and dislike of the preachers, had long since been drawing closer to the State religion; in the choice of the Protestants he smelt the illiberality of the petit bourgeoisie, and while the Huguenot assembly was offering him the command of its army, he accepted from the King, to their crushing disappointment, the conduct of the campaign against them, and shortly afterwards consummated his conversion. He paid for his acceptance by the winning side by flinging all his influence into securing for Luynes the rank of Constable.

The Huguenots now turned to the Duc de Bouillon and the Duc de la Tremouille; also to Châtillon. Bouillon refused; La Tremouille inclined unequivocally towards the Court; Châtillon would have nothing to do with a post which was trammelled by the admonitions of preachers and the decisions of councils; he was resolved either to command or stand aside. Against La Force, who was also asked, the whole Béarnese nobility were united; they hated his family as intruders into their country. By the exclusion of everyone else young Henri de Rohan, Sully's son-in-law, who had fomented the Huguenot resistance, now assumed command as a matter of course along with his brother Soubise. The Protestants, incapable of really uniting, proceeded to attack the King at a moment when the Counter-Reformation was making triumphant progress in all Europe, and when only the Crown could protect them and preserve their liberties.

The royal army once more set out and occupied Saumur on August 18, 1621; then it proceeded to lay siege to Montauban. La Force defended the place stubbornly. Luynes, of whom people said that as Constable he avoided danger even more anxiously than before, wanted to negotiate with Rohan at the first sign of resistance. Everyone who wore a sword in France laughed at him. That Mayenne lost his life during the siege so embittered the people of Paris that there were attacks on the Protestants and their churches. The Catholic party would gladly have torn Luynes to pieces for his weakness; Bérulle said it was not to be believed that God wished to carry out His work of exterminating heresy by such a contemptible instrument. Father Joseph visited the Constable in person to instil courage into him. Louis's confessor began to inveigh against the favourite, and of the gratitude which Louis still had for his deliverer from the shameful bonds of his youth there was just enough to prevent him from dismissing Luynes at his confessor's demand. But there was no longer any choice; everyone turned to Richelieu as the coming man, the man whose strength appeared in its real impressiveness now that Luynes proved himself so weak.

The fortress of Montauban resisted. Luynes had to raise the siege, and this exhausted the last reserves of the influence he possessed over the young King. Lesdiguières had advised against the siege; Luynes had insisted upon it.

Everyone was now unjust to the unfortunate man. He had reinstated the monarchy in the person of the King, and through the errors of his enemies he had succeeded in destroying a great aristocratic coalition. Though hesitatingly, he had taken up again the struggle against the redoubtable power of the Huguenots. But to break them a leader was required whose character contained fewer weaknesses. Richelieu said that at this time Luynes was like a man who had reached the top of a tower alone; his next step would lead him into the empty air.

It was the beginning of winter when the siege was raised. No preparations had been made for the bad season, neither equipment, nor provision, nor hospitals. The roads were no longer passable; it rained perpetually. Luynes put the blame on everyone but himself; he once more attacked the Queen-Mother; he wrote violent letters to Condé. After his defeat he did not dare to conduct the King back to Paris. He sought an easy success. Montauban had resisted; he attacked the little Huguenot castle of Monheurt; but here, too, success evaded him. Like all men who believe in their star, he was deeply disturbed by his change of fortune. He was overtired; at last, after lying down in bad quarters he fell ill. To his friend Contades he said: "We have come to this now; Montauban has escaped us; we are unable to take Monheurt; the feeble Huguenots are defying the great King." Contades tried to comfort him; he spoke of the bad season, the sickness, the rain. "No," replied Luynes in an exhausted voice, "no, my friend, it is something else which I cannot utter." Richelieu, who was informed of the conversation, added that the Constable no longer felt that God was on his side.

In the beginning of December Luynes was lying in a high fever. Because of the risk of infection no one was prepared to nurse him; the doctors diagnosed scarlet fever. Finally, he was reduced to the offices of the adventurer Ruccellai, who remained with him to the end, which came on December 15th; on the 13th Monheurt had fallen and been razed to the ground. Without any escort Luynes's coffin was conveyed by laborious stages through a flooded country to his duchy of Luynes. Fontenay-Mareuil tells how he met the funereal train; the soldiers had stopped for a rest, and while they let their horses graze they played cards on the lid of the coffin. The lovely Montbazon, Luynes's widow, married three months after his decease the Duc de Chevreuse of the house of Lorraine. The great favourite had died with the death of his favour, and Louis XIII was the richer by a deep disillusionment which left behind it only emptiness, fear, and mistrust.

CHAPTER X

RICHELIEU DRAWS NEAR TO THE KING

When after Luynes's death the young King set out on his return journey to Paris, letting everything drop, he was joined by Condé; but on reaching Paris he found his mother already awaiting him there, and the question once more arose, who was to exercise power. Richelieu had met him at Orléans and had sought to convince him how necessary it was to give the Queen a voice in State affairs again, to cease from ignoring her great experience, and to forget Luynes's prejudices against her. Richelieu could at need speak as the priest.

The Ministerial Council which Louis found waiting for him in Paris consisted mainly of spiritual descendants of the old men whom Concini had once called the "barboni."

The president Jeannin, the Chancellor Brûlart de Sillery and his son Puisieux, the Foreign Secretary, the Cardinal de Retz, and the Master of the Great Seal De Vic still pursued the Spanish policy of the Regency and of Luynes.

Richelieu's admonition to the King had results; he gave his mother good words and promises for their happy collaboration. On January 27th their first meeting took place, and Consini, the Apostolic Nuncio, declared that the one man who had the capacity to manage both mother and son was Richelieu.

In March Louis again left Paris. The Huguenot leader Soubise, Henri de Rohan's brother, had taken the offensive, and encouraged by Condé, Louis set out with his feeble forces against the enemy. His mother impeded him with discouraging warnings and admonitions. All summer the two sides fought with changing success; Condé became insufferable to everyone because of his exacting arrogance. In a moment of weakness he confessed to Fontenay-Mareuil that, encouraged by the King's childlessness, he still had hopes of the throne.

Against him and his influence the Ministers sought the support of the Queen-Mother and Richelieu. They urged in Rome that Richelieu should be made cardinal at once.

Events worked on the side of Condé's enemies. As Luynes had besieged Montauban, so the Prince now besieged Montpellier, and with the same unsuccess and the same losses. At last Lesdiguières offered his mediation; the two sides came to an understanding; the peace of Montpellier signed on October 18th confirmed the Edict of Nantes, granted the Protestant clergy liberty to assemble without receiving the royal permission, and allowed political assembly on the condition that the King's assent was first received. Rohan and Soubise were pacified with governorships and pensions. Insulted and humiliated, Condé left the country and retired to Italy. At last the field was free for the Brûlarts.

Puisieux was a pupil of old Villeroy. Sillery, his uncle, the brother of the Chancellor, was ambassador at Rome; the most important diplomatic position at that time. Lesdiguières supported the designs of this family who worked into each other's hands.

Richelieu was nominated as cardinal on September 5, 1622.

He thereupon took charge of the opposition against the Ministry. All the forces of foreign policy worked for him.

The circumstances which in Richelieu's first term of office had made him pursue an anti-Spanish policy now forced the hesitating interregnum Ministry in the same direction. Dependency turned quickly to enmity, and at a time when the country was even less prepared for a decision by arms than it had been in 1619, the year of Henry IV's death.

Apart from working upon Louis XIII through his mother, the Cardinal made free use of the journalists, and above all of a paid pamphleteer, Fancan, the Canon of St. Germain l'Auxerrois. Fancan had been for twenty years a collaborator of

Richelieu's friend, the famous advocate Denis Bouthillier de Fouilletourte; Bouthillier had taken over the clientèle of Richelieu's grandfather, La Porte, at his death. At first Richelieu had employed Fancan from time to time on his own affairs, but later took him completely into his service; he soon recognized the man's unusual talent as a journalist. He instructed him to write in the name of the so-called "good Frenchmen" or "politicians" of the nationalist group. Fancan poured scorn on the Brûlarts in a pamphlet entitled : "France on its Death-Bed, a dialogue between Gallia, Chancellor l'Hopital and the Chevalier Bayard." The avarice of the Minister was described with great gusto, and Richelieu himself said that the portrait was a lifelike one. All that Fancan wrote on foreign policy was in accordance with the ideas in Richelieu's memoirs. No open conflict with Spain and the Emperor, Richelieu insists there again and again; from which it may be assumed that he and the "good Frenchman" Fancan were even then engaged in that concealed war which Richelieu conducted with such faultless skill once he attained power. But on one point the Cardinal and the journalist were not agreed. Fancan was a sworn enemy of all internal and religious wars, in this being an advocate of the theories of the "good Frenchmen." Here Richelieu had other ideas. On the one hand, during Brûlart's ministry he encouraged the Protestants not to keep the peace of Montpellier; Luynes and Condé had been disposed of by such means, and they could be used at need against the Brûlarts as well; on the other hand, he was resolved to wage the religious war to the utmost, to the destruction of the enemy, for in the Huguenots he saw a danger to the stabilization of any future régime in France.

The Brûlart Ministry recognized the threat that lay in Richelieu's new connections with the Protestants; dismayed by the growing difficulties of the international situation, which had intensified since Philip IV mounted the throne, and discouraged by the King's frequent condemnation, the Queen-Mother's opposition, and adverse public opinion, they no longer felt equal to the situation. Hitherto the honest Schomberg had been Minister of Finance; knowing his character, Condé had secured him the post; but Schomberg was not proving yielding and adaptable enough, and he was replaced by the Marquis de la Vieuville on conditions which showed that, like Concini and Luynes, the Brûlarts were set chiefly on increasing and establishing their possessions and their power. La Vieuville was a superficial mediocrity, quick and lively, but in no way remarkable. He too, like Luynes, came from the petty gentry, and had risen to influence as a falconer. He was handsome, his manners were agreeable, and he had made a rich marriage. The Brûlarts tried to play him off against Richelieu; but Richelieu saw him as a glittering soap-bubble at the mercy of every wind; there was no need to fight him; he would burst on the first hard obstacle that lay in his way. His father-in-law Beaumarchais, the most important tax-farmer of the second decade of the century, gave La Vieuville good advice, and his administration of the finances was fairly successful. The King tried to advance him, so as to have someone on whom he could rely, for the Cardinal, whose rise was generally now regarded as inevitable, was repugnant to him. "He has done too much against me," said Louis. "He is false through and through." And that was not all that he said. But he could feel the man inexorably approaching. The Venetian Alexanador reported: "In everything that the Minister does or decides upon, he finds Richelieu confronting him."

For the people of Paris that winter was a wretched one; the Sillerys encountered failure after failure in their foreign policy. Intrigue at the Court was more busy than ever; every human relation was poisoned, wrote a contemporary. The plague raged in the city; the Court left. Louis XIII had no longer anyone on whom he could rely. His relations with his wife grew worse and worse; he felt perpetually at a disadvantage with her; she had smiled at his stuttering; she surrounded herself with a court of beautiful, gay, and licentious women. Luynes's widow, the lovely Montbazon, was her chief friend; all the elegant youth streamed to her Court. But Louis avoided it; with his wife he was awkward, harsh, cutting, querulous, and even abusive; he tried by a false show of authority to make up for his failings as a husband.

Now that he was deprived of all friendship, and his confidence had been destroyed by Luynes's failure, he slowly and reluctantly drew closer to his mother, as if seeking protection against the vitality of the young Queen; he clung to Marie's powers of passive resistance and her perfect readiness to take part against Anne of Austria, who was edging her out of her former position. Marie de' Medici now sat again in the Ministerial Council; she once more had a voice in the policy of the State. Puisieux gave her to understand that her position would be still more powerful if she could bring herself to sacrifice Richelieu. The King, too, made shrewd remarks on her dependency on the Cardinal. But Marie knew that they were afraid of her adviser, and she was proud of it. Slowly, step by step, Richelieu advanced. Cardinal de la Rochefoucauld had been called to the Ministerial Council; as a prince of the Church he claimed the same seat and rank as princes of the blood. The Brûlarts objected strongly, and declared that with a cardinal in the Ministerial Council no secret would be safe in future from the Curia in Rome. But Marie supported La Rochefoucauld with emphasis. Everyone knew who counselled her in this. The Venetian Ambassador reported about this time that it was in Richelieu's interests to maintain a cardinal in the Council and undermine the influence of the Chancellor.

In the midst of all these silent machinations with their countless hidden dangers, the relations between Louis and his mother became more and more intimate. The King was afraid and sought protection, and he found it in her. After the flight of the Court from the plague, when everyone was at Saint-Germain or Fontainebleau, there was great surprise at the prolonged solitary consultations between mother and son. It was impossible to work any longer with the Ministry, paralysed by inner dissension. Sillery and Puisieux were fighting out a bitter family feud. The King resolved to settle accounts with these people. On New Year's Day he abruptly ordered Sillery to hand back his seal of office. Sillery protested; Louis became peremptory. In February 1624 the Brûlarts vanished and retired to their estates in Champagne. After their fall Louis clung to Vieuville in order to postpone once more the hour of the Cardinal, who now overshadowed everyone else. Richelieu bore silently his gnawing impatience, and hardened his resolution. Not for long; for Vieuville was no match for him; there was no need to employ against him the weightier weapons, the Protestants or the nobles; the mere course of affairs, particularly of foreign affairs, would dispose of him.

War threatened. La Vieuville did not know where to turn. At last, as he now scarcely dared to express an opinion before the Cardinal, so deeply did he fear his better judgment, he resolved to forestall the unavoidable and offered the dreadful man a post. He proposed that in consideration of the extraordinary complication and gravity of the international situation a new Department of Information should be created, which should concern itself exclusively with foreign affairs; he offered Richelieu the control of the new department.

We have the Cardinal's reply to this proposal. He wrote: "The Cardinal does not know how to express his thanks to Monsieur de la Vieuville for the trust and goodwill which he has shown towards him. He will take every opportunity to show his appreciation, and the interests of the Minister will be as dear to him as his own. But as regards the present proposal, it seems to the Cardinal that in such a form he could neither serve His Majesty usefully nor advance the good relations between the King and the Queen-Mother; the skill which the said Cardinal has acquired in a few years is too small; also his health is so uncertain that he would prefer a private and secluded life to a great position in the public eye. In affairs of such importance the decisions required are so grave and far-reaching that it is to be assumed that none except His Majesty and his wise counsellors are capable of making them. And it is not inconceivable that while the Cardinal came to certain decisions as Councillor of Information, the cabinet of His Majesty might come to diametrically opposite ones."

This letter is one of the most insolent documents in the official correspondence of the time; the last sentence in particular is a direct insult to which the parody of courtesy adds only a keener sting. To rid himself of Richelieu and at the same time secure his services in the increasingly confused situation, La Vieuville next proposed to send him as ambassador to Madrid. But Richelieu declined; he was not to be caught. While these half-measures were being suggested to everyone's dissatisfaction, Marie de' Medici kept urging her son and the Minister to offer Richelieu all or nothing; the Ministry of Foreign Affairs, but not such improvised temporary makeshifts. In Compiègne La Vieuville turned upon her at last and said: "You ask for a thing that will mean my downfall. I fancy Your Majesty may yet regret some day having advanced a man of whom at bottom you know so little!" But he yielded; he himself suggested to the King that Richelieu should be taken into the Ministerial Council, yet with the ludicrous qualification that he should have no voice in it, but only a consultative function.

Richelieu still showed no eagerness. He once more insisted on his bad health. Finally he accepted "in obedience to the command of my master," but he requested to be absolved from any party discussions; he could not bear seeing crowds of people daily, and any serious work was bound to suffer from useless and protracted discussion.

Meanwhile the pamphleteers with Fancan at their head went on attacking La Vieuville. They seized upon Beaumarchais, his father-in-law, who wished to enjoy his enormous fortune in quietness and began to be alarmed. The journalists also inveighed against the rich marriages of the nobility, which lent support to these shady figures of high finance. La Vieuville was made ridiculous, a fact that kills a man in France more quickly than failure itself.

The King became impatient; he summoned Richelieu and asked his advice. As was his way, Richelieu first said the opposite of what had for a long time been virtually understood between the King and himself. He was afraid, he said, that these perpetual changes in the Ministry might produce a sense of insecurity. Nevertheless, if the King's decision was unalterable, if he was really resolved to dismiss La Vieuville, he, Richelieu, was prepared to form a new Ministry with Schomberg, Marillac, Champigny, Molé, men of substance. The King accepted.

La Vieuville combined the faults of Concini, Luynes, and the Brûlarts, a pamphlet of the time asserted.

A few weeks after Richelieu assumed office the King summoned La Vieuville to Ruel; he informed him that he was dismissed; then he had him arrested.

Richelieu became Minister in April of 1724.

"So far as it is given to us to foretell the future," wrote the Venetian Ambassador, "it seems certain that the new structure will be more difficult to overthrow than the preceding one."

The system erected by the Cardinal and maintained by him against severe opposition was to last from 1624 to 1642, the year of his death.

CHAPTER XI

RICHELIEU'S FIRST TASKS

When on April 29, 1624, in the old castle of Compiègne, Louis XIII led Richelieu into the chamber where the royal Ministers were gathered and introduced him as the new member of the Council, everyone was completely taken aback. They had been prepared for this happening, but no one thought that it would happen so soon.

Louis had had to overcome an old and strong repugnance before he decided at last to allow the priest he distrusted so much to achieve his aim and seize the conduct of foreign affairs. What decided the King was his clear realization that extraordinary intellectual capacity was required if France was to be extricated from its difficult position; that, and the Queen-Mother's persistent efforts on Richelieu's behalf. She had appointed Richelieu as superintendent of her property; through her he had become rich; now she wished him to attain the highest position in the kingdom. She had worked on La Vieuville; to escape from her admonitions he had suggested the post of Councillor of Information; he knew that it would mean the end of his own career if he allowed Richelieu into the Ministry, and he had stiffly opposed his candidature. Others also were of his opinion; old Lesdiguières spoke his mind plainly to the King. Anyone but this man Richelieu, he warned him, who would seize all the power into his hands, raise trouble everywhere, and bring the Crown into disrepute. But Louis replied: "I will keep my eyes open; but I must advance the man for the time being to please my mother."

The nomination was made in profound secrecy. On the

night of April 28th the King made an appointment with the Cardinal on the walls of Compiègne, where they formed a sort of terrace in front of the royal apartments. A man in a cloak was seen arriving there in the darkness and stopping before the dimly lighted window, but it was thought that it was the German leader Mansfeld who had come to have a secret talk with the King of France. Next morning Louis went to see his mother and confided his decision to her, requesting her to say nothing about it. Marie received the news with indescribable joy, and repeatedly assured her son that it was a fortunate day for the country, and that France had acquired a great servant.

Richelieu was not, as has often been asserted, nominated as first Minister. It was merely given out that, as the Cardinal de la Rochefoucauld was unwell, he had been replaced by Richelieu. The Ministerial Council now consisted of the Queen-Mother, the Constable Lesdiguières, the Master of the Great Seal d'Aligre, the Marquis de Vieuville, who had succeeded Schomberg as Superintendent of Finance, La Rochefoucauld, and Richelieu. Sillery was Chancellor, but was to die in six weeks' time and to be replaced by d'Aligre. Along with these six Ministers there were also the four Secretaries of State, who were present at all the sittings.

Immediately on Richelieu's entry into the Council there rose a dispute on precedence. The Cardinal, as befitted his spiritual rank, demanded a higher seat, that is to say, a seat nearer the presiding King, than Lesdiguières; Lesdiguières on his part threatened to leave the Council if he was not given first place. As La Rochefoucauld on account of his age had hitherto taken without any question the first place after the Queen-Mother, he was appealed to, and decided that Richelieu should be given the place next to his, and therefore above Lesdiguières; and as La Rouchefoucauld had soon to forsake the council chamber for good on account of his health, Richelieu was advanced as a matter of course to the first place. With that he was first Minister, without having achieved a nominal superiority in rank over the other councillors. The King later called Richelieu his "chief Minister," which, however, was merely a mark of appreciation and not an official title.

That La Vieuville vanished a few weeks after Richelieu assumed office was not entirely Richelieu's work. The King had long before decided on getting rid of him. He was disturbed by the fact that La Vieuville was the son-in-law of the greatest financier in the country, regarding whom stories of embezzlement on the grand style were always going about; if a tenth of what was said in them was true, it was enough to ruin the name of any Minister.

Louis had been enraged for months by La Vieuville's placid inefficiency, and when shortly after Richelieu's accession to the Ministry irregularities in the administration of the finances came to light, he had him arrested without more ado and imprisoned in Amboise. Richelieu pled that the unfortunate man should not be cast into the Bastille. Ultimately La Vieuville succeeded in escaping from Amboise. A long and wearisome law-suit was started, in which both La Vieuville and Beaumarchais vanished as in a dense thicket.

Richelieu at once recommended Schomberg as La Vieuville's successor. But Louis declared that that excellent soldier had failed once already in finance; he would gladly have him as an advisory Minister in his Council, but not in the Ministry of Finance, which he was resolved to entrust to Champigny and Marillac. With Marillac a man enters the stage who in the coming years was to become Richelieu's bitterest enemy. In Schomberg, on the other hand, Richelieu was to find the firmest support thenceforward; among all these busy, changing figures he was the only steadfast one; and he was the only Minister with whom Richelieu, as the controller of the foreign policy of France, discussed his deepest plans.

The point on the European map on which Richelieu had his eye fixed was the Valtelline. In that remote valley in the southern Alps he saw a decisive strategic point in the European system of Spain. The Valtelline was formed by the course of the Adda which, springing from the Ortler, flowed first towards the south, then turning towards the west held in that direction for some fifty miles, passing through Tirano and Sondrio and ending in Lake Como. Difficult paths led from the Grisons into this valley with its vineyards shut in by high mountains, which formed a pathway from the Inn and the Danube lands and Germany to Italy.

Richelieu was in no doubt about the importance of that gathering point of Alpine passes. The Valtelline remained a key position for Spain to the day when the fortress of Bresach on the Upper Rhine fell, an event which was profoundly to alter the whole strategic constellation in Europe. The reason for the decisive military value of this remote valley was easy to perceive: the Valtelline formed the only avenue from the Austrian lands to the Spanish territory on the other side of the Alps which did not march with neutral territory. Since the time of Philip II the duchy of Milan had belonged to the Spanish Crown; the Inn valley and the Adige valley belonged to the Emperor; but the Duke of Milan, Maximilian Sforza, had left it under the protection of the Swiss confederacy of the Grisons.

Everything for the Austro-Spanish power now depended on whether the mountain republic of the Grisons, torn with dissension, composed of incompatible elements, would give Austria and Spain freedom to pass through its lands; Spain in that case could at any time send troops to Germany to assist her Austrian ally in the work of Counter-Reformation, while Austria could quickly intervene in favour of Spain's policy in Italy. Troops could be poured without resistance into the Austrian Trentino not only through the Wormser Pass and the Stilfser Pass, but through the Tonale Pass as well.

The position of the Valtelline population under their protectors was a hard and difficult one; it became unendurable when the majority in the Grisons went over to the new faith, and overseers, drawn mainly from the lower classes, supported by a crowd of fanatical preachers, began to impose it without mercy on the dwellers in the valley. All the internal quarrels of the Grisons, including the family feuds of its nobles, particularly that between the Catholic pro-Spanish Plantas and the pro-French Salis, exploded violently in the wretched Valtelline; the population of the valley was frightfully reduced by oppression and misery. All this was bound to lead to some popular outburst. A supporter and relative of one of the Plantas, who had suffered wrong at the hands of an arbitrary Protestant Court, raised the Valtelline people against the oppressors and demanded revenge. On July 1620 he fell on Tirano with a hired mob, occupied all the gates of the town, and set all the bells ringing in the early dawn; the Protestants rushed out of their houses and were all cut down; the same thing happened at Teglio, where the Protestants were massacred in their churches; the terror lasted for fifteen days. The prefectures of Bormio and Valtelline flung off their Alpine overlordships. Chiavenna alone remained faithful.

The Spanish Governor in Milan, the Duke of Feria, embraced the messenger who brought the news. And now emerged the plan which had been behind these massacres: Austrian troops occupied the Münster valley and erected a fortress at St. Maria, which overlooked the pass leading to Bormio, the Wormserjoch. The Spaniards occupied Valtelline. The Adda road was in their possession; if they succeeded in bringing more Swiss territory under their power, they would have control of the route from Lake Como to Lake Constance. The Pope had not collaborated, for though he approved of Spain's services to the Counter-Reformation, he feared the extension of Spanish power in Italy.

As for the population of the Grisons, they were paralysed by their religious dissensions; the same cause made the intervention of Switzerland end in failure, in spite of subsidies from Venice. The Valtelline question might easily have led to civil war in Switzerland.

Even before Richelieu's assumption of office the foreign policy of France regarding the Valtelline had been unobtrusively returning to the anti-Spanish line which Henry IV had thought out so thoroughly and held to with almost foolhardy boldness.

As may be seen from all her actions, Marie de' Medici felt deeply bound to the house of Spain. Luynes had been anti-Protestant in his policy. Nicolas Brûlart de Sillery, Louis's Minister and once an ambassador of Henry IV to Switzerland, had followed the policy which had been initiated during the Regency. He was a prudent and circumspect man, who looked a long way ahead; but though he indefatigably worked for the power of France, he saw as the aim of his life the advancement and enrichment of his house. He was a Nestor, a pacific patriarch, and even so he could not quite accept responsibility for the political aims of the Queen-Mother.

The events in the Valtelline had roused every power in Europe which was hostile to Spain. Savoy, Venice, even the Curia were united in their resolve to resist. Everyone urged that France must now settle her internal quarrels and confront the approaching danger. Lesdiguières, who still kept alive the ideas of Henry IV, demanded that peace should be made with the Huguenots, though he himself had now become a Catholic. The Duke of Savoy and the Venetian ambassador pled with Louis XIII; it was agreed and decided that Spain must be compelled to reinstate the *status quo* in the Grisons. In 1621, on Luynes's instructions, Bassompierre had taken up the Valtelline question at the Spanish Court. The treaty of Madrid had been signed by Philip III. Under the pressure of European opinion Spain had then agreed to return the conquered territory, but certain clauses were added which were so equivocal that the Grison authorities would be bound to find insuperable difficulties in carrying them out. Spain's partner to the agreement was not the Grisons alone, but the thirteen Swiss cantons. The Catholic elements in Switzerland, worked upon by Spanish agents, refused to subscribe their signature. In this way time was won for Spain. Then, in 1623, under the Brûlarts, an offensive and defensive alliance was concluded between France, Savoy, and Venice, in which these powers pledged themselves to see that the terms of the Madrid treaty were kept. But Sillery was not the man to act boldly in such uncertain circumstances. In Rome and Madrid he sought a friendly accommodation, while simultaneously threatening Spain in public and arranging for an offensive campaign. And this policy seems to have been successful; Spain yielded, evacuating the fortified places she had held or leaving them in the hands of the Pope. In Rome negotiations were next set going to reinstate the *status quo* in the Valtelline. Papal troops, it was decided, should first guarantee the freedom of the Catholic faith in the whole valley. Madrid was alarmed at the violence of the European reaction; before the French-Protestant front which the Pope had also joined, it gave way. Spain surprisingly renounced most of her claims; but insisted on retaining the crucial one: the right of free passage. The immense following of the Counter-Reformation in Europe would gladly have seen the Valtelline in the permanent possession of Spain, but the Pope, resolved to protect his territorial power against Spanish attack, refused to be moved by Catholic opinion; he yielded only on the question of free passage, and with qualifications: free passage would be permitted to troops from Italy to Germany, not from Germany to Italy, and even that would be allowed only on certain conditions. Great importance was attached to this qualification in view of the approaching religious war in Germany, now awaited by all Europe. The Sillerys, father and son, with no consideration for their allies, declared themselves satisfied with this solution.

In her world-embracing policy Spain found in her path, like Louis XIV and Napoleon and the German Empire much later, a stubborn and ubiquitous enemy in England. As in the reign of Louis XIV, England in its natural role of permanent opposition to the most powerful continental State claimed the justification of a religious motive; it took the Protestant side. In the constant, inextricable, antithetic criss-cross of national, political, and religious motives in the seventeenth century, it is instructive to note, first, how seriously Spain estimated the hostility of England, and how hard she tried to neutralize it by minimizing grave religious questions; and secondly, that the means she used, a policy of dynastic alliance by marriage, still enjoyed enough prestige to be assumed to outweigh all countervailing disadvantages. Under Lerma's influence Spain set out to arrange a marriage between the Prince of Wales and the Spanish Infanta.

What fears, what hopes were involved for all Europe in this possibility the following facts make plain: the Calvinist Elector Frederick V of the Palatinate, the chosen King of Bohemia, had been ejected from his throne by the Emperor Ferdinand II after the battle of the White Mountain, and had fled through Germany to Holland, as an outlaw, while his electorate was laid waste; Bohemia's harsh fate was settled; while the Alpine lands had lost their religious liberty. All this had made the hopes of the continental Protestants turn towards England and James I, the father-in-law of Frederick V. The foreign policy of that King, who was always at odds with his Parliament, seemed extremely vague, seen from the distance. After the hubbub caused by the Gunpowder Plot in 1605, everyone thought that the King would take up a clear, Protestant, anti-Spanish policy, but they were to be disappointed. Just as Walter Raleigh had had to pay with his life for his attack on the Spanish colonies, so the King now refrained from giving any assistance to his son-in-law; it was as if he regarded any interference with the plans of Spain as completely out of the question. More, he sought to ally himself with the Spanish system, going directly against the national development of his people; the mysticism of absolute power was still strong in him. Before his Parliament he upheld repeatedly his superior rights as a king; he advanced step by step towards the position which his son Charles I was later to occupy, and which was to lead to his death.

Many of the Stuarts never gave up, even when they were Protestants, a scarcely avowed hope that there would be a Catholic reaction in England. James I, the son of Henry Darnley and the unfortunate Mary Stuart, though he had sacrificed his mother's cause by the treaty of Berwick and married a Protestant Danish princess, remained nevertheless attached to those ideas of his time which were to throw up absolute rulers of the scope and temper of Louis XIV. The rocklike authority of the Roman Church, the enormous seeming power of the Spanish Empire attracted him. When Spain suggested a marriage between an Infanta of the Spanish House and the English heir-apparent and visibly began to court England's favour, James I calmly allowed the Spaniards to take the last uncaptured fortress in the Palatinate. To him there seemed more chance of his outlawed son-in-law being reinstated by those who had driven him out than by their enemies.

James I was a scholar and a theorist, a voluptuary and a pedant; he had the will of the obstinate man, the weakness of the coward at the mercy of his frailties, the melancholic irascibility, the slight absurdity of an arbitrary ruler who could not really punish and, easily charmed, succumbed again and again to his favourites. His political behaviour has never been better characterized than in the words of his greatest subject, Francis Bacon: "Magis in operatione quam in opere."

Bacon had foretold the Cromwellian Parliament, with its passion for redressing abuses and punishing offenders, which could already be divined in the Parliament of 1621. That assembly passionately attacked the scandals of finance, justice, and administration. The patriotic ardour of the members announced a power which was to create a new age. The representatives of the Commons declared that they would give their lives and their goods not only for the defence of their country, but for the Protestant cause in Europe.

But the King continued to rule against the wishes of his people. His eldest son Henry, a young man of fine intelligence, who might have altered the course of events, died while still young; Charles, later to be Charles I, was heir to the throne; and James was resolved to marry him to the Infanta, the sister-in-law of Louis XIII and the sister of Anne of Austria. The Parliament sent a deputation to the King imploring him to wed his son to a Protestant princess. But the King forbade them to interfere; the popular representatives entered their protest; the King in a rage dissolved Parliament, tore up the protest with his own hands, and once more took up negotiations with the Spanish Court.

At this point the affair was given another turn by the private influence of Buckingham. The journey which the Prince of Wales embarked upon with Buckingham was a secret romantic pilgrimage such as was fashionable in the stories of the time. In 1623 the two Englishmen travelled incognito through France. Wearing false beards they reached Paris, where they changed their disguise and appeared at Court as distinguished strangers. There they saw the Queen, whose young charms were so sadly thrown away, and Louis XIII's young sister Henrietta Maria, now fourteen. But that was merely a passing impression on the way to Madrid.

The marriage plan had come from Spain; the pressure of English public opinion and of Parliament had forced James I to treat it with caution, almost with reluctance. The leading Minister of Philip III, the Duke of Lerma, took it up anew. In his opinion the policy of Spain must be founded on friendly relations with its two most dangerous neighbours, France and England. Count Gondomar was Spanish Ambassador at the Court of James I, and he gave comforting assurances. He considered that there would be no risk of Spain's insisting harshly on religious qualifications should the Infanta be married to the Prince of Wales; on the contrary, the King could rest assured that Madrid would show the greatest consideration for his conscience and honour and the feelings of his people. A Papal dispensation would naturally have to be obtained, but that would present no difficulty. James was at bottom disposed to make the concessions required by the Vatican so far as his Protestant allies and his subjects would allow it.

But now the complications in the Palatinate had to be faced. As already hinted, James believed that there was more hope for his son-in-law to be reinstated by the power which had driven him out than by a Protestant coalition, which must set Europe on fire; also he showed his kinship with the large ideas of the Renaissance in regarding an understanding between the houses of Spain and England, an agreement between personages of his own rank, as of far more importance than the deepest conflicts of opinion. He believed that the friendship of England would change the whole balance of Spanish policy and weaken its connection with Vienna. He accordingly advanced his conditions, and while a Spanish army occupied the Palatinate, he made the return of that Electorate to his son-in-law the first requisite of further negotiations. He went far in the highly personal, highly curious development of his plans; to the savage Huguenot leader, the Duc de Soubise, he said that if the marriage took place, he and Spain together would espouse the cause of the French Huguenots. He sent a special ambassador to the Infanta Isabella in Brussels. Actually, after much hesitation, he was resolved now to circumvent his Parliament, win a backing in Spain against the ever-growing wave of Puritanism, and, as he conceived it in his torpid, tortuously methodical way, use his Spanish backing simultaneously to pursue a more vigorous Protestant policy in Europe.

The Prince of Wales and the Duke of Buckingham reached Madrid, in disguise and without an escort, on the night of March 7th. Charles held the horses in the shadow of a well, while Buckingham with some difficulty managed to effect an entry into the English embassy, where the sleepy attendants would not at first believe the sensational news that the King of England's son had suddenly appeared in the middle of Madrid in the company of the hated favourite. The Spanish Court was at first flattered by the Prince's personal courtship of the Infanta. But that journey, embarked upon so romantically, and carried out with the brazen insolence which was natural in Buckingham, soon became in the eyes of the Inquisition and of the Court itself with its strict etiquette, a painful, slightly dishonourable and almost menacing enterprise.

The Prince once saw the Infanta as she passed him in a carriage; he was introduced to her, but the Princess had been instructed word for word what she was to say. He now tried to emulate the heroes in the romantic stories; one day he clambered over the wall of the garden in which the Infanta was walking in Moorish seclusion; only the fact that an aged courtier who accompanied the Princess begged him on his knees to withdraw, or he himself might have to pay for the incident with his head, induced Charles to return by the way he had come. Such behaviour was scarcely calculated to advance the business as James conceived it. Entertainments were of course provided for the distinguished guest; Lope de Vega wrote stanzas in his honour; but in spite of this nothing was decided, so quickly had the position changed to the detriment of England; without some result to show for his courtship Charles could scarcely leave Spain; it was therefore for England now to make concessions. The demands of the Spaniards rose; they asked that the Infanta should be at liberty to practise her religion, that the children should be brought up by the mother and her suite until they reached the age of ten, that the English laws against the Catholics should not apply to the royal children, which meant nothing more nor less than that the King's grandchildren would be Catholic. These demands were accompanied by certain secret clauses whose aim was to abolish entirely the disabilities of the English Catholics, at least as far as freedom of private worship was concerned. That was certainly in accordance with James's unspoken wishes; nevertheless he hesitated, he must have time for consideration; he argued from the bargaining standpoint that he could not concede everything without further ado, while the other party had in its hands the Palatinate and now the heir to his throne as well. The Spaniards, who at first had made genuine advances to him, now made none at all; and in spite of his reluctance he gradually gave in, and finally confirmed, on July 20th, his acceptance of the Spanish conditions in the presence of the Spanish ambassador. His decision at once began to have practical results; the English Catholics were released from prison; preachers who denounced Popery were immured instead. A Catholic movement seemed on the point of setting in all over the country; families, whole groups, who had till now concealed their beliefs, came to the fore. The Protestants were alarmed and assembled in their churches to call on God's help against the new danger. The Archbishop of York intervened; since the King was resolved simply to set aside by a proclamation laws passed by Parliament, he appealed to the constitution of the country. These first disturbances in England were called forth by the measures designed to bring about the Spanish marriage, measures which had been decided upon between the heir to the throne, the King and Buckingham, without consultation with anyone else, merely to shorten the negotiations; for from the utterances of the Prince of Wales himself it was clear that he did not seriously intend to keep these promises.

James's object was to regain the powerful dynastic position which the Tudors had held in Europe. But though in doing this he took the gravest domestic risks and showed little appreciation of the forces which were changing his time in comparison with what he saw as the dynastic reality, he could do nothing to gain his main point; Spain, as before, made no reference to its great pledge, the Palatinate. The high conception which James had of the Madrid Court made him assume that Vienna would toe the Spanish line; if Spain spoke unmistakably, it would be an easy matter to make his peace with the Emperor. And with the Emperor, too, the policy of dynastic marriage would help to bridge religious differences; James planned to arrange a marriage between the eldest son of the Elector Frederick and the daughter of Ferdinand II.

But Ferdinand wss a believer from his heart in the Counter-Reformation. He was the Holy Roman Emperor, and his mission was to lead the Germans back to unity with Rome. Compared with his stern seriousness in pursuing his sacred task, James's policy, circumscribed by his insular outlook, seemed almost mercenary and heathenish. The Emperor was closely bound up with his task; all the German Catholics relied upon him; the Duke of Bavaria, who might at any time be lost to the Empire through a French alliance, must not be alienated. During the whole *ancien régime* there was always a Bavarian party in France, and never was it more wide-awake than in the first half of the seventeenth century. The Emperor had accordingly to keep his promises to Bavaria. In February he solemnly transferred the Palatinate Electorship to Maximilian of Bavaria; and with that the Catholics had a majority in the Council of Electors. The question has often been canvassed whether Spain played a double game with England and had secretly signified its agreement to the Emperor. This was not so; at Regensburg the Spanish ambassador spoke out strongly in the name of his King and the Infanta Isabella, and prophesied that the Emperor's act would have the gravest consequences; it was as if he already saw before his eyes the awful self-destruction of Germany, the epochal crisis which was to overtake both the Hapsburg system and the Empire. More, he went so far in his resistance that the Nuncio complained. But in spite of everything the Emperor remained unshaken; in his ecumenical dignity he stood for the clean-cut and militant world of the Middle Ages. His schooling by the Jesuits while a youth had made his resolution as firm as a rock; no storm could shake him; and even though the German lands were brought down by it, never was the will of the Counter-Reformation more absolutely embodied than in this Hapsburg. His work was a last great attempt to create religious unity in the German-speaking lands, to save the Empire and establish the rule of one sovereign house above all the others.

From the reports of the Imperial ambassador in Madrid, Count Khevenhüller, it was quite clear that the Viennese Court laid great importance on appearing completely independent of Madrid in the eyes of Germany. After the Emperor's decision on the Palatinate question the Duke of Lerma still advocated James's idea of a marriage between the son of the

Elector and the Archduchess, and the extraordinary proposal was made that after Frederick's reconciliation with the Emperor the electorship could be held alternately by Bavaria and the Palatinate. But Vienna bluntly refused to send an ambassador to consult concerning such a marriage.

It was chiefly because of this curt refusal that Lerma fell. His partisans held out for a while longer; Gondomar, the former ambassador at the English Court, was included by Philip in his ministerial council; with Cardinal Zapata he and Don Pedro de Toledo flung their whole influence into the scale; an alliance with England was in their eyes of the first importance. Their policy was a purely Spanish one; to them the colonial empire meant more than European prestige. But Khevenhüller, the Imperial ambassador, showed adroitness and tact; after the fall of Lerma his supporters multiplied. The Emperor's victory in Bohemia had an incalculable effect on Spain's decision; once more the mirage of a Spanish-Catholic world-monarchy rose before people's eyes. Olivares, who had the complete confidence of the King, and the Marquis de Aytona advocated a strict dynastic policy—the establishment of that Hapsburg strategy operating from twin poles which was always regarded by North Germany with such distrust and by France with a deep alarm lasting to our own time. In the State council Olivares declared bluntly that the King of Spain could not afford to break with the Emperor even if he were insulted; a friendship with England could be embarked upon only if Vienna approved it; the preservation of Christendom, of the Catholic religion, and of the royal house demanded unity with Vienna. And if these three prime necessities required it, they must simply break with England. A calamitous decision for Spain, which was to have far-reaching consequences. For twenty-five years Spain had based its actions on policy; now it once more flung its full energy into the service of an idea. After all, Philip IV had once himself declared that he intended to resume again the plans of Charles V: the first aim of his house was to restore Catholicism in Germany.

With that the marriage between the Infanta and the Prince of Wales became impossible, for James I was bound to insist before his Parliament and his people on the return of the Palatinate, yet it was just this that Olivares declared to be unacceptable. Proud, young, and high-spirited, he had exchanged sharp words with the haughty Buckingham on this question, and relations between the two men had become distinctly cool, even strained. The position of Charles and his friend at the Madrid Court grew more and more invidious and painful. He was treated as a relation, it was true; Philip actually addressed him as brother-in-law in a letter. The Papal dispensation arrived; the marriage could now take place, but the Spaniards were silent regarding James's one condition. There was still no actual break, but Buckingham began to fear public ridicule and the loss of his authority in England; the Protestants there were no longer to be restrained; the people who had always hated the Spanish marriage felt now that their King and his son had been insulted. James urged Charles and Buckingham, the two men whom he loved most, to return at once. He became impatient and made his request a command. For a time it was feared that the Spaniards might keep them by force; never before had the English looked with a more anxious eye at the weather-cocks and the clouds than during these days. Adverse winds delayed the departure; at last, on October 5th, after an absence of almost eight months, the Prince of Wales stood again on English soil. The people had ceased to hope for his return; there had been wild rumours that the Spaniards had thrown him into prison and wished to convert him by force. Now he was back, and after his frivolous and disastrous adventure he drove like a victor through London; the whole city rejoiced, bonfires were lit, the shouts of the crowd drowned the ringing of the bells. Even the hated Buckingham was received with favour.

It was at the moment when Spain finally turned towards the Empire that Richelieu came to power. The vacillating policy of the Sillerys and their successor La Vieuville was on the point of dissipating the advantages won in the Valtelline, and that key position seemed about to fall to Spain. Richelieu intervened at a moment when with the failure of the English marriage both a great danger and a great hope had vanished: the danger of an understanding between England, Spain, and Austria which would be disastrous for France; the hope of detaching Spain from the Hapsburg system and continuing a policy of accommodation. After the contemptuous treatment of James I by the Madrid Court, the position was now clearer. France held once more the line between the two Hapsburg empires, while England was free, and behind England stood Protestant Europe. Accordingly France must once more turn to England as in Henry's time; and once more the rapprochement took a matrimonial form. If France could be sure of England, an energetic policy in the Valtelline would become possible, all the more so as in view of the threat to the territorial power of the Pope in Italy a widening split among the Catholic forces in Europe and an anti-Spanish policy by the Curia itself could be counted upon.

On September 5, 1624, Richelieu renewed at St. Germain the treaty with Venice and Savoy. He also promised that the King would intervene in the Valtelline only as the protector of the Grisons, without raising demands of his own. Louis entreated the Pope, Urban VIII, if Spain should fulfil the treaty of Madrid within three months, to raze all the fortifications in the Valtelline and to restore the position which had existed before the massacres. But the Pope refused to give up the places occupied by his troops and to evacuate the valley. Louis's tone grew sharper; on December 6, 1624, he wrote to the Curia saying that he could no longer leave his allies to their fate, and that he would act. Hannibal d'Estrées, the Marquis de Coeuvres, marched to the Grisons with a force of 500 horse and 3,000 foot; he proceeded victoriously through the Valtelline, took Tirano and Sondrio, drove out the Papal troops, advanced to Chiavenna, and in January 1625 laid siege to Ripa. Spanish Milan was held in check by Savoy and

Venice. Charles Emanuel of Savoy had great plans; he claimed Milan and Naples for the French heir-apparent Gaston of Orléans, as well as Genoa, the great Spanish port on the peninsula. Richelieu stirred up every power in Europe that was hostile to the Hapsburg. He gave huge subsidies to Holland. He supported Mansfeld, the Protestant enemy of the Emperor, with money and troops. He hounded the King of Denmark into the war. And finally he took the decisive step; he tried to win England over. Everywhere success seemed to meet him. But when the anti-Spanish front was formed, it was to be ruined once more by the Huguenots. The narrow fanaticism of a movement concerned exclusively with internal affairs can alone explain an act so obviously against the essential interests of the Huguenots themselves.

No one could have reckoned beforehand with such a paradoxical possibility. Neither Richelieu nor the English, who were now quickly coming over to the side of France. Scarcely had Buckingham returned from Spain when he sent a secret emissary, a barefoot monk, to Marie de' Medici. At dinner the monk was to whisper to her that he brought Buckingham's warmest homage, that the Duke as ever felt friendly to France, that he had been mortally insulted by Spain, and that there was nothing against the resumption of the negotiations for a marriage union between the houses of England and France. Marie conversed graciously with the monk; she thanked the Duke, she said, for his kindness; she had always had the warmest sentiments for England while she reigned—the parenthesis had a somewhat bitter ring—it had been clear to her then that the English King desired peace with France; while public affairs were still in her hands, the English King had suggested such a marriage to her, but now things at the French Court had changed very greatly. It was Richelieu who had instructed the Queen to receive the monk so encouragingly, and who had put these words into her mouth. The English marriage had been a part of his plans for a long time; he records in his memoirs that in the March of

1623, when Charles and Buckingham stopped at Paris on their way to Madrid, the Queen-Mother had spoken to Louis XIII of the great danger to France should the Prince of Wales marry the Infanta.

Soon after Richelieu's assumption of office Lord Carlisle and Lord Holland appeared in Compiègne to pay their respects to the King. They had instructions from James I to ask the hand of Henrietta Maria of France, Louis's sister, in marriage to the Prince of Wales. The English ambassadors were received with great pomp; in the Ministerial Council Richelieu addressed the King on the answer which should be given. If his predecessors had treated the proposal hesitatingly, his own judgment was perfectly clear. He had considered the question for a long time, and his exposition was lucid and convincing. First, he enumerated the advantages which Spain would have derived from its connection with England: the prime reason for Lerma's pro-English policy he saw in the military state of the Netherlands. The kernel of the Dutch army, he said, consisted of its six English and Scottish regiments, regiments both well-disciplined and inexpensive, which could be superseded neither by German nor Swiss troops. If the King of England had withdrawn this assistance and forbidden recruiting, the Netherlands would have been weakened at one blow in their struggle with Spain. The second reason for Lerma's attitude was also connected with the Netherlands; their shipping, he said, was completely dependent on England; free entry to English ports was the prerequisite of their whole marine trade, their constant connection with the Mediterranean countries and the Indies. The whole Spanish colonial empire was endangered by such a strong maritime power, the Indies above all. The third ground for an alliance between England and Spain lay in the great influence which the King of England, as the real head of the German Protestants, had with the Danes and the Poles; all the Baltic peoples acknowledged his power. James I was the brother-in-law of the King of Denmark, who was both Duke of Holstein and next-door neighbour to

Holland, and so in a position to appropriate its influence with the Hanseatic cities. This last consideration was decisive; the Hanseatic cities were vitally necessary to the Empire, and the influence of England and Denmark with these rich and powerful towns could be effectively exploited, if England allied itself with Spain, to extend the power of the Hapsburgs in North Germany as well.

After outlining the advantages which would accrue to Spain from an English alliance, Richelieu went on to say that for England itself friendship with Madrid would be disastrous, for it must lead to complete dependency, while a Francophile policy was clearly in its interests. Spain was like a cancer which ate into the flesh of all who came in contact with it; if such a thing were to befall England, its internal religious conflicts would make it an easy prey. After this declaration, Richelieu came to the main point of his speech, and said that an alliance between England and France was a very different matter; France was such a rich and fertile country that any idea of conquering England, such as the Spaniards secretly contemplated, was as far from its mind as the acquisition of new territory in Italy; France merely sought its own security and preservation; an alliance between England and Spain would mean a complete reversal of English foreign policy, while France, on the other hand, was a member of the same international combinations as England. So much for England. As far as concerned France itself—and here, after so much cold objectivity, Richelieu introduced a religious note which he knew would appeal to Marie de' Medici—as for their own policy, they must carefully consider whether a genuine gain could be expected for the holy Church of Rome, and whether the soul of the Princess whom they were entrusting to the great English barque for the rest of her life-voyage, might not suffer shipwreck. There were two points to consider: they must ask themselves what a marriage alliance would mean for religion, and what repercussions it would have upon the State. And he went on confidently to say that the marriage

must be auspicious and fortunate for the Church, since one of
its conditions would be that Catholic persecution ceased in
England, and it must be for the good of the State because
England in future would not be able to support the Huguenots,
and must instead give its assistance to the monarchy and the
Catholics of France. The essential thing was not to yield by a
single inch to the Protestants, for not only would it be a grave
sin to consent to the conversion of the Princess and with open
eyes consign a Christian soul to destruction, but quite apart
from any religious considerations, it was clear that the Huguenots would in that case see their real sovereign in a Protestant
princess of France; even if she should remain true to her
country at heart, her position as a princess of France would be
weakened in England's eyes by such a conversion, for a
Protestant Queen of England could never act as the advocate
of French, in other words of truly Catholic interests.

He went on: "We have the right to demand freedom of
conscience for our Princess, for in France we permit it to an
upstart sect; it is the least we can ask of England that it should
allow the same freedom to a religion worthy of all honour,
the *corpus christianum*, from which the English derive their
own faith, as they must admit." And the Cardinal began to
work out the details of Henrietta's life in England: pious
ladies must accompany her, her almoner and confessor must
be a bishop, learned theologians must be in her retinue, a
church must be put at her disposal. Great hopes would be
set on these things by the persecuted Catholics in England. It
was politically important that the religious conditions of the
agreement should be strictly observed; it was also a matter
involving prestige. When the Savoy ambassador had tried to
arrange a marriage between the heir-apparent Victor Amadeus
and Elizabeth of England, he had shown great complaisance in
the religious question, and that had given rise to a feeling
almost of contempt for him among the English, while on the
other hand they had been impressed when Zuniga declared in
the name of his King that if the Prince of Wales became a

Catholic he would send him the Infanta with a magnificent dowry, but that if he remained a heretic he would not send him the humblest chambermaid.

Then Richelieu summed up: "In these circumstances we must accept; the alliance of England has always been of the greatest advantage to France, and always will be; England forms a bulwark to our kingdom; no one recognized that more clearly at one time than the Dukes of Burgundy. We must consider which is greater: the advantage which we can win against Spain from the new alliance, or the fearful disadvantages which we shall have to face if we reject England's offer and do not succeed in preventing an agreement between the Madrid Hapsburgs and the Stuarts from taking place after all."

Richelieu carefully set down all these arguments in his memoirs, and as the importance of the European factors involved was evident in every sentence, he later buttressed his arguments by facts drawn from history. He pointed out among other things that the Spaniards had not succeeded in conquering Navarre until they had formed in 1511 the Holy League with England, Venice, and Switzerland.

Now that Spain had decided to follow in collaboration with the Emperor a policy involving the whole destiny of Europe, the Cardinal weighed the scattered forces of the Protestant world, and gradually, with many setbacks, began to shape them into a force which was destined to break the world power of the Hapsburgs and prevent a revival by violence of Catholic Christendom as the Middle Ages had known it, under the rule of Spain. He at once proceeded to make Protestant alliances; the first was the English one; an alliance with Holland immediately followed; and they were the beginning of a great system out of which a new Europe was to emerge. But grave setbacks were in store for him before that.

CHAPTER XII

THE ENGLISH MARRIAGE

Henrietta Maria, Henry IV's daughter, was now fifteen, a sensitive and charming girl. All who knew her wrote with delight of this young princess, whose fate was to be such a hard, almost unendurable one, and who in spite of her faults always showed a gentle yet firm strength and feminine wisdom, a capacity to renounce at the right time, an original and judicious understanding, and a knowledge of human nature which had been trained in a school which was to produce Madame de Sévigné.

Henry IV himself in his struggle with Spain had tried to bring about an English marriage. His eldest son, the future Louis XIII, was to have married an English princess, and his sister, Elizabeth of France, had been destined for Prince Henry, the eldest son of James I. To upset the policy of France, rob it of the English alliance and the Protestants of their predominance, Philip III of Spain had sought to arrange a marriage between Prince Henry and the eldest Infanta, Anne of Austria. Henry's death put an end to everything, and the suspicion that Ravaillac had assassinated Henry IV on instructions from Madrid seemed more than probable at the time.

When Marie de' Medici quite renounced the anti-Spanish policy of her husband and under Concini's influence seemed about to withdraw under the shadow of the Spanish Hapsburgs, the change was clearly expressed in the royal marriages which followed: Princess Elizabeth became the wife of the Prince of Asturias, and Louis XIII married Anne of Austria, once intended for Prince Henry.

"Ya no divide nieve Pirenea
A España pue con Francia se desposa,"

Lope de Vega wrote at the time.

Prince Henry died, and James I's daughter married the unfortunate Frederick V of the Palatinate, the Winter King. Now the second son Charles remained, and the whole game of foreign policy for ten years is reflected in the history of his marriage.

"That this matter of the English marriage is in such a bad state is La Vieuville's fault," Richelieu had said to the King. Yet a month after his assumption of power the marriage was consummated.

The sensation of these festive days in Paris preceding the marriage and the departure of the young Queen was Buckingham, who had followed the special ambassadors, Lord Carlisle and Lord Holland, to Paris in order to escort his Queen to her new home. When some years before James I had sent Lord Carlisle to Paris to congratulate Louis XIII and Anne of Austria on their marriage, the Englishman's magnificence had astonished the Paris people. Nothing was stranger to them than magnificence squandered on one's own person, and they retorted to it with fear, amazement, or hatred; even a century later the monarchy had to pay for the pomp of Louis XIV, which was more native to Spain than to France. To the frugal French people any senseless or histrionic display appeared contemptible, ludicrous, and barbarous. Carlisle had ridden over the bad surface and puddles of the Paris streets on a magnificent Spanish charger, which in executing its stylish caracoles kept throwing off silver horseshoes, whereupon a blacksmith in brilliant livery belonging to Carlisle's retinue sprang down and fixed on new ones, which were flung off in turn among the crowd. Buckingham's twenty-seven gala suits were long remembered by the Paris people, particularly the suit of white velvet sewn with diamonds, from whose shoulders as the Duke strode through the halls of the Louvre strings of pearls fell and rolled over the marble floors to be picked up by poor courtiers and lackeys.

A reception was held in the great gallery of the Luxembourg. Marie de' Medici received the guests surrounded by twenty-one huge pictures by Rubens, in which that great painter had employed all his skill to glorify the reddish-blonde, vacuous, somewhat ample charms of the banker's daughter from Florence, displaying her in golden armour, in a blue robe worked with lilies, or as Juno, queen of that long-vanished heaven with whose denizens it was no profanation to compare oneself. This was one of these epochs that reflect the antique past and seek to make it live again, and so the old gods, in whom forces so mighty were once incorporated that even in the broad light of day they could find darkness enough to envelop them and let them vanish from men's sight for ever—these old gods once more were made manifest, yet this time not as forces; a god was now but a mask, an attitude, a name, with which the great ones of the earth could deck themselves for festival, though moving all the time on the verge of an abyss of fear, repentance, guilt, penance and the austere forgiveness to be obtained in a heaven accessible, not to pride or state or magnificence, but to humility alone. This contradiction ran like an irreparable rift through the lives of the upper classes of that age; they sought to escape from the religious struggles of the sixteenth century into the serene brightness of a world of beauty where the measure of all things should be the resplendent "virtù" of the Renaissance, a world from which they were always driven again by the dark-shadow that their Augustan splendours cast upon it: the Christian conscience.

On June 2, 1625, the young Queen set out for England. Louis XIII was at Fontainebleau; the Queen-Mother and Anne of Austria had set out for Boulogne by a different route, as etiquette demanded; they would meet the young Queen again at Montdidier. During the eight days which Buckingham had spent in Paris, his reputation had become unbearable;

cursed, envied, loved, he was the subject of every conversation, and he passed through all the stages of that kind of success with dispenses with respect; the women were for him; the men, while ridiculing him, aped him; to the respectable he was an evil, to the people a new sensation every day; but his thoughts were occupied with one thing alone: the fair-haired, feminine Anne of Austria, neglected by a sick and morose husband. His mind was possessed by her; she was the ideal woman, he said, whom he had always been seeking in his countless love affairs. She was the eldest daughter of the King of Spain who had slighted him; she was the first lady of France; and the vanity of men so unsure of themselves as Buckingham always strives for some signal mark of justification. Everyone had noticed the impression he had made upon the Queen; she actually sought his company; her friends did their best to assist her, treacherously and without shame, in that hopeless love affair.

Richelieu had informed Louis XIII of the "constant familiarities between the Queen and the Duke." "The freedom of communication between them from the very first day was such that they might have known each other all their lives," wrote someone belonging to the Queen's suite. Louis gave strict orders that their meetings in future should be confined to purely official occasions.

In Montdidier his orders were observed. In Amiens the ceremonies attending the Queen's entry lasted for hours; improvised gardens, ornamental fountains, allegorical representations had to be viewed, speeches and poems composed by the city poets listened to. Then followed a solemn *Te Deum*; thereupon those who had come to say goodbye to Henrietta filed past her, followed by the guilds bearing gifts: twelve flasks of white hypocras, then all sorts of living wild birds in cages: six swans, six peacocks, six pheasants, three dozen partridges, three dozen turtle doves, six dozen snipe, wood pigeons, hares, rabbits—half the creation. After that there was a ball, and the cynosure of all eyes was Buckingham. He tried again and again to approach Anne of Austria; he did not succeed, and acted like a man in despair; he could not sleep, and filled his lodgings with his lamentations. Then came a fine summer night; the Queen went for a walk in the park of the palace which had been put at her disposal. Lord Holland, who was in love with one of her court ladies, conducted Buckingham by a secret path to the gate; there was only a court chamberlain with the two ladies, who were talking in an arbour; he withdrew at the arrival of the Englishmen. In the falling dusk the two couples wandered along the paths, Holland with the lady-in-waiting, Buckingham with Anne of Austria; they lost each other, the last faint light still illumined the great, dark eyes of the young Queen, so often praised for their beauty; then suddenly, as in some classical opera, there was a loud cry for help, the chamberlain, with his sword drawn, was quickly at the side of his Queen; he made to seize Buckingham, but in the confused throng of courtiers and court ladies who had streamed to the place, Buckingham tore himself away and hastily vanished.

This little episode, though trivial, was yet to have great consequences, and was to influence high political events from a side which Richelieu in his Cartesian calculations concerning the prospects of the English marriage had not taken into account. The memoirs of the time are full of contradictory details regarding the adventure in the garden. In any case it was now high time for Buckingham to leave; the Queen-Mother accordingly gave orders that Henrietta should proceed on her journey.

The last person to whom Henrietta said farewell was Anne of Austria. The carriages of the two Queens halted a little distance from each other; Buckingham stepped over to the French Queen's carriage, and after the custom of his country fell on his knees. The onlookers thought he was asking the Queen's forgiveness for so impatiently insisting on his departure. But when he rose again he had to conceal himself behind the curtain of his carriage that his tears might not be seen.

Scarcely had he reached Boulogne when the pain of separation became unendurable. Cold and windy weather prevented the convoy from setting out. Couriers kept coming and going between Henrietta and her mother in Amiens, and the constant communication worked Buckingham up to desperation. One day he snatched the pretext given by a letter from his King to the Queen-Mother; he jumped on his horse and along with Lord Holland rode straight to Amiens, a distance of thirty miles, without stopping. He announced himself to Marie de' Medici; she was indisposed and confined to bed, but she received him. When Anne of Austria was told of his return she cried: "What! Here again! I hoped we had got rid of him for good." When he begged her to grant him an audience she asked her mother-in-law whether it would not be inadvisable to see him, since she, too, was confined to bed after blood-letting. "Why on earth not?" replied Henry IV's widow, "I've just seen him myself."

Buckingham was admitted, and in the presence of all the Queen's ladies flung himself on his knees again, desperately protesting his love. With finely assumed wrath, Anne of Austria ordered him to leave. He obeyed, but the very next day he appeared again before her, this time, however, in the presence of the whole Court and without addressing a word to her.

These doings might not have had very serious consequences on the relations between France and England if a third person, an intriguer, had not now appeared: this was Lady Carlisle, who was hopelessly in love with the Duke. Our authority for what followed is La Rochefoucauld. His pessimistic mind must have found in Lady Carlisle a justification for his gloomiest views of human nature. He moved in the society in which all this was happening; in 1625 he was twelve, and until 1628, the year on which La Rochelle was besieged, Buckingham's intrigue with the French Queen was the chief topic of scandal in Court circles. La Rochefoucauld must have heard a great deal of talk concerning it, and his sure eye for human weakness makes it highly probable that what he relates is near the truth. According to him, Lady Carlisle, driven by jealousy and desire for revenge, became a spy in Richelieu's service; and considering the attitude prevalent at the time to such things as money presents and pensions, and the constant money embarrassments of the nobility, it is not inconceivable that she was in the pay of France. La Rochefoucauld relates: "Buckingham took great pains with his adornment when he appeared in public. One day Lady Carlisle, who had so many opportunities to observe him, noticed that he was wearing with ostentation two diamond studs which she had never seen before. But to make certain she waited for the chance to be alone with him at a ball in London; she managed to cut off the studs unobserved and take them away with her, intending to send them to the Cardinal." But the same evening the Duke discovered the theft; the thief could only be Lady Carlisle, for no one else had been so near him, and only she had any interest in making profit from the theft; in a few hours the studs would be in Richelieu's possession, and the Queen of France would be hopelessly compromised. Confronted with this predicament, Buckingham at once ordered all the ports of England to be closed; no one after a given hour was to be permitted to leave the country. In great haste he had two studs made to resemble as closely as possible those which had been stolen; he sent them to the Queen by an official messenger, at the same time explaining what had happened. Buckingham's precautionary measures kept Lady Carlisle in England, and she realized that the Duke had stolen a march on her. In this way Anne of Austria escaped the revenge of her jealous rival, and the Cardinal lost a sure hold over the Hapsburg woman who sat on the French throne, for the studs had been a present from Louis XIII.

The favourite's French adventure brought no good to Henrietta Maria. Her arrival in England was sad; everything was disappointing, the future uncertain; she was hounded through never-ending ceremonies, and given bad accommodation in uninhabitable castles; she was subjected to a whole chain of fatigues, and in the midst of all this her marriage was consummated as a State act. Charles was strange, suspicious, and completely under Buckingham's influence; it seemed that the Duke wished to revenge himself on the young Queen for the failure of his vain and foolhardy adventures at the French Court. Soon the religious conflict, as was to be expected, burst out again. Henrietta's clerical suite, with their insistence on the removal of the laws against the Catholics and their Counter-Reformation spirit, the devout French ladies who surrounded the Queen, were a cause of much embitterment to the English. The King, taken by surprise, had to give way to popular feeling; against all the clauses of the marriage contract, religious persecution was once more resumed as a gloomy accompaniment to a joyless marriage. The little Court of the Queen, who felt she was an exile, lived in a state of siege. Buckingham played idly and irresponsibly with the fate of the young girl; he so chose his words that Henrietta soon became insupportable to the vacillating King, who submitted all his judgments to those of his friend and servant, apparently so rich in experience. Furious outbursts of anger against his wife alternated with periods of complete indifference; and then the lonely King would yield completely to Henrietta's charm. She was always so disarmingly right; her words were such a mixture of proud feeling and quick intelligence; she was a true daughter of Henry IV. When Charles made it up with her, Buckingham would intervene again; but having parted them, he would himself woo her with all the resources of his charm, surrounding her with a world of shadowy seductions and pleasures. An account of an entertainment given by the Duke has come down to us. In his country house on the banks of the Thames, while the guests sat in the spacious halls open to the summer air, the food was borne in by male and female dancers to soft music; the courses were changed as by magic; the King was served by Buckingham himself, the Queen by Lord Carlton. Then a wall disappeared and a play began: it showed the court of Neptune, and Marie de' Medici appeared, as Rubens had painted her, on the waves that separated France from England; she advanced towards the ruler of the seas, surrounded by her three daughters and her three sons-in-law, the King of Spain, the King of England, and the Prince of Piedmont. While such entertainments were being given people were dying by thousands of the plague in London. An effigy of Buckingham the spendthrift was hanged on the gallows in the sailors' quarter. But he went on, as if his personal importance were the measure of all things. He began to hate Henrietta as soon as he felt she was slipping from him and winning over the King; he so far lost control over himself as to be brutally disrespectful to her. He shouted at her once that he would no longer treat her as a queen; another time he forced her to beg the pardon of his wife, whom she was supposed to have offended. Finally, he succeeded in inducing the King summarily to dismiss her French Court (he was particularly incensed at the Duchesse de Chevreuse, who was supposed then to be in Richelieu's confidence), and all her spiritual advisers. He hoped by this to win back his lost popularity; and in fact Henrietta's spiritual advisers had been unwisely zealous; they had encouraged her to make a penitential pilgrimage through London to the spot where the conspirators implicated in the Gunpowder Plot had been executed.

Buckingham, who had just concluded an alliance with the Netherlands, Buckingham, who fancied that he now had Parliament in his hands, after arresting this member and distributing rich places to that, decided to strike. The Queen's Grand Almoner had been to France and returned with new instructions from Richelieu, mild and pacific in nature: but all in vain. Buckingham was both spoilt and revengeful in a feeble, ineffectual way; he found it unendurable that he should fail in the art of seduction, of which he regarded himself a master; yet that intoxicating conviction was only his when he saw himself as the great seducer in the eyes of whose who surrounded him. He, too, needed justification, though in a different way from Luynes, for with him there was no measure; for the sake of his love affairs he not only had all the English ports closed, not only upset the present and the future course of his King's life; he went farther, he used the fluctuations of world politics to serve the petty masquerade, the empty, glittering ballet of his worthless life.

He still had power over the melancholy and awkward King, who greatly admired his vulgar assurance. "Ill-bred, boastful, empty," so Richelieu summed him up. But men of Buckingham's kind do not exert influence by the sum of their qualities, independently of the society around them; they become effectual only in circumstances where they can charm someone in power by their fleeting brilliance, insinuate themselves into great affairs, and having by some happy stroke of fortune reached the source of power, proceed to set vast enterprises going at the bidding of their whims. Yet if one looks more closely one sees that they serve their whims only in appearance, and that in reality they have to obey a far deeper will, quite unknown to themselves. Buckingham, the enemy of the people, the belated heir of the Renaissance in a world of growing Puritanism, persistently opposed Richelieu's plans for the most absurd and irresponsible reasons; yet in reality he did nothing in the sphere of foreign affairs which did not express the wishes of the English people and of English Puritanism, though the English never knew it.

Finally, he induced Charles I one day to take his wife by the hand, lead her from her friends who were standing round her, conduct her to her room, and there, having locked the door, inform her of his unalterable decision to send her French suite back to France without delay. At this news she fell to the floor and could not speak for a while; then she began to sob, clung to his knees, kissed his feet, begged him to forgive her people, and reminding him of his promise, his oath, called on the vengeance of God. In vain. Charles's orders had been given; she could already hear the cries and protests of her friends; they grew louder, rising from the little inner courtyard of the palace to her window; suddenly she leapt up and beat her brow against the opaque window-panes until it bled, clinging desperately to the window-bars; but the King took her by the shoulder and pulled her away. Guards appeared; she was a prisoner. Her French household left London, sailed down the Thames and across the English Channel, as eleven years later the Spanish household of the Queen of France were to return across the Bidassoa.

The brave and witty Bassompierre was sent on a special embassy to London to alleviate the Queen's situation if possible. Compromises were arranged to smooth over the painful incident, but for the moment all the hopes that Richelieu had set on the marriage were lost. And Buckingham was not content even with that; he now proceeded directly against this personal enemy who had crossed his path; he lent his hand to the first French conspiracy against the Cardinal's life; like a blind fool he opposed himself to the onward march of a great force which would soon seize and destroy him.

The European situation seemed to be favourable for the rebels in France.

Bassompierre's diplomatic mission improved the relations between the royal couple, but produced a fresh tension with Buckingham. He had received the famous hero with the most scrupulous marks of honour; Bassompierre was the perfect symbol of a world which he himself strove to represent with such an extravagant expenditure of pomp, but from which he was stubbornly excluded by the will of his country and of its nobility. He accepted from Bassompierre much that he would not have tolerated from anyone else. But he could not get over Louis's instructions to his ambassador, which had been dictated by none else than Richelieu. Buckingham had proposed that he himself should proceed to France personally to settle the questions that existed between the two countries. What he really desired was an opportunity to see the French Queen again. He wanted to get out of England, away from an atmosphere which grew more unbearable and more dangerous day by day; he wanted to be absent during the sitting of Parliament, to forget the hostility of the people, and wait until a pamphlet called "The Duke and the Devil" had been forgotten. He paid no attention to the warnings which Lord Holland, the friend of the Duchesse de Chevreuse, sent him from Paris; he was accustomed to play for big stakes, and he deserved the reputation of being one of the bravest men of his time. In a transparent code in which the lily stood for Louis XIII, the heart for the Queen, the anchor for Buckingham as the admiral of the English Fleet, Holland had written saying that Louis was filled with suspicion, that the Queen returned his love, and that all the hotheads in Louis's entourage had sworn to make away with him if he ever set foot on French soil. All this had no effect on Buckingham; he was resolved to go. Bassompierre delayed his answer; and he had not yet answered when he set out on his five days' return journey across the English Channel, a stormy passage in which twenty-nine horses belonging to him died of thirst, and two carriages filled with dresses to the value of 40,000 livres, which he was bringing back as presents, were swept overboard. On December 22, 1626, he landed again on the soil of his adopted country; but scarcely had he arrived when he was ordered by the King to inform Buckingham that his proposed visit to France was not desired. The Cardinal also expressed his opinion on that question. "Buckingham's presence in Paris," he wrote, "would be harmful for the King, harmful for the State, and prejudicial to the relations between the two countries." And he added that Buckingham's share in the late conspiracy and his hatred against those who had foiled it were only too well known.

Bassompierre wrapped up his answer to Buckingham in silk; he wrote that it was impossible for the King to receive such a highly-placed ambassador from England until the violation of the marriage contract had been made good; moreover, when Louis XIII received an ambassador from his brother-in-law, he did not want to discuss complaints with him, but rather to celebrate their friendship.

Buckingham was deeply insulted, and determined to revenge himself on the Cardinal.

CHAPTER XIII

REVOLTS

In every province of his activity Richelieu was resolved to continue the policy of his great master, Henry IV. But he could now apply to the plans of that great improviser the scientific methods which expressed the spirit of the age in politics, as the work of Descartes expressed it in pure thought. The masses which Richelieu had to set in motion were human lives.

His hazardous attack on Spanish world-power required as its condition an agreement of all the parties within France, a concentration of the national effort. But that was far from existing; since Henry IV ground had been steadily lost; the Regency of Marie de' Medici and the first few years of Louis XIII's reign had senselessly squandered the efforts of centuries to achieve a central authority for the monarchy.

All that Henry had aimed at had to be won all over again, and the internal requirements in the country for the great external task which now could no longer be postponed had enormously worsened. In spite of Louis's domestic successes, both the Protestants and the feudal nobles seemed more threatening than ever; foreign policy had to be carried on without any real military backing that could be relied upon; an open conflict with the Hapsburgs would still mean certain destruction for France. And so those vast indirect methods had to be fashioned by the Cardinal which were to lead to the defeat of Spain by the ruin of Germany.

Scarcely had Richelieu assumed office in 1626 than the conspiracies of the nobles began again, and the external enemy was informed of its most intimate ramifications. Buckingham

GASTON, DUC D'ORLÉANS
(*From the painting by Van Dyck in Longford Castle*)

HENRY, DUC DE ROHAN

(*Portrait by J. Frosne*)

[*Cabinet des Estampes, Bibl. Nat., Paris*]

was closely involved. A peculiarity of these plots was the large share that women played in them.

Condé, in spite of his collaboration till now, was still the silent, watchful enemy of the King. He lay at Bourges and kept a watch on Paris, where his old mother fought for him, though the moving spirit of his enterprise was his wife, Charlotte de Montmorency. There was also Louis of Bourbon, the Comte de Soissons, who had so stoutly supported Marie de' Medici in her fight with her son; now that Richelieu, the Florentine woman's creature, dropped his mask and revealed himself as an inveterate supporter of the monarchical principle, Soissons became one of his boldest enemies. Besides, he never forgot an insult; he had asked for the hand of Henrietta of France; now that her fate had been left to the mercies of the Cardinal, he turned to Marie de Montpensier, the sole heiress of the estates and titles of the ancient collateral branch of the Bourbon family; but Marie de' Medici had long since reserved the princess for her second son, Gaston of Orléans. The reasons were therefore mixed which animated Soissons against the King and his strong Minister. The Condés were joined by Henry IV's bastard sons. The sickly, morose King had always hated those provocatively vigorous sons of his father's happiest years, when he had lived with the most gay and brilliant of his mistresses: Gabrielle d'Estrées. César, the Duc de Vendôme, was the eldest; he was governor of Brittany; his wife belonged to the house of Penthievre, and by virtue of this César laid claim to the ancient Breton dynasty. The Grand Prior Alexander, his younger brother, worked quietly and diligently to further the intrigue.

After the princess and the bastard brothers the first noble in the kingdom was Henri de Montmorency, Admiral of France. He hesitated; he was worked upon, on the one side, by his sister Charlotte de Condé, and on the other by his wife, Marie des Ursins, who was related to the Queen-Mother. Favourable to the Queen-Mother, too, were the members of the house of Lorraine, who really belonged to the Empire;

they were attached to France only by their interests, and being Guises they could always change sides in accordance with them. But associated with their house was the most astonishing figure among all the intriguers, a woman who possessed in the highest degree all the great qualities needed for the exciting and dangerous game she played: Marie de Rohan, the daughter of old Montbazon, Luynes's widow and now the Duchesse de Chevreuse, the closest friend of Anne of Austria; sometimes indeed she seemed to rule completely over that gentle and quiet princess, whose silent plans were seen through by no one but the Cardinal. But the Duchess never achieved complete control over the Queen's mind; she never succeeded in leading that solitary woman farther than the verge of destruction, for a deeply feminine and assured power, an inborn sense of propriety and dignity, always recalled her to that patience and renunciation which Madame de Motteville in her memoirs has described with such gentle and convincing force. Richelieu had encountered the Duchess when she gave her youth and her riches to Luynes at the height of his ephemeral splendour. After Luynes's death we encounter her again in that garden in Amiens; she was the lady-in-waiting who, through her lover, Lord Holland, led Buckingham to the Queen; and in England we find her once more as Buckingham's enemy, encouraging the young Queen to resist her husband, and initiating her into a thousand feminine arts; it was she who at this time scandalized all the English by swimming across the Thames; that accomplishment was later to stand her in great stead, when she jumped into the Somme, flying for her life, and swam to the other side. Saint-Simon has described her: "Her grace and beauty are great, her wantonness still greater, but all these are surpassed by her intellect, and over that reigns her insatiable ambition. She has a clear mind, sure and resolute, always charming, always inventive and never at a loss for a hundred ruses; no reverse can break her energy and elasticity; her character has a masculine strength. In spite of her constant adventures she remains faithful at heart; with her husband and children she lives in unalterable accord. The Duc de Chevreuse in his magnanimous way bears with all the changes of her nature and admires her in everything. Anne of Austria remained deeply devoted to her all her life, and yet the Duchesse was the source of all her misfortunes."

The episode in which the Duchess was involved shortly after her return from England, or rather which she herself set in motion, was short and gruesome. A young scion of the house of Talleyrand, the Comte de Chalais, twenty-seven years old and "maître de la garderobe" to the King, was a mixture of youth, energy, wit, and amiable impudence such as is often found in the youth of men who later develop into sordid failures or great figures. Chalais hoped to be made general of the light horse; he had just achieved a deed which was in everybody's mouth; he had killed the famous swordsman, the Comte de Pontgibaud, in a duel. The duel was the fever, the disease, by which the nobility, grown more and more useless, now began to exterminate themselves in a kind of collective suicide. Since the death of his brother there was nothing which could wound Richelieu more deeply in his most vulnerable spot than a boastful success in a duel. There may have been another reason as well. Little is known of any passionate connection between Richelieu and a woman. He was now forty, he was a cardinal, and he was burdened with the cares of the State. He knew his new master; and he had noticed again and again how much that taciturn young man was impressed by free and pagan natures who loved and killed with equal lightness. Young Chalais was always in the King's retinue, as the falconer had once been; and a new favourite would have risked all that Richelieu had won. More, Richelieu, who had learned silence and concealment in his hard days at Luçon, had once given way to his feelings when the Duchess, whom he had carefully watched in England, exerted her charm on him after her return. He had emerged from his reserve; something impetuous had blazed up in him. But she had repulsed the sick man with the astonishment and ruthless contempt which was to be expected in a woman of her abounding vitality. And scarcely was she back at Court when Chalais became her latest lover; that could not make him more liked by Richelieu.

Madame de Chevreuse had inherited all the revengeful passions of Luynes and the Guises, and she was an indefatigable fighter in the ranks of the doomed feudal nobility. She naturally flung in her lot with the cabal of the Condés, the bastards, the nobles, and the Guises: more, she became the incarnation of all the energies of the conspiracy.

But now a representative figure was needed in whose name they could fight, and he was easy to find in the person of the successor to the throne, the eighteen-year-old Gaston of Orléans, at that time Duc d'Anjou. He stands before us as a thoroughly spoilt, thoroughly weak, thoroughly despicable youth, who, however, could find an answer or an excuse for every rebuke or difficulty; a little brazen fellow with his hands always in his pockets, and a habit of whistling to himself as he pirouetted on his high heels. He was naturally the favourite of his mother; the fact that there seemed to be a certain vitality in his folly, a certain humour in his impudent retorts, pleased her; but there were also other grounds for her preference. Gaston was an excellent foil to the severe and morose King, his brother; the mother hoped, too, that she might yet revenge herself through him, for she could never forget, far less forgive, in spite of all her vows and protestations of reconciliation. In any case, Gaston must be married off as soon as possible; as the father of an heir to the throne he would virtually be King; in that case, France might yet see a new Regency, a new revolution of policy, a new Spanish friendship, a complete rehabilitation of the revengeful mother. But Gaston was not only weak and easily led; he was faithless as well, and had the perverse cruelty of the worthless, which was capable of making others commit themselves by raising flattering prospects, thereupon to betray them one after another with an astonishing coldbloodedness, sometimes quite inhuman, or warmed only by a faint glow of sarcastic enjoyment and a sense of his own apparent power and invulnerability. Louis XIII remained in his heart true to his father and observed for a long time a strict morality astonishing for the age; he feared adverse judgment, and he broke through his shy and cold nature only at rare times, when his feelings drew him to a man like Luynes or to young Chalais, as it was to draw him later to Cinq-Mars. He was a huntsman and a soldier of great personal courage; his brother Gaston had none of these qualities; there had been frequent scandal at his nightly excursions from the Louvre to visit brothels; all his life he sheltered behind women whenever there was a risk of danger.

Gaston was always dependent on someone; his favourites were his tutors as well, and even when he changed them, as he often did, he swore by the teaching and the word of the latest one. His steward Ornano was the ugliest man in France, but desperately vain, and accordingly very susceptible to the apparent interest that the ladies of the Court showed in him. The conspirators seized on this and sent the Princesse Charlotte de Condé and Madame de Chevreuse to him; in the whole country no two women could have been found whom an old colonel would have more difficulty in resisting. Ornano accordingly agreed to oppose the marriage between Gaston and the Montpensier, and instructed his pupil to make a bold resistance to his mother's plans.

For understandable reasons the marriage was not very welcome to Louis either. But the Cardinal won him over; he supported the standpoint of the Queen-Mother and dynastic duty and the good of the State, and here, too, took the opposite side from his sworn enemies.

Richelieu had tried at first to detach Gaston from the conspiracy. He induced the King to nominate Ornano Maréchal of France. The new Marshal was delighted with the honour done to him, but he went on intriguing, and refused to give up his visits to the Princesse de Condé; he must see the

Princess; he loved her, he said quite openly. He went farther; he entered into correspondence with Vendôme, who was arming against the King in Brittany. He next insisted that Gaston should be at the Ministerial Council, and tried to get permission to stand behind the Prince's chair and himself take part in the consultations. Richelieu said at the time that Ornano was aiming at his post.

The heads of the conspiracy were unanimous that the King's complaisance in allowing Gaston to be present at the Council could only damage their cause; they tried therefore to detach Gaston from the Court and put him under the protection of the rebel army.

Vendôme openly offered him the crown; Buckingham, in collusion with Spain and Savoy, supported the plot.

Only rumours of all this reached Louis XIII. He consulted with Schomberg and Richelieu; both decided that in such cases it was impossible to have exact evidence. "One never knows everything about a conspiracy until it has succeeded, and then it is too late." They were consequently for immediate action.

The Court was at Fontainebleau. One morning Louis XIII reviewed a regiment of the guards in the courtyard called "la cour du cheval bleu," and going over to Ornano, tapped him on the shoulder, and casually pointed up at the window of the room in which Biron had once been a prisoner. On the evening of the same day Ornano was incarcerated in Vincennes. Richelieu undertook the full responsibility for the arrest. Gaston's excited protests to his mother were unsuccessful. This was on May 4th. The conspirators at once struck back. They tried to find someone bold enough to assassinate the Cardinal. Madame de Chevreuse had once more to exercise her arts; the boldest was also the man most attached to her, the young Comte de Chalais. He was to do the deed; the details of the plan had still to be worked out. Blind devotion to his lady was a matter of course to that romantic and chivalrous young man.

Six days later, on May 10th, Richelieu received an unexpected visit, and was given information which threw a sharp
light on the state of the conspiracy.

A Maltese gentleman, Monsieur de Valençay, appeared along
with his nephew; the nephew was none other than young
Chalais. He now made his confession. Valençay stood by him
and gave him moral support in that hard task. He informed
Richelieu that Gaston and a few other conspirators intended
to visit him next day, at the Château Fleury, to breakfast
there before the day's hunt. During the meal a quarrel was
to break out among the huntsmen, swords and daggers were
to be drawn, and the Cardinal was accidentally to receive a
fatal blow. Chalais was himself in the plot; it was he who was
to deal the blow.

Richelieu listened calmly to the confession; then he thanked
Chalais and promised that he would fulfil his wish and appoint
him master of ordnance to the light horse. Then he commanded
him to go to the King at once along with Valençay and inform
him also of the plot.

Louis XIII made the necessary preparations. About midnight thirty gendarmes and the same number of light horse
reached the Château Fleury. They were on guard when about
three in the morning Gaston's kitchen staff appeared to prepare the meal. Richelieu greeted the household officers, handed
his house over to them, and with an escort of twenty men
rode off in the early morning to Fontainebleau.

Having reached the palace, he at once proceeded to Gaston's
apartments. The dumbfounderment of the young prince when
he suddenly saw the Cardinal, whom he thought at Fleury,
entering his room at such an unusual hour, was so great that
for a while he could not utter a word and quite lost his countenance. But Richelieu behaved as if nothing had happened,
and handed the Prince his shirt, as was the etiquette at such
"levees," saying casually how sorry he was His Royal Highness
had not informed him beforehand of his intention to honour
Fleury with his presence, in which case he would have done

all in his power to entertain his men; as it was, he had withdrawn so as to leave his house at their disposal. From the Prince's apartments Richelieu proceeded to the King, and no doubt said to him what he wrote fourteen days later from Limours, where he had retreated to recuperate from so much excitement: once more he begged that he might be permitted to resign; at any time, if the good of the State and of His Majesty required it, he was prepared to sacrifice his life, but this continual creeping danger was unendurable. The King begged him to remain in office, and gave him a strong body-guard.

Chalais's confession had an interesting history. He had done everything hitherto that his lady had commanded him, but the responsibility for the assassination was more than he could bear. He poured out his difficulties with ingenuous ease to Valençay. Valençay was an honest man; he let Chalais speak, and then told him that he would have nothing to do with such things; only complete frankness could now extricate Chalais from such a serious position. They must at once put things right, and so he took the young man by the arm and conducted him to Richelieu.

For the time being Richelieu did nothing to expose or punish Gaston and his confederates, for that did not matter.

But he went on fighting persistently and with the most careful choice of means. Nothing could be done against the heir to the throne, so Richelieu decided to reconcile him with the King. Gaston still felt uneasy; the man had appeared suddenly like an evil spirit when he was rising from bed; how much did this uncanny priest know? What was he concealing, for what was he waiting? Richelieu worked on Gaston through his fears; he drove him into a corner and made him beg the King's forgiveness on his knees. But Gaston was certainly the most worthless of the conspirators; to settle with him was the easiest part of the task. Richelieu himself drew up the declarations and promises which Gaston had to make to the King; he would not only love Louis XIII, but reverence him as a father, as his supreme sovereign and master; never would he come to a decision without informing him of it, he swore it in the name of his father Henry IV. Then Richelieu requested the King, the Queen-Mother, and Gaston to put their names to a document in which they vowed everlasting peace and allegiance, a promise which was empty air to Marie and Gaston.

Condé was won over in a different way. That man so experienced in conspiracies was intelligent enough to recognize the completely different tone which now ruled at the Court, and considered it expedient for the moment to seek an accommodation. On Richelieu's advice the King showed indulgence to his cousin's change of front, and the Queen-Mother and he consented to be god-mother and god-father to Condé's first-born son, who was one day to be known as the great Condé, the victor of Rocroy, the man who completed with the sword Richelieu's work against Spain. On the day of the baptismal ceremony Condé received word of Ornano's arrest. The moment could not have been better chosen. The Prince swallowed the blow without a word.

Now it was the turn of the Vendômes. Richelieu did not know at first how far he could go; they were after all the sons of Henry IV, and half-brothers to the King. Confronted with the impossibility of dealing incisively with these princes, he again proffered his resignation, supporting his request by the plea of bad health. But in the nature of things Louis had to sacrifice the bastards. No pity was to be shown, he told the Cardinal, and there was no question of his resignation. The two brothers were lured to the Court by fair words on June 11th, arrested in their beds, and imprisoned in the Château Amboise.

After this act, Condé paid open court to the Minister; never, he vowed, had the Crown possessed a less self-seeking counsellor or a greater; in the Valtelline question, in the Italian question, he had set the fame of his King above his own dignity and the interests of the Church; nothing, neither the criticisms of the ignorant, nor the libels of the pamphleteers, had made him deviate from the right way as he saw it.

Now only the conspirators of the second rank remained, and they still refused to believe that the game was lost. In spite of his confession, Chalais had not succeeded in freeing himself from his bonds; he was more deeply in love than ever. The heir-apparent had complained loudly to him of the burdensome pact with his mother and his brother, into which Richelieu had forced him. The Chevreuse intrigued tirelessly; Gaston's position was shameful, she said, the oath had been extorted from him; it would be dishonourable of him now to leave his friend Ornano in the lurch. Chalais vacillated, and when he reached the bitter turning-point in his affair with the Chevreuse, which seemed harder to bear than any other evil in the world, he began to visit the Prince at night, and, as he thought, unobserved; he argued with him, went over repeatedly what he had been asked to say, kept at him about Ornano, and discussed plans of flight, nothing that could be seized upon, mere possibilities; at one time they played with the idea of fleeing to the citadel of the Huguenots, La Rochelle, another time of leaving for some foreign hostile country; once more high treason was in the offing. The idea of a counter-King at the head of the Huguenots had been hatched by the Comte de Soissons. But Gaston was not to be had for such daring plans; he was afraid of the Huguenots, and if there was a next world, the game was much too risky. Another plan was much more to his taste: the commandant of Metz, La Valette, was requested to shelter the Prince in his powerful frontier fortress; he handed on the suggestion to the Duc d'Epernon, who was Governor, and the Duke immediately informed the King.

Meanwhile Richelieu had had Chalais constantly watched. Every day he reported on him to the King. Louis along with his Court was now in Nantes, at the assembly of the estates of Brittany. On July 8th he had Chalais arrested. He appointed a commission to try him, consisting of certain councillors out of the Ministerial Council and some parliamentary councillors of Rennes; to preside over it he named the Master of the Great Seal. It was the first time that a royal commission had dealt with a case of high treason; this was to happen often during Richelieu's term of office; but to this procedure, whereby the judges were chosen by the King, there always clung something offensive to men's sense of right, though the King was regarded as the fount of justice.

Chalais stood charged with high treason and *lèse majesté*; Gaston, who had tried to flee on July 10th, was left quite unmolested. He had broken his vow, but the King was reconciled with him, and when pressed his spoilt brother poured out everything, exonerated himself, and blamed everyone else, Ornano, Vendôme, above all his friend Chalais: he had been to blame for everything, had advised and incited him, had never left him in peace; and to crown his perfidy, Gaston tried to cast suspicion on Anne of Austria, knowing that nothing could wound his brother more deeply and make him more angry.

Chalais was in prison, and things looked bad for him. Richelieu, it was true, had visited him in the first days of his imprisonment and asked him to take heart, offering him pardon and the rehabilitation of his honour—on his life, he had assured him. But this was before Gaston's damaging testimony. And Chalais was still bound by the passion which had led him to captivity. He wrote letters to his mistress in the exalted style of the time, in which can be read a despair which had nothing to do with his approaching sentence. "If my complaints touched the hardest hearts," he wrote, "at a time when the sun of my life no longer shone for me, who is there that would not weep with me now that I lie in prison far from the rays of that star, without power to let my beloved know of my tortures. . . . I no longer know myself, except in the unalterable constancy of my prayers for her." This first letter is quite in the style of the "Amadis," but in the next brief note nature breaks out: "As my life depends on you, I do not fear to risk it by saying how much I love you. Accept this small token of my feelings, and do not condemn me for my boldness. If your fair eyes deign to read this letter, I shall accept it as a good omen for my fate; if it is otherwise, then I no longer desire my freedom; it would only mean the greatest torture to me." There followed a third and last letter; Chalais succeeded in smuggling these epistles out with great difficulty through a faithful servant. The Duchesse de Chevreuse left all these letters unanswered, as prudence demanded. When the third letter had gone without response, and Chalais received no sign of life, he was seized with despair and the fear of death, and he, too, began to confess. In the interrogation he answered the questions which were put to him about Madame de Chevreuse, but with reserve. His general testimony, on the other hand, was damaging. There had actually been thoughts of murdering the King; this one and the other had uttered the criminal words.

But these belated confessions were of little avail, and Chalais's remorseful letter to the King was equally vain, for Gaston continued to maintain that it was Chalais who had advised him to flee, Chalais who had planned to raise Paris against the King, Chalais who was deep in the most secret councils of the conspiracy. Gaston's behaviour seemed particularly contemptible, since at the same time he was imploring his mother to do all she could with the King for Chalais; he depended on it, he said, and that was a point which the King could appreciate, for if as heir-apparent he did not stand by the prisoner, he would never find anyone again who would consent to serve him.

The King only needed these last words to spur him to final action. The Cardinal, who had now and then advised that Chalais should be treated mildly, made a gesture of resignation. Chalais's fate was sealed.

At this Gaston gave way without opposition. He agreed to marry the rich and pretty Montpensier, at once if necessary. He was reconciled with the Cardinal, who was lying ill with exhaustion during these hot July days. He set out on his journey to meet his bride: it was a succession of entertaining adventures by boat, carriage, and horseback; there were expeditions to shoot sea-gulls on the Loire; a nobleman in his eagerness was left stranded on one of the islands; it was all very amusing, as, for instance, the entry into a small town, the Prince on a horse without a bridle, his suite on asses without saddles, and great confusion when the guns fired the salute. And everything went off excellently; the King invested Gaston with the dukedoms of Orléans and Chartres and the earldom of Blois, with a hundred thousand livres in rents and a yearly allowance of five hundred and sixty thousand pounds for the upkeep of his position. The wealth of the bride was fabulous. In such circumstances the eighteen-year-old Prince quite forgot his friends' counsel to insist on the release of Ornano and Chalais before he consented to the marriage. He was crammed with money until he became silent. On the evening of August 5th he was married in the Church of the Oratorium in Nantes. The Cardinal solemnized the marriage in the presence of the nobility and the Court; next day he celebrated Mass in the Church of the Minorites.

Richelieu gave instructions that Chalais should be informed of Gaston's marriage. Since the day when he had visited Chalais in prison and told him to pluck up heart, he had read the letters which the prisoner had written to Madame de Chevreuse; he read everything. He had Chalais casually informed that the Duchess spoke of him in the most contemptuous terms, and that she had taken a new lover. Again Chalais's love was turned to hatred, again he gave damaging evidence against the woman who possessed his mind. His evidence was taken down. At last the Duchess, realizing that Chalais's life was in danger, overcame her prudence and fears, went to the Cardinal and begged for the life of her lover. In answer Richelieu merely handed her the protocol containing Chalais's evidence against her. In the torments of jealousy he had tried to drag her into the dungeon which he would leave only for the scaffold, and now, as a last bitter drop in his cup, he had to appear a traitor and coward in the eyes of the woman he loved.

Richelieu still tried to prevent justice from running its full course; to the King he said that men were weak creatures and fell easily, their vices had often slender roots and could be bettered; admonition was to be preferred to punishment. Perhaps he remembered that Chalais had saved his life; perhaps he recalled the words which he had spoken to him in prison. But he did not intervene with any great energy to save Chalais; he let things take their course; an example had to be made.

Ornano, of course, remained, but he stole a march on justice; he fell ill and died. "The King was vexed," Richelieu wrote in his memoirs, "that God's justice forestalled his own."

Who else could have been indicted? The conspirators were all of too high rank; the half-brothers of the King who had Henry IV's blood in their veins could not be touched; they were in captivity, and to have put them there was itself a great deal; it was not expedient to show that men of royal blood could be executed. It remained for the English to demonstrate that to an astonished world. The other conspirators, such as Madame de Chevreuse, were connected with powerful foreign houses. No, there remained only Chalais; he had known of several murder plots, and of Gaston's treasonable understanding with England. On August 18th the court gave its verdict; on the ground of *lèse majesté* Chalais was sentenced to be publicly executed, his head to be stuck on a pike above the town gate of Sauvetout, his body to be quartered, the parts to be hung in gallows in the four chief streets of Nantes; he was to be tortured before execution, his estates were to be confiscated, his successors to lose their titles.

His pious old mother wrote to the King. "Have pity, Sire," she wrote, "his past ingratitude will only demonstrate more gloriously Your Majesty's mercy. I gave him to Your Majesty in his eighteenth year; he is the godson of the late King, and the grandson of Marshal de Montluc and President Jeannin. His family serve Your Majesty every day; if they do not fling themselves at your feet, it is because they fear to displease you. In all humility and deep devotion they beg you for the life of this unhappy youth."

The King was merciful; he absolved Chalais from all his penalties except that of execution.

When he was told of his sentence Chalais became quite calm; all his confused hesitations and hopes left him; he was past them. He forgave everyone; he took back his damaging evidence; he had given it out of fear for his life; now that was over. He was cheerful and brave as if he were going into battle. His mother was kneeling in prayer in a chapel, where she intended to wait for the carriage which would bring back his dead body. He sent an archer belonging to his escort to her. "Tell him," she said to the man, "that I am filled with joy and gratitude for his steadfastness in dying in God; that alone is my comfort. As I fear that the sight of me may rob him of his composure, I shall stay here and pray for him, though my heart urges me to be beside him to the last."

Chalais's friends hoped up to the very end. The hangman could not be found anywhere. Gaston had bribed him and he had disappeared. The rumour went that the Cardinal was in the plot. But two convicts who were to have been hanged next day were pardoned on the condition that they should act as executioners.

"Do not make me suffer," said Chalais to the one who held the sword in his hands; he was a cobbler by trade. At the first blow Chalais fell down, scarcely hurt. Three times more the man struck him; Chalais opened his eyes; the priest bent down to him and said: "If you are still conscious, show that your thoughts are with God." "Jesus Maria, regina coeli," murmured Chalais. Then they turned him on his back and cut his head off with a gully.

This event made a deep impression on the nobility. Hitherto rebels had been bought off; that a member of the house of Talleyrand could be beheaded as an example meant a profound change for the worse for them.

CHAPTER XIV

THE HUGUENOTS

In May of 1625 Richelieu wrote a memorandum intended for the King, which expressed his resolution to break the power of the Protestants. The crucial sentence ran: "So long as the Huguenots in France are a State within the State, the King cannot be master within his realm, or achieve great things outside it."

Richelieu made comprehensive preparations for the great stroke. Shipping was important; he extended his powers, already too great; he got the Queen-Mother to grant him control of the city and harbour of Brouage, and he purchased the control of Havre and Honfleur from Villars. He abolished the office of Admiral of France and himself took over its functions, becoming General Controller of Shipping and Trade. Shipbuilding was begun at once, and Richelieu founded the shipping company of Morbihan. It was a question of defeating the rebels from the sea without the help of foreign fleets; Richelieu attacked the shipping question and soon had all the threads in his hands.

Ever since the fifteenth century England had stirred uneasily as soon as a continental ruler extended his sea power.

Since England's weeks of vacillation between a Spanish and a French marriage, Richelieu had handled the relations between the two countries with the utmost delicacy, but these relations involved such powerful contradictions that they were bound to end in rupture.

Times had changed; English kings were no longer able to keep their promises. The Parliament which the Tudors had been accustomed to control with a firm hand was now the controlling power, and the Stuarts were under its tutelage. To quieten the Parliamentary opposition, Charles I in the beginning of his reign had withdrawn his protection from the Catholics. Then there was Buckingham, who was not only a brilliant and dashing figure, but the very embodiment of a type which the people had hated in all ages, as soon as they recovered from their first gaping admiration. Along with her good qualities, too, Henrietta of France had others: a dangerous assurance, a casual and yet arbitrary generosity, which advanced dangerous friends and servants without accepting any obligation for them, for she easily forgot all about them. Her position in England was infinitely difficult; every mistake she made was used against her by Buckingham; and the fact that France had intervened over the violation of her marriage contract made things still worse. All that was required was a palpable *casus belli* to terminate relations between the two Courts. The personal tension between them was merely a minor symptom of a much greater divergence, which was to lead to the France of Louis XIV and to the England of Cromwell. Richelieu had not reckoned with the rapid progress of that development; he did not foresee that Buckingham would make himself the instrument of English Puritanism, and that by supporting the rebellious Huguenots he would seize the initiative in foreign affairs.

In 1625 there were some four hundred thousand Huguenot families in France, strict, instant in work and in prayer. Inwardly and outwardly they were harsh and difficult to move, and even the worst of them were prepared to put their cause to the hazard. They lived in a heroic preparedness, and the gloomy philosophy of the doomed Greek *polis*, of the Stoa, permeated more and more deeply their Christian faith. They struggled untiringly for their rights. Those granted them by the Edict of Nantes no longer sufficed them. In the sixteenth century their great predecessors had given a political direction to all their actions. The Huguenots regarded themselves as the inevitable coming class; the weakness of the Crown during the minorities of Francis II and Charles IX increased their strength, and the betrayal of St. Bartholomew's Night increased it still more. In Henry III's reign they fought for the King against the ambition of the Guises. Henry IV by his Edict tried to win for them the position of a national opposition. Honours and offices fell to them. The man whom they regarded as their leader, Henri de Rohan, was made a Duke, peer of France, and commander of the Switzers; he married Margaret de Rosny, Sully's daughter. The so-called "edict" chamber for the Huguenots in the Parlement of Paris was founded; another chamber arose in Castres, still others in Grenoble and Bordeaux. The Protestants were granted what the nation itself had never possessed: regular provincial assemblies, and every three years a general assembly which chose by vote six deputies whose names were proposed to the King, of whom he had to select two for attendance on his person; their office was to represent directly the interests of the reformed religion. This arrangement clearly contained the elements of a political constitution of a democratic character, a constitution through which the primacy of the royal power was frequently called in question. The stability of this arrangement rested on the power which Henry IV had given the Calvinists by leaving strongholds in their hands; behind their fortified walls they exercised complete sovereignty; their communities stood in the relation merely of vassals to the Crown. Now under Louis XIII began the fight for absolute power, the struggle to reclaim or seize by violence all the rich pledges which Henry IV had given. The resistance of Montauban, the siege of Montpellier ended in honourable treaties of peace; the fact that the peace conditions were held by neither side led to the revolt of La Rochelle; that proud city on the Atlantic Ocean now became the scene of the swift, brief, and pitiless final struggle.

All that had led to the Huguenot rising of 1621 was involved in that final struggle. Where the trouble began is quite clear;

much as the Edict of Nantes had reassured the Protestants, the murder of Henry IV had flung them into the deepest uneasiness. The child Louis XIII showed no sign of possessing his father's great qualities. The mere name of the Italian Regent reminded them of the darkest days of religious persecution; Sully had fallen into disfavour; the nobles were plundering Henry's state treasury, conspiring and extorting; uncertainty again ruled everywhere; their rights and treaties were once more in question. Who was to guarantee the Edict which was their contract with the King? What could be expected from Condé's treacherous antics?

After the blow sustained by them in the death of Henry IV, the Huguenots pulled themselves together again under the leadership of Rohan, Sully and the last of the really independent feudal lords, the Duc de Bouillon, who in Sedan, with his German Calvinist allies behind him, intervened like an independent ruler in the affairs of the Huguenots. They tried now to adjust the manifold dissensions in their own camp, to put their fortresses in a state of defence, to gain new ones, and extend certain rights granted them under the Edict. Their policy soon became more violent and lawless in the general disorder; a Huguenot army with leaders and a high command, almost an independent government was created; open war began, accompanied by victories and defeats and peace treaties which both sides vied with each other in breaking: the Court in any case could never be expected to keep faith. For a while Condé was an ally of the Protestants, but he betrayed them; their leaders walked with equanimity into the Bastille; with indifference they watched the fall of Concini and the rise of Luynes. They felt their strength; all these favourites were masters of the King and the kingdom only for the time being. Concini was assassinated; a strong Huguenot fortress and a great Huguenot general, Henry de Rohan, were sufficient to break Luynes's power.

When the nobles slowly began to forsake the Calvinist cause, Rohan remained faithful. He, too, disliked the political complexion of the Protestant assemblies, but he did not desert his friends, he was a sincere believer and in deadly earnest. His inborn gift for rule found the collective pressure of these assemblies led by fanatical pastors and deciding everything by vote hard to bear. He was attacked both in print and by word of mouth, vilified and abused. At an assembly in Languedoc he exclaimed: "You are all republicans! I would rather preside over a gathering of wolves than a gathering of ministers!" The other nobles who had given their blood and riches for the Protestant cause during the sixteenth century fell away, crossed over to the Catholic Church, and became realists. Rohan, though the most vilified, remained faithful, and tried to carry on the struggle under the greatest difficulties. The assemblies lost the leaders who were in close contact with the central Government; they also lost freedom of action; they were paralysed by internal squabbles. It was parliamentary anarchy that destroyed the Huguenots.

After the skirmish whose chief incident was the siege of Montauban, the King had taken precautionary measures against the Protestants. He had left a strong garrison in Montpellier; a small fleet under the command of the Duc de Guise kept watch over the island of Rhé and La Rochelle. One of the King's favourites, Thoiras, threatened the city from Fort Louis, which had been erected outside its very walls. According to the treaties all this was impermissible. Rohan, who after the last campaign had withdrawn to his château at Castres, where he broke in wild foals, read the antique authors, and occupied himself with his estates, indefatigably and respectfully kept reminding the King of the Huguenots' violated rights. He demanded the recall of the fleet, the withdrawal of the garrison, the demolition of the fortress, and the restoration of the "edict" chamber at Castres. As Castres was Rohan's own town, and immediately under his control, the choice seemed a judicious one; the place could easily be reached from the Cevennes and lower Languedoc, where the Protestants were strongest. But the King refused to listen to Rohan's suggestions; he replied violently that he would never consider any request of the Huguenots which reached him by such an intermediary. Since the last peace treaty the Court had used every means in its power to win over the Duke, especially through his wife, who in morals was a true child of her age. During her stay at the Court she had enjoyed high favour; her stern faith had not hindered her from following the usual life there. But as soon as her husband attracted unpopularity by his fidelity to his religion she shared his exile with him, and willingly assumed fatigues and dangers; later, just before her death, she is said to have uttered certain words which show how truly she belonged to the world of Henry IV: "I have certainly sinned, but I have never had more than one lover at a time." Rohan himself was a strict liver, but even in his case we must take into account the ideas of the age; it seemed to him a natural thing to receive palpable reward in return for any agreement with the enemy. His younger brother Soubise was very different. His nature was changeable and rash; at bottom he remained a rebellious noble, and a Protestant only in the second place. Protestantism was merely a means to achieve the personal power for which he strove. In the late civil war he had been taken prisoner; he had been released on his parole; he now broke it. He took advantage of the international difficulties which had followed Richelieu's first measures as a Foreign Minister. He secretly got in touch with Buckingham, manned five small warships, raised soldiers in Poitou, and in January 1625 occupied the island of Rhé. From there he sailed to Fort Louis and captured five ships belonging to the Duc de Nevers, which had been intended for Father Joseph's crusade. The Governor of Brittany, the Duc de Vendôme, quickly raised the neighbouring nobles and tried to shut him into the harbour; but he escaped on February 6, 1625, seized the island of Oléron, which was garrisoned by royal troops, and occupied it too.

The Huguenots of high rank in Southern France had first disapproved of Soubise's uncalled-for breach of the peace;

he had reckoned on a general rising; it did not come. Yet, as his brother Henri wrote with justice: "When they heard of his heroic expedition from the harbour of Blavet and saw that he was the incontestable master of the sea, they changed their minds and perceived that he was something more than a pirate." They fancied that they had found a leader, and after that daring and successful feat Rohan, feeling that the iron must be struck while it was hot, went from town to town in Languedoc, accompanied by a band of ministers. He had the Holy Scripture borne before him, and sermons were preached in the public squares. The Huguenots rose and followed him.

At this point Richelieu had been in office for a year. He had intervened decisively in the Valtelline; he had arranged Protestant alliances with England and Holland. Now everything was in question. The Protestant powers would not support him in a struggle against their fellow-believers; the nobles would join forces with the rebels, and Spain, likely enough, with the nobles. Either, it seemed, he would have to sacrifice the Valtelline, concentrate on crushing the revolt, and make terms with the Hapsburgs, or else give new concessions to the Huguenots. They had chosen for their uprising a moment of grave external danger. Richelieu called the two Rohans "Antichrists"; but for the moment he had not the power to meet them; he needed time.

At the end of Henry IV's reign La Rochelle had been one of the most powerful and flourishing cities in the country. It had an incomparable position on the Atlantic Ocean; it lay in a great bay guarded by three islands, Rhé, Aix, and Oléron. At flood tide the harbour was accessible to the biggest ships, at ebb tide only to light craft; a lighthouse tower at the end of the harbour wall pointed the way to the proud city; strongly manned watch-towers, joined by detachable chains strung across the entrance, made any attack from the sea hopeless. Ocean ships and coasters crowded the harbour. The town traded with England, Scotland, Flanders, the ports on the

North Sea and the Baltic, Spain and Portugal, Canada and Newfoundland. It was as handsome and clean as a Dutch town; the wide, cobbled main streets were flanked with arcades. Rich burghers and merchants, with country houses in the neighbourhood, lived here in well-built Gothic palaces which in recent times had acquired ornate Renaissance façades. In all the squares the citizen army went through their drill, and as they marched through the echoing streets they could read on either side of them texts from the Bible carved in stone above the doors and porticoes. The Town Hall, richly embellished with Renaissance sculpture, the Palace of Justice, the fine street where the nobility lived, were the pride of the whole town and the talk of travellers. The city walls, now too small for the town, were five hundred years old; the city had increased by a third since the beginning of Henry IV's reign. The new fortifications were modern and regarded as impregnable. To the west lay the sea; to the north and south stretched impassible salt marshes, through which well-kept roads ran away in all directions.

Behind the walls lived the community with its strong communal spirit which embraced everything, stamping on every citizen an unmistakable imprint, wherever he might go in the world. The Rochellois were filled with that strong and sometimes bitter love which binds all true citizens of a town to their narrow and unique home. They had something to guard which, once lost, could never be created again by any later generation; the unique mystery of the "polis," which is so great because it prolongs backward into the past and forward into the future the life of those who share in it, and because everyone is at liberty to serve it, bound in that great chain which extends from the past to the future, till the day of the blasphemer comes and the mystery goes up in flames. Every citizen in Calvinist La Rochelle was a soldier, as once in Geneva. The men who were capable of fighting were divided into companies, ready at any moment to rush to arms. The Mayor was the chief military commander. The mercantile craft were constructed in such a way that they could at any time be transformed into warships.

At the beginning of the sixteenth century La Rochelle could boast a history of five hundred years. Two nations, two political parties, two religions, had fought round its walls, which had witnessed many sieges; the list of heroic resistances lengthened from generation to generation. The English and the French had struggled for the possession of the town in the twelfth and the thirteenth centuries; but until the hundred years' war La Rochelle had remained French. Later it changed hands frequently, and it was said that it had claimed the right in one day to be three times English and three times French. The English were no strangers to these seagoing people. In the long conflict English and French lords alike had endowed the town with rights and liberties. Its independence and pride grew; it refused to have its trade trammelled by the legal restrictions of the central authority. That La Rochelle embraced the new faith was as much due to the stout and independent character of the inhabitants as to political necessity.

On the hundred years' war followed the religious wars. In 1573 La Rochelle was besieged by the united Catholic armies under the command of the King's brother, the Duc d'Anjou. Queen Elizabeth of England sent the besieged money and cannons. Henry IV at last succeeded in giving the city peace. But after his death everything once more became insecure.

CHAPTER XV

BUCKINGHAM'S ATTACK

A capacity which Richelieu possessed in an unusual degree was the sense for ripeness; ripeness in men, in times, in circumstances; he never intervened until the moment was ripe. Everyone, the Catholic party, the Curia, the King himself, urged him to strike now, and proceed with the instant extermination of the Huguenots; even his enemies among the discontented Catholic nobles, the friends of Spain, offered their services to him; the Catholic party seemed strong, and the Protestants weak; but Richelieu said to the Nuncio: "Patience. I must go on disobliging the world for a while yet." For the moment he had only one aim: La Rochelle, England's gateway to France, must pass into the King's hands.

When the advocates of war against the Huguenots said that the moment was auspicious, things seem to justify them: Soubise had fled to England; Rohan still held out, but he was isolated, without real support; La Rochelle had no fleet, and the Rochellois were apprehensive and doubtful, and apparently ready to yield. People doubted Richelieu's penetration; they were surprised that he did not see all this, that he did not act at once; now or never was the time to remove this revolutionary menace, this perpetual danger to the health and stability of the monarchy. A violent anti-Protestant movement began which recalled the worst days of the League. Rome supported the Catholic party with secret encouragement; Spain took advantage of the new possibility of civil war to gain its ends in neighbouring countries; a civil conflict would further the Counter-Reformation on the one hand, and destroy the Cardinal's alliances with Holland and England on the other; the King of Spain offered financial help, and Olivares was presently offering it to the Catholics and Huguenots alike; he hoped that out of the exacerbation of relations the party of the League would rise again and with it his influence in France. He assumed that the Cardinal must fall as a result of all these things.

Richelieu saw it all and found the strength to restrain himself and wait.

He watched every slightest movement, he judged, with the profundity which he always showed in such things, the new power that was rising, a power once so badly misjudged by James I: the popular movement among the nations. He saw that the lower classes were indissolubly associated with the Protestant cause. In Amsterdam riots had broken out; hand-workers, sailors, harbour labourers had called loudly for the withdrawal of the ships which cruised before La Rochelle; in England Soubise was loudly cheered in the streets, and public opinion forced Charles I to refuse the return of the ships the French leader had captured and towed to Plymouth; all that Charles could do against the popular clamour was to refuse an official audience to the rebellious Frenchman.

Richelieu did his utmost to avoid a break with the sea powers; he hoped to let the Huguenot conflict die down and thus gain time. When on November 21st the Protestant deputies handed the King at St. Germain-en-Laye the document outlining their conditions, the King replied in words dictated by Richelieu: "I incline to peace, and I shall assure Languedoc and the other provinces to you. But as for La Rochelle, my intention is different."

Of Soubise nothing was said; Richelieu wished to isolate his case; his popularity was rapidly growing in England, and Buckingham, obeying both his personal impulses and public opinion, now openly declared that he was resolved to send the whole English fleet to the help of La Rochelle. The Cardinal was informed reliably of this between November 21st and 26th.

The Huguenots were deeply disturbed by the King's reply regarding their most important city. They urgently asked to be heard again. The King received their delegates, but this time his answer was sharper, for now Richelieu no longer believed that he could prevent England's defection. And he acted accordingly.

On the 26th Louis replied to the delegates: "You have behaved badly and disrespectfully towards me; I forgive you this one time more; but I shall inform you of my conditions through the mouth of my Chancellor."

The conditions were harsh. There was no longer any mention of destroying Fort Louis. On the other hand, all the new fortifications erected in La Rochelle were to be razed to the ground; the city was to withdraw within the walls it had possessed in 1560, and the citizens were required to recognize a royal superintendent appointed by the King as their final legal authority. No warship was to enter or leave the harbour. For the rest, the city could retain the privileges guaranteed to it by the Edict of Nantes.

An interval was granted to convey the conditions to La Rochelle and the Protestants in Languedoc. During that short time Soubise succeeded in getting news through to his sister-in-law in Paris, the Duchesse de Rohan, which surpassed the wildest dreams of the rebellious Huguenots; he reported that the King of England promised his full assistance; he would intervene in three months, with the beginning of spring; Rohan must be informed at once, and the Protestants must hold out at all cost.

When Rohan received the news he found himself in a difficult position. If the alliance of the French Protestants with England were to be successful, if a super-national Protestant front were to come into existence, there must be in France an army of Huguenot warriors prepared for the utmost. But that condition was lacking. The will to unity which their great enemy the Cardinal possessed was wanting among these Calvinistic individualists. They were disunited, and their differences were almost sectarian in violence. There were two main groups: the first would hear nothing of the new revolt; the second refused to separate their interests from those of the Huguenot capital; they would not sacrifice La Rochelle. This simple difference might have been overcome; but the countless minor disputes over leadership and alliances, particularly over Rohan himself, wrought confusion and paralysed the party. Rohan was everywhere; he went from town to town, where the crowd, singing psalms, followed him into the churches. He threw all his energy into rousing and inspiring the Protestants. He had a secret agent in Madrid; Spanish gold was promised him; emissaries from England were ready to help him. He spoke energetically at the assemblies. "You have as many views as preachers!" he once shouted at the squabbling ministers. Among these zealots there was now a demand for a republic. Rohan knew what such an unconsidered demand would mean: first of all, the withdrawal of the English King from any participation in the Huguenot cause, for with anyone in the position of Charles I the word "republic" would have to be avoided like the plague. Suddenly a wave of hope swept through the suspicious and downcast Protestant towns. Several important places which had recently joined the common cause, Nîmes, Uzes, Alais, decided to prepare for the struggle. Rohan at once saw that they were put in a state of defence; he requisitioned the royal monies in the reformed communities, and raised five regiments of one thousand men each, and a sixth of five hundred.

After hostilities had broken out in several places, violently in the neighbourhood of Nîmes, Richelieu concentrated his whole attention on his relations with England; he no longer believed that the alliance could be saved, but he wished to postpone the break as long as possible, at least until the increasing tension between Holland and Spain should make the General States so dependent on the power and help of France that the break with England would not involve a break with Holland and the German Protestants as well. An astonishing situation in which for a time it looked as if Spain with her plans for a Counter-Reformation world-monarchy would exploit the Huguenot revolt to bring the Protestant powers over to her side and along with them put an end to the French monarchy.

The negotiators whom Richelieu employed were carefully chosen with an eye on Buckingham: a woman and a witty and elegant man of the world, a great favourite in French society, the Bautru of whom Rohan wrote in his memoirs: "He was subtle and possessed the gift of giving to lies the pure colour of truth." The woman was the Duchesse de Chevreuse, Lord Holland's mistress, who was to reappear in Richelieu's path in so many changing roles. Buckingham had confided to her his mad hopes, his hopeless passion, and this gave her a hold over him; he needed her, he could not do without her, until he discovered that she regularly reported everything he said to the Cardinal.

In the beginning of 1626 the difficulties of the royal marriage, the observation of the contract, the question of the Catholic friends of the young Queen, were once more gone into, and the outcome of Bautru's mission was a delegation led by Lord Holland and Lord Carlton, who returned to Paris with him and consulted at once with the ambassadors of Holland, Venice, and Savoy, the result being that a stronger front was shown for the time being against Spain. The consultations of the diplomats frequently took place in the Palais Rohan, where the Duchess was still staying; they were often conducted in her presence and that of the delegates from La Rochelle. These Calvinists from their city on the Atlantic Ocean held firmly to one thing, and refused to budge: they demanded daily the destruction of the fort erected under their walls.

But in the internal conflict which had seized France, Buckingham had won the initiative. He counted on the alliance of the Duke of Savoy, who was always to the fore when there was something to be gained; the support of the Duke of Lorraine seemed certain, should all the discontented elements in France rise at the same time. He sent Walter Montague, a son of Lord Manchester, on a special mission to the Continent. Then he himself put out from Portsmouth on June 27, 1627, with a fleet of several hundred ships and five thousand soldiers, and appeared before La Rochelle on July 10th.

Richelieu had been counting on the attack ever since February, and had strengthened the forces occupying the islands of Rhé and Oléron.

Scarcely was Buckingham within sight of the French coast when he sent Sir William Becher to La Rochelle; Becher was accompanied by Soubise, and their mission was to inform the city of the English fleet's arrival. The two men found the city gates barred; the burghers feared open collusion with the enemy. To overcome their hesitation Rohan's old mother, who was living in La Rochelle, set out; their resistance yielded to the great respect in which she was held; they could not refuse her leave to see her son again; she had the gates thrown open, greeted the two men, and led them amid the loud acclamations of the people into the city, while the mayor and the town councillors looked on with apprehension. In the Town Hall Becher conveyed his King's message to the city magistrates; he promised energetic assistance by sea and land against the tyranny of the French King's councillor; the sole condition the English King required was the city's promise that it would conclude no alliance and no peace without his knowledge and consent, and this condition was to work reciprocally. But the mayor and councillors returned an evasive answer; they begged Becher to convey their thanks to the King of Great Britain for the confidence he had shown in the French Protestants, but declared that it was impossible for them to conclude an alliance, for they were only a part of the Protestant Church, and without its assent they could do nothing.

Rohan blamed their lukewarmness; the burghers, he said, feared a war; they were slack and unwilling to fight. An oppression lay on the inhabitants of the town; it was as if they divined the fearful destiny that awaited them. The Rohans hounded them on; they were now their sole leaders; Bouillon was dead; his sons Frederic and Turenne, the future commander, were twenty-two and sixteen respectively. La Force and Châtillon were serving in the King's army as marshals. La Trémouille was on the point finally of going over to the Catholic Church.

To the very last the majority of the Huguenots had refused to believe that without firm alliances England would fling itself into a continental war for the Protestant cause. Now the improbable had happened, and the Protestants were filled with incredulous amazement.

From a strategical standpoint it was essential that Buckingham should take steps to raise the Huguenots in a general revolt. Many of the Huguenots held that he should have landed on the mainland near La Rochelle; the French fleet could not have prevented him; the real point of dispute between the Government and the city was Fort Louis, which was feebly manned; he should have attacked it and then proceeded with his assembled forces to La Rochelle itself. But Buckingham was thinking of his line of retreat; the hesitating and cold attitude of the city itself forced him to do so; he was resolved to gain possession of the island of Rhé, occupy it with his army, and from that point of vantage control the shipping of the Loire and the Gironde. There were strong French forces on Rhé. Caught between them and the mainland, Buckingham did not feel safe. He regarded the conquest of the island as his first task.

A later marshal of France, Thoiras, was in command of the narrow, seven-mile-long island which lay at the mouth of the bay. The main French force was concentrated in the strong Fort St. Martin; there was a second, weaker stronghold, Fort Pré. The island was manned with two hundred cavalry, almost all belonging to the nobility, and two thousand footmen belonging to the "royal Champagne" regiment. Directly opposite La Rochelle was a place called Sablanceaux; there dunes fell down to a wide sandy beach which abruptly ended in quite deep water, so that at ebb tide big ships could come within pistol range of the shore. Here Buckingham landed his troops.

As soon as the enemy sails appeared Thoiras had posted his troops along the dunes. Before the landing was completed he had already suffered losses from the ships' fire. But he took the landing to be a feint; the real attack, he thought, would be made at another point on the island. He waited too long; two thousand of the English were ashore before his doubts were finally dispelled. He saw that the English troops were hesitating; after the fatigues of a voyage lasting a fortnight, they refused to follow their officers. Buckingham himself rushed through their ranks, striking the reluctant with his cane; they remained sullenly standing on the beach. Thoiras gave the sign to attack. His cavalry made their way at a foot pace through the deep sand of the dunes; when they reached the firmer wet sand on the shore, they put their horses to the gallop and charged. Under the cannon fire from the ships and the musket fire of the English footmen the attack broke; the English who were still on the ships hastened to the help of their companions. The French foot also found it hard to advance through the dunes; they were discouraged by the superior numbers of the enemy; Thoiras had to sound the retreat: Buckingham had won his first victory. The Huguenots were exultant; the news flew like wildfire through all the Protestant towns in the country. A third of the English officers were put out of action in that first battle. But the losses of the French were much heavier. "The flower of the French nobility have fallen," the Duke wrote to Charles I; Thoiras's brother was among them, and promising young officers such as Noailles, Montaigne, Savigny.

The English completed their landing, waited for a few days to rest their horses, and then began their march into the island. Fort Pré was ignored; Buckingham declared it beneath him to besiege the weaker fortress. Now volunteers from La

GEORGE VILLIERS, DUKE OF BUCKINGHAM

(*From the portrait by P. P. Rubens*)

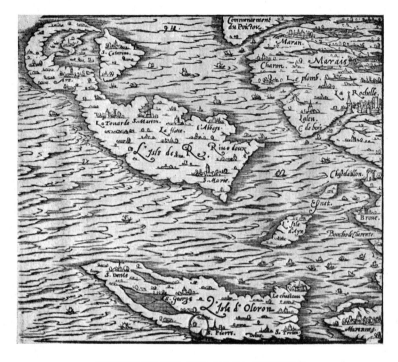

CONTEMPORARY MAP OF LA ROCHELLE

[Cabinet des Estampes, Bibl. Nat., Paris]

Rochelle joined the English army. They sat down to besiege
Fort St. Martin, into which Thoiras had withdrawn with all
his men. The fortress was built on a rock; to mine it was a
hopeless task. Thoiras must hold out at all cost and delay the
English until Louis's armies had occupied strong positions
round La Rochelle. And it was at once clear that Thoiras
would hold out for a long time. If there was no help for it, he
would have to be starved out; but the loss of time was serious
for the Duke. He set his hopes on the effect of his first victory
in England—a victory for Protestantism; but the people's
hatred of him was greater than their zeal for their fellow-
believers. They remained silent when the news was brought
them. Buckingham blocked all access to the fortress by sea,
while day and night free passage between La Rochelle and the
island was assured by swift English pinnaces. A flotilla was
detailed to watch the isle of Oléron, where French troops, it
was said, were concentrating.

The enemy commanders surpassed each other in reciprocal
courtesies. Three wounded French noblemen in the fortress
wrote to Buckingham begging him to grant them a free escort
and permission to return to their castles on the mainland so
as to recover from their wounds. Buckingham granted their
request. The three Frenchmen were conducted in a sloop hung
with purple through the English fleet, while a band played
cheerful dances for their enjoyment. A trumpeter and a foot
soldier thereupon escorted two English hostages to the Duke's
camp; Buckingham gave the Frenchmen 50 gold pistoles each.
At this Thoiras set free four English prisoners and gave each
of them six pistoles. Buckingham, through a member of Parliament, requested the surrender of the fortress. Thoiras sent
him back with a proud refusal and a load of presents. In his
talk with the Englishman he had asked whether there were still
any melons on the island. In an hour's time an orderly of the
Duke appeared at the fortress with a dozen melons, and he in
turn did not leave with empty hands; Thoiras gave him
twenty gold pieces, and next day there arrived at Buckingham's

tent six bottles of orange-flower water and twelve boxes containing *poudre de chypre.*

But the battle did not cease in spite of all this; each side knew how to die. The bombardment went on: the attacks followed each other. There seems actually to have been an attempt to assassinate the Duke; on a deserter who asked to speak with him, ostensibly a Protestant who had been pressed into the King's service, a sharp broad-bladed dagger was found. Buckingham sent the dagger to London, where it was openly exhibited, so that the Duke might appear a martyr for his religion.

The English erected outworks; the French strengthened their fortifications. But soon the besiegers proceeded to sharper measures; time pressed. In the open town of St. Martin they assembled the wives and children of the men shut in the fortress; they drove them towards the gates with naked swords; a trumpeter conducted them; any who turned back were shot down. Thoiras and his soldiers took pity on them and let them in. There were now a few more hungry mouths to be provided for. The water began to run short. A guard was set on the draw-wells. Thoiras alone kept their spirit of resistance alive.

On August 30, 1627, Buckingham issued an ultimatum. "As I do not wish to subject you to greater hardships, I offer you and your garrison an honourable withdrawal . . .," he wrote. "I should be sorry to employ the extremer measures which I have at my disposal." And he signed himself Thoiras's humblest and most obedient servant. Thoiras replied: "The courtesy of Your Highness is known to the whole world, and as it is guided by clear judgment, those who achieve honourable deeds can above all reckon on your approval; and I know no better deed than to lay down my life in the service of my King. . . ."

But in spite of all this, Buckingham had to end the siege before winter came; the extreme measures of which he spoke proved insufficient; without telling anyone he sought a way out. He proposed to Thoiras to treat in secret with the French King. If Thoiras would provide one of his officers as an escort, he was prepared to send his own cousin, young John Ashburnham, to the Court in Paris. Thoiras agreed. The two men, Ashburnham and La Mothe-Fouqué, were landed near La Rochelle during the night and rode to Paris. The King received La Mothe-Fouqué in solemn audience in the presence of the Queen-Mother, the princes of the blood, the cardinals, the dukes and peers of France. In this way Thoiras was able to inform the King circumstantially of his position. But the Englishman was not admitted. "What does this step of the Duke mean?" asked Louis. "Weakness," retorted the Cardinal; and then he dictated the answer: "The King will not treat while there is a single English soldier on his territory, and he reserves his judgment should the English decide to withdraw." Ashburnham requested a free passage to England in order to inform Charles I of the position and obtain his peace proposals. The request was refused; there must be no rumours of peace. The two young men returned to the isle of Rhé. But this time Buckingham refused to let La Mothe-Fouqué return to the fortress; he had received instructions from the King for Thoiras, and he must not be permitted to deliver them; he was detained by force, but treated with the utmost politeness; he dined daily at the Duke's sumptuous table.

The famine in the fortress grew worse; Thoiras fell sick. Mutinies had broken out and had with difficulty been suppressed. One day the soldiers assembled under the governor's window and demanded that the fort should be surrendered. Thoiras had himself lifted from his bed; he addressed the troops and won them completely over. But the garrison was sadly depleted, while the English received reinforcements every week; they had command of the sea, and Holland provided them abundantly with supplies.

In La Rochelle itself no decision had yet been reached; the councillors were still waiting. From the beginning they had been for remaining within the law; the extremists who were for revolt and the English alliance were led by the Rohans and some ministers; they were supported by the hand-workers, the sailors, and the harbour labourers. The counsel of a few experienced politicians was: "Neither submission nor revolt; the city must mediate between France and England." But this wise standpoint was ignored.

It was English gold which had most effect on the masses. Good profits were made on the food which they sold to Buckingham's army; yet in selling it they considerably reduced the supplies of the city itself, and suddenly there was no time left to make good the deficiency.

In the beginning the city was merely watched. The royal army, which was under the command of the Duc d'Angoulême, Charles de Valois, a natural son of Charles IX, consisted of 7,000 men, with 600 horse and 24 cannon. A further four thousand men were to arrive under the King's command: old, experienced regiments. In July the relations between Angoulême and the city authorities were still courteous. "If the citizens," he said, "are prepared to show themselves good Frenchmen, they have nothing to fear." In August the troops moved and drew up in position round the city. The Duke justified the manœuvre by the necessity to guard the coast against the English. In the city there was great alarm when on August 10th two companies of guards appeared before the gates; the councillors went out to meet them and assured them of their loyalty to the King. Valois himself addressed friendly words to the black-robed magistrates; several of the French officers were actually allowed to enter the town and make purchases. But henceforth the Rochellois were prepared for anything. In spite of every assurance, certain measures of the army began to have a daunting effect. No one was allowed to bring food into the town; no citizen could gather his harvest outside the gates. All summer the English were astonished that with the power at his disposal Angoulême did not prevent the rebels from strengthening their fortifications. Buckingham began to wonder whether the inner position in

France was such that the Government could not dare to intervene vigorously. He did not see through Richelieu's policy, did not know that it was merely the Cardinal's will that kept Angoulême's army inactive. Richelieu submitted everything to the main axiom of all his policy, which was that the King must remain in the right, must seem to be the non-aggressor. Any unjust act would have unified the Protestant party and provided incalculable material for propaganda abroad. He calmly waited for the moment when the Protestants would be disunited and the town break into open revolt. On August 5th the King despatched a message which reached La Rochelle on the 15th. In this communication the English attack was condemned as an attempt on the French Crown and the honour of the nation; all good Frenchmen, whether Catholic or Protestant, were summoned to give their lives and goods for the general cause. The letter described Soubise and his followers as traitors who had broken their word. But the King assured loyal Protestants, on the other hand, of his special protection.

The result of this letter drawn up by Richelieu was to sharpen the divisions in the Huguenot camp. The majority of the high magistrates left the town; they did not want to wait for the open outbreak of the revolt; and that revolt had all the marks of a revolt of the masses, inflamed by the Rohans. The Parlement of La Rochelle was officially transferred to Marans. Only seven judges were left in the town to attend to the business of justice.

But the Rochellois continued energetically to strengthen their fortifications. Their engineers erected strong redoubts in the marshes, connecting the town with the already existing outworks, and when they proceeded to strengthen these outworks in turn Angoulême swore that the first thud of the first spade was like a declaration of war.

Henri de Rohan, and the Protestants in Guyenne and Languedoc, remained in anxious communication with the town. The negotiations with the royal army ran their course.

A few burghers who had ventured to appear outside the walls met an officer of the royal army, a Monsieur de Comminges. He spoke to them of hopes for an accommodation. Charmed by his amiability, they informed the Mayor word for word of the conversation when they returned. The town authorities sent a courteous invitation to Comminges to come and lay his views before the Town Council. Comminges succeeded in getting permission from his superiors, appeared one day and gave a short speech in the council chamber; the King, he said, merely desired peace in the country, peace with his Protestant subjects. The assembled councillors and burghers replied that they were prepared to attack even the English if the King would observe the articles of the treaty of Montpellier, if he would put Fort St. Louis under the command of Marshal de la Force, or alternatively of the Duc de Châtillon or the Duc de la Trémouille. These names were symbols in which the Huguenots still believed: La Force's father had been murdered in the St.· Bartholomew's Night massacre; Châtillon was a nephew of Coligny; La Trémouille, who was connected with several reigning houses, was a son of one of the most able Protestant generals of the religious wars. But the accommodating Comminges could not promise such things.

Buckingham himself was at the same time urging the councillors and burghers not to intervene for the moment. "Wait," he advised them again and again, "until Fort St. Martin has fallen; then I shall come with my whole force to your aid, and blockade all the estuaries and harbours of France; Savoy and Lorraine will not fail to join us." On September 1st a party of burghers returned from the island quite dazzled by such prospects.

The question has often been asked why Richelieu let the whole summer go by without destroying the very palpable possibility of a victory for Buckingham. The answer is connected with many complicated factors of foreign policy; but it was clear that everything depended on the attitude of Spain; Spain could not be allowed to go over to England's side, and to prevent this Richelieu needed to conciliate the "devotees" in France. Another decisive fact was that Louis XIII was sick, and that questions of rank and precedence among the generals paralysed any decision; and finally the Cardinal wished to gain time so that the internal disputes among the Huguenots might become crucial.

The question, Who was to command the army? had wide-ranging implications. If the King because of his illness could not conduct the siege in person, he could be represented by no one but his brother Gaston. Only he had a rank which set him beyond the reach of jealousy. It was still less than a year since he had, though reluctantly, played with the thought of joining the Huguenots, and, with La Rochelle as his centre, defying his brother. He must now be finally exposed in the eyes of the Protestants; that was clearly necessary. No chance to do so could be better than the present one; he must be given the command of the army operating against La Rochelle. To leave him behind in Paris would not have been safe. He was accordingly nominated, appeared with the troops in the middle of August, and for the time being was rendered harmless.

But war had not yet been declared. The Rochellois were certainly feeding and supplying the enemy, sailing under the English flag, and being paid by English money, but no act of war had yet been committed; the troops who had gone over to Buckingham might be regarded as volunteers.

On Friday, September 10th, in the late afternoon, it was seen from the town walls that the outworks of Fort St. Louis were being repaired. Fort St. Louis had always been the real stone of offence to the Rochellois. For weeks they had lived in a state of exasperated tension; the citizens had not gone out unarmed for a long time; a slight incident would be enough to change their apprehension into terrified rage. All the artillery of the town had for long been posted on the walls. When the councillor Tesserand, on watch with his battery, saw the workmen busy with their trowels and hammers at the hated fortress, he could not resist his fury; he commanded matches to be lit and discharged a volley at Fort St. Louis. The fort replied at once, and balls of stone and iron were hurled from all the mortars and cannons; the towers of Saint Sauveur and Saint Bartholémy roared and spewed fire: the war had begun.

After these cannon shots the town of La Rochelle considered that it had the right to full freedom of action. It begged Buckingham to send a garrison of two thousand men, coined its own money, and made a treaty of alliance with England. The remarkable thing is that in this document the Rochellois still declared in the sight of God and man that they would remain immutably faithful to the King of France whatever might happen, even in the desperate situation which now threatened them. The King of England had been summoned only as a protector in their need. But they were prepared to accept Buckingham as their military commander in the town, and the war fleet was put under his charge.

Gaston was no formidable enemy; the siege did not really begin until the arrival of Louis and Richelieu himself. Scarcely had they come when Gaston became eager to leave; he did not want to play second-fiddle, he said; he was bored; he was also attracted by the thought of being in Paris while his brother had to endure the winter storms on the edge of the Atlantic Ocean. On the top of Gaston's moods, came Bassompierre's and Schomberg's refusal to serve under Angoulême: they would serve on equal terms with him, they said, or not at all. When after the reconquest of Rhé Thoiras appeared with his fame new upon him, the disputes over precedence became still sharper. Thoiras requested Marillac, the Keeper of the Great Seal, to secure promotion for certain officers who had served under him at St. Martin; but caution and sobriety were in the air. Richelieu said several times that he was displeased by this insistence of the generals on their services; Thoiras must be content as he was. Marillac said to the victor of St. Martin: "You fought magnificently, but there are five hundred gentlemen in France who would have behaved similarly in the same 'situation." Thoiras answered: "France would be much to be pitied if it could not show two thousand men capable of achieving what I achieved, but do you not also know of four thousand men in the country who could fill the office of Keeper of the Great Seal just as well as you?" So Thoiras, too, was annoyed with the Government; he had many talks, not intended for the ear of the Cardinal, with Bassompierre, who treated all military matters with great nonchalance, broke in horses, directed orchestras, and held banquets; but Richelieu heard everything that was said all round him, and he had a faultless and very long memory.

At the beginning of November Louis XIII received a deputation from the Parlement of Bordeaux. The spokesman said in his address: "La Rochelle has always been the moving spirit in all rebellions in Your Majesty's kingdom. Public peace has always been shipwrecked on that rock on the sea; that happened more than fourteen times during the religious wars." An aged officer wrote to Louis at the same time: "Your France, Sire, has so many great nobles who are never quiet, that only a green prince of the blood is needed as a pretender, for them all to pin their hopes again on this town of La Rochelle." The King knew it, yet nevertheless he, too, hesitated.

In many of Richelieu's notes one can feel the fire that was devouring him at this time, as when he writes: "While the Cardinal was employing all the powers which God had given him to make the siege of La Rochelle successful, to the glory of God and the good of the State, while he was labouring far beyond his physical strength, one might have thought that the ocean and the tempest, these powers so favourable to England and the islands, had conspired to work against him."

Now he subordinated everything to one aim; he was resolved to capture La Rochelle quickly and without delay. He saw that this would be decisive for the general situation; every means must be employed to achieve it; "on the capture of La Rochelle depends the good of the State, the peace of the country, the stability of the governing power." There was only one question: "Should there continue to be a State within the State, a perpetual ally of hostile foreign powers, an open wound in the flank of France?" He refused to be diverted from his purpose by any setback, any offer of mediation, any temporizing at Court; the key of this Huguenot town was well suited to open the cabinet which had thus far resisted all his efforts, the cabinet of French policy. Against that will stood Rohan and his handful of Huguenots; their strength, even if they were defeated, would still be as great as the depth of their faith.

The Cardinal worked without intermission on his preparations for the campaign. In August, during the King's illness, he flung his whole private income into the war chest. It was a good thing, wrote a Huguenot, that Richelieu was no longer a bishop, otherwise he would soon be without his kissing ring; everything was being sold or melted down. His first aim was to relieve Thoiras, elude the blockade and furnish the fortress with munitions and food supplies. He offered a high prize to anyone who succeeded in that daring enterprise. For it he employed personal friends of Thoiras, people whose hearts were with the besieged garrison; he also employed priests, friends of his own; he turned princes of the Church into naval officers, people like the Bishop of Maillezais, Henri de Sourdis, whom he called his "Deputy on the sweet and bitter waters."

One day in October he received a letter from Thoiras. The general had sent off three strong swimmers during the night. They carried the news for the Cardinal in a bullet; if anything happened to them they had only to detach the bullet, which would sink without a sound. One swimmer became exhausted half-way across and drowned; the second was captured by the English; the third, after being pursued for a long time, diving, and swimming under water, got through. The message from Thoiras was brief: "If you wish to save the place, send me pinnaces with food supplies before the evening of October 8th. After that I shall have no bread left, and must surrender."

On the evening of the 7th a dense fog covered the coast and

part of the bay; the wind had fallen, but the sea was still high. Forty-six swift pinnaces set out blindly towards two beacons which, Thoiras had said, would be burning on the citadel over the sea. At eleven o'clock the island was still free of mist.

Some days previously Thoiras had sent to Buckingham to discuss the conditions for the surrender of the fortress. Now the deliverers whom Richelieu had chosen, man by man, were noiselessly drawing near. The commander of the flotilla was called Beaulieu-Persac. The moonless night was pitch-black. Several of the boats had crept through the English patrol ships when the sound of their oars betrayed them, and the alarm was given on Buckingham's ship. The pursuit began, a confused pursuit in which it was hard to tell friend from foe. The English lit countless flares on their ships, set stacks and sheds on fire on land to confuse the French boats. The French password was: "Long live the King; get through or perish!" The English patrol ships drove the French into the half-circle formed by their bigger ships, which were bound together by strong cables. Beaulieu-Persac with half his boats let himself be taken in the trap; he sailed straight at the cable, the fight began, the English flung themselves on their easy prey. Beaulieu fought like a lion, drawing as many ships as he could; the English hastened up from every side and completely relaxed their vigilance; they thought they had captured the whole flotilla. Meanwhile the transport boats, twenty-nine in all, crept past the blockade and reached their destination; Thoiras was saved, and now Beaulieu-Persac could surrender.

The English in their camp outside Fort St. Martin knew nothing of this, for next morning they marched out. They expected the fort to be surrendered, and Buckingham and his soldiers stood as if struck dumb when from the battlements they saw capons, turkeys, and great hams displayed on the points of pikes and halberds.

Buckingham paid a visit to Beaulieu-Persac in his captivity; the two men exchanged a dialogue which has come down to us: "Were you under sentence of death that you attempted such a mad and hopeless deed?" asked Buckingham. "In my country bold deeds are not achieved by condemned men, but by free men," replied Beaulieu.

Richelieu celebrated the success of the exploit in Bassompierre's quarters.

On October 12th the King arrived at the camp outside La Rochelle. The artillery of the besieging army fired a salute in his honour. He established his quarters a mile south-west of the town, in a vineyard overlooking the little village of Aytré, where two roads joined. Richelieu settled in a lonely house south-west of Aytré, between the sea and the road to Saintes, at Pont-de-la-Pierre.

He had prepared, seen to, and executed everything, down to the smallest detail; he now felt the pulse of the European powers, and quickly improvised an intelligence service; in addition to his public diplomacy he had his secret diplomacy at work too. He knew all the relations between the various groups in the besieging army, and the temper of the troops. When Provençal sailors would not man the pinnaces, he had to train musketeers to do it. Everything depended upon him, had to be seen to by him. Bassompierre, for example, appeared and declared that he was returning to Paris; he refused to command along with Angoulême. There were always these eternal squabblings, these personalities, this inability to believe in the general goal and submit to discipline. Richelieu had no means to force these people; he begged, implored, he even wept; he promised that the King would grant a written petition of the Marshal, if he sent it in, and astonishingly enough the King had to keep the Cardinal's promise. One of Richelieu's spies repeated to him some muttered words of the proud Bassompierre: "We nobles will never be so stupid as to take La Rochelle." Contarini, the Venetian ambassador in London, reported on January 9, 1628, a saying of Lord Carlisle: "Without the fever of (Protestant) revolt France would become too powerful and intimidate all the other States." But what Richelieu was after was that very power which intimidated Carlisle. And step by step he worked to create it. At the moment the other island, Oléron, was his chief concern. From the start he had reckoned with the failure of the attempt to reach Thoiras. In that case, after the surrender of the fort, Buckingham must next turn his attention to the greater and richer neighbouring island. There he could go into winter quarters with his whole army; he would have sufficient supplies. Oléron had no fortifications; months before Richelieu had strengthened the feeble garrison, had created great arsenals of munitions and food supplies, and the reports which had reached Buckingham of a concentration of troops on Oléron had been perfectly true. Richelieu's first task now was to defeat the foreign enemy, and then proceed with energy to besiege the town. Every day he had impressed this upon the King, and with convincing arguments had dissuaded him from embarking on quicker and ostensibly easier measures. Daily he had to exert on his sovereign the silent pressure of will which during his whole term of power he never exercised on the populace but always on that young man, so easily won, and so quick to withdraw again or to be discouraged.

After the success of Beaulieu-Persac's exploit, Buckingham had been plunged into dejection. He became gloomy, and looked around him for someone on whom to put the blame. The winter was approaching; dysentery had broken out among his troops. In England no one heeded his advice, now that he was no longer there in person. He had no money to pay his men; his reinforcements did not appear; he and his expedition seemed to be forgotten. He sent couriers to London; he wrote: "If you do not support me vigorously now, after the successful commencement of the campaign, it will be an indelible blot on me and on the nation." He threatened and exaggerated; important as he was, he spoke of condign punishment and the gallows. At last Charles I promised that reinforcements would be sent at once. But after a month in which nothing was done he sent his favourite a letter of apology which breathed complete despair. The English finances were in a wretched state;

the people were groaning beneath their taxes; Buckingham was to blame for everything; he had dragged the country into this senseless war, this senseless adventure, and religion had been merely a pretext; so the pamphleteers and the street-corner orators were shouting. The Duchess herself wrote to him saying that the popular fury against him was mounting; it was not worth his while to give his life for such a rabble.

Panic seized public opinion in England; the people felt they were in the hands of gamblers; the worst was to be feared from a policy so completely without all seriousness. There were still English soldiers in Holland and on the Elbe: what would their fate be? Rumours flew about; the French, it was said, were planning an attack on Jersey and Guernsey. A fleet made up of Spanish and French ships would attack the English coast; the ports must at once be put in a state of defence, the Isle of Wight must be fortified.

At the end of October Sir William Becher at last set out with a small fleet for Rhé. Public opinion was now definitely hostile to Buckingham. The captains of the mercantile fleets grew suspicious, the English no less than the Dutch; several ships had been seized by force in Rhé, and the sailors pressed into war service; the mayor of Bristol refused permission for a ship with food supplies for the expedition to sail. The weather grew cold; the soldiers were without clothing, and most of them without shoes. The burghers of La Rochelle agreed to take a thousand sick English soldiers inside their walls, but it was a heavy burden for the besieged town. Buckingham suffered in his own way; everyone found him very greatly changed. He had arrived with horses and carriages in his fine ship, which was as richly furnished as Cleopatra's barge. Now he had to spend most of his time in open trenches; and on board his ship he passed many sleepless nights listening to the howling of the autumn winds. He became a soldier. He began to brood on the approaching return of his inglorious fleet, the strongest in the world, with which he had not succeeded in mastering a little island.

At the same time Richelieu was tirelessly building up the army which was to relieve Thoiras and drive the English out. The commander of this force was Comte Henri de Schomberg, the son of Caspar Schomberg who had served under Charles IX, Henry III, and Henry IV as a German condottiere. Contemporaries said of him that he was the most honest man at Court; he was both brave and prudent, humanely mild, and yet princely in his nature and views. While the other German, Bassompierre, only deigned to continue in the command given him by the King, Schomberg remained completely faithful and did his duty to the last. The King and the Cardinal chose the volunteers who were to attack Buckingham's army on the island. Louis gave the horses from his state carriages for the transport of arms and food, and the nobility were not to be outdone by their master.

The little château near Pont-de-la-Pierre where Richelieu had taken up his quarters belonged to a Huguenot, a former mayor of La Rochelle, Jean Berne; the lonely house could easily be reached from the sea, where the enemy fleet cruised. Berne knew secret paths into the grounds; on his advice it was decided to abduct the Cardinal. A traitor divulged the plot to Richelieu for pay. As once before at Fleury, the Cardinal left the house, while a company of musketeers were posted among the dunes. Behind the château were concentrated two squadrons personally led by the King, who loved martial adventures. The burghers of La Rochelle tacked about half the night, but did not dare to land. They were townsmen, heroically stubborn in defence, but as Bassompierre in his memoirs once scornfully said of the Strassburgers, "like all such people, no good at all in attack." Richelieu had Pont-de-le-Pierre fortified.

On November 6th Buckingham risked his last throw; he resolved to take the fort by storm, in the face of expert opinion that such a thing was impossible. At seven in the morning an officer entered the ship-cabin where Beaulieu-Persac was imprisoned. The officer greeted him and said: "May I invite you in the name of the Duke to watch the assault on the fort from the upper deck?" "Assault?" replied the Frenchman, "God preserve us!" And he quickly followed his conductor on deck, into the light and the sea air.

Three artillery salvos were fired at short intervals. The first gave the signal to fall in, the second to march, and the third to begin the assault. Beaulieu admired the impetuous force of the attack, but he knew that it must fail. The outworks were taken in the first charge. Thoiras had scarcely bothered to defend them. Now forty scaling ladders were planted against the smooth walls of the sea cliff, crowned with its bristling fortifications, whose foot was dry at ebb tide; the attackers clung on stubbornly, the foremost reached the battlements, their hands grasped the walls, they swung themselves up; but beyond the wall was a moat, and beyond it a second, stronger bastion. The English were now within musket range; the order was given to fire; the living targets were sharply outlined against the sky; almost every shot took effect. From the scaling ladders the foremost of the English plunged down, carrying the others with them, to be dashed to pieces against the foot of the cliff. New waves of men ascended over those who had fallen; none reached their goal; dead bodies piled up on the edge of the sea which was rising again and washed away with it many of the dead and wounded. More than three hundred men were lying dead and shattered on the beach or in the moat; for two hours the assault went on without stopping. Where the moat was not deep enough the French fought on the outside wall, seized hold of the ladders and dragged them along with the men clinging to them into the fortress. Beaulieu stood on the bowsprit of the ship and gazed on breathlessly; he was filled with admiration for the senseless bravery of the English, for Thoiras's quick presence of mind, for the courage of his men, now reduced to a third of their numbers, and for the sick who dragged themselves to the wall, "gave four musket shots, lay down and died." The village of St. Martin was one great hospital; no preparations had been made for the wounded.

Richelieu now acted promptly. The King ordered all Schomberg's volunteers to confess and receive absolution. The whole nobility wanted to join the expedition; a Comte Harcourt belonging to the house of Lorraine was among them, two Rohans all the more eager to show their fidelity to the King since their cousins were leading the revolt; they sprang into the first ship. At last the King said to the jostling nobles: "Am I to remain behind alone?" He forbade a brother of Thoiras to go; two other brothers of that brave soldier had already fallen.

Buckingham seemed now resolved to withdraw to his ships and leave the island, if one can speak of resolution in a man filled with fear, love, and a desperate desire to distinguish himself, who was at the same time so lightminded regarding the business in hand. One thing told Thoiras with certainty that the English intended to take to their ships; they no longer buried their dead, but flung them into the trenches and hastily covered them up.

On the night after that bloody day, a November storm rose from the Bay of Biscay; it was pitch-black, heavy seas swept over the English ships; to keep a patrol was hopeless. That night Schomberg crossed with his army, horse and foot, in the shelter of the islands. He had succeeded in making small landings in the previous nights; undisturbed by the English he had flung troops into Fort Pré, the small fortress which Buckingham had refused to capture until the main one had first fallen. In the early morning of November 8th there were four thousand French troops on the island. The English cavalry attacked; they thought they had merely to do with a sortie from Fort Pré. But when the situation became clear the English sounded the retreat; the enemy were too greatly superior in numbers, and the English had been weakened by the long siege and the attack of the previous day. Quickly but in good order they began to withdraw westwards past Fort St. Martin towards a tongue of land which formed a natural inlet where even in rough weather there was promise of getting off safely to the ships; but the point was narrow and swampy. In spite of every warning, Buckingham had not provided for the possible need for a sudden withdrawal. At first his men retreated in good order, but then they left everything behind, their wounded, their ammunition, and their food.

Schomberg now set his expeditionary force in motion. He himself rode at its head. After half an hour a single horseman advanced towards him on a Barbary stallion. It was Thoiras. The commander of the unbeaten fortress introduced himself; greetings followed; Thoiras's first enquiry was for the health of His Majesty the King.

A council of war was held. Marillac, who was regarded as an excellent tactician, suggested that flying enemies must be helped on their way and not retarded with iron shot. Thoiras urged instant attack; the English must be given such a lesson that they would never want to return again; the French had the advantage, their troops were fresh, and the English were exhausted. His advice carried the day. Schomberg ordered his men to follow slowly and delay their attack until the English had reached the narrow passage between the swamps.

This was done. Six hundred men from the fortress joined the advancing troops. A bridge spanned the first swamps and ditches; beyond the bridge the road led through a dense thicket where only two horsemen could ride abreast. Buckingham had fortified only the bridgehead on the opposite side, and that weakly.

Schomberg waited until half the English army was squeezed into the narrow defile. Then he sounded the attack and himself charged at the head of his cavalry. The English cavalry, which were acting as a rear-guard, were overthrown; their leader, Lord Mountjoy, was taken. On the bridge there was indescribable confusion. Sir Pierce Crosby, one of the officers who survived, wrote to Buckingham afterwards: "The French had merely to choose whether they would kill us, drown us, or capture us." Forty banners and all the artillery fell into the hands of the victors; the English dead amounted to eighteen hundred men, almost all of them officers. Buckingham, every French witness declared, fought like a lion; he escaped; he was the last to leave the island. Soubise, on the other hand, had taken as little part in the rear-guard action as in the assault on the fort. He was with his mother in La Rochelle. Gaston of Orléans, who was no hero either, but who knew how to turn a phrase, said at the royal table after the victory: "Honour thy father and thy mother that thy days may be long in the land." During the night what remained of the English army set out in complete confusion for the ships. Buckingham released all his French prisoners, Beaulieu-Persac among them. Soubise reached the English fleet early in the morning. The disaster was complete; the flower of the English nobility had fallen; there was hardly a great English house which was not in mourning. Contarini wrote to the Doge: "Fortune, which treated Buckingham like a mother at Court, has suddenly become a murderess."

Schomberg's report to the King was brief: "Yesterday I effected a landing in Rhé; I have raised the siege of Fort St. Martin and annihilated the English army."

The storms of the past few days had blown over. The winds were favourable for the return voyage; the news of the disaster had not yet reached England; on the high seas Buckingham's fleet met a fleet led by his friend Lord Holland, which had at length come to his help with a collection of old, unseaworthy craft. It was too late. If the weather had been stormy, the remnants of Buckingham's fleet would have been lost as well; it had provisions only for a few days, and water for only a few more; and the decks and cabins were crammed with the sick and wounded. In the night of November 12th the ships landed on the English coast wherever they could, without a single salvo in their honour. At midnight the Admiral's ship, the *Triumph*, with its purple hangings, arrived in Portsmouth with Buckingham.

CHAPTER XVI

THE SIEGE OF LA ROCHELLE

In spite of the collapse of the English attack and the risk of being so far from Paris, the centre of operations, Cardinal Richelieu did not leave the army. In the beginning of 1628 the besieging force numbered 30,000 men, for that time a great army. Protestants also were serving under the King's flag; they were regarded with a certain suspicion, but they proved their mettle; their presence and their bearing demonstrated that among the Huguenots the nationalist idea was growing stronger than the religious, and that the passion which had gone into religion was now seizing on the new concept of Nationalism, and shaping the religion of Patriotism, which also has its martyrs.

Among the Protestants in the besieging army were former leaders who had fought against the League, such as La Trémouille, who at the end of the campaign went over to Catholicism.

Richelieu saw to the equipment, clothing, and accommodation of the troops in a manner they had never known before; he made sure that at the end of every forty days each infantry captain received 300 livres, each lieutenant 100, each ensign 60, and each sergeant 30. The soldiers had their wages paid weekly; their bread was free. The effective strength of the army was regularly tested by inspections; the men's pay was not handed to the chief officers as was customary, but given directly to each man. Food was cheaper than in Paris. The Cardinal instituted strict hygienic regulations. It was a feat at that time to keep a large army in the field for a whole winter without the outbreak of some pestilence. Looting was strictly forbidden; all food had to be bought from the civil population. Capucin priests attended to the spiritual needs of the troops. The Cardinal saw to it that the soldiers attended Mass regularly.

But this army, which in discipline was unrivalled by any military force of the century except the first armies of Gustavus Adolphus, was of no use if the blockade from the sea proved impracticable; and in spite of all the Cardinal's efforts the fleet proved unequal to that task. So he had recourse to another expedient and decided to block the harbour entrance. Already in 1621, during the siege conducted by the Comte de Soissons, an Italian engineer, Pompeo Targone, had suggested this plan. His proposal was now taken up; he appeared in the camp to sponsor his ideas; but his scheme of floating batteries and pontoons linked together with chains could not be carried out. Then an old enemy of France, the Genoese Marquis of Spinola, who was immortalized by Velasquez, visited La Rochelle to pay his respects to the French King. The plans of his Italian compatriot were laid before him, but while he was astonished at Targone's inventive gifts, he saw no hope whatever of executing his ideas. Spinola had the name of being the most skilful siege commander of his time; he had stormed the strong fortress of Breda while simultaneously defeating the army sent to relieve it. His opinion was that the harbour should be blocked by ships sunk in the entrance. Richelieu discussed every detail of the project with that sober expert, a man who slept in his clothes with his sword at his side and spent much of his time praying and fasting. Spinola made a deep impression on him; eight days after his departure he wrote of him: "He is a man of rare virtue, and of intellectual powers equal to it."

Two Frenchmen, Clément Métezeau, an architect in the King's service, and Jean Thiriot, the chief master-mason of Paris, put their services at his disposal. Their proposal was to keep the sunk ships in position by driving piles through them, at the same time building a strong stone dike along this stockade from both arms of the land, leaving in the middle a narrow passage for the ebb and flow of the tide. This narrow passage could easily be guarded by a chain of floating batteries. It was decided to protect the walls of the dike against the pressure of the sea by breakwaters and wide embrasures. The Cardinal had all the plans laid before him, and as soon as the construction of the dike was begun simultaneously from both ends, at a point where the haven was very wide and beyond the reach of the La Rochelle artillery, he appeared daily to supervise the building.

The arms of the dike lengthened, the first from Coreille, the other from the point on the shore which to-day bears the name of Richelieu. The King often accompanied the Cardinal on these rides. At Richelieu's insistence he ordained that the workers on the dike should be highly paid; once, to encourage the soldiers and peasants toiling in the icy water, he himself put his hand to the work.

To provide for the expected fleet, a new harbour near Fort Louis was being simultaneously constructed under the supervision of Bassompierre. In January the fleet created by Richelieu arrived under the command of the Duc de Guise. But hardly had it anchored when an old familiar difficulty arose; the Duke announced that the command of such a trifling sea-force was beneath his dignity. Richelieu promptly appointed a substitute, and preparations to repel the English attack were made. Two hundred and fifty ships and more than six thousand sailors were detailed to guard the dike, the coast and the approach from the open sea. In La Rochelle the churches were filled daily with the faithful, who prayed for the return of the English and the arrival of Rohan with a Huguenot relieving force.

In January Richelieu had written to the Queen-Mother: "Though we are living in a dismal bog here, amid wind and rain, the King remains as cheerful as if this were the most beautiful place in the world." But in February the King's

artificial gaiety ceased somewhat abruptly; the thought of
the stag- and fox-hunting waiting for him gave him no peace;
his courtiers urged him to return to Paris. Gaston, they kept
telling him, was assuming the airs of a ruler there, and his
supporters were increasing. For Richelieu the situation was
more anxious than ever; if the disgruntled King were to
remain all winter in camp, the responsibility of his counsellor
must be heavy; and if the slightest thing went wrong, it
would be the end of the Cardinal. His position was like that
of a man who keeps his balance over an abyss only by a
miracle, by mere force of will, for if the King left, half France
would see in it a condemnation of Richelieu's policy and the
failure of the whole enterprise; his departure would demoralize
the troops; it would give new courage to the beleaguered
garrison and all the other Protestants in the country; it would
encourage the English to intervene again, and Holland,
Venice, Savoy, and Lorraine might send help to Rohan. Also,
the King if far away in Paris might be induced to discard a
policy entered upon with so much thought and even proceed
against his Minister. From La Rochelle nothing could be
parried or circumvented; valuable time must elapse between
each new problem created by circumstances and the measures
taken to deal with it.

The Curia was following intently the progress of the siege
of La Rochelle. Giovanni Francesco Guidi, a son of the
Marchese di Monte Bello and Laura Pompeia Colonna, was
Archbishop of Patras and had formerly been Vice-Legate at
Avignon. The Pope had sent him as Nuncio to the French
Court, and Francesco Guidi despatched reports of the military
operations before the Protestant stronghold. At the beginning
the passionate supporters of the Catholic cause were concerned mainly with the question whether the King would
have the patience to remain with the besieging army and
renounce his comforts and pleasures, the greatest of which
was the daily hunt which had become a lifelong habit. In
October 1627 Guidi was already reporting that Louis was

bored. In January of next year he wrote that the difficulty of the siege, the lack of means, the faint desire which the King showed to continue, made it likely that the whole enterprise would be dropped; and he added that Richelieu and the Queen-Mother desired to continue it, but it was to be feared that the Cardinal would lose his power over the leaders of the army as soon as he was no longer supported by the personal authority and presence of the King. Rome replied that the King would expose himself to the contempt of all Christendom if he renounced such a task at the last moment, when it was so near success. Among the means employed to induce Louis to persevere, one of the strongest was this letter from the Pope, which he was allowed to read. Louis grew sick of the whole business; he declared that he was sorry he had ever embarked upon it; the Cardinal and Bérulle in particular, who at that time was in the closest touch with the Nuncio, kept working upon him. On February 25, 1628, the Nuncio wrote to Rome in deep dejection, for the King, in spite of all this persuasion, had decided to leave for Versailles with a whole crowd of bored young nobles who had been imploring him daily to go. In a month, he promised, he would return. But Louis was to keep his word in spite of the sneers of his courtiers and Gaston's sarcastic reminders that he must not forget to hurry back to La Rochelle, since the leave which the Cardinal had granted him had now expired. By Easter he was back at headquarters again; he had progressed slowly, one stage at a time, and while his subjects in the besieged town slowly died of starvation he was indulging in staghunts during the journey. Yet who had believed in winter that he would ever return? Even Richelieu had regarded his promise as a mere formality. After the King's departure he had fallen into great trouble of mind and had a kind of collapse.

Once more he was shaken by fever, for which no herb known at that time was any help. But he worked on; he had a comfort which kept him going: power. For the King had given him supreme command of the provinces of Poitou,

Saintonge, and Angoumois, and set him over the experienced Marshals Angoulême, Bassompierre, and Schomberg. The Cardinal did not hear until later, when his position was unassailable, that the King after this appointment had said to his followers: "They are as likely to obey him as to obey the kitchen boy." The King and his great servant parted on bad terms; Louis suffered from remorse when he left, and put the blame for it on the Cardinal. But hardly was he at a good distance and no longer listening to his Minister's admonitions, hardly was he in Paris when he felt moved by an inner compunction towards his counsellor and a certain warmth animated his letters. Richelieu issued his commands from his sick-bed and as a true child of his time read Quintus Curtius's *Life of Alexander the Great*, containing the story of the dike which the Macedonian ruler erected outside Tyre.

Yet he had moments of impatience in which everything went too slowly; too much was at stake if this town were to stand out for months to come; he could not depend on reducing it by famine alone. He listened to many a venturesome plan and finally decided to take the town by surprise. There were traitors within the walls. A Catholic citizen of La Rochelle deserted to the King's army and brought a proposal with him: they should steal into the town through a sewer under cover of darkness. A wooden grating which guarded this underground drain must be broken down. In the night of March 12 and 13, 1628, Richelieu waited in the icy cold, his mail over his cardinal's robes, at the head of one thousand horsemen and four thousand foot; he was resolved to lead the attack himself and lay the conquered town at the King's feet on his return. Creeping through the sewer, a small troop of daring spirits would penetrate into the sleeping town and after overcoming the guard throw open one of the great town gates, which was quite near the other end of the sewer. With his small force Richelieu would burst upon the sleeping town. The night was windless, and it seemed endless to the impatient Cardinal; the tension became unendurable;

249

in the east the sky was already beginning to brighten. Where could Marillac, the leader of the storm-troops, be? "Perhaps his nose is bleeding," the Cardinal said bitingly, sitting stiffly in his saddle.

Marillac had set out at eleven; he had had to improvise two bridges to get himself across the marshes; now he and his men were waiting for the gunners, whose task was to burst the grating guarding the sewer. Hours passed, but these men did not arrive with their appliances; they had lost their way in the darkness, and when they appeared at last it was too late.

The people of La Rochelle, when they learned next day of the fearful danger which had hung over them, thanked God in their churches for their miraculous escape. On the other hand, the Cardinal wrote in his memoirs that Providence was not pleased to let the rebels off so lightly; they were destined to suffer greater punishment than the sword could inflict upon them.

This attack through the sewer was not the only attempt to take the town by surprise; nevertheless every other project of the same kind miscarried.

Bad news arrived from Paris. The Queen-Mother, who in one of her moods had once incited the King to persist in the siege, had now become the centre of opposition to the Cardinal. His playing at war was ridiculous, she declared. After all, he was nothing but her creature. What would he have been without her? What talent did he have but morbid ambition, a mania for exercising authority? He knew nothing whatever about military affairs; he should hold his tongue about such things. The siege had been wrongly set about from the start; the Huguenots should have been attacked along the whole line in all the rebellious provinces; instead Richelieu had sat down like Luynes before an impregnable fortress. Such as these, and still sharper, were her strictures.

Richelieu had an access of discouragement in which he felt tempted to forsake the besieging army. News from abroad looked more and more threatening; the accommodation, food supply, and health of the troops were no longer in February what they had been in December; the roads to the camp were bogged in mire. For a moment the Cardinal considerd pushing the blame upon someone else, dismissing the siege as a matter of secondary importance, entrusting the Duc d'Epernon with the command of the besieging army, and seeking laurels elsewhere. It was Father Joseph who diverted the Cardinal from this design. In the last months of winter and the early spring, while Richelieu was assailed by doubts, the besieged began to show the courage of desperation. They often made forays with seven or eight hundred men; small troops of cavalry actually appeared. The town had its heroes, such as the master-weaver La Forest, who was given a solemn burial at the public expense; his coffin was covered with a pall on which martial weapons were embroidered, along with the words, worked in gold: "Fortitudo nobilem fecit"; the whole town followed the funeral procession, the sister of Rohan walking beside the wife of the mayor.

Now and then noblemen belonging to the besieging army were challenged to single combat by one or more of their own rank in the town. Richelieu instructed Angoulême and Schomberg strictly to forbid the acceptance of such challenges; the bearers of them were hanged out of hand.

But soon hunger put an end to such gestures from the besieged. The diversion of provisions to the English in autumn, food which could not be replaced, now left them in cruel want. Secret speculation was already beginning; the authorities had to insist with severity on the fair distribution of all stores of food and to supervise its sale in the open market. In February and March there were many cases of scurvy, which disappeared towards Easter when vegetables became available again. The Mayor's request to the King to allow a proportion of the women and children permission to leave was refused. The number of deserters was increasing, those who were caught trying to escape were executed.

Treachery was rife; abortive attempts on the lives of the magistrates had been made several times. The English garrison which had remained inside the walls began to murmur and demand higher pay. After Louis's return to the army the struggle became more merciless; no communication was permitted with the royal army, two trumpeters who appeared to announce a herald were sent back again. In La Rochelle people began to give up all hope of help from the Huguenots of Southern France. But they still waited tensely for what England would do. On March 3rd they received their first letter from England; the first report from the delegation they had sent there the summer before. A tailor brought it; after his sea journey he had wandered about on foot for twenty days with the code message sewed inside a cloth button. The note promised that the relief fleet would arrive in April.

At the end of March a La Rochelle sea-captain returning from Southampton succeeded in breaking through the blockade; during a violent storm, at flood tide, he made his way by night through the blockading ships and the breach in the dike. At one moment he thought he was lost and flung the letters from England into the sea; but in the confusion another and faster sailing ship managed to follow him after rescuing the package. A draft agreement between Charles I of England and the town council, burghers, and citizens of La Rochelle was among the papers which he handed to the Mayor. It was signed at once. On Thursday, March 30th, the authorities and personages mentioned in the English agreement were called to assembly by the ringing of all the church bells. Gravely and solemnly they listened to the proposals from London and swore on the Holy Scripture to observe the conditions put forward by the King of Great Britain, gratefully to accept his protection, but at the same time to violate in no way their duty and allegiance to their own sovereign lord, the Most Christian King.

The rumours of renewed intervention by the English helped materially in deciding Louis XIII to return to his army; he was convinced, not without reason, that his presence alone would prevent the nobles in the camp from abandoning the siege.

On March 31st the besieged townsfolk took an important step; they elected as their new mayor Jean Guiton, an experienced seaman, one-time Admiral of the port in its struggle against the Duc de Guise. Guiton was a strong character, with all the ruthlessness of the Calvinist and the sanguine resourcefulness of the medieval guild brother; a short, sturdy figure with a rugged face, shrewd and yet frank, kindly yet stern, modest in his piety and simple in his habits, an opponent such as the magnificent Cardinal had rarely encountered. And while Richelieu was bound to regard the siege of La Rochelle as a mere episode among countless others, an operation which he had to perform in accordance with his analysis of the situation before turning to much more serious tasks, Guiton was wholly committed to it; he stood or fell by his achievement in this terrible though limited struggle; he became an incarnation of the destiny of La Rochelle, a symbol of its vitality; even to-day he can be recognized as such in the memorial erected to him by his fellow-townsmen.

With such a man to lead them, the citizens of the township stiffened themselves and began to feel new hope and courage. The women gazed out to sea from their high gabled windows and saw, as a chronicler records, five white swans flying towards them over the roofs of the houses, which they took as a favourable omen; soon, they averred, countless white sails of English ships would cover the sea between Oléron and Rhé. They were not far wrong; two days after the flight of swans the new English expeditionary fleet commanded by Buckingham's brother-in-law came into sight.

After his defeat at Rhé Buckingham had met with contumely from the English populace, but was received by his King with undiminished friendship. Charles showered gifts, rewards and comforting words upon him, making no reflection on his failure except to complain of the people in England who had prevented timely succour from being sent.

To his credit it must be said that Buckingham made no attempt to blame others for the ill-fate of his expedition; he accepted the whole responsibility and insisted on singling out by name those of his officers and men who had distinguished themselves.

Deputies from La Rochelle who had arrived in England with the remnants of Buckingham's troops were officially received by Charles I. The King assured them that their cause was his own; he went so far as to tell these black-gowned Calvinists that the plight of his fellow-Protestants in France haunted him in his dreams.

But it was clear enough that neither sentiment nor the honouring of pledges provided the real motive for English intervention, which was rather to be sought in the traditional principle of England's foreign policy: to weaken France through encouraging the French Protestants, who were the best allies at hand for this purpose. The English believed that Richelieu's various moves, his show of friendship for England, the marriage of Henrietta, the alliances with Scandinavia, Holland, the North Germans, and the Swiss, were primarily intended not to set up checks to the Spanish system but to ensure a free hand in France for a final reckoning with the Huguenots. In this spirit they now interpreted his offer of an alliance with England. Conway, the Secretary of State, summed up the matter when he said that honour and practical common sense alike made it necessary for the King to help the Rochellois once more; and it was the common sense on which the emphasis was laid. So Charles I discovered that the dynastic policy he was relying on to strengthen him against his own Parliament in the struggle for absolute power which he had inherited from his father, had to give way to the national policy of England; against his will he had to deviate into action conditioned by the nature of things, into a policy designed to keep France weak and divided. It was ironical enough that Buckingham's romanticism should be ready to further that deviation; his real interests, like Charles's, were

utterly opposed to any rupture with the French Court, however much his private fantasy might expect to benefit from it.
Once he attacked the French monarchy in the name of Calvin,
he turned his back on everything his world represented, and
the stucco-and-plaster magnificence of his baroque façade
was bound to crumble. Whatever he did was done for the
English Puritans; it was for them he had landed on the island
of Rhé, for them he had fought Thoiras, for them scaled
the fort of St. Martin. Yet all that he did appeared contemptible
in the eyes of these same English patriots, since it seemed that
he took up arms against France merely for the Queen of
France's sake. The relationship between a man like Buckingham and the English middle classes could never be unravelled
into simplicity. The citizens were right in mistrusting him,
but for the wrong reasons; Buckingham fancied that he was
serving both himself and the kingdom of his dreams, while
he was really serving his country's interests and harming his
own. In the end, this most sociable of good companions
found himself playing alone on a deserted stage before a
hostile audience from which his murderer was to emerge.

Buckingham entered into negotiations with the deputies
from La Rochelle, but his conversations with them were
mysteriously complicated. It was as if he were trying to
entangle both himself and them in impossible conditions.
There were rumours of a private intrigue with the enemy.
In fact, Richelieu had sent a messenger to Buckingham with,
it was said, a letter written by Anne of Austria under compulsion, in which she had charged him, by all the oaths he
had not ceased to swear to her, not to allow any further
intervention; his compliance would be a proof of his devotion.
Whether this was true or not, Buckingham propounded
astonishing conditions to the deputies, telling them: "If we
are to intervene again, we must have guarantees that you will
not suddenly conclude a separate peace, so we demand hostages from you; send a certain number of children from your
best families to England, and we shall keep them at the King's

charges and give them a good education." The deputies rejected this condition; for children to live in exile was too hard, they said, and for parents to be bound by such a pledge was too bitter. The Duke then made another proposal; the town of La Rochelle must pledge itself to give shelter at all times to English soldiers and sailors. That too was refused by the Huguenots; and when one considers the state of extremity to which their community was reduced, their answer is very significant, betraying, as it does, how they were torn between devotion to their religion and to their country. They answered that under the pretext of finding shelter in La Rochelle the English might seek to master the town as they had done before, and then the war would go on for ever, since France could never allow a part of her coastline to pass into the possession of an alien power. They themselves had to fight out their quarrel to the bitter end, but they had also to remain the subjects of their hereditary and rightful sovereign; no other outcome was possible.

In the end, however, a pact was concocted in which either side pledged itself to assist the other within the limits of La Rochelle's allegiance to the King of France. The citizens promised to help Charles's forces with all the troops and munitions at their disposal; Charles promised to send provisions to relieve their distress and to prosecute the war until their ancient rights were again recognized under seal by the King of France. This was the draft pact which the mayor and magistrates of La Rochelle consented to sign. And now at last Buckingham seemed to take the matter seriously; a schooner was sent off with a cargo of wheat. Yet on hearing the rumour that a new French fleet was putting out to intercept the cargo, the captain brought his schooner back. Day after day the deputies urged that something should be done, but now it was argued that for the moment money was lacking. In London there were daily processions of protesting sailors who had received no pay at all from the time of the first expedition; they marched three or four hundred strong on Buckingham's palace and would have stormed it but for the Royal Lifeguards.

This opposition apparently kindled Buckingham to greater enthusiasm; the time had now come, he said, to widen the scope of English intervention; he spoke of attacking Calais and achieving what Mary Tudor had failed to accomplish. An unfathomable man! The Huguenot deputies were bewildered. Large sums of money could be obtained only through Parliament, but while the King's advisers thought a summons to Parliament rash and impolitic, Buckingham, who had most to fear from the country's representatives, was insisting on it. Charles tried to raise money from the bishops by frightening them with tales of the Pope's growing influence in France and Germany, and from the sale of Crown lands and the imposition of new taxes, which merely spread disaffection without bringing in much. In March he was at last compelled to give way to Buckingham's insistence and summon Parliament. Instead of passing legislation to secure the means for helping the Huguenots, the Commons began at once an offensive against the Government on the score of illegal impositions, and a concerted attack upon Buckingham. A member called Coke denounced the Duke of Buckingham as the cause of all the evils in the kingdom. Revolt was in the air. On the King's side there was talk of dissolving Parliament and arresting the Opposition in a body; but in the end Charles agreed to hear a "Petition of Right" read in his presence, a kind of re-statement of Magna Charta and a summary of existing grievances. On the King's acceptance of the Petition, Parliament granted him some subsidies for the expedition, yet not without recapitulating its objections to Buckingham. Once more the King had to shield the favourite, but the temper of the populace was rising and the royal authority was being undermined.

Buckingham, apparently unmoved, seemed to devote himself wholly to the expedition, which was now made possible, at least on paper. Old ships, badly found and badly manned, were placed under the command of Buckingham's brother-in-law, the Earl of Denbigh; mouldering grain and half-rotten provisions were rushed aboard them with ridiculous haste; and with the same precipitancy the expedition set sail. On Thursday, May 11th, early on the afternoon of a clear, fine day, the white sails of the English fleet were espied by the burghers of La Rochelle, now in more desperate straits than ever.

The Cardinal's dike had not unduly scared them, since storm and tides kept making breaches in it which Richelieu had to repair. And now, with mounting excitement, they expected the fleet of their sea-faring allies to break the blockade once and for all during the night. Guiton and his predecessor Godefroy rushed from group to group, manned towers and harbour walls, and ordered the disposition of troops and ships in such a way that the English should be assisted to the utmost. The batteries of the French army, which now opened fire on the English, sounded like music in the ears of the Huguenots: those who had any food left sat down to a double ration that evening. In the night the English ships would force their triumphant way into the port, and next day at dawn the deliverance would begin.

But the night passed; the French fleet took on more volunteers, while the French army leaders seemed not in the least discomposed and the English stayed where they were, although there was a full moon and a high flood tide. The Huguenot deputies who had accompanied the English fleet begged and implored the Admiral to take the risk of setting his ships against the dike. He refused, saying that his orders were merely to convey them within reach of their town; he had not been instructed to give battle; there was news of a Spanish fleet coming up to help France, and in these circumstances the risk was too great. The deputies urged him at least to let the transport ships advance towards the breach in the dike, and promised to pay in weighed-down gold the value of any ship that foundered. Until three in the morning they implored

him, but in vain. Then they shut themselves in their cabin
and wrote a letter to the Mayor. One of their train, a captain
of La Rochelle, got into a small boat with two English sailors
and in the darkness slipped safely through the French fleet,
asking every ship he encountered for the whereabouts of a
certain small sailing-vessel, until he reached the harbour. The
townsfolk were all out in the streets in the warm May night,
and crowded round him as he sprang on land; he gave them
gay answers, praised the strength, spirit, and devotion of their
English allies, exhorted them to keep up their hearts, and so
arrived at the Town Hall.

But when he was face to face with the Council and Guiton
the Mayor, behind closed doors, he handed over the letter.
An oath of secrecy was sworn on the Evangel, and Guiton
read the letter silently, his face betraying nothing of what he
felt. Guiton then bade the captain speak, and the captain
briefly described the situation. In complete silence the letter
was read aloud; it urged the Council to arrange for terms of
honourable capitulation with the King of France, if at all
possible, that being their sole hope, and to do it at once while
the English fleet was cruising before the town. The Councillors stood in mute despair, while the cheers of the exultant
crowd outside swelled and died in the air.

Guiton then began to consider and decide what was to be
done in the altered circumstances; a messenger must at once
be sent to Denbigh to make a last attempt, another must set
out for the faithful in Languedoc; at the same time he must
get quietly in touch with the King, and for this task he chose
a former mayor of the town now in opposition, who had once
raised his voice against resistance and an English alliance, a
patrician called Paul Yvon de Laleu. Guiton's predecessor,
Jean Godefroy, was in touch with this gentleman, who now
lived in retirement and had lately sent a petition to the King
to be allowed to leave the city for good; the permission had
just been granted. Godefroy asked Laleu to undertake the
difficult mission to the King. Laleu agreed; one Tuesday he

left the town unobserved during the early morning service; he had arranged with the authorities that if the conditions were inacceptable he would himself return, that if they seemed acceptable a drummer would appear outside the royal tent, and that if they were warmly received a trumpeter would appear instead.

The authorities could not let it be known at any price that they were negotiating with the King. The people were still elated at the sight of the English fleet cruising before the town; but that elation gradually turned into surprise and impatience, and finally mistrust; the dreadful thought of treachery with all its attendant perils was in the air. So no one was informed of the mission to the King; even the commanders of the guards knew only that Laleu had left the town. And when the royal drummer appeared, a captain of the guards on one of the towers immediately gave orders to fire; a musket bullet burst the calfskin of the drum and negotiations were at once broken off. Denbigh still tacked idly about; he made one or two attempts on the palisades of the dike with fireships and floating mines; eight of the English lost their lives through a premature explosion.

On Thursday, May 18th, the starving people stood on the city walls and shouted, as if they hoped their massed voices might reach the English out at sea, when suddenly the fleet was seen in motion and coming nearer. Now the decisive moment seemed to have come at last. The English ships fired a broadside at the French army and the dike, then slowly swept past until only their poops could be seen; the wind was blowing from the land, the distance between the town and the ships lengthened, the fleet got under weigh, its course became more and more clear, the sails smaller and smaller and disappeared beyond the horizon.

It is said of Charles I that he often wept, venting his impotence in tears, and he wept now when he heard from Gobert, a burgher of La Rochelle who had hastened before the fleet in a fast sailing boat, of Denbigh's shameful and incompre-

hensible conduct. Orders were immediately given for the fleet
to turn back and fight. Gobert himself and Lord Fielding,
Denbigh's own son, were sent out to intercept the fleet.
They missed it, tacked about, and returned without success;
and on June 7th Denbigh arrived, his forces reduced by three
ships which had been lost in the English Channel in a fight
with the French. Denbigh had only failure to show; one of his
commanders had attacked some ships belonging to Hamburg,
England's ally, on the voyage back, and in return pirates
had captured several of the lighters intended for La Rochelle.

For two days the King remained invisible; he refused food
and drink; he looked upon the failure of the expedition as a
personal humiliation. But he exacted no punishment; hidden
influences paralysed him. The hatred of the English for
Buckingham became inveterate; it was openly said that he
was at the bottom of the whole wretched failure; he was
dazzled by the Queen of France; he would sell anything, the
King, the nation, the future, for his vain and impossible lusts.
Only a few sober observers still maintained that the tactical
preparations of the French army, the building of the dike,
and the numbers and discipline of Louis XIII's troops had
made landing or any attempt to relieve the town impossible.

Buckingham once more resolved to play for the highest
stakes and challenge the King of France on his own ground,
and he began to prepare a third expedition on a scale not yet
attempted. He would lead in person this last and mightiest
expedition, would conquer and prove everything at one blow:
his fidelity to the good cause, the people's injustice to its
greatest leader, the wisdom of the favour which two kings
had again and again shown him, his own bravery, whose
trophies he would lay with the pride of a war-god at the feet
of the forsaken Queen in Paris; in short, he was resolved to
justify himself before his contemporaries and history, and at
the same time drown his fears and doubts. It would not have
been fitting for a Denbigh to prevail where a Buckingham
had failed.

During these events which revealed to the world more and more clearly the weakness of the English monarchy, Richelieu remained at his post. There were frequent brushes between him and Bassompierre, whose cheerful serenity drove him sometimes to adopt a tone which the Lorraine nobleman regarded as discourteous, regrettable, and surprising. There were heated disputes over questions of precedence: "Who is commanding, I or you? Is it the King or Maréchal Bassompierre who decides?" But after violent letters and sharp protests the Cardinal had always to invite the unmanageable man to sup with him; the old marshal was too disarming; Richelieu had to forgive him again and again, swallow his own humiliation for the time, and nurse it until a later day, to wreak it then on its cause, with the excuse that such carefree and arbitrary personages had no place in a strictly ordered State. Men who were so certain of their courage and health that they feared neither death nor the devil and took everything as a game were of no use to Richelieu now, faced with his overwhelming task. He was daily dinning into the King's ears: "If La Rochelle does not fall now, it will never fall, and the Huguenots will be more unbearably arrogant than ever." Soon the first anniversary of the beginning of the siege would arrive, and the dike was not yet finished; how was such a huge army, how was the King, how were the countless nobles to be kept together before the walls which shut in such a volume of misery during these summer days? "If you conquer the city, Sire," Richelieu wrote, "Your Majesty will be the mightiest king in Christendom, and its arbiter. After the fall of the city we must raze the fortifications of many other towns as well. But we must keep these plans strictly to ourselves, otherwise we may risk finding ourselves confronted with closed gates."

In May the besieged had made a despairing attempt to rid themselves of their women and children. A palefaced crowd appeared at the city gate with their hands raised in supplication and walked towards the enemy lines; they were driven back at the point of the sword. The town seemed empty now; the survivors no longer filled it. They died in hundreds, then in thousands; at the approach of autumn the mortality increased greatly; on October 18th alone four hundred perished. The dead could no longer be buried; the survivors had not the strength to carry the corpses; they dragged them by ropes over the mouldering cobbles, between which the grass grew on which they kept themselves alive.

Two English soldiers who had been wounded on Rhé and sent to be nursed in the town prudently arranged and paid for their burial in advance; they paid sixteen shillings each, naming the day of their burial, and one of them at least punctually kept his appointment.

Finally the dead were left lying where they fell, in some house, at some corner, no matter where. Guards in the towers and on the walls broke down, no longer being able to hold their muskets. Outside the walls the King's soldiers cooked savoury food over their fires, whose smoke blew over the walls; they stuck juicy titbits on spits and held them up, while the starving men on the walls turned away or flung themselves down with their faces in the dust.

But they did not surrender; Guiton, their faith in the next world, and their hope of English aid, kept them going; for they had not yet given up all hope of the English, and when the news came that Buckingham was himself preparing a fleet in Southampton, their hope crystallized into a fixed despairing hallucination from which there was no escape for them thenceforward. It was as if the death of so many of their friends meant nothing now, as if in their town perishing of hunger the dead still kept watch under an invisible mayor, singing psalms in the dark churches and praying as they had done weekly since the beginning of the siege for their anointed King, whose men were setting fire to the meagre crops which they had sowed under cover of night among the salt marshes, hoping the thin ears would not be noticed and might be reaped unobserved.

The Mayor and the eight pastors of the town were resolved to hold out at any price; the former Mayor and the high judges demanded surrender. There were deserters almost every night during those summer months. Women of the town crept out to the first lines of the enemy and gave themselves for a piece of bread. The Cardinal ordained that soldiers who lent themselves to such proceedings should die on the wheel.

A young girl of good family in the town sent word to a handsome young lieutenant that she had a dowry of 30,000 livres, and that if he would save her from starvation and certain death she was prepared to renounce her faith and marry him. The lieutenant petitioned the King; Louis laughingly granted his request; the lady succeeded in escaping and a gay marriage celebration followed, with martial sports, music, and abundance of food and drink.

But that was not the rule. Most of the refugees from the town were strung up without ceremony. There were spies everywhere; the town was devoured by suspicion, and neighbour watched neighbour.

Guiton remained unmoved: if they surrendered and opened the gates the town would be looted, the population butchered or violated; none but fools and children could count on mercy.

A sailor appeared at the Mayor's house and offered to assassinate Richelieu. Guiton answered that he could not advise him, it was a matter of conscience; he sent for a theologian, the pastor Salbert, who declared that such an act would be a shameful and deadly sin; God did not approve of such ways of delivering the town.

Richelieu continued to press the town with all the means at his disposal: the sharpest methods were the mildest in such a case, he said, because the quickest. He distributed sheets in the town, in which he asserted that "a tyrannical minority" were coercing the unfortunate citizens; these men were "food profiteers," and they regarded with indifference "the lingering death of the poor"; if they had any public feeling, they would "distribute their food stores"; they could not advise or act disinterestedly while they possessed more than their fellows.

These vilifications were not without their effect; there were attempts on the life of the Mayor, and several patricians joined forces with the lower classes and exploited their misery. Fire was set to the Mayor's house, but the fortitude shown by that man paralysed the arms which were raised against him. Twice he fainted while attending divine service, for he too suffered from hunger like everyone else; but when he came to himself he was as resolved as ever and had the firmness to walk unmoved past some women who flung themselves before him, holding up their famished children. The old Duchesse de Rohan stood by him; along with her unmarried daughter she had endured all the hardships of the town; she had exhausted all her food bit by bit; in the early summer she had had her two carriage horses killed, and now she was using the leather of her easy chair for soup. People were reduced to eating their hats and boots during those days.

In September Guiton, that his responsibility in the sight of God and man might be endurable, sent two deputies to the Cardinal to ask what terms the King would grant if the city surrendered. The two citizens have left a description of Richelieu: they said that he looked like a commander and a prince of the Church; under his black, gold-braided hat his yellow face with the dark eyes, quick to read and to dismiss people, looked uncanny; his slim almost boyish body was clad in purple silk under the glittering breastplate; he wore stockings worked with gold, and red shoes. His behaviour was a mixture of brusque, touchy arrogance, and meditative goodwill. He did not have the mild persuasiveness which might be expected of a priest; he had broken into their speeches as if by deliberate intent, with rude martial ejaculations such as "by my word as a cardinal," "by my honour as a nobleman." He refused to talk to them about the King's conditions; he enquired what their proposals were, and when they had none to make asked them vehemently what he was to think of men who had come ten miles to see him without anything definite to say; he worked himself into a rage, but his anger soon cooled, and he informed them briefly that the town could still hope for the King's mercy. If they surrendered they would be assured full freedom to practise their religion. They would also retain such privileges as did not clash with the royal authority. La Rochelle was the natural capital of these coastlands, and in favourable circumstances could become a trading port like Lisbon or Antwerp.

On their return the two deputies were first heard in secret; the Mayor hesitated to inform the war council, and at last decided to keep silence; what had been offered was not enough; the restriction of the town's privileges implied in the King's demands was far-reaching and dangerous; moreover, fresh news of the English preparations had reached the town. After their experience of Denbigh's fleet, it was senseless of the Rochellois to expect a miracle from Buckingham and the King of England. But simply because it was senseless, they awaited it as they might have awaited the fulfilment of a prophecy.

"By unexampled endurance," the La Rochelle ambassador told Charles I, "La Rochelle has held out now for a year under the tortures of famine, and all this to give Your Majesty time to send the promised help. . . . The fact that your fleet appeared at last in spring, and was seen for several days, and sailed away without doing anything or making the slighest attempt to do anything: even this has not shaken the resolution of the citizens. . . . Will future generations read in the history of Your Majesty's reign that the town was destroyed while in your royal hands, and that from the goodwill which Your Majesty assured the citizens he nursed for their cause, the only reward they reaped was the pitiless enmity of their own sovereign, from whom without that goodwill they might have hoped to find mercy?"

And Charles promised, worked, implored, and lost his sleep thinking of the fate of the besieged. Buckingham went on with his preparations; people remarked how much he was changed; he thought of nothing but his work, he was reserved, serious, indefatigable, and seemed to have forgotten the vainglory of his youth. He now saw through the trick which had been played on him by the secret message from the French Queen. He felt encompassed by danger; even the King's limitless confidence in him seemed to be waning; the hatred of the people, nursed on legends and fantasies, had become habitual and demanded a victim; they spoke openly of his treachery; and now that he tried to break through all these snares and prove himself finally, he was met with fresh suspicion from every side. Not attack but defence was required, people said, for the safety of the country; France was making preparations for an invasion; this was the outcome of Buckingham's half-measures which had miscarried so wretchedly. International diplomacy now entered the lists against the relief of the besieged town; the Venetian and Dutch ambassadors, hostile to Spain, were strongly averse to it; Richelieu's agents had impressed on all the European Courts the fact that to weaken the King of France was to strengthen Spain. Yet these influences could have been overcome; the real obstacles lay in the enterprise itself; all the commanders who had taken part in Denbigh's expedition declared with one voice that it was impossible to force an entrance to La Rochelle; the Cardinal's dike was impregnable. The sailors loitered about the streets of Portsmouth in a mutinous, threatening mood; the hopelessness of Buckingham's position undermined all discipline. Several ships escaped from the port and took to piracy. A letter was sent to Buckingham telling him that he must come to Portsmouth in person, only his presence could save the situation; he appeared and battled with his difficulties. He had now reached a point in his life where only incontestable success in the new enterpsise could save him. But there seemed to be not the slightest prospect of such a success, and no time to organize it.

A necromancer and horoscopist, a certain Doctor Lamb,

was regarded by the people as Buckingham's friend and evil genius. They maintained that he was the devil in person, to whom the Duke had sold himself to secure his rise to power. "The King rules the realm," a pamphleteer declared, "the Duke rules the King, and the devil rules the Duke." In the taverns ribald songs were sung, and everyone knew that Buckingham consulted with Jesuits and Catholic Scots in the presence of Satan; they were all in the pay of France. Nothing more was needed to drive the Puritan masses to violence. On Sunday the preachers spoke in scarcely veiled terms of the Duke's sins, dreadful sins, dyed in sacrilege.

Lamb was crossing the street one day when a crowd gathered, became threatening, and began to shout that he was the Duke's evil spirit. Lamb tried to escape, but the crowd pursued him and stoned him.

From that day Buckingham believed that his hour had struck. He was warned, he was advised to wear a breastplate under his doublet, but he would not abandon the role he had played for so long, and caution did not suit it; from now on he was imprisoned in his part until the end of the play, and that was soon to come. On August 22nd he narrowly escaped from the hands of some mutinous sailors. On August 23rd, after dinner, he left his dining-room and went into the entrance hall, where he remained talking with some friends. A man, covered with dust, a messenger he seemed to be, pushed his way up to Buckingham; his face was known, many recognized him; it was John Felton, an officer who had fought at Rhé and had once been recommended for promotion by Sir William Becher. Then he had been forgotten or passed over; for a long time he had haunted the taverns of London without employment or pay, listening to the scurrilous songs about the Duke and reading the pamphlets; now and then, in his much-darned, threadbare clothes, he had listened to some sermon in which Buckingham was referred to as the viceroy of Satan. Shame, poverty, the rebellious spirit of youth, the deep wound to his pride, and his loathing for a man accused of blasphemy, combined to spur him to action. He rushed up and plunged a dagger into Buckingham's breast. "God have mercy on your soul!" he cried to the dying man, who had reached for his sword. Then he disappeared in the confusion. Someone cried "A Frenchman!" as they crowded round the dead man, but John Felton had left his hat behind him; bareheaded, he stepped out of the kitchen of the house where Buckingham was staying, clearing a path for himself with his dagger. "I am John Felton," he announced. The name was also found in two notes tucked inside his hat, one of which ran: "If I am murdered, no man shall pass sentence on the murderer, unless he should do so himself. Our hearts are hardened with our sins and grow insensible." The other ran: "He who fears to give his life for the glory of God, or for the good of his King and his country, is unworthy of bearing the name of a gentleman and a soldier." Stern, curt words of a man driven to desperation, who in his arrogance regarded himself as the instrument of God.

As for the dead Duke, it was hard to say more of him at that moment than that for years he had been deeply loved by those who were nearest to him. Two kings, father and son, had been devoted to him; they had seen him daily, and the love and friendship which they showed for him to the end were a measure of his value in their eyes. Charles I never entirely recovered from the loss of his friend; he was at church and in prayer when the news was whispered into his ear; he made no answer and continued immovably in his posture, but the blood rose to his face, "so that it grew as dark as his doublet"; then he got up and rushed to his room, locked himself in, and flung himself weeping on the bed.

Richelieu had deeply despised Buckingham. He showed an almost physical loathing for the man's ostentatious splendour and charm, his senseless courage which always ended in failure. He has described him in his memoirs with the harshness of instinctive dislike. "Buckingham was a man of low birth," he wrote, "of ignoble mind, without honour, without knowledge, ill-born and ill-bred; his father was deranged in mind and his brother so insane that he had to be shut up. He himself stood half-way between madness and sense; he was extravagant, possessed, and without measure in his passions."

As soon as the news reached him, Charles I ordered all the English ports to be closed, as Buckingham had once done for Anne of Austria's sake. But a messenger got through and appeared at the tent of Louis XIII, where he reported what had happened; he was disbelieved at first and put under arrest, but when the news was confirmed the King gave him 1,000 talers. This man was in the personal service of Henrietta, the Queen of England; she regarded Buckingham as her personal enemy and the enemy of her native land, to which she always remained faithful; his death meant for her an alleviation of her domestic troubles and gave her hope that her husband might change his anti-French policy.

In France, too, there were hopes that the tension between the two countries might now slacken. There was a chance that the preparations in Portsmouth would be broken off. It was reported that all interest in the enterprise had vanished, and whole detachments refused to march to the port.

Charles had foreseen this eventuality and acted with a despatch foreign to his nature. He requested prayers to be read in all the churches for the success of the expedition. The post of Admiral was left vacant, as if Buckingham's shade were still too near. A naval commission directly under the King was set up. A resolute man, Robert Bertie, Lord Lindsey, who had distinguished himself when fifteen against the Spaniards, was entrusted with the command of the fleet. A hundred and fourteen ships were ready to sail. A whole expeditionary force, eleven regiments in all, was embarked; the ambassadors from La Rochelle, Soubise and his friend and rival Laval, accompanied it. Everyone knew that many of the ships were scarcely seaworthy. But that was ignored; a haphazard haste must make up for such difficulties and dangers. In September the fleet set out. On the 28th its arrival was reported on the French coast. As on the previous occasion, volunteers assembled from all over France; the King took up his quarters in Bassompierre's camp; the news had roused him from his apathy; he always needed excitement —the hunt or war.

Round Gaston of Orléans a sort of Anglophile clique had formed meanwhile, to which the Duchesse de Chevreuse belonged. It had made a cult of Buckingham and intrigued freely. But when the news came of the English expedition, the whole clique, with Gaston at its head, broke up and made for the French camp by the quickest route. The army was posted all along the coast. And now the French once more had to wait, for again the English fleet remained inactive, though this time for different reasons. Lindsey did not vacillate like Denbigh; he urged an immediate attack and gave orders for it, but the officers refused to obey him.

In La Rochelle the surviving defenders still stuck to their posts; in six months eight thousand of the population had died of famine, two thousand in the last two weeks. But Guiton and the preachers still held out. They ordered flags to be displayed once more from the empty windows of the dead streets, and the bells were heard again. Guiton had now to fight his hardest battle. He knew, as he had known in spring, that this was his best chance to negotiate with success, but he also knew that to negotiate would break the spirit of the people entrusted to him, who had endured such terrible conditions. Also, on the first news of negotiations, he feared that the English would turn about and give up the whole business.

This time the torture of waiting did not last so long for the besieged town as in May. With threats and blows Lindsey brought his fleet to the point of giving battle. On October 3rd his ships advanced in fighting order against the enemy. The whole shore was black with troops, we are told; the infantry were drawn up in squares, the cavalry stood "bridle to bridle." The tradesmen who had set up countless booths round the camp sent a delegation to the King with the humble request to be allowed to fight. An ancient fortress facing the sea was given them to defend. Whole processions of fine carriages approached, containing ladies eager to watch the fighting.

Lindsey's plan was first to attack the French fleet, and not to begin his assault on the dike until it was put out of action. A whole flotilla of small coasters of shallow draught were to encircle the French ships and drive them towards the main English fleet; meanwhile the two warships at either end of the crescent in which the English were disposed had to account for the coast fortresses. Lindsey himself, in his flagship *St. George*, conducted the smaller craft in their encircling movement. But the men had no fighting spirit. The nimble English boats kept out of gun-range, so that the French ships wasted all their ammunition in the air. Night put an end to this curious sea-fight.

Lindsey threatened his ship-captains with the death penalty, and at dawn next day the battle again began. From four in the morning Richelieu and the King were in the fighting line. Once they came under strong artillery fire, and cannon-balls fell all round them. But this day was as unsuccessful for the English as the previous one; towards noon clouds blew up, the fleet had to make for the open sea, rough weather set in, the ships tacked about far out and could no longer be seen from La Rochelle, where the autumn tempest howled through the forlorn streets, as if announcing a second winter of famine.

Yet the citizens received a message; Lindsey urged them to hold on; his fleet was as fit for battle as ever; his orders were to bring food to the town, and he would do so if he had to dash all his ships to pieces on the dike. He warned the citizens not to go too near it, since mine-layers would be sent in front to clear the way for him.

But the fleet would not obey him; the English were pregnant with revolt. His orders were not passed on; the bonds of ordinary discipline were severed; no one had any longer the

CHARLES I

(*Portrait by Van Dyck in the Dresden Gallery*)

FRANÇOIS DE BASSOMPIERRE

(From an engraving by B. Moncornet)

authority to punish. It was clear that a Cromwell would become necessary.

At last the resistance to Lindsey broke out in such tumults that that resolute commander, whom Soubise in his despairing letters to Charles I lauded as a hero, consented to attempt negotiation with the enemy. A fortnight's armistice was agreed upon. Montague, the English ambassador to Savoy and Lorraine, who had been seized on Lorraine territory by French cavalry, was empowered to appear before Louis XIII and discuss conditions of peace. In the name of the English King he begged Louis to show mercy and forgiveness towards his subjects in La Rochelle and grant them freedom of conscience and belief; also he asked for a pardon for Soubise and Laval and the free withdrawal of the English garrison. Louis refused to accept foreign mediation; he would treat only with his rebellious subjects themselves, he said, on the subject of capitulation. The English garrison would not be permitted to withdraw until the town was surrendered.

This reply was not softened by the fact that Richelieu gave Montague an official banquet, sent him fruit and wine, showed him every possible mark of honour, and escorted him to his sloop with torches.

Slowly the last surviving Huguenots in La Rochelle, who day in and day out had gazed out to sea, descended from the walls and towers in their dead city.

The first to decide on negotiation were the representatives of the town who were with the English fleet. Richelieu informed them that they would receive very different treatment if the town surrendered while it still had food for three months, as was asserted, instead of waiting until it was in a state of naked want. To confirm the assertion that the town still had stores of food, he suggested that royal commissioners should accompany the two ambassadors back to the town. But they made excuses; "such a thing," they said, "was impracticable, for most of the food was carefully hidden by the owners," and they added that "the resolve of the citizens, shown a thousand times, to die for their cause, must also be seriously taken into account." The Cardinal gave no promise, except that he would inform the King. In parting the two men mentioned the royal fleur-de-lis which still remained unscathed on the city gates. "We know it and bear it in mind," replied Richelieu.

Guiton was informed by two letters in cipher of the interview and of the general situation. The second letter said that Lindsey had put five of his ship-commanders in irons, and that in such circumstances the fleet was no longer capable of action.

On October 26th, a Thursday, the Mayor summoned the councillors to a meeting in the Town Hall. The consultations were brief, for everyone was too feeble to waste words. It was over. A prisoner, an officer of the King, was requested to proceed to the royal camp and say that the town was prepared to surrender unconditionally, and begged for mercy. Richelieu informed the King. Louis XIII hastened to his Minister; a royal council was called in the château of Sauzaie. Three views were expressed. The first demanded that a fearful example should be made of the rebels; the second pled for mildness; the third asked that the ringleaders should be severely punished and the others treated with mercy.

Finally the Cardinal spoke and said: "Seldom has a prince been given such an opportunity to distinguish himself by his mildness before the world and future ages; mildness and pity are the qualities in which kings should imitate God, for they can be His true representatives on earth only by good deeds and not by destruction and extermination. Also, the deeper the guilt of La Rochelle, the more glorious must appear the monarch's greatness of heart; he has broken the town's resistance by his invincible arms and forced the rebels to fling themselves on his mercy and that alone; but still greater will seem his victory over himself if he now forgives them. The name of this town will carry his fame over all the world and spread it among future generations."

At the beginning of the siege La Rochelle had had twenty-five thousand inhabitants; there were still five thousand alive. If there was any question of punishment, it seemed that the punishment had been already executed. The King himself seemed to be moved by the heroic endurance of the citizens, and by the proud thought that it was his own subjects who had achieved such glorious feats.

On the day following the meeting in La Rochelle and the decision of the royal council, four representatives of the town appeared before the Cardinal. He briefly informed them that next day, the 28th, at three in the afternoon, he would expect definite proposals from them; after that date they need expect neither consideration nor mercy. They duly appeared, were fed and given lodgings, and on Sunday they were received by the assembled royal council.

They were informed that their lives and goods would be granted them, and their liberty of worship assured. They tried to bargain concerning the fate of Rohan's mother, the Huguenots in Southern France, and their fellow-citizens who had joined the English fleet. They were told that they had no claim to concern themselves with the rebels in Southern France; as for the Duchesse de Rohan, the King would decide what was to be done with her; in his mercy he was prepared to treat her still as his relative. The Huguenots in the English fleet had already been pardoned. When the La Rochelle delegates showed astonishment at this last news, Richelieu ordered the door of the council chamber to be thrown open, and Vincent and Gobert, the town's indefatigable representatives at the English Court, appeared; they were greeted with tears by their fellow-citizens. All that had guaranteed the individual existence of their town for centuries, their privileges, their free self-elected authorities, their mayors and councillors, was now lost for ever; State officials would govern them in future. La Rochelle would become an ordinary French provincial town with all the grey uniformity of such places. "We shall have to break down many more walls before we reach our goal," Richelieu had said to the King.

The town delegates next had an audience of the King. A hundred yards from the château in which he was residing they painfully descended from the horses that had been provided for them. Bassompierre greeted them and spoke cheerfully to them, as if nothing had happened; the Cardinal, the Keeper of the Great Seal, and the members of the royal council went out to meet them and conducted them into a large chamber, where the King sat surrounded by princes of the blood and great nobles. At the very door these Calvinists, so little used to kneel, fell on their knees. In a feeble voice their spokesman began his address, in which he did not dare to ask for more than mercy.

The occupation of the town followed under strict discipline; there was no act of violence or provocation; troop after troop entered in silence; nothing was heard but the words of command, nothing shown but the spectacle of naked, crushing force. Behind the troops came the food transports; it was strictly ordered that the food should be sold at the same price as in the camp. For that age such a degree of discipline was astonishing.

The first delegates of the town to be received by Richelieu had spoken about him on their comfortless return in a way which had aroused surprise and coldness and finally incredulous indignation; they had found him a man, they said, who judged their situation with calm measure and understanding; he was the real agent in all that had been done against them; the dike had been his idea, the army, which was without an equal, had been created by him; in everything his mind could be felt, no matter where one turned: he had something great in him.

When Richelieu rode into La Rochelle by the side of the Papal Nuncio, the Mayor appeared to greet him in the name of the town. In accordance with ancient custom, his halberdiers marched before him. The Cardinal refused to listen to his address, told him that his office was abolished and that none would hold it after him, and ordered the halberdiers to be disarmed and to disperse. So vanished Guiton, Richelieu's great enemy, from history. He was exiled from his native city.

On Wednesday, All Saints' Day, Richelieu celebrated Mass in La Rochelle. At the same hour Louis XIII in his camp exercised the ancestral magical right of the French royal house: he "touched" the scrofulous, and many who believed in the healing power of his consecrated hand were freed from their sickness. The cures were put on record.

Towards two o'clock in the afternoon the King made his entry. It was followed by great ecclesiastical ceremonies. All Counter-Reformation measures were forbidden; Capucin priests, who had appeared in crowds, were sent out of the town again.

At once Louis set about demolishing the walls and towers. The royal authorities installed themselves in the Town Hall. The ancient town bell was melted down. The justices who had resisted Guiton remained in office.

On November 6th, 7th, and 8th a high gale blew in from the sea; the tide rose so high and so violently that it opened great breaches in the dike, and the breakwaters were shattered and washed away; a Flemish ship of two hundred tons, driven by the storm, made the harbour. If the citizens had waited for a few weeks longer, they could have provisioned themselves.

The English fleet still cruised about inactively; peace was not yet concluded with Charles I. But the Frenchmen who had entered the service of England were pardoned by the King.

The Catholic religion was once more introduced in La Rochelle. No foreigner and no Protestant who was not already a burgher of the town could settle in it without royal permission.

The King left the broken Calvinist city on November 18th, but four regiments remained behind him to superintend the demolition of the fortifications, until the plough could be driven over the ground where its walls had stood.

Hundreds in La Rochelle continued to die for weeks after the surrender of the town. A squad of sappers was kept busy doing nothing but bury the dead.

CHAPTER XVII

THE POLITICAL BACKGROUND

The resumption of Henry IV's policy by Richelieu was much hampered by the uprising of the French Protestants. It is one of his greatest achievements during his early tenure of office that he succeeded in so minimizing the commitments which he had hastily made against Spain that the defection of England from the French side was counter-balanced on the part of Spain by an attitude which at times could almost be called friendly, though it remained uncertain to the end, and might easily veer to hostility.

France had incurred the displeasure of the Curia by its favourable settlement with the Huguenots in 1626, and above all by its intervention in the Valtelline. Now at last, with the attack on La Rochelle, the policy of Louis XIII was entirely aligned with that of the Vatican. The situation which resulted from Richelieu's assumption of power indeed put the Papacy in a stronger position. It was bound to create difficulties for the Vatican if Spain claimed a monopoly of the Counter-Reformation, for Spain's territorial possessions in the Apennine peninsula were a constant menace to the Pope, and made it hard for him to see eye to eye with the policy of Madrid; but if Louis XIII and his army were beleaguering La Rochelle, there were hopes at last that France would join the Catholic front. That was an enormous relief for the Curia, and gave it some freedom of action against Spain. And the change was timely, for, as a contemporary political writer said, the highest favour that the Holy Father could expect from Philip IV was that which Polyphemus had designed for Odysseus: to be devoured last of all.

The approval with which the Pope regarded Richelieu's attack on the Protestant stronghold can be measured by the tireless vigilance with which the Curia followed the most minute fluctuations of party feeling in France, and the fact that Papal influence induced the French clergy to contribute one million gold francs to the expense of the siege. Rome employed all its powers to damp the persistent attempts of Spain to take advantage of and foment the French rebellion. Spain had naturally the liveliest interest in the Franco-English war. Officially Madrid seemed inclined during the first few months of the siege to follow the lead of Rome and support Louis XIII in his Catholic campaign. When Holland, to whom Richelieu turned for naval assistance, made difficulties, Don Diego Messia de Guzman in Paris offered Spanish help, on the condition, it was true, that his king should be given a French harbour and a French fortress as a pledge for his fleet. Richelieu had to refuse; but when help was then offered without conditions he eagerly accepted. Yet an actual alliance such as the Spanish party in Paris desired, and were prepared to purchase with high concessions, he would not consider; he would not go a single foot farther than the practical demands of the moment required. When the English were preparing for their great expedition against France, rumours flew about Madrid of a purposed attack on the Spanish ports, and there was general relief after the landing on the Isle of Rhé. It was reckoned in Madrid that the two strongest enemies of the Hapsburgs would now be kept busy destroying each other for a long time, and that Buckingham on the Isle of Rhé and Louis XIII outside La Rochelle would go on indefinitely with their inconclusive combat.

Richelieu's diplomacy in Madrid kept tirelessly insisting that it was in accordance with Spain's most sacred traditions to support France in the struggle against the Huguenots; for Louis XIII's bold enterprise was not merely a matter involving France. What was happening at La Rochelle was the first step in a complete extermination of heresy, in Holland and Germany as well. The Cardinal dared say this, though in his campaign against the Huguenot stronghold he had done his utmost to enlist the support of the German, Scandinavian, and Dutch Protestants. Once he hectored the Spanish ambassador: "You Spaniards always have God and the Holy Virgin on your lips and a rosary in your hands, but you never do anything except for worldly ends."

As for the help offered by the Spanish fleet, it was highly desirable, considering France's weakness, that the English should be driven from the Isle of Rhé. Operations were discussed with the Spanish ambassador in Paris; the high sea and canal fleets of the Catholic King, united under the command of the Duke of Toledo, were to operate along with the French navy against Buckingham: so it was agreed. But Madrid showed no haste in executing the decision; flying its purple banners dreaded on all the seas, the Spanish fleet arrived three weeks late before La Rochelle, three weeks, that is, after Buckingham had left.

Now began some of the wordless and perilous mummery of etiquette in which that age was so rich. Daily Richelieu issued strict instructions regarding the precedence to be accorded to the various Spaniards; the harbour of Morbihan, and the best place in it, was reserved for the Spanish fleet; the form of salutation was precisely defined, and countless banquets were arranged in honour of the guests. Richelieu chose to preside over these receptions a number of men of high rank who were well thought of in Madrid, and appointed a special master of ceremony to supervise everything. One scarcely dared to breathe lest the honour of the Spaniards might be offended; anything might serve as a pretext for a sudden misunderstanding and lead to some outbreak. The foreign warships in Morbihan were now not only dangerous but quite useless; they were merely costing money. Richelieu accordingly invited the Duke of Toledo at least to join France in a demonstration before La Rochelle. Toledo agreed, but during the first reception by the King the long-feared mishap occurred; the Duke declared that his honour was deeply insulted because Louis XIII had not requested him to keep his hat on as beseemed a grandee of Spain, a thing which Philip IV had never omitted to do. Toledo at once asked permission to leave; he seems also to have had secret orders on no account to be involved in a fight; his fleet had arrived without ammunition, ill-manned, and ill-equipped; now, after an empty demonstration, it sailed back again into Spanish waters. Toledo's assurance that he would return in the event of a renewed English attack was taken seriously by no one.

But how scrupulous was the courtesy which continued to be shown in the French camp towards the Spaniards, in spite of all this, can be gathered from the reception given there to the Marquis of Spinola shortly after Toledo's departure.

Through Spinola the Court in Madrid presently learned that against every wish and expectation La Rochelle would actually fall, and that the English were incapable of hindering the success of the French army. At once and with the greatest secrecy Olivares again got in touch with the French Huguenots, and at the same time tried to make a diversion in Northern Italy, of which more will be said. Olivares' secretary, Don Carlos Bodequin, put himself in communication with three emissaries of Rohan, La Milletière, La Boussilière, and Campredon, through whose hands great sums of Spanish money passed. With England's approval, Louis Clausel, also called La Roche, left on Rohan's instructions for Madrid, where by English influence he was put in touch with the Savoy ambassador, the Abbé Scaglia, so as to further the anti-French alliance which Montague on Buckingham's instructions was trying to bring about in Venice, Holland, and Savoy, and for which Spanish money was now to be sought. The attitude of Spain was completely equivocal; if the States of Lorraine and Savoy, on France's frontiers, dared any provocation, Buckingham held that the full power of the Hapsburgs would be involved in open war against France. For such an eventuality he wanted to keep Venice and Holland neutral, so that after the collapse of France England might join them in arranging the peace. But here as elsewhere Buckingham miscalculated. The counter-resources of French diplomacy were too powerful, the threats which Richelieu already had at his disposal too strong, and besides, in all these States, behind the possibility of immediate success against a France threatened on every side, there was a deep fear of a Hapsburg hegemony. This was most clear of all in the case of Venice.

In the mellow splendour of its sunset hour Venice lay at that time before the astonished world like a golden mirror reflecting the last brief glory of Renaissance man before his slow descent into eternal night. Shakespeare had held up this mirror to the peoples of the North, and the light it threw affected them like magic, for it came from a land beyond their own horizon, beyond the truth for which Europe fought its unresting battles.

The empire of the Venetian Republic in the East was crumbling, in spite of the most desperate defence. The sea-fight of Lepanto had been a victory for Venice, in which she had shown her old spirit, but Cyprus was no more to be wrested from the Turk.

In vigorous collaboration with the orders of the Counter-Reformation, the Curia began to put pressure on the Republic. Paul V had intervened emphatically in its domestic affairs, and in 1606 had laid an interdict on Venice; almost all the priests had obeyed the orders of the Signoria, and continued to exercise their priestly office; but the Jesuits, the Theatines, and the Capucins had refused to do so and had been expelled.

It was Henry IV of France, grateful for the part which the Republic had played in his reconciliation with Rome, who succeeded in bringing about an agreement; the French cardinal Joyeuse solved the problem in favour of Venice. But there were other considerations which made it advisable to keep in with France. Venice had more to fear from the Spanish Haps-burgs than any other State in Italy. In Rome the daunting effect on Venice of Spanish proximity was well known, and though

Rome regarded with suspicion and fear the growth of Hapsburg power in Italy itself, it nevertheless took advantage of the situation to treat the Doges in a manner which in former times would have been unthinkable.

Venice was brought almost to the verge of destruction by the subversive propaganda carried on there among the discontented lower classes by Madrid and Vienna. The plot hatched by the Spanish ambassador Bedmar in 1618 was very nearly successful; an uprising was to have broken out in the town, and simultaneously the Governor of Milan was to have appeared with a strong army, while the Vice-King of Naples was to have advanced through the lagoons with a fleet. The authorities intervened speedily and silently; the conspirators were executed, the ambassador was immediately recalled. Life in Venice after that became stricter, less care-free. The republic looked round it for a protector, and France seemed the only ally who could save it from the threat of Hapsburg world-monarchy.

The remarkable crusading temper which persisted through the era of the Renaissance in France and lasted into its classical age, the plans of Father Joseph, the fact that the first attempt to liberate Greece had come from France—all these things raised hopes of a common policy in the East, which might yet save the possessions which Venice had won there during the Crusades.

Never had the incomparable instrument of Venetian diplomacy worked with more subtlety than during these days when it set itself to further Richelieu's policy. No observer of the political occurrences of the time could be compared with the ambassadors of Venice. They followed the course of events in the camp outside La Rochelle down to the slightest vacillations in the relations between the parties. The news of the fall of the Protestant stronghold was received with joy in Venice. In solemn audience, in the presence of the Doges, the councillors and the French ambassador, an oration teeming with mythological terms was delivered on Louis the Conqueror. The freedom of Italy and the possibilities of an alliance with France against the unbelievers were openly canvassed.

During the whole conflict England had done all in its power to win Venice to its side. On his way to the Duke of Savoy, the French Huguenots and the Duke of Lorraine, Montague had stopped in Venice. Sully's daughter, the wife of Henri de Rohan, had also settled there, and was working for a Huguenot-English policy; she was treated with great honour; she was allowed to worship according to the Calvinistic faith in her house, a privilege which was permitted only to ambassadors. Richelieu was keeping a sharp eye on Venice; the Huguenots had received money from the republic, and he was afraid that under English influence it might turn against him. But with scrupulous caution Venice constantly kept in mind its anti-Spanish standpoint, and simultaneously grasped so completely Richelieu's general policy that it now urgently insisted on an immediate peace between France and England; all this with the definite aim of joining the great anti-Spanish system, which could not arise at all unless France and England were agreed. The only thing that made the Venetian attitude somewhat cautious and tentative, whenever the Doges were sounded regarding their mediation, was their fear of Buckingham's incalculability; the senators of the republic despised his lightness of mind, and in his habit of giving his agents official instructions which were completely incompatible with any policy they saw a danger to all international relations.

Contarini, the republic's ambassador to Charles I of England, had been instructed to shake the King out of the alluring fantasies woven by Buckingham and confront him with facts. Contarini's reports from London spoke pessimistically of the whole north of Europe; Denmark he regarded as lost, Germany as having no freedom to act, the Baltic as already in Wallenstein's, that was to say, Hapsburg, power. He held that the Emperor would claim both Bohemia and the Imperial crown for his successors, and accused Ferdinand II of being a traitor to Christendom, who to maintain the power of his house was ready to sign peace with the Turks. The Hanseatic city of Hamburg at the other end of the Empire, he said, was also coming under the influence of Spain; now that Holland seemed to be weakened and La Rochelle was on its last legs, it was backing toward the Infante. But neither Charles I nor Buckingham would listen to Contarini's arguments; Buckingham smiled when the Venetian urged how necessary was a quick peace between England and France in a situation which would soon mean universal empire for the Hapsburgs. Charles dismissed the ambassador with cool generalities, while Buckingham insisted that England was bound to win; France would be involved in civil war for several decades, and its foreign trade would be completely ruined.

Zorzi, the Venetian ambassador in France, had quite a different impression; he was convinced that Louis XIII was perfectly aware of the general European situation and was prepared at any moment to sign an honourable peace.

In Savoy, on the other hand, there was no sign of any wish to mediate. Charles Emanuel I hated Richelieu and dreaded his policy. He had no desire to see either the French or the Spaniards in Italy. Savoy, poor and royalist, always menaced by powerful neighbours, had maintained itself for centuries by a constant struggle. Seated astride the Alps, it throve on the jealousies of its stronger neighbours. Its princely house, immutably true to its own people, crafty, even faithless to the great neighbouring States, had welded the tough but able upper class into the most capable martial and political aristocracy in Italy. Among these princes and their nobles there existed a loyalty to the State and a political realism which in many features resembles that of Prussia. Flung to and fro by the Italian policy of Spain and France, the mountain state defended itself as best it could. During the first twenty years of the seventeenth century Charles Emanuel of Savoy had seized every chance he could to weaken the royal authority in France, exacerbating difficulties when they arose, and where there was internecine revolt supporting it; he had maintained a vigilant balance between France and its enemies, ready at any moment to come down on either side. He had backed the Comte de Soissons, the most dangerous of the princes of the

Fronde; had given him sanctuary and concealed him, had furnished him with arms and advice. But all Charles Emanuel's enterprises were hampered by lack of money. To the French ambassador at the Court of Turin he seemed to be like "a fish on dry land." He had plans; along with Soissons he had hoped to stir up the nobles of the Dauphiné, march in two columns to Toulon and the mouth of the Hérault, capture the royal galleys there and join up with an English squadron. But without money such things could not be done. At this time Spain, even if it should establish itself in North Italy, did not seem so dangerous to him as France, whose policy in Italy in the first years of the century had never been forgotten by his house. If France sought a way into Italy, it would have to secure Savoy first, while he calculated that the Hapsburgs in Italy had an actual interest in leaving Savoy as a mountain buffer state between the plain of the Po and France.

Buckingham naturally did all he could to exploit these ideas at the Court of Turin. He approved Soissons' intentions and encouraged him to make a drive through the Dauphiné. And if English money had arrived, this attack might have been a serious danger to France. In the spring of 1627 Montague appeared at Turin on a special mission; two days after Buckingham's fleet set sail he was in London to report; he was immediately despatched to the Continent and to Turin again with new instructions. Rohan's wife also appeared at the Court of Charles Emanuel; she found encouragement, and her reports convinced her husband, that great Huguenot condottiere, of Savoy's support."

"If Savoy follows my advice," he wrote to his brother Soubise, "our enemies will have a hard job of it. He has four thousand cavalry and ten thousand footmen. He will find no effective resistance in Provence and the Dauphiné.

But at the moment when the foreign policy of France seemed immutably committed to an anti-Protestant policy, an old and ever-recurring idea again cropped up in Savoy, and on that idea the negotiations between Savoy and England came to grief. By heavy sacrifices Savoy had again and again vainly sought to extend its rule both over North Italy and French Switzerland. The ancient Burgundian policy of the house of Savoy contributed to this. Hardly thirty years had passed since the "escalade," the abortive attack on Geneva; now or never, Charles Emanuel thought, was the chance to capture the city of Calvin once and for all. What a blow for the Protestants if Geneva fell at the same time as La Rochelle! At the moment France simply could not intervene; both military and moral considerations made that impossible while she was besieging La Rochelle. Madrid and Vienna and the Curia must regard such a glorious deed as a providential gift for the Counter-Reformation. Berne would be bound by its agreement with its Catholic compatriots; also it was keeping an anxious eye on the Rhine, from which Switzerland was gravely threatened.

It was England that raised sharp remonstrances against this plan. Until England's defeat was certain Savoy, which had ventured so far on the English road, could do nothing against the wish of Buckingham, and Buckingham declared: "The main aim of the present war—or at least its ostensible aim—is the strengthening of Protestantism; it would look more than strange if one of our allies chose this moment to attack the capital of Calvinism." He could not answer for it to the English Protestants.

Accordingly, Buckingham's first defeat was celebrated in Turin as enthusiastically as his first victory over Thoiras had been. But Savoy was now restrained from actually betraying England by the consideration that France's hands were no longer tied. So negotiations were once more hastily resumed with the Court at Whitehall; the Abbé Scaglia went as special ambassador to London. This priest was high in Buckingham's favour; after the landing at Rhé he had compared the Duke to Scipio, and wished him Caesar's fortune and Alexander's glory.

If Savoy could occasionally afford to adopt a bold policy, Lorraine, the other frontier State, certainly could not. Louis did not love the Guises, yet he had a kind of affection for

Charles IV, the Duke of Lorraine and Bar; the two princes had been brought up together. Richelieu has devoted one of his sardonic thumbnail sketches to the Duke; he was fiery, young, vain, and inexperienced, he wrote, and yet continually dreamt of great conquests. This madness, he went on, was fed and inflamed by a very dangerous person, the same Marie Anne de Rohan who was the wife of Claude of Lorraine, Prince de Joinville and Duc de Chevreuse. Since the conspiracy of Chalais she had been living in banishment in her castle at Dampierre; she was forbidden to appear in Paris. Daring as ever, she had escaped to Lorraine with a small following; in a very short time the Duke was completely under her influence and did whatever she wished. He did it the more willingly in that her wishes coincided with the political needs of his territory, the old western borderland of the Holy Roman Empire, imperilled so gravely by the expanding and growing power of France. Now, if ever, was the moment to escape from the meshes of France and join an anti-French coalition. "This business," wrote Richelieu, "began with a love affair and ended in Lorraine forming an alliance with England." In sober fact this was what the Duchess achieved; when Montague stopped in Lorraine on his way to Savoy he did not fail to pay his respects to her at Bar-le-Duc; and she presently wrote to Buckingham that the alliance was as good as settled; the Duke of Lorraine would furnish ten thousand footmen and fifteen hundred horse, and the Emperor had promised six thousand men; the construction of fortifications against France had already begun. Richelieu kept a sharp eye on all these doings, and when he reprobated them the Duke, as was to be expected, answered evasively that they were mere precautionary measures in view of the unsettled times.

But Lorraine was too weak to hold its own against France, and the Emperor, who should have offered his assistance now or never, was paralysed by the struggling German Protestants of the North. Any independent movement by the Court of Nancy would have been answered by a blow in the face from France.

Francis of Lorraine, the Bishop of Verdun, was resolved to assist his cousin's policy. He undertook to prevent the erection of a French citadel at Verdun, the first French defensive work in that fateful city. He excommunicated the French officers and the workmen who were labouring at the citadel, and threatened to raise the whole population against their project, which was to be of so much moment in years to come. But the King's officers ordered the letters of excommunication to be burned by the public executioner in the open square; they expropriated the Bishop's possessions; the imperial eagle was chipped fromt he walls of his palace and the fleur-de-lis carved instead on the sandstone. The Bishop was forced to seek safety; he fled to Nancy, and after that to Germany.

This provocation, too, brought no reply from the Emperor or the Duke of Lorraine; the Duke was as helpless before it as before the violation of international law which followed when Montague was seized by French troops on Lorraine territory. Montague was flung into the Bastille; the confiscation of his papers apprised Richelieu of the complete foreign policy of Buckingham. In vain the Duke of Lorraine protested, even sending a personal appeal to the Queen-Mother; the tone of the reply he received proved how little his sovereign rights were now estimated. The men implicated in the seizure of Montague, Marie de' Medici wrote, would not be punished, but rewarded; Montague would remain in prison; the seizure had been made on the King's orders; the fact that his officers had trespassed three miles into Lorraine territory was of no consequence; they had known that Montague would never dare to set foot in France. And she added, with that insulting ruthlessness which characterized her family when it dealt with a weaker opponent, that it was very fortunate the arrest had been made in the territory of such a powerless prince, who was also one of the enemies of France. Already in Switzerland every step of Montague had been observed by French agents.

Shortly after Montague's arrest the French forces in Champagne were concentrated on the Lorraine frontier.

And soon after that came the success of Rhé, which threw all the small States adjoining France into apprehension, since the Emperor was still involved with his own affairs. Richelieu began to threaten. He wrote to the Duke of Lorraine that he knew of his plans against France; Lorraine must now put his cards on the table; he was free to join the enemies of France; but if, like his fathers, he kept faith, the King would graciously extend his protection to him.

The success of the French arms made Savoy and Lorraine hesitate, and after the failure of the second English expedition they yielded. Charles IV of Lorraine sent an embassy to Paris, which included his cousin and brother-in-law, the bastard son of the Cardinal of Lorraine, the Prince of Pfalzburg. This embassy was successful in two matters which were highly important to Charles; it obtained permission for the Duchesse de Chevreuse to return to France on condition that she never saw the two Queens and resided outside Paris; it also succeeded in effecting Montague's release. Yet nothing of real political importance was achieved, and the Duke of Lorraine himself had to go to Paris; he waited on the Queen-Mother, gave assurances of his loyalty, and set himself to dispel any doubt of his goodwill to France. But Richelieu remained mistrustful, and after Charles had returned again some of Marillac's friends thought out, in the May of that year, 1628, a curious method of dealing with their uncomfortable neighbour. A captain of light horse, a certain Baron Blaigny, pledged himself to seize the Duke, who often rode out without an escort, by broad daylight, and bring him to Paris. But the Cardinal would not hear of it; his policy and all his measures —he insisted on this as an axiom—must always have an appearance of complete good faith, must always be conducted in such a way that the King was in the right and his enemy in the position of a wrongful aggressor. He was well aware of the persistent harm arising from an appearance of being in the wrong; and this policy, which began as astuteness, had a genuine moral effect when it stopped real injustice from being done. Nancy and Turin drew in their horns and waited for the issue of the war between France and England. They also watched carefully for a turn in the incalculable affairs of the Emperor, and above all for Spain's decision; but towards the policy of Madrid they stood on a very unequal footing; for Savoy felt itself threatened by Milan, while Lorraine, on the other hand, preferred a Spanish predominance in Franche-Comté. Spain remained the great unknown in these political combinations, and because of Spain the anti-French league with England never came to anything. Richelieu tirelessly impressed on all the European Courts that whoever attacked France would strengthen Spain; and his propaganda was effective because it was true; no one could doubt it.

But the complications of the situation in the Netherlands were still graver. In these independent republics the populace clamoured that assistance should be sent to their threatened co-religionists in La Rochelle, while the Governments knew quite well that for the time being they could oppose the Spanish hegemony only by lining up with France. Yet an uncanny premonition warned the Dutch that the claim to European hegemony might yet pass from Spain to France and so endanger Holland even more gravely than did the antique Spanish monarchy, now slowly fading into the shadows. On the General States of Holland were fixed the eyes of all the free political organisms which, surviving from the Middle Ages, had in the name of liberty or of their liberties maintained their separate existence, setting up against the emergence of one great power the idea of federation. Richelieu knew very well that this federal idea must lead the small States in the end to the Emperor, since he alone had preserved the loose political structure of Charlemagne's Empire. French policy had recognized this danger ever since the time of Francis I, and was to recognize it until Louis XV's Foreign Minister, Fleury, in the reign of Maria Theresa, thought that the rise of Prussia had put an end to it. For these reasons Bourbon propaganda and policy ever since the time of Charles V had always sought to characterize the Empire of the Viennese Hapsburgs as the devourer of federal liberties, which subordinated everything, in true Spanish style, to the power of the dynasty. This striking formula, which worked so effectively on the fears of the single States, was immensely strengthened in its effect by the religious schism; the word Hapsburg became in great stretches of Europe synonymous with Roman Catholicism. In this quandary Holland managed to find a solution to which there are few parallels in European history. Federalism is a Germanic principle which has been perhaps most fully realized by England, and at a very early stage France was opposing to this idea of a federated Empire the idea of herself as the protector of small nations. It was Sully who first envisaged a League of Nations as a substitute for the Holy Roman Empire.

The great sixteenth-century controversy over the relation between the State and the subject, in which the Calvinists, the Jesuits, and above all the advocates of monarchy had each played a part, was interrupted by the threatening actuality of the Counter-Reformation and the Spanish bid for hegemony. In this emergency the clear-cut idea of royal absolutism based on national feeling seemed the only political form equal to the tension of the age. The Dutch alone, with their love of freedom, went on to find real a solution for the problem theoretically formulated by Calvinists and monarchists: that is their imperishable achievement. In their resistance to Philip of Spain they became a pattern among nations, an example for all Europe during the whole seventeenth century. In Holland appeared the modern credit system, with its strange mixture of good and evil and its widespread consequences; the naval and mercantile fleets of the General States ruled the sea for decades, and in the controlled freedom of a rich intellectual life Dutch painting spontaneously flourished. Two generations raised Holland to security and fulfilment. In their fight against Spain the Netherlands had saved the liberty of the peoples. By their victory they had achieved an equal recognition for nations regardless of their size or religious affiliations. Ruccellai's and Machiavelli's idea of a balance of power among the principalities of Italy became a reality for all Europe, and took the form of a union of all States against the menace of the strongest.

During the French religious wars of the sixteenth century the Huguenots had been assisted by English money as well as by Dutch and German troops, all directed against Spain; for until 1648 the Counter-Reformation and the Spanish bid for hegemony were regarded as identical. Through its war with Spain the Republic of the Netherlands had become the great Calvinist power. But in the beginning of the seventeenth century, at the time of the siege of La Rochelle, wealth and growing security, desire for peace and comfort, had gradually blunted the warlike spirit of the Dutch burghers; their half-paid soldiers idled about the frontiers, without discipline and without thought of danger. The Dutch democracy with its monarchical apex and urban-republican aristocracy began to rest on its laurels instead of advancing. For a time the opulence of Holland's flourishing culture concealed its political decline; prosperity and production were still increasing; the Dutch colonial empire was being added to, and its acquisition still showed some of that daring which had marked the wars for freedom. Antwerp in the south still stood at the peak of the baroque triumph of the Counter-Reformation, to be immortalized by Rubens. In the north, in Holland itself, a yet greater figure appeared: Rembrandt. Throughout the Netherlands flowed the powerful energy of a people who, having reached the summit of their capacities, but now on the point of imperceptible decline, attracted the admiration and astonishment of all nations. Wherever, in the beginning of the seventeenth century, liberty was threatened, people looked towards Holland as towards the promised land.

At the very beginning of the siege of La Rochelle the French Protestants had set their hopes on the General States. In Holland the threat to their fellow-believers had created a party strongly in favour of intervention. From every pulpit the ministers declaimed against the King of France, and Frederick

Henry of Orange agreed with them. How could he do otherwise? This son of William the Silent was half a French Huguenot; his mother was Louise de Coligny, and she had supervised his education; his sister, Charlotte Brabantine of Nassau, was the Duchesse de La Trémouille, and her son, the Comte de Laval, the Huguenot leader, was always a welcome guest at The Hague. On the other hand, a long and indecisive struggle between France and England was bound to be highly profitable to Dutch trade; consequently, in view of the still existent threat from Spain, and of Spanish and English competition, the only safe friend was France. There was sometimes great anxiety in Amsterdam concerning the possibility of a Franco-Spanish alliance against England, which would have completely destroyed the balance of power.

In Richelieu's talks with Langerach, the Dutch ambassador, the difficulties of this situation became evident. The Dutch were prepared to let the King of France have ships, but only on condition that they would not be used against England; on the other hand, when the combined employment of the French and Spanish fleets came into question, Richelieu exerted all his diplomatic arts to prevent the Dutch from engaging Spain at sea.

During the whole course of the siege the citizens of La Rochelle tried to obtain help from the Stadtholder. Several emissaries appeared at The Hague, and an audience given to a certain Vivier by Frederick Henry of Orange caused great annoyance at the headquarters of Louis XIII, particularly as about the same time a former treasurer of Mansfeld, now in Buckingham's service, had made large purchases of arms and horses in Holland.

The strong popular movement in Holland in favour of the Protestants of La Rochelle was not unknown in England, and hopes were built there on it. When Carleton was sent on a special mission to the Hague in 1627 with instructions to prevent any Dutch move to help France at sea, he confidently relied on the argument of Protestant solidarity. But Richelieu's direct negotiations with Langerach were more successful. By the extension of the alliance of Compiègne between France and the Netherlands for another nine years, the Cardinal won a decisive diplomatic victory. By this treaty the King of France had to pay the General States a million livres yearly, in return for which the States pledged themselves to sign no peace without the consent of the French King; they also promised help to France in men and money as well as preferential treatment in the delivery of ships; and they gave their word not to assist any enemy of France directly or indirectly, while in case of war both parties claimed the right to pursue enemy ships to within firing distance of the ports of either country.

There were ample obstacles to such far-reaching assurances. The Dutch tried to modify several of the clauses; the Catholic, pro-Spanish party in France raised objections; but in spite of everything the treaty was signed.

As a consequence, the General States did not come to the decision in favour of La Rochelle for which all Europe was waiting. They also reaped the equivocal harvest of a neutral country which delivers war materials. Their trade flourished. They supplied ships to France, and arms, munitions, and horses to England. They fished in troubled waters. An English squadron blockaded the harbour of Amsterdam, hoping to capture certain ships intended for Louis XIII; when the ships did not sail, the English invaded neutral waters and after a fight of six hours captured a French warship. Diplomatic protests re-echoed. Hostility between Holland and England deepened and did not vanish again until much later, before the common danger of Louis XIV's predominance in Europe.

The great idea of a community of nations living together in amity had been profoundly harmed in the German Empire. By many classes in Germany the house of Hapsburg, so long identified with the Empire, was regarded as the representative of a Spanish power hostile to the German spirit. For the German Protestants the Jesuits, who in the seventeenth century were to a great extent Spanish, typified a spirit inimical to the highest qualities of the nation.

So in the German lands the attitude to the Franco-British conflict was confused and contradictory. Those who supported the House of Austria were elated by the struggle, which involved both the religious and political opponents of the Emperor. Austria was still at peace with France, but all the old causes of dissension between the two countries had revived again. If the Duke of Lorraine had been more resolute, and the Emperor's prompt help more certain, the towns of Toul, Metz, and Verdun might have been won back from France. But his difficulties in North Germany kept Ferdinand from intervening, and Richelieu fomented these by every means in his power, since he needed to keep the Emperor's armies fully occupied in Germany. The Stuarts of England had supported the Prince Palatine until now, but after Buckingham's landing on the Isle of Rhé, Charles I could put only a few regiments under the command of Colonel Morgan at the disposal of the Winter King, thus enabling the Hapsburg armies to extend their gains in North Germany. If England continued at war with France, the results would be disastrous to the German Protestants. One half of the German Empire was looking towards Spain, the other towards France and England. The Empire had never recovered from the shock of religious division. Large stretches of it had not yet revived from the economic crisis of the sixteenth century. The German peoples in their despair sought for some new order, and they were attracted by order in its simplest form, that which rallies round a banner.

Naked necessity drove men to the markets where they could sell their flesh and blood. There was ample opportunity for this in Hungary, where Bethlen Gabor, who had grown grey in forty pitched battles, was carrying on his fight against the Hapsburgs and the Turkish Empire with the help of adventurers who streamed to his standard from every corner of the globe. But still greater, still uncannier was the gathering of armed men in Germany itself, drawn together by sheer necessity. It was as if an irresistible power were attracting all the fighters in the world to the lands between Stralsund and Klagenfurt.

The Augsburg agreement of 1555 had been only an armistice. Each of the three new Christian confessions in the German countries was still striving to achieve the unity of a church; each held that that unity could be gained only through the strict observance of its own creed; each insisted on its own demands; each carried out its own propaganda. The Zwinglians and the Calvinists were militant; Lutheranism, on the other hand, operated by its mere spirit, knowing that it profoundly mirrored the essential nature of the German people. But the Catholic Counter-Reformation had operated in Germany just as powerfully as in France, and ten years earlier. From the first it had never ceased to carry on its persistent work; the Society of Jesus was its Storm Troop, with which it achieved marvels of organization. What the Kings of France had undertaken, and Louis XIII and Richelieu carried out, was begun in Germany by the Hapsburg Emperors. They, too, in their own way fought against all the forms of destructive particularism, against religious schism and political treachery, against the overweening power of the feudal nobles. They set themselves the same aim which Richelieu was to achieve: a harbour of refuge from the breakdown of medieval society, a unity where the fluctuating, manifold, erratic, daring Nordic spirit, longing for a glorious downfall, an end, should be integrated by the ancient Roman wisdom of the Christian spirit, which would thereafter rule north and south in unity for all time. For long the Counter-Reformation struggled in vain; for long Protestantism triumphantly advanced. But after the first victories of the Hapsburgs over the Protestants in their own territories, the prospect of their ultimate triumph in Europe was considered so probable that Spain, already on the point of disavowing the Austrian branch of its dynasty and coming to an understanding of its own with the Western powers, suddenly returned to the policy of Charles V: collaboration with Vienna. As if awakened by the Hapsburg successes in Bohemia, Olivares and Philip IV envisaged once more the possibility of coercing Europe; and when they began to support the policy of Vienna, the Counter-Reformation in Germany took on a Spanish character; the gloomy and sanguinary element which the religion of redemption had acquired in Spain in its struggle against Moors and Jews, in its extermination of the cultures of America, became an unnatural ingredient of German Catholicism. What, a lifetime later, the German Protestant sects, so long at odds with each other, combined to oppose was this same Spanish Jesuitism, which no longer expressed the balanced serenity of the medieval faith but expended itself in aggressive and intolerant action. Richelieu himself had recoiled from the Spanish ferment in the Counter-Reformation, and when in 1628 in the Valtelline he tried to cut the knot that bound Spain to Germany, he was not committing treachery against the cause of Christian unity, as is often said. He kept that unity in distant view; but he meant it to be fulfilled in the French spirit and by the power of France; he was incapable of seeing it otherwise.

The independence which France in its own fashion desired, the separate territories within the German Empire were demanding for themselves under the spur of religious dissension. In the sixteenth century religion had been the ultimate value. The princes had fought each other in its name, and in its name the peoples rebelled against the Emperor. But the increase of trade barriers between region and region was now alarming; the Empire as a whole, thus threatened and paralysed, could give no protection to German trade abroad, and its internal commerce was strangled by a thousand obstructions.

The hardship was terrible, and for a long time expert observers of European politics in France and Italy had been prophesying that the tension in Germany could be resolved only by a grave internal crisis, which in all probability would bring down the Empire.

Buckingham has been blamed because, while he fought at La Rochelle for the Protestants, he did not succeed in detaching the Protestants of North Germany from French influence, and in forming them, along with Denmark and Sweden, into a great German-Scandinavian block. Those who say this forget that the English could not come to an understanding with the German Protestants, if only because they were vitally concerned in preventing the large deliveries of shipping material from North Germany to Spain, for which purpose they had blockaded the Elbe estuary. A fleet sent out by Hamburg, Lübeck, and Danzig in the summer of 1627 was destroyed by the English. Without English support, North Germany had no alternative but to turn to France; much French gold, it was reported in Venice, had gone to the adventurer Mansfeld, one of the military leaders of the Protestants. The Elector Palatine, the Dukes of Brunswick, Saxony, and Württemberg, the Prince of Anhalt, the Margraves of Brandenburg and Baden-Durlach turned to Richelieu in their struggle against the Hapsburgs; Bethlen Gabor, the Transylvanian Calvinist, did the same. In March of 1628 a nephew of Bethlen had a private audience with Louis XIII.

Among the Protestant powers, only the Hanseatic cities stuck to the Hapsburgs for reasons connected with their world trade.

In 1625 Christian IV of Denmark had made an alliance with England and Holland. For a time he received subsidies and some assistance in troops from them against the Imperial armies, which were nearing his frontiers. But soon both his allies failed him, and he found himself and his country hard-pressed.

As he saw his only hope in France and an England at peace with France, he made desperate attempts to mediate between London and Paris. His ambassador Rosenkrantz laboured for a time in both capitals; then Thomassen and Brahe were sent to help him. But the King's endeavours were fruitless; he was rebuked in England for advising that his fellow-Protestants should be sacrificed, and in Paris—where he was considered to be in a cleft stick, being the King of England's uncle—his proposal for a peace congress at The Hague was laughed to scorn. His ambassadors were invited instead to concert measures against the Emperor.

Christian's northern rival, the King of Sweden, was troubled with the same fears: against the establishment of the Hapsburgs' power, a united Empire under the Hapsburg sceptre, he was bound to fight with every means in his power. The Emperor was growing too dominant, and his power was being increased by a man whose name even in the countries of Western Europe was beginning to have an uncanny prestige: Wallenstein.

Gustavus Adolphus, the son of Charles IX of Sweden and Christine of Schleswig-Holstein, the grandson of Gustavus Vasa, the saviour of German Protestantism, the founder of the North German ascendancy in the Empire, lives permanently but far less vividly in the memory of the Germans than his great enemy who fought for another German world, a world which, with its Mediterranean possessions, its world-wide relations from Constantinople to Madrid, has long since dropped into oblivion.

Gustavus Adolphus made his entry into German history as the ally of France against the House of Hapsburg.

Since his sixteenth year this king had been a soldier; since 1611, when his father conquered Esthonia, he had fought for the possession of the other Baltic provinces; the Baltic had been his scene of action from his early years, and he had waged a perpetual struggle against the Poles and the Russians. The dethroned King of Sweden, Sigismund Vasa, Gustavus Adolphus's cousin, and now King of Poland, was his enemy in more ways than one. Their hostility had a double cause: Sigismund wanted to win back the Swedish throne, while Gustavus coveted Ingermanland and Pomerania, and in addition to these Livonia, Courland, royal Prussia, which belonged to Poland, and ducal Prussia, which was a Polish fief ruled by the Electors of Brandenburg.

The antagonist who was in the end to confront Gustavus on a road which carried him far beyond his original intentions was the Imperial commander Wallenstein.

In 1625 Ferdinand II, feeling himself threatened by the growing European coalition, had given Wallenstein powers to recruit twenty thousand men, had appointed him commander of that army with the title of Commander-in-Chief, and had raised him to the rank of Duke of Friedland. On April 25, 1626, Wallenstein defeated Mansfeld, who was subsidized by France, at Elbbrücke, and drove him to take refuge with Bethlen Gabor in Transylvania, while Wallenstein's reserve army, uniting with Tilly, flung itself against Christian IV. By 1627 Wallenstein had freed Silesia from the Danes. He thereupon induced the Emperor to declare the Dukes of Mecklenburg-Schwerin and Güstrow high traitors, and have their lands transferred to himself; he had already been endowed with the Duchy of Sagan in Silesia. With that the Hapsburgs had established a foothold on the Baltic; a united empire under their sceptre seemed to be on the verge of accomplishment; a quick decision seemed imminent which would have given Germany its share of the world; but the fateful year of 1628 brought all these plans to nothing.

In 1628, the year in which Richelieu was besieging La Rochelle and refusing to be turned aside from his purpose either by external or internal dangers, the year, in other words, in which he set the seal on French unity, Wallenstein sat down to reduce the Protestant city of Stralsund, which was supported by foreign fleets. And history still loves to relate how by their heroic defence the stout burghers of that old city defeated Wallenstein's and the Emperor's designs. It is true that the burghers of the town held out sternly and bravely, yet it must be added that the decisive factor was that Wallenstein's judgment failed him, and with that his grasp of the whole situation, at the bidding of more questionable desires. It was he who pressed for a hurried peace with the King of Denmark. Yet the day that saw him give up the siege of Stralsund, the gate to the North, while Richelieu continued to besiege La Rochelle, saw the destiny of Germany decided for centuries, no less than that of France. France was to be united, Germany split asunder.

In any case, Wallenstein was waging war not only for the cause of Catholicism and the Empire, but for his own advantage and his princely ambitions. He was now master of Mecklenburg, and in accord with Pomerania and Brandenburg. As if he could find no fulfilment in his own life, his ambitions were set on his heir and his house; he resolved to work for them, and that was what gave him the strength to maintain victoriously, through right and wrong, through violence and treachery, against the resistance of the whole German world, the power of the Emperor and the Church.

In Lower Saxony, Upper Hungary, Silesia, Mecklenburg, Pomerania, Holstein, and Jutland he had achieved a German solution for the Hapsburg. But 1628 was to be his fatal year; in that year, when by his failure before Stralsund he sacrificed all that he had won, his sole heir, his son, died.

Having no fleet, he had resolved to wrest the Baltic from Sweden, Denmark, and Holland with the support of Spain and the Hanseatic cities. The Baltic must become Catholic. Before him hovered a vision of a great empire stretching from the Adriatic to the Baltic; he would crush these territorial princes who had once been mere stewards of the medieval empire; with a grandiose flouting of all logic he planned to maintain the power of himself and his house in a central European Empire which would become a unified kingdom like France, and like Richelieu he would suppress its liberties. Through these fantasies there shone again and again one of the most persistent dreams of his age: the destruction of the infidels and the erection of a great Christian imperium whose frontiers would be those of ancient Byzantium. This unified Christendom did not have for him the shape which it had for Father Joseph; he was opposed to all compulsion in matters of faith; his essentially modern mind envisaged rather an agreement among the most varied beliefs; he belonged to the

Renaissance generation of Henry IV, but without its clarity and cheerfulness. What brought his ideas so close at times to those of Richelieu's Franciscan was the ancient Byzantine dream first summoned up by Gonzaga, the dream of a crusade issuing like a lightning flash from the vanished empire of the Hohenstaufens. The mind of this sleepless man who could bear no noise, who posted guards at night to drive away barking dogs, was visited with strange intuitions; and in the silence which he commanded around him his agonized spirit wandered restlessly, aware of no better dwelling-place than the body which so often seemed contemptible to him, but which he was to forsake so reluctantly, praying his murderers to spare him with his last breath.

He was a Leader, because he was at once so remote from and so near to common men; he could regard them as driven herds and yet feel with them; he could be both small and great, both human and inhuman; he was a magician who could step outside his circle and yet always had to re-enter it, free and yet fettered, an authentic mediator between the masses and their destiny. He lacked only the constancy of love and the simplicity of faith, else he would have achieved great things. His own lust for power always entered as an element into the service he rendered to powerful institutions; the colossal success that attended his first campaigns intoxicated him; he would not admit that circumstances had any share in the credit for them. A grandiose melancholy, rising like a vapour from within himself, shrouded the far-spreading landscape of his career, veiling the immediate aim, the tactical objective, although he could see it in a flash, quicker than other men; but, having seen it, a dreamer obsessed by dreams he forgot it at once, in his preoccupation with the final question: to what end? This was what hindered him, not from achievement, for he was a man of action, but from the logical consolidation of his achievements.

He must have cast a glance now and then at the work of his great contemporary Richelieu. He tried to eliminate the fruitless religious struggles in Germany and initiate a constructive

HENRY DE SCHOMBERG, DUC D'ALLVYN
(*From* Le Livre de Louis le Juste)
[*Bibl. Nat., Paris*]

RICHELIEU
(*From the sketch by Claude Mellan*)

Vraye effigie du R. P. Joseph de Paris predicateur
Capucin Prouincial de Touraine superieur des missions
estrangeres et de Poitou fondateur des Religieuses de
Caluaire. A rendu l'esprit entre les mains de ses
superieurs le 18. decembre 1 6 3 8.

FATHER JOSEPH

(From the sketch by Claude Mellan)

policy. It has been said that Ferdinand II's religious policy, being bound up with Spain and an European Catholic hegemony, prevented him from accomplishing this. But it must be remembered that Richelieu in his own land did not achieve unity by eliminating religious differences, but by a trenchant operation, by an unequivocal decision for one religious confession. Wallenstein, who had assumed in turn the beliefs of the Moravian Brethren, of Lutheranism, and of the Catholic Church, could not do such a thing. He served every age and none; he shaped no epoch; something timeless in his nature hindered his work from realizing itself on the actual plane, but raised it to the spiritual, so that as long as the German language is spoken the dark and majestic tones of his nature will be part of it.

His fate is indissolubly bound up with that of his great enemy Gustavus Adolphus, who brought into the German conflict the diametrically opposite qualities, the concreteness of North German Protestantism.

Wallenstein, with his prophetic insight and his capacity for separating his own designs from the general purpose, could view with equanimity the appearance of Gustavus on German soil with his new instrument of a perfectly disciplined army furnished with the latest weapons, which was quickly followed by the destruction of the Catholic opposition in North Germany in two years, and the subjugation of great tracts of the South. It was Wallenstein who opposed the restitution edict of March 6, 1629, for he had seen in it only an incitement of the vanquished to renewed resistance. What made such an exclusively Catholic policy seem hopeless in advance to him was the attitude of Bavaria, that Catholic country in which the desire for political and religious independence by far outweighed the common religious interests of the Hapsburgs and the Wittelsbachs. In his policy of disintegration, Richelieu found instruments in the Catholic Bavaria of the League as well as among the Scandinavian and North German Protestants.

As to the means by which Richelieu came to an understanding with Gustavus Adolphus only a brief summary need be given here.

During the siege of La Rochelle, in the course of a reception given by Bassompierre, Richelieu fell into conversation with a certain Hercule Girard, Baron de Charnacé, an able diplomatist and a much-travelled and clear-sighted man. He knew Russia and Poland intimately; Richelieu listened to him with tense interest while he spoke of the rising star, Gustavus Adolphus, "who had waged war on all his neighbours and won several provinces from them." Richelieu digested this chance piece of information concerning that remote figure; he ruminated over it for some time, and then made Charnacé a proposal. Christian IV of Denmark, first link in the chain of allies which France had fashioned round the Empire since the time of Francis I, had failed him. Next ally in importance was Poland. It struck him that the powerful Swedish king should be enlisted in place of the Dane; but to make that possible France must try to mediate and make peace between Sweden and Poland, both of them struggling for the control of the Baltic. This task the Cardinal now entrusted to the man who had described the great Gustavus so vividly; he appointed Charnacé special ambassador, and gave him instructions to reconcile Gustavus Adolphus with Sigismund III, and thereupon encourage him to invade Germany so as to secure his Baltic conquests. On October 21, 1629, Charnacé was with Gustavus Adolphus in Upsala.

While Wallenstein was besieging Stralsund Gustavus had sent help to the town, but had not intervened in person at the head of his army, for his hands were tied by his conflict with Poland, and he could not venture to challenge the Imperial forces while the Baltic question was still unsettled. If he were to invade Germany his rear must be secured, also he could not fight alone against the inexhaustible reserves of the Empire; he required the help of the Germans if he was to wage war on the German Emperor, and France suggested that the best propaganda for the great new German war—the greatest act of fratricide known to history—would be to publish far and wide that the King of Sweden had come to save Protestant-ism. But that this pretext should be a perfectly genuine one to Gustavus Adolphus himself the Cardinal never imagined, and the irresistible onset of the Swedish king, which in a few months created a completely new situation in Europe, was soon to cause him deep alarm.

France, however, extricated Sweden from its war with Poland. Gustavus Adolphus wanted peace, and he responded warmly to the offer of mediation. The questions to be settled were mainly questions of etiquette, extremely important in that age of ceremony, which lingered out negotiations for a long time. From the start Gustavus Adolphus and his chancellor Oxenstierna treated the French with great independence; they insisted on retaining complete freedom of movement. Nevertheless it was the work of Charnacé that Poland, with the Emperor at its back, agreed to a six-years' truce, to last from 1629 to 1636, which left Sweden in possession of Livonia and several posts in Prussia, while Mitau went back to Poland. The peace came just in time, for Gustavus was convinced that after the defeat of Denmark Wallenstein would attack Sweden next, that, as he said, "the Imperialists will appear in Stockholm, if I don't get in first while they're scouring Italy for booty."

But towards France the King remained as reserved as ever. He would not take the first step. When in the November of 1629 Charnacé tried to persuade him at Upsala to send a special ambassador to Louis XIII, he declined almost rudely.

Charnacé's instructions, dated December 24, 1629, and signed by Louis XIII, empowered him to offer Gustavus a yearly subsidy of 600,000 livres, in return for which the King must pledge himself to secure the freedom of the German princes and cities against the Emperor, to force the King of Spain to withdraw his troops from Germany, to raze all the Imperial fortresses on the Rhine frontier and in the Grisons, to disturb in no way the members of the League, in particular Bavaria, to foment no discontent against the Bavarian house, and never on any account to oppress the Catholic religion.

Gustavus Adolphus is supposed to have laughed heartily over that programme; France's attempt to combine regard for the Catholic religion with her anti-Hapsburg policy seemed to him incomprehensible, ludicrous, and out of date; the Machiavellian spirit of the West excited his merriment. He was no half-savage henchman of the Bourbons. He had no intention of breaking with Spain, for Sweden's trade with Spain was flourishing; he had no intention either of spoiling his relations with Protestant England by standing up for Bavaria's right to the Palatinate. All these clauses in the French proposal were completely against his intentions; he was resolved merely to wage war on the Hapsburg power which was threatening his country, not to become dependent on France. He broke off the negotiations. In March 1630 he sent new troops to Stralsund and occupied the island of Rügen, and four months later he landed at Peenemünde on the island of Usedom on the Pomeranian coast.

Whether with or without a treaty, the events which now began, the horrible conflict between the North and South on German soil, the great deeds of the Protestants under the Scandinavian king known to his time as the Snow King, were indissolubly bound up with the policy of Richelieu. Bavaria was the chief obstacle to a final agreement between France and Sweden. Gustavus Adolphus sent Lars Nielson to Louis XIII to secure an agreement inimical to Bavaria on the long-standing Palatinate question. But the influence of Father Joseph was exerted again and again in Bavaria's favour. He warned his master against a too thorough collaboration with Sweden. "Certain things," he said, "must be used with caution; in small quantities they act as a counter-irritant, in great they are a deadly poison."

During his first Swedish mission Charnacé had achieved considerable results; he had shown adroitness in dealing with differences between Sweden and Poland, but he had failed in inducing Sweden to assume the French yoke, and Father Joseph was glad of it, for he felt sure that without encourage-ment from France, out of mere necessity, Sweden must invade

German territory; he hoped, however, that the war, while restricting the Emperor's power, would not go too decisively against the Counter-Reformation. Richelieu now sent Charnacé a second time to Gustavus Adolphus, and this time, the money question having become urgent, the Swedish king consented to sign an agreement with France, on January 23, 1631, in which he guaranteed the civil and religious freedom of Germany and complete equality of rights between Catholics and Protestants, also to maintain an army of thirty thousand foot and six thousand horse; against which France promised an annual subsidy of 40,000 talers. Sweden had now ceased to be independent of France, and France's policy of expansion to what it called its natural frontiers began with the help of Swedish arms, a policy directed against the Empire, which was to raise openly the long dormant question of the future of Alsace and Lorraine.

To soothe the feelings of the Catholic party in France, who had been deeply indignant at Richelieu's alliance with the Protestant king, French diplomacy now devoted itself to Bavaria. Richelieu assured the Catholic League of his full neutrality if they would withdraw their troops and give up their alliance with the Emperor. If the League accepted this proposal, Austria would be greatly weakened against Gustavus Adolphus's attack; if they did not accept it, Richelieu had at least fulfilled his duty towards the Catholic party, and was no longer responsible for what happened beyond the Rhine. But Maximilian of Bavaria held to his alliance with the Emperor, and sought now to turn against Gustavus the help which Richelieu had offered him against the house of Hapsburg. The negotiations had still reached no conclusion when news came that the Swedish king had already won decisive victories over the Imperial army.

But before these events were to affect France vitally, the first open conflict between the houses of Hapsburg and Bourbon broke out, and Richelieu had now himself to assume command both in the diplomatic and in the military field.

CHAPTER XVIII

MANTUA

During the siege of La Rochelle Vincenzio II, Duke of Mantua, died; as his successor he had chosen a representative of the younger line of his house, Charles of Gonzaga, Duc de Nevers, whose emergence during the nobles' revolt under the Regency and whose Philhellenic plans had brought him in contact with Richelieu and Father Joseph.

Hardly did the Mantuan succession come into question before it seemed about to precipitate a grave European conflict. The territory involved comprised Mantua and Montferrat, and both territories were Imperial fiefs; now they were to be allotted as their prince a born subject of the King of France. The Duc de Nevers at once took possession of his inheritance; he moved into his residence and sent his homage to the Emperor. He was not to enjoy his sovereignty undisturbed for long; other claimants emphatically announced themselves: among them the Duke of Guastalla, followed by the Dowager-Duchess of Lorraine, herself a Gonzaga, and lastly the Duke of Savoy, Charles Emanuel, who had no wish to see a French prince on his southern as well as his northern frontier. He immediately demanded Montferrat for his niece Margaret, a daughter of the elder brother and predecessor of the defunct Vincenzio II. Without the support of Spain the new policy of Savoy could not be carried out; Spain had to protect its Alpine corridor and its Northern Italian territories, and the danger of a forward push by France turned Savoy into an important strategic point for Madrid. The negotiations were soon concluded. In January 1623 the

Spanish ambassador and Charles Emanuel agreed upon the partition of Montferrat; to support the project Madrid next exerted strong diplomatic pressure on the Emperor, requesting that he should declare openly for it. Ferdinand resisted, but the treaty of 1617 was appealed to by which the Viennese Hapsburg Philip III made good his claims on Bohemia, Hungary and the crown lands, and promised in return to leave his Spanish cousin all Imperial fiefs in Italy which should fall vacant thereafter. Here was another excuse for the German Protestants' distrust of the Spanish-Hapsburg system, but here, too, it became clear that an Emperor sure of his power and supported by his whole Empire might have answered in a very different way the claims of the Spanish line of his house.

In the matter of the Mantuan succession Spain and Savoy proceeded at once to acts; they flung themselves on their easy prey while the French forces were still held up before La Rochelle. Charles Emanuel occupied the territory on the left bank of the Po between that river and the Stura; Gonzalez of Cordova, the Governor of Milan, proceeded to besiege Casale.

For Richelieu these incidents, like any open conflict with Spain, were untimely; he was still at the beginning of his concealed war, but now his hand was forced; he could not look on and do nothing without French prestige being gravely damaged and France losing all influence in Italy; and on prestige alone he would have to rely for the next few years in his designs on Germany. Casale and Mantua, the two strongest fortresses in North Italy, were key positions; if he left them in the hands of Spain, he would lose at one stroke all the diplomatic advantages he had won so hard in the Valtelline. While La Rochelle held out he had been thrown back on negotiation; but now that the army was free again, the position was different.

Such was the problem in main outline; Richelieu's real difficulties began in the circle immediately surrounding the Crown. Gaston, the King's brother and a pampered mischief-maker, had lost his young wife, the Montpensier; she had died after giving birth to a daughter who was to become the heroine of the Fronde during Louis XIV's minority. Gaston made up his mind to marry again, and his choice fell on the daughter of the Duc de Nevers, who was now so uneasily reigning in Mantua. The Princess's name was Maria of Gonzaga. The Queen-Mother of France was passionately against the connection; she had thought of a Florentine princess of her own house for her son, one of her two nieces; but the elder was already engaged to the Duke of Parma, and Gaston would have nothing to do with the other. Marie de' Medici had an abnormal capacity for taking offence; for months, for years, she could carry about in her dull mind a chance word, without humour and without understanding. She had always spoken with contempt of the Duc de Nevers, and was never tired of assuring her son Gaston that the Gonzagas were quite small people. Nevers, when told what she said, replied proudly that he was conscious of the respect which was due to the mother of his King, but everybody knew that the house of Gonzaga had been a princely one when the Medicis did not belong even to the petty nobility. Naturally this was at once conveyed to the Queen-Mother, and she felt so deeply insulted that for many years, almost to her death in Cologne, the words rankled in her mind.

Richelieu, who was engaged in striking at the roots of the power of the territorial princes inside the Kingdom, could not regard with equanimity a connection between the irresponsible heir-apparent and a house standing in such complicated relations to French sovereignty and Italian territorial problems. When the King tried to divert Gaston from his marriage plan, Gaston, always volatile, declared he was prepared to strike a bargain. He would agree if he were given the command of the army to invade Italy, also 50,000 talers; after that, Maria of Gonzaga could leave France within fourteen days. The talers presented no great difficulty, in spite of the shortage of money and the cost of maintaining the army, but the thought that his brother might win military fame beyond the Alps made Louis XIII ill; his extraordinary jealousy, which rose from doubts of his own masculinity and influenced all the acts of his life, was further inflamed during the days of decision by an incident at the hunt, where he usually forgot his repressions; Gaston's pack beat the King's in the woods of Fontainebleau: a trifle, it may be said, but a King's trifle may become a people's destiny.

Louis XIII sometimes acted at the bidding of his most personal moods in coming to important political decisions. With intense circumspection Richelieu exploited the pecularities of his master for the good of the State, both guiding him and circumventing him.

On December 26, 1628, the King summoned a council on the Mantuan question. The Queen-Mother, Richelieu, Marillac, Schomberg, the Secretaries of State and Cardinal Bérulle, at that time a great confidant of the Queen-Mother, were present.

Richelieu opened the discussion and advised the King to intervene; Schomberg supported him. The opposition was led by Marillac, and again, as at the beginning of the year, by Bérulle; both in the matter of the English marriage and of La Rochelle Richelieu had already encountered the antagonism of the great theologian. Bérulle declared that they had no money, the royal troops were exhausted; a winter campaign after crossing the Alps was unthinkable; they were isolated, without an ally; moreover, the Huguenot revolt was by no means crushed. Southern France was bristling with arms; Montferrat and Mantua had no significance for France; and it was senseless to provoke Spain and the Emperor, make the Duke of Savoy an irreconcilable enemy, and stake the peace of Europe on such a transparent pretext.

Richelieu judged by other standards; in his testament he called Italy the heart of the world. In profound earnest he pled for intervention. It was a matter entirely, he said, of international esteem; if they did not intervene now, they would lose more morally than they could gain by being cautious; they had not yet settled with the Huguenots, but there was ample time to cross the Alps, raise the siege of Casale, return by Languedoc, reduce the Protestants between May and July, and be back in Paris by August. The present opportunity must not be let slip; Italy with its Alpine passes was the key position in the Spanish system; if they gave way at this point many of the advantages won by France would be nullified. Richelieu could not afford to renounce the work he had begun in the Valtelline. The risk he was taking, the wide-reaching consequences which might follow from the enterprise, were quite clear to him. "In this question," he concluded, "only the King himself can decide; the possible dangers are too great." Louis XIII rose and declared that he would undertake the campaign; more, he would himself lead the army. Bérulle once more prayed to be heard; he begged the King to take three days for reflection. After the three days Louis was still resolute, and three weeks later, on January 15, 1629, he set out. With twenty thousand footmen and two thousand horse he proceeded to the frontier. The besieging army of La Rochelle followed through the Auvergne and the province of Lyons, led by Thoiras. The King marched through Burgundy and on February 14th reached Grenoble; Richelieu and Schomberg followed on his heels. A hard campaign was before them; heavy snow set in.

A firm Spanish-Savoyan alliance was threatening; Richelieu had done all he could to counter it by diplomatic means. He had advised the Duc de Nevers to buy off Charles Emanuel's claims with a sum of 12,000 livres, knowing that Charles always suffered from lack of money. He had actually gone the length of suggesting to the Duke of Savoy the possibility that his State might be elevated into a kingdom. But while the Governor of Milan was laying siege to Casale, Charles Emanuel and his son, the Prince of Piedmont, had already reduced the fortresses of Alba and Moncalvo. To these hasty dealings of the enemy the only answer was deeds.

Louis XIII's warlike designs were blamed not only by

Bérulle; Richelieu had to maintain them against the whole coterie of princes and courtiers. As soon as Gaston of Orléans saw that he was not to have the command of the campaign and that the agreement which he had extorted had been broken, he again went into opposition. "Orléans and his followers," wrote Richelieu, "hated the Cardinal because his master loved him—a usual thing in Court life; but the hatred was like that of demons raging to enter a soul which God has filled with His grace. They hated the Cardinal out of envy of his growing fame and because he had foreseen things truly and maintained his opinions; they hated him because success was granted him and because that success was contrary to their wishes."

During this, his first great martial undertaking in the grand style, Richelieu had always to count with the same domestic enemies at his back: the feudal nobles, the Catholics, the inheritors of the League, who during these twenty years of the seventeenth century were known as the *dévotes*—Bérulle was regarded as their leader—and last of all the Southern French Protestants with Rohan, not yet crushed, at their head, and ready to make an alliance with any enemy of the State.

Now for the first time the need became clear for what has been called the greatest act of ingratitude in Richelieu's life; that was, cautiously to begin breaking with the royal personage to whom he owed his rise to power, and proceed at last against the Queen-Mother. That ambitious and sluggish-minded woman, so moody and so hard to influence, reverted over and over again to the policy of her Regency: the policy of agreement with Spain. At the start she, as well as Bérulle and his party, had greeted the siege of La Rochelle as a blow for the Counter-Reformation; but when it became clear in the course of that difficult operation that Richelieu might use against Spain the inner freedom which the nation had won at the expense of the Protestants, she and the whole clerical group changed sides and began to obstruct and cast suspicion on the enterprise; she was immediately joined by the dissatisfied feudal nobles, and Bassompierre's words, which Richelieu was never to forget: "We would be fools to take La Rochelle," became the device of the Queen-Mother and her followers. Only the opposition to England and the blunders of Buckingham, apart from the Cardinal's undeviating will, held the domestic front precariously together till the fall of the Huguenot fortress. But now, confronted with Richelieu's Italian plans, all the concealed opposition suddenly emerged with trenchant clarity. The Queen-Mother, proud of her Hapsburg blood, the Queen, Anne of Austria, Infanta of Spain, the incalculable, incomprehensible, perverse Gaston, the Guises and the other great nobles who had taken part in the conspiracy of Chalais, united once more with the *dévotes* against Richelieu and his policy; and while the Cardinal was in Italy with the King, he was in daily apprehension that they might betray him at home and ally themselves with Rohan and his Huguenots for Spanish ends, thus sacrificing the victory of La Rochelle and with it all the international prestige that he had won.

Here Richelieu once more staked his life and all that he had achieved to win the game. Again everything hung on one thread, the perseverance and fidelity of the King; Richelieu was quite isolated, and the precariousness of his position gave him many sleepless nights, whose terrors, whose temptations to give everything up and flee, were banished only by the thought that he must continue his work.

It was the suggestion of Richelieu, made with a profound knowledge of the person involved, that the King before his departure should make Marie de' Medici his Vice-Regent over all the provinces beyond the Loire. By giving her power and satisfying her in that way, he was protected for the time being against any irresponsible conspiracy. Before Louis XIII left Paris, Richelieu did all he could to secure his base: Marie de' Medici was the chief of his anxieties. To put pressure on Louis, the Cardinal once more proffered his resignation. If there was uncertainty in his own camp, he could not embark on great operations; one thing he must be sure of, that the King was entirely with him; that was axiomatic. In every emergency he had always to struggle with the eternally procrastinating, never quite foretellable mind of the King; he had perpetually to circumvent his suspicion, his hasty and revengeful .timidity and a thousand other idiosyncrasies, to charm away the mad ideas which swarmed in his mind, and constantly to explain, begin at the beginning again, conceal his real intentions, and when they were discerned pretend that the King alone had penetrated them, and then offer them as a fictitious tribute to the King's uncertain opinion of himself.

On January 13, 1629, two days before his departure, Richelieu begged the King, in the presence of Anne of Austria and the King's confessor, for a final assurance against domestic intrigue and treachery. He went far, for what he demanded was a guarantee against the failings of Louis XIII himself, against his lack of perseverance, his changeableness, his sudden fits of depression, his equally unaccountable lightness of mind. To show what was involved, Richelieu explained his plans, and first of all the part most likely to please the King: the extermination of heresy, the reduction of all the Huguenot fortresses in Southern France, the destruction of all strongholds in the country, except for bridgeheads, the strengthening of the Government, the suppression of the influence of the Parlements and the nobles, the elevation of the clergy in a spiritual and moral sense, and then, after these projects so near to the King's heart, his more ambitious European plans, first clearly formulated by Henri IV, though they had existed ever since the time of the Capets; the secure fortification of the French frontiers, the construction of points from which the neighbouring estates could be attacked, and unsleeping and ubiquitous precautionary measures against the Spanish system, against the manifold, confused and disintegrating German Empire, perpetually blind to the advantages of its position.

In that interview of January 13, 1629, the name of the German city Strassburg came up. "We should advance on Strassburg," said Richelieu, "quickly, silently, unobserved, and at once acquire the sovereignty of Neuchâtel from the Duc de Longueville, turn Geneva into an outwork of France, and build a Mediterranean fleet to instil respect into the Italian princes." But he did not stop at that. He spoke of the mastery of the sea, which formed a road to all the countries of the world, and he added that they must never forget that Navarre and Franche Comté were also French territories. The astonishing thing about all the great periods of French history up to the Revolution is the clear definition of the Government's plans and the impenetrability which marks their execution. Richelieu had to play a Protean and nerve-wracking game to keep to the clear line of his policy amid the wretched confusion of party and Court relationships: the most difficult problem of all was the King himself.

In order to speak the truth to the King on January 13th, the Cardinal took refuge behind others and adduced their words instead of his own; he went very far; he played upon the "concealed pleasure in suffering" by which Louis occasionally purchased a moment of freedom from his repressions. "It is unfortunate," said the Minister, "that so many believe that Your Majesty inclines more to harshness than to mercy. Luynes himself once said this, though I have not noticed that quality in you up to now; rulers must be strict, but they must not even for a moment take pleasure in harshness." And he went on to refer to the King's ingratitude for and forgetfulness of great services which had been rendered to him, and with an adroit turn roused all his feelings of inferiority, feelings which he knew would go on working, by speaking of the person to whom Louis was most closely bound by fear, hatred and love: Marie de' Medici. The disconcerting "unwillingness to act" which marked the King, Richelieu said, might be due to various causes, but this quality was, sad to say, an inheritance and an influence bequeathed by his mother; the King was often overcome by a stale feeling of satiety during the greatest enterprises, no matter how glorious the fruit he was about to pluck; before he raised his arm he was paralysed by disgust. All this was hereditary and the result of a will broken too soon; the inability of the Queen-Mother to persevere in any undertaking could be recognized as the cause of this malady and weakness in her son. "Her Majesty the Queen-Mother," said the Cardinal, "shows firmness in great decisions, but the merest irrelevant trifle can daunt her and divert her from her aim; her wishes can never be foreseen." She had no sense of proportion; she was incapable of "putting the interests of the State above her personal whims." It was a subtle poison that he dropped into the King's ear, and its effect could be depended upon, since it was founded on truth. For years Richelieu had had again and again to correlate his experience of Marie de' Medici with a series of failures. He had wasted years in doing this; now too much was at stake for him to do so any longer. At the end of his astonishing speech the Cardinal spoke of his own health, of the burden of hatred which he had to bear, the dislike of the heir-apparent, who to-morrow might be his master. The greatness of the purposed undertaking, he said, made him wish that a less-hated man might take his post, even a weaker man, for he might be supported and upheld by the great aim they had in mind; he would be freer, would know less and fear less, and could therefore speak more freely and act more boldly.

The strangest thing about this interview was that not only Louis XIII himself but the Queen and Suffren, the King's confessor, listened in silence to the extraordinary words of the Cardinal. Anne of Austria was to fear the Cardinal all her life; he seemed a supernatural figure to her, and her dislike of him always turned in his presence to terror. Louis XIII, with the inborn dignity which was always his in hours of resolution as of weakness, dismissed his servant after this speech with the brief and cool answer that he would strive to profit by what had been said; but he did not want to hear again any word of the Cardinal's resignation.

Furnished with such advice, Louis set out on January 15th on his campaign, which had so suddenly been decided upon and which presently took him to Grenoble, where he was joined by the Cardinal.

Before leaving Paris Louis had asked Bassompierre, his father's old comrade-in-arms, to send him some of his excellent cider from Normandy for the journey; the Marshal at once sent twelve flasks, and Louis summoned him to the Louvre in the evening to thank him. "Betstein," he said to him—for he always called him by his German name—"you've given me twelve flasks of cider; I shall give you 12,000 talers in return; d'Effiat will pay them over to you." In his camp outside La Rochelle Bassompierre had laid out 28,000 talers on banquets; as so often in his life, which fluctuated between cheerful ostentation and gay poverty, he had been on the verge of destitution.

The royal munificence was not merely one of those high gestures by which Louis showed now and then that he was his father's son; he had other reasons for his action. From Chateaumorant Bassompierre travelled to the front with Gaston of Orléans; the way was long and it was filled with talk. Gaston grumbled as usual: "I'll get no command; the Cardinal will take over both my post and the King's. . . . He persuaded the King into this business against his will, simply to rob me of the command promised me." Bassompierre did his best to mollify the Prince, but he appeared on February 19th at Grenoble without him; the offended Gaston had turned back to Paris. It was a triumph that Bassompierre himself was willing to assist in the campaign without conditions. Money could not bribe him, especially when it was handed over to him in such a lighthearted way. But the others! They would all crowd round Gaston again; the nicknames which the Cardinal gave them describe them well and show that he had a satirical gift which exaggerated some of the traits of these incredible people into the grotesque, perhaps to make them comprehensible to himself. His name for d'Epernon was "Cacofin"; he took every opportunity to ridicule the former boy-friend of Henry III, but he also knew from the time of Concini what an influence the man had among the officers of the whole realm, and from the first day of the campaign he kept him under strict supervision. Vendôme, the half-brother of the King, who had been in captivity since 1626, he would gladly have set free, as he considered him harmless, but his brother the Grand Prior he regarded as capable of leading "Hébertin" and "Saint-Ursin"—his names for Gaston of Orléans and the Comte de Soissons—into bad ways again. There are notes upon all these men, which were dictated by Richelieu during the campaign. The Grand Prior did the realm a service by dying in the Bastille on February 28, 1629; now Vendôme could be released with an easy mind. An indication how anxious Richelieu was to avoid anything which might give rise to the idea that he persecuted his enemies out of personal malice may be seen in the fact that when the King offered to give him one of the best abbacies of the defunct bastard, he refused it and asked that it should be granted to Cardinal Bérulle; and by this he seems to have attracted that favourite of Marie de' Medici once more for a time to the King's side. Finally Condé, who was fighting Rohan and who had made his peace with the Cardinal during the Fronde, while not yet being granted permission to return to Paris, was rewarded by the King with Rohan's dukedom and empowered to preside over the assembly of the estates in Brittany.

In such ways, bit by bit, Richelieu secured his rear. But he pushed on the campaign with the utmost speed, in spite of mist, snow and frost. Again nothing was ready; money and munitions were lacking; but again, as before La Rochelle, Richelieu organized unceasingly, day and night. By the beginning of March the army was ready for attack and the troops assembled at Chiamonte at the entrance to the narrow mountain-pass of Suze. The King asked the Duke of Savoy for permission to pass through his land. Charles Emanuel, as in duty bound, refused to agree to such a proposal unless Louis openly declared war on Spain and at the same time permitted himself, as the master of the Alpine passes, to seize Genoa and Geneva. But Louis would not hear of either proposal. On the first of March he crossed Monte Genevrino, and faced with further difficulties raised by the Duke, resolved to force a passage through the country. A declaration of war was drawn up; Richelieu enumerated the list of Savoy's offences which gave a pretext and justification for the attack: the frontier fortresses of Valence, Montélimar and Toulon which Savoy had tried by secret ways to undermine, its dealings with the rebel Soissons, its incitement of Lorraine to form a coalition, its machinations in Holland to alienate the General States from France, ally them with England and reconcile them with Spain, the insolent letter to the King of France in which the Duke claimed to be the sole guardian of every entrance to Italy: all this was included in the bill, and the bill was presented by a king at the head of an army of thirty-five thousand men. Louis's brother-in-law, the Duke of Piedmont, the brother of Charles Emanuel, tried to gain time by half-promises, but Richelieu insisted; the army advanced to the village of Chaumont; an emissary of the Duke's, who demanded a French stronghold as a pledge for the yielding of the pass, was ironically offered Orléans or Poitiers by the Cardinal. The Duke, wrote Richelieu, treated with the King as if he were at the head of fifty thousand men and Louis at the head of only ten thousand.

On small mountain-sledges and on foot, in deep snow, Louis and his army penetrated higher and higher into the mountains, sometimes in danger of avalanches. The valley through which they climbed was the valley of the Doire, which led in the direction of Suze. According to Father Joseph, the Duke had constructed three defensive positions, one behind the other; the first barricades of tree-trunks and

branches were comparatively feeble; then came a stronger
fortification supported by the Piedmont Fort Gelassé, powerfully furnished with artillery, which overlooked the whole
pass, and also the third defensive position.

As a daring surprise was the only hope, Bassompierre was
given command. At half-past three in the morning Louis set
out from Chaumont and presently reached the Savoy frontier
barriers. Bassompierre sent a member of Parlement, a certain
Comminges, to the first barricade along with a trumpeter.
The commander of the position came out to meet him with
two hundred men, and Comminges requested permission to
prepare quarters in Suze for the King of France, who came
as a friend. The commander retorted: "It will be a great
honour for His Highness the Duke to entertain His Majesty,
but as the King of France has such a numerous escort, you
must allow me first to inform my master the Duke, who is
only five hundred yards away." And he added: "We are
not Englishmen, and we will know how to defend our passes."
Comminges had heard enough; he returned and reported
without waiting for any further answer.

At that moment Bassompierre approached the King with
the well-known words: "Sire, the guests are gathered, the
fiddlers are in their places, the maskers are at the door. If
Your Majesty pleases, we can begin the dance." The King
replied: "Are you aware that we have only five pounds of
lead in our arsenal?" Bassompierre said with a laugh: "This
is a fine moment for remembering that. Because the mask is
not ready, are we to miss the dance? Let us begin, Your
Majesty; everything will go splendidly." "Do you vouch
for that?" asked the King, and the Marshal answered: "It
would be foolhardy to guarantee such a high stake. Either
we shall conquer gloriously, or I shall be dead or a prisoner."
Here Richelieu, who had been silent till now, intervened.
"Sire," he said, "from the expression on the Marshal's face
I think we can count on a fortunate issue."

Thereupon the attack began. The Switzers did the main

work by clearing the heights; the King's Guards took the barricades by storm, and the Savoyards were chased to the town of Suze. Suze was taken and again, as at La Rochelle, Louis XIII kept stern discipline; there was no pillaging.

On March 11th the Cardinal and the Prince of Piedmont signed an agreement guaranteeing free transit to the French armies; in return for which the King, as was customary after any defeat of the house of Savoy, offered the Duke an extension of his territory by giving him the town of Trino, and an indemnification of 15,000 gulden in gold. Louis guaranteed that he would make no conquests in Italy, and he assured the Duke of protection against any attack. Secret clauses which were signed on March 15th laid down that Casale was at once to be furnished with corn and wine, and the Prince of Piedmont promised that Charles Emanuel would get in touch with Gonzalez de Cordova, the Governor of Milan, for the purpose of raising the siege.

Richelieu had quickly reached the first aim in his programme. The Princess of Piedmont had been a great help to her father-in-law the Duke of Savoy, the Cardinal wrote a few days later to Marie de' Medici, for, he went on, it would have been an easy matter for the King to confiscate all the lands of the Duke. Actually the meeting of Louis XIII with his witty sister, Christine of France, had helped to relax the tension. The encounter is known to us in all its details; we know how the young Princess, dressed in the French fashion, with her long English curls and pear-shaped ear-rings, was lifted from her litter, how she fell on her knees before her brother, how he leapt from his horse, raised her and clasped her in his arms, then rode for a long time beside her litter, and more and more charmed by her conversation permitted her to plead for Savoy. It was a pleasing and very private account of the exact execution of his own policy which Richelieu sent to Marie de' Medici, but it was nicely calculated to please her wishes. His invariable moderation, his resolve to achieve his hidden aim and nothing more, without being tempted to snatch a sudden success, he now represented as being due to the power of a brother's love and the "natural kindness" of the King: they are his own words. Less amiable, considerably sharper, was the encounter of the Cardinal with Charles Emanuel. The Duke had bent his knee to the King of France as his conqueror; but when he met the Cardinal he did not descend from his horse, and Richelieu also remained in his saddle: an exact definition of the position according to the symbolic ceremonial language of the age. "The two gentlemen bowed to the very necks of their steeds," wrote Fontenay in his memoirs, "their greetings were curt, their bearing more than cool, above all that of the Duke, who hated the Cardinal like poison, more than any other man in the world, because he had to do with one who insisted on plain speech and plain dealing, which was not at all the way of the Duke."

Charles Emanuel was one of those men who mingle with all their actions a too obvious cunning, a caution and craft which in concealing one weak point easily lays bare another. Richelieu always disapproved of finesse as a diplomatic method, though during his own rise to power in the narrow circle of the Court he had been reduced to it; in foreign policy he used deception only in very important cases, and for the smaller ones employed an almost dumbfounding frankness, sudden attack, hard truths. The Duke of Savoy was cunning in a way which was always a puzzle to the Cardinal; behind his obvious wiles and transparent changes there worked the indestructible craft of the mountain peasant, amenable to no logic.

On the day of that cool encounter Louis XIII himself received the Duke in the castle of Suze. Charles Emanuel took the opportunity of addressing to him a few phrases of that massive Baroque courtesy which the age delighted in. As the two princes entered one of the halls, they were followed by so many nobles that Louis, who heard the floor creaking suspiciously, urged the Duke to hurry. Charles

Emanuel laughed and said: "The floor will not collapse under me, though it well may under the feet of Your Majesty, to whom the mightiest powers of the earth have to bow."

The two princes conversed only for a short time; in half an hour the Duke proceeded to the Cardinal to talk business, and that evening Louis wrote to his mother: "After that conversation Charles Emanuel could not praise enough my cousin Monsieur de Richelieu, and the words they had together. I have heard nothing yet of the substance of the conversation, for Richelieu is indisposed to-day." To others, too, Charles Emanuel said: "As soon as the Cardinal opens his mouth it is hard to resist him." It is certain that the talk was a hard test of nerves for both men. Charles Emanuel behaved as if he were the victor, and even when he cringed and promised everything he was asked—with the firm intention of not keeping his promise—he tried to extract palpable results from the situation far greater than he could have expected from his alliance with Spain. He now importuned the King to attack Spanish Milan; he sought to drive him into a war for which there was a distant and uncertain end; he returned again to his wish to attack Geneva. "He wants," wrote the Cardinal, "to get France to attempt everything at once, so that at the end he might have all the gains for himself and leave us nothing of consequence. His mind is restless and turns more swiftly than the spheres; in one day he makes a girdle round the earth thrice; he would like to hound every prince into war, so as to snatch everything out of the confusion." Charles Emanuel insisted especially on attacking Genoa. Richelieu considered for a moment both proposals, that concerning Genoa and that concerning Geneva. As for Geneva, was it expedient to take more Counter-Reformation wind out of Spain's sails now, after the fall of La Rochelle? There was much to be said against it: France had a permanent league with Switzerland—the cantons were the soil on which grew the soldiers of the Bourbons; just now, in the mountain fight, the Swiss troops had contributed decisively to victory.

No, it did not seem advisable to deliver Geneva into such uncertain hands. As for Genoa, it would be foolhardy to attack it while the revolt in Languedoc was still alive, and the pretext of just dealing by which Richelieu tried to safeguard all the King's actions might be endangered by such a move.

The first thing was to reach Casale by forced marches and relieve it. But four days after the signing of the agreement with the Duke of Savoy, the news arrived that the Spaniards, alarmed by the French victory and the approach of the French army, had raised the siege on the night of March 15th and 16th. The town was delivered and the campaign had achieved its purpose.

Richelieu furnished the town with food and strengthened the fortifications against a new attack; Thoiras with three regiments was entrusted with its defence, and on April 28th, after a month of waiting, the King set off with the main army for Languedoc. The Cardinal remained behind in Suze with a strong force; he was appointed General; it was the first time, says Ménage, that the title "Generalissimus" was employed.

A few days before his departure from Suze the King signed a peace treaty with England which strengthened still more the position of France. At the moment when Richelieu was considering where to give the death-blow to French Protestantism, Charles I delivered it into his hands.

The French troops were now distributed over Languedoc, Vivarais, and Provence, wherever the Protestants still held fortified places. Rohan fought like a lion; the Cevennes swallowed him and his men again and again; the daring band vanished to break out in some unexpected place and hour, to fall on some small troop or transport, after which it spread fire and slaughter for miles around. But in spite of the brilliant strategy of his mountain warfare, Rohan had in the end to submit to superior force. Town after town of the Huguenots was razed. Even to-day, as one descends the valley of the Rhône, one can see on the hills, behind olive woods, the ruins of the former strongholds of the Calvinists lying like white bones bleached by the sun. Richelieu himself had worked out the plan of campaign against the rebels; Schomberg expressed his admiration of the feat.

In September 1627 Rohan had been chosen at Uzès as the commander of the Protestant troops by an assembly drawn from the evangelical towns. He had gone much farther than the burghers of La Rochelle; he had negotiated not only with England but with Spain as well; he had actually sent one of his noblemen, Clausel, to his Catholic Majesty asking for immediate assistance, in return for which he had promised to support all Spain's political aims. He spoke of separatism; he acted not like a rebel, but like an independent sovereign. An agreement was signed in Madrid on May 3, 1629, and Rohan was guaranteed a yearly subsidy of 40,000 gold ducats. Intercepted papers informed Louis XIII of this act of high treason. Not till six years later was Clausel apprehended and hanged. As for Rohan, Louis had him condemned *in contumaciam* by the Parlement of Toulouse; his privileges as a Duke and a peer of France were declared null and void. But before that sentence could affect the unbending Rohan, he must be captured. Richelieu's plan was to divide the Huguenot towns and conquer them separately; they were strung in a thin line from Privas to Montauban; Nîmes on one side, and Montauban and Castres on the other, must be cut off from all communication with each other.

But for the time being Richelieu was still in Suze, and as soon as Louis was away from his adviser power and success seemed to desert him. He besieged the town of Privas, but it defied him; disorder spread in the royal camp; the higher officers executed their orders carelessly or not at all. Louis wrote to the Cardinal urgently: "I await you with impatience, and it seems to me that it is months since I saw you." Richelieu left Savoy at the head of nine thousand men; he knew that the agreement with Charles Emanuel was only an armistice, and that he would soon have to return to take stronger measures. On May 19th he reached the royal camp; on the 21st the gates of the town were opened; Richelieu advised lenience, but this time Louis ordered the town to be burned; and he forbade the surviving inhabitants ever to set foot on their native soil again. And now everything went quickly; St. Amboise, Alais, and Anduze were taken. Yet the fate of the towns which fell into the King's hands was less terrible than that of those which were captured by Condé and d'Estrées. In spite of Richelieu's desire for moderation, which he showed again as in La Rochelle, the butchery was dreadful; Condé permitted looting everywhere; in some towns he hanged the whole male population or sent them to the galleys.

At last the accumulation of horrors bowed the will of Rohan; he sued for peace and promised to raze all the Protestant strongholds in the Kingdom. On Richelieu's advice a Calvinist assembly was called; the peace must not be settled with Rohan alone, but with the assembled representatives of the French Huguenots; and he did not treat with them, he dictated. On June 9th Louis XIII rode into Alais. Marshal d'Estrées was wasting the land round Nîmes; the Duc d'Epernon was exterminating all life round Montauban. All that Rohan could still hope for was to hinder the towns from making a separate peace; the league of towns as a whole must submit to the royal commands. Now all the country which spoke the beautiful Provençal speech lay at the feet of the King; one of the most lofty European cultures had been exterminated there in the Middle Ages; but still proudly conscious of their ancestry, the peoples of that beautiful southern land had allied themselves with the Reformation in their deep rejection of the existing order; they had become Calvinists in their struggle against the King of France, like the peoples of Transylvanian Hungary in their struggle against the Hapsburgs of Vienna. Now the bitter end had been reached, and in spite of the toleration which Richelieu desired to show for reasons of foreign policy, for the sake of England the Netherlands, and the German Protestants, the dark period of French Protestantism began which was to reach its worst point under Louis XIV.

Up to Richelieu's time rebel leaders, on submitting, had usually been granted territory, power, fortresses, and money by the French kings. These times were past; Rohan was banished and fled to Venice, though his ancestral titles and privileges were returned to him by a royal act of grace. According to Richelieu, he also received 100,000 talers, a sum which represented only a small proportion of the value of his mutilated woods and burned castles and fortresses. The grant made it possible for him to live in Venice in accordance with his rank; it seemed that some use might still be found for him, and at the moment the Cardinal had plans which that incomparable strategist might help him in executing. The Cardinal never lost sight of men of intelligence; he knew how rare they were.

Besides, he must husband his powers; in Italy the Mantuan conflict was showing signs of breaking out again, and in France Gaston of Orléans was causing new difficulties.

The peace treaty of Alais was signed on June 28, 1629; all Protestant fortifications in the kingdom must be razed; but also, and this was Richelieu's work, Henry IV's wise Edict of Nantes was once more confirmed in all its scope.

Richelieu was himself present at the destruction of the proud walls and towers which had grown for centuries, as if he were resolved to supervise the execution of the peace treaty to its minutest detail. He rode from town to town, his mail over his purple robes, like the incarnation of the idea of the State, following through Southern France the road of the Roman legions. Everywhere the people thronged to see him and pay him homage; from their castles the nobles streamed to join him; before the gates of the towns the magistrates greeted him with Latin orations; the high clergy and the representatives of the universities surpassed one another in his praises.

Everywhere Richelieu held before him like a shield the shadow of the King's majesty; he made himself inconspicuous and withdrew. All the glorious deeds which had been done on the coast of the Atlantic Ocean, here and in Italy, had been achieved, with God's help, by the anointed King of France. The Cardinal had a peculiar gift of directly and sagely impressing upon the people who approached him as suppliants the immediate, constructive suggestion which served most obviously the general interest. Everyone was amazed to find this man whom rumour had made terrible so humane and helpful.

On August 20th he reached Montauban and made his solemn entry. Montauban—how often the royal will had had to bow to that powerful city; La Rochelle and Montauban had been the twin citadels of the new faith. Now the city fathers appeared with bare heads, bearing the city keys on a velvet cushion. Bassompierre had entered the town the day before with three regiments. Twelve thousand horsemen followed the Cardinal, among them one thousand nobles from the vicinity. The Archbishops of Toulouse and Bordeaux, seven bishops, sixty spiritual princes rode in his train. A portable baldachin in the form of a canopy was brought forward, but Richelieu forbade it to be elevated over his head, also that the magistrates should walk round his horse with bared heads, as such honours were suited only to monarchs. Wherever he could he eased things, tried to smooth over disputes, soften penalties, and avoid acts of revenge.

It was his first great moment of outward success; he was spoken everywhere as the pacifier of the kingdom; he had ended the struggles of religion which had rent the country for centuries. From the Rhône to the Pyrenees he had won the country back for the Catholic monarchy. He had defeated England; he had made Spain and the Emperor feel the power of France. It seemed for the moment as if he were now the undisputed leader of his country's fortunes; from all sides people wrote to him that he enjoyed the complete goodwill and confidence of his King. Marillac, who was soon to pass over to the ranks of his enemies, reported with what love and respect the King spoke of him, and Bouthillier, who was always to remain his friend, said to him: "I can give you no conception of the warmth and admiration with which the King speaks of you." And indeed Louis spoke in a way in which no one had ever heard him speak before; he confessed that he had a genuine passion for his Minister, and he assured him: "I shall love you till I die." To a friend of his brother Gaston he said: "The Cardinal must be shown the honour that is owing to him; all our successes inside and outside the kingdom are due to his wise and bold counsel."

Richelieu was one of those men who are prone to take every sequence of good fortune, all goodwill expressed by others and especially by the great as an omen of approaching disaster, and who always count upon a change of fortune; he relied on nothing but the pursuit of his work, the redoubling of his caution, the intensification of his concentration of purpose, which he knew must become keener and more singleminded to the end, until it achieved the destruction of his personal wishes, and left merely the attained end, not the personal enjoyment of power and honour.

There was one circumstance, difficult to over-estimate, which again and again made it impossible to place any reliance on his relation to the King, though everything to the smallest detail depended on the royal goodwill. It may not seem much, but Richelieu, who had an extremely delicate and sure sensibility, sharpened by his illness, never escaped from the compulsion to take it into account: he felt that at certain moments the King had an almost physical repugnance to him, to his sickliness, and to the compulsive, intellectually exciting quality which breathed from all his words and actions, but which roused the King's opposition. Richelieu suffered under this, for it was beyond his power to alter it; he wrote once: "This loathing which suddenly rises in the King and whose cause is hidden from me, sometimes wounds me so deeply that all my courage cannot get me over my profound discouragement."

Like all men who are unsure of themselves, Louis XIII was very touchy; sometimes a mere word or turn of phrase would annoy him deeply; then he gave rein to his vexation and made his power felt by a haughty displeasure of bearing. An instance of this had occurred at Nîmes shortly before the end of the camapaign against the Huguenots. It was hot in the south of France during these summer months; one day Louis declared that this sultry heat was insupportable, he would return to Paris at once; besides, cases of plague had occurred in the district. Richelieu replied that he was of the same mind, if His Majesty would deign to make his entry into Nîmes at the head of his troops, and added: "It is important that the Huguenots should see the King on the spot, as a conqueror who keeps his pledged word." But Louis was wildly indignant at the word "if." "What does the man mean? Who does he think he is? If! Does he make conditions with me? Does he dare to treat me like a schoolboy?" Richelieu at once requested an audience and outlined a plan which he had thought out to spare the King the troublesome entry into the town. Louis listened to the proposal and agreed. Next day, as Richelieu was lying sick in bed, the King suddenly entered his room and informed him that he would make his entry into Nîmes, and at the head of the French Guards and the Switzers too; he strongly advised no one to dissuade him; anyone who advised him against it now would incur his anger just as strongly as those had done who had tried to force him to do so.

Richelieu repeatedly declared that the irritation of this relation was the cause of his illness. The King was perpetually watching for confirmations of his jealousy and suspicion; his hostility against his Minister sometimes reached the point where in imagination he dismissed him, exiled him or even delivered him to his enemies; then suddenly he would waken as if from an anxiety neurosis, annul all that he had purposed, punish the Cardinal's detractors, ask the Cardinal's pardon, reward and honour him, and transform all his repulsion into cordiality, almost into love. There was something uncanny in that relation, above all when we consider the difference in public consequence between the two men, when we reflect that the one was master and the other saw in that master the sole embodiment of the spiritual power which he served with all his mind—the State. Richelieu had nervous breakdowns; foreign ambassadors wrote of fits of weeping. He vouched for all that the King did, for his irresponsibility, his ruthlessness; the general aversion was turned against him and was made still more bitter to swallow by the fact that the King constantly blamed him for his growing unpopularity. The pamphleteers knew how uncertain Richelieu's position was. In a libel by Mathieu de Morgues the Cardinal was addressed in the following terms: "Though you are to-day master of the liberty of millions of men, take care lest to-morrow you be in the care of an insignificant prison warder! A brief moment may lie between the blandishments of a crowned head and the hook by which men are dragged to the place of execution." People liked to remind the Cardinal of Concini's fate.

In the times of his most brilliant successes there was always an increase in the tension between Richelieu and the King. Behind all the cordial words which Richelieu received from Louis himself or through friends and informants, there was gathering in Louis now, after the fall of Montauban, renewed suspicion and annoyance which could be seen at once in his face if the Cardinal were mentioned, above all if any reference were made to his approaching return.

In spite of this, Louis was fully aware of the scope of the success that had been won. The whole world spoke of it; Spinola, who had seen Louis at work at La Rochelle, said in the anteroom of Olivares in Madrid: "The King of France has fulfilled his whole task as a soldier and a prince." Everywhere in Madrid at that time the portrait of the King of

France could be seen. When Olivares was not present, everyone envied a King who had such a servant as Richelieu.

But all this was only the first beginning of Richelieu's labours on the foreign policy of his country. For six months he had been away from Paris and the centre of affairs; he now hurried back with his reserves of strength quite exhausted. He took ship on the river Allier and with a whole flotilla sailed down the Loire. Two squadrons of mounted guards escorted him on either bank. His ship with its tapestried cabins was followed by two barques containing his table silver.

Richelieu rested during the quiet journey; he had to harbour his strength to the utmost; behind drawn curtains, listening to the whispering of the water, he considered what must be done next.

Already at Privas he had written to Marie de' Medici, knowing that what he had long seen coming, and had been preparing the King for, had now unavoidably arrived: the Queen-Mother had turned away from him, openly, in her rash, defiant way, joined his enemies, exchanged her fading love for the young priest, her creature, for hate against the prince of the Church, the victor, the counsellor of her son, who was taking a path so different from the one she desired. Everyone who came in close contact with Louis XIII was hateful to her because of her jealous wish for sole mastery over the uncertain and divided spirit of her son; her hatred of Richelieu was particularly violent, for it was she herself who had discovered him and maintained him for a long time against the resistance of the King, until, having reached his goal, and thus having demonstrated the rightness of her judgment, he had made himself indispensable to Louis. Scarcely had Richelieu established his position with the King, when her aversion at the thought of any close relation between her son and him ousted every other consideration; all the more as in Richelieu, and in the trend of his policy especially, there reappeared traits of her husband Henry IV, whose work she had tried to nullify almost before she achieved power, and whose free bearing and cheerful nature she hated from the bottom of her gloomy resentful heart even after his death.

In such psychologically difficult situations Richelieu had always sought adjustment or relaxation by calling up past memories or by frankly discussing the situation, unless he found that impossible. The postulation by romantic nineteenth-century historians of an antithesis between Richelieu's apparent friendship and sudden treachery is baseless on a closer view; after exhausting all the means of adjustment, he acted in hopeless cases quickly and sternly if the good of the State demanded it, because any half-measures would have been disastrous.

From Privas Richelieu had tried to avoid the incipient conflict. He wrote to the Queen-Mother: "I have so much confidence in your kindness and such a strong consciousness, not so much of the services I have rendered you, as of my sincere endeavours to render them, that I cannot believe Your Majesty can have altered your opinion of me. I must admit, however, that rumours are going about to that effect." Cardinal de La Valette, who delivered the letter, reported how well the Queen had taken it; without doubt, at the moment, she wished their former harmony back again; also she feared the struggle; but her original impulse was stronger, and quick-witted intriguers among the Cardinal's enemies soon realized that a word was enough to rouse her hatred of him at any time.

On his return from the south of France Richelieu was seized by repeated violent attacks of fever; he received many marks of symapthy from the Court; a letter from the Queen-Mother spoke of her deep sorrow, and he had to read the truth between the lines.

During her short Regency in winter and spring Marie de' Medici had intervened in an important sphere of Richelieu's policy. After parting from Bassompierre, Gaston of Orléans had not returned to Paris but betaken himself to his principality of Dombes. From there he informed his mother that in return for the command of the Italian campaign and the money pertaining to it, he had agreed that Maria of Gonzaga should leave France and return to Mantua. He had now heard that the Duke of Mantua had recalled his daughter and that she was to leave France at once, without his having received the command in Italy; this was against the understanding, and he consequently proposed to abduct the young Princess, who was staying with her aunt in Coulommiers. Marie de' Medici, who would not hear of such a marriage for her son, at once sent several carriages with an escort of forty horse to Coulommiers and had the Princess transferred to the castle of Vincennes, where she was given the royal apartments to reside in. Louis XIII and Richelieu ratified this act, as there was no choice. But then the Queen-Mother changed her mind. Her second son had no quality which she, from her own point of view, could find fault with; Louis was far too often in the right against her, but with Gaston it was quite the contrary; she had always to be forgiving him and comforting him, so that she invariably felt the stronger of the two, which pleased her. Now he appeared again full of lamentations; he enumerated all the wrongs that had been done to him; he spoke of his loneliness, declared that they were gravely mistaken in the Cardinal if they regarded him as a friend—in short, he won her ear and heart, and she suddenly released the Princess and virtually left her at Gaston's disposal, caring little what happened as long as it resulted in a blow for the Gonzagas. She was now all on fire for Gaston's claims; as a compensation for losing the command of the Italian campaign, she demanded a provincial governorship for him and a seat in the royal Council. Her passionate partisanship was still more inflamed when she heard that Richelieu really supported the marriage and was consequently very jealous of the Princess's honour; this touched her in her most sensitive spot; whatever happened, there must be no marriage; no Gonzaga must be granted such a distinction; and as always, when she felt that her honour was threatened, she fell back on the

337

reflection that she was a descendant of the Hapsburgs and hated Richelieu's anti-Spanish policy more than ever.

The Cardinal left his ship at Briare on September 11th; on the 13th he was in Montargis. Many dignitaries of the Court had come to meet him, among them the cardinals Bérulle and La Valette, also Chevreuse, Montbazon, and La Rochefoucauld. Richelieu felt at once that something was in the air; a certain embarrassment, an excessive, chilly politeness, a menacing commiseration shot with irony greeted him.

After his long months on the battlefield, where action followed immediately on decision, the Cardinal journeyed through the woods of Fontainebleau, already autumnal, to the manifold restrictions of his civil functions at the Court, where everything shifted like a quicksand, and where the same figures, as if in a silent fury to prevail or seem to do so, reappeared in ever new combinations, and one day was never like another. The opposition which had made itself felt during the debate on the Italian campaign was still alive; during the Cardinal's absence it had grown freely and powerfully.

A violent pamphleteering campaign had started again. Some bitter observations of the Cardinal date from this time. "Base and common natures," he wrote, "whose hearts are wrung by the successful achievements of others, and who know only one aim, to destroy, to pull down. . . . And the more despicable their hatred, the more inveterate it is also." One is almost surprised that after the path he had trod, after his knowledge of the intrigues of men, he had any attention for such things; but it was his task that he was concerned with and for which he fought a bitter fight: the erection of a State authority from which his generation recoiled in fear, and whose stability now and in the future he regarded as necessary in view of the ever increasing danger of the nations.

At the reception given to the Cardinal at Fontainebleau the labours of the opposition and the complete reversal of the Queen-Mother's attitude became clear to every eye. Marie de'

Medici treated the conqueror with coldness; she had warm words only for Marillac, whom she now counted with assurance among the inveterate enemies of Richelieu. She enquired ironically regarding the Cardinal's health; wounded in a spot which his will could not protect, he replied in a quivering voice: "I am better than many people would wish me to be!" But at once, with a vestige of the long vanished familiarity which had existed between them, he approached the Queen-Mother and softly whispered words of jealousy to her as Cardinal Bérulle entered the room; the pretext was harmless enough; she had laughed at Bérulle's white boots and short doublet, which went strangely with the cardinal's hat. Richelieu's awkwardness in handling women had increased since his fortieth year; when he was young he had sometimes shone as a wit; later, all that had vanished under the burden of public care, the importance of the matters with which he had to deal, and his illness which never allowed him any sense of physical assurance. In the young Bishop there had been memories of his martial training; but in the Cardinal traits of his childhood seemed to emerge at times; people turned away when he tried to be gay or tender in the exalted style of contemporary poetry. When he was tired it sometimes happened that, without falling out of his part, he seemed to act against his essential nature, with its almost painful clarity, elevation, freedom, and genuine humanity; but suffering and constant anxiety about his work had brought out this other side of his nature, which could not be reconciled in harmony with the dominance of his great soul; with women he had an unhappy, clumsy and sometimes violent hand, and occasionally there appeared for a moment, only to be burned up again in the pure fire of his genius, something low in his bearing, composed of uncertainty and anger. If, after looking at the profile of the Cardinal, with its fineness, daring and nobility, one contemplates his full face, one can remark a touch of weakness, even of malice, about the mouth; but these traits never predominate; the minor qualities remain

339

subordinate, fully mastered by the higher ones; and that is what matters.

In the middle of September the solemn declaration of peace with England was made. The two Queens attended the ecclesiastical ceremony. Richelieu drove to it along with Marillac, the Keeper of the Great Seal; an armed peace reigned in the carriage which carried them to the celebration of peace. Mediation between the Queen-Mother and Richelieu had been attempted from various sides; the King, appealed to by Richelieu, had promised to do what he could; Richelieu had shed tears; he wept easily in such circumstances; a profound, apprehensive melancholy was never far from him.

But apart from his illness and his weakness, he knew with unshakable clarity that there was no going back, no hope of adjustment in his relations with the widow of Henry IV. Anything gave her a pretext for insulting remarks. Once it was the arbitrary discontinuation of a pension, another time it was certain intrigues against Richelieu's nieces, who were in the Queen's service. Richelieu was still chief superintendent of the Queen-Mother's household; this connection was dissolved by her; she told the Cardinal that he made himself "insupportable." Richelieu at once offered to resign from his offices of State as well; he induced his relatives to resign their service with the Queen-Mother; he became violent, there were agitated scenes, and the Queen-Mother screamed in the peacock voice which her husband had feared: "You're mistaken if you think I'm your slave!" When the King tried to make peace, she admitted that he still required the yellow-faced, arrogant invalid for his foreign policy; she had no wish to interfere in that; but she desired once and for all to have nothing more to do with the man. Nothing made Richelieu feel more insecure than these secret dealings between mother and son; what might they say, what might they hint regarding the past, or hatch in the present? He wrote at once to the King; he humbled himself; but in his protestations of loyalty there was a turn which was bound to impress the

King deeply, and it did. "Perhaps," the letter ran, "Your Majesty will remember that in cases where I have had the honour to be asked to act as arbitrator in the differences between Your Majesties, the Queen-Mother has refused my help with the objection that I am all too devoted to your service, Sire." A sentence which brought an answer which, once given, was a pledge. Louis XIII gave it with both hands. "Think of nothing," he wrote, "but your affairs of State." And then: "Rather than dispense with you, I shall settle for good with the Queen-Mother and the whole cabal." A far-reaching utterance! But to the King, too, the development of the crisis was painful; he too had moments of acute depression; yet Richelieu showed how greatly the firmness of the King surprised him, how much he admired it, how strongly he felt supported by it. The advantage fluctuated in that silent struggle, public opinion following it. In late autumn the Court began slowly to go over to the Cardinal; there were still some vacillators and a few counter currents, but on the whole the sharp-witted and agile now drew near to Richelieu. Not for long.

From the letters which Bérulle wrote to Richelieu during 1629 little can be discerned of the almost wordless struggle between the two men; all these communications are couched in a conventional, almost obsequious style; yet they were written by a cardinal to a cardinal, also from one great personage to another. What really actuated Bérulle's clumsy loyalty to Marie de' Medici was the essential power which he embodied: the cause of the Church, the cause of Christianity, the unity of the seamless garment which was more to him than all else, so that nation, State and everything for which Richelieu worked seemed shadows to him. The *victa causa* which Bérulle and Marillac represented has been sharply condemned by most historians of Louis XIII and his great councillor. In this they overlook many things and among them the essential one: that the vision of an integral France in the service of Catholicism towards which Bérulle strove in mystical exaltation was to be realized in the same century under Louis XIV, was to reach its consummation in the revocation of the Edict of Nantes and to lead to the disastrous war of the Spanish Succession in which France stood alone against the coalition of the Protestant world, which by a strange fate was to be led from Vienna by the house of Hapsburg. But Bérulle's deeds were not of this world; as a young noble, his mother had already seen that the administration of his estates could not be left in his hands, for he was incapable of distinguishing even the commonest coins from one another. During the siege of La Rochelle he had spoken again and again against the construction of the dike, since he claimed to have been told by inspiration that the fortress would fall not by human agency, but by a sudden miracle. He had honestly endeavoured to buttress the purity and simplicity of his imaginings with those more equivocal worldly conceptions for lack of which men reproached him; and he once wrote in connection with the negotiations in the Valtelline: "They are bad theologians who assert that a man loses his right to the rulership he possesses if he loses the right faith, or that one may not support with a good conscience heretics, whether as nations or princes. The rights of States cannot be measured by ordinary standards, and they obey other rules than those laid down by the university of Salamanca." He was trying to convince himself, but one feels that he did not succeed. Richelieu's political direction was completely contrary to his, and he made no secret of his inward resistance to the powerful Cardinal, least of all before the Queen-Mother. Zorzi, the Venetian ambassador, noted on November 6, 1629, that Bérulle alone was to blame for the estrangement between Richelieu and Marie de' Medici; but the judgment was superficial. In the relation of Bérulle to Richelieu it is idle to seek for any reason founded on jealousy; to do so is to belittle both the man and the spiritual background of his actions. What impelled Bérulle was a universal ideal, completely hostile to Richelieu's. Richelieu saw the rise of conscious

and separate and exclusive nations as an unavoidable law of
the near future, and set himself to prepare for it by erecting
the centralized State; while Bérulle's spirit was timeless; he
dreamt of a human order in which all earthly things would
be subordinated to eternal law, a new birth of Christianity,
and, like all the members of the League and the whole party
of the *dévotes*, he believed in the possibility and necessity of
working along with Spain and the Hapsburgs. His opposition
to Richelieu was to the politician who set the nation above
the Counter-Reformation. This was Richelieu's own judgment, for he wrote of Bérulle: "That pure spirit made all
those violent attacks on me . . . not in the least out of dislike for me; he did not know what it was to hate anyone:
what made him so obstinate in his ideas was his conviction
that they were in accordance with the will of God." By his
zeal and his sudden inspirations Bérulle had ruined the political effect of the English marriage and worked against
Richelieu at La Rochelle; by his fanaticism he had roused
the Queen and all her followers against Richelieu, that enemy
of Spain; as a man already half-withdrawn from the world
in divine contemplation, he had raised his voice along with
Marillac against the Italian campaign. Louis XIII said of
Bérulle that he was terrified of everyday things, he had no
practical sense; and the King considered sending him on a
special embassy to Rome, so as to be rid of his political
influence in France. Bérulle forestalled all such plans; he fell
ill and lay down to die, and before he did so spoke words,
never forgotten by those who heard them, on the vanity of
all earthly things; he passed away on October 20th, a great
figure of Catholic Christendom, which he had stamped with
the inmost national spirit of France without having ever
grasped the truth known to Richelieu, that the happiness of
countries lies in the simultaneous development of people,
nation, and State.

Now only Marillac remained. With him Richelieu was on
very different ground, easy to survey; here there was no

difficulty which could not be settled in the ordinary course affairs. Richelieu built and destroyed for the sake of a future which could not be conceived by a single generation: Marillac, on the other hand, was merely a mediocre, well-schooled reactionary. He was also a realist who could not imagine the vast intellectual resources of a man like Richelieu; he kept repeating what was actually the truth: that France had no money, that the army was unreliable and disorganized, the leaders and men faithless, the nobles merely waiting for a treasonable opportunity, the economic state of the land wretched; and his final guarantee for the truth of this was always Bérulle's words: "Many pious spirits foresee that this State will be punished if it does not avail itself of the means which God has put in our hands for the final extermination of heresy." For him Armand de Richelieu, Cardinal of the Roman Church, was a traitor to the true faith, but for whose work the plan of the holy Ignatius, which the Emperor Ferdinand was executing in Germany, would have led to complete success and the salvation of mankind. As for Richelieu's national aims, he did not believe that they could be achieved; Spain was too powerful, Hapsburg too great, France too weak, and dangerously threatened on all her frontiers; the will of God was against such a policy. But though Marillac claimed the will of God for policies so narrow and so conditioned by his time, he could not conceive the scope of a human will such as that of the great Cardinal, which, working within the bounds of an actuality that seemed narrow and trivial in the world's eyes, could fulfil the destiny of a nation.

Richelieu was wrested from the confusion of these animosities by the renewed breaking out of the Italian conflict. The agreement made in Suze he had always regarded as no more than an armistice. Now, as he had foreseen, Olivares refused to ratify the agreements made by his representative in Upper Italy and ordered Spinola, the Duke of Lerma and the Marquis of Santa Cruz to resume hostilities in the valley of the Po and besiege Casale once more. Simultaneously the Emperor was urged to send his best troops to Italy; the forces of both branches of the house of Hapsburg must be speedily mobilized to crush the Duke of Mantua before help from France could reach him.

Richelieu at once had the matter at his finger ends. He had been abundantly informed of all the movements of his enemies by an efficient secret service. The Emperor would pour twenty-two thousand foot and four thousand horse through the plain of Po; Spain would send fifteen thousand foot and three thousand horse under the great Genoese general, Spinola, the man who had judged most quickly and justly the genius of Richelieu. Spinola replaced the former Governor of Milan, Don Gonzalez de Cordova; the Imperial troops were led by Collalto.

This was no mere military expedition; it was war on a large scale, though the wisdom of contemporary custom permitted the intervention even of large bodies of troops for or against a third party, without postulating a general war between the intervening powers. To meet the Hapsburg threat France would at least have to produce an army of fifty thousand men, for the ideas of the first half of the seventeenth century a very great force. Where it was to be had, how it was to be furnished, who was to be entrusted with the command when so many of the generals could not be relied upon, was the problem. The Cardinal's relations with the Queen-Mother had been outwardly re-established at a reception given in Richelieu's Paris residence, where Marie de' Medici was present. Now the vast preparations of Spain and Austria seemed to have outdone all Marillac's prophecies, and the danger appeared irrevocable. What would happen if Spain attacked from the Pyrenees at the same time? The peace party hardly dared to think about the danger from Germany. The abuse of the pamphleteers fell thick about the Cardinal's ears. "He will repent of his madness, this man who had only one thought: the ruin of the house of Austria!" "He will bring about universal war; the barbarians will sweep over the fields of France." Marillac was now more insistent than ever; it was a matter of avoiding the worst; he protested, he admonished, he importuned the King daily. At last, in order visibly to renounce all responsibility, he spoke to Richelieu in November of resigning. "Why?" asked the Cardinal. "Is the Government acting wrongly?" Marillac replied that for twenty years he had wished to withdraw from public affairs. But Richelieu ignored his protestation and persisted: "Is it the death of Cardinal de Bérulle?" But Marillac refused to be drawn into a personal explanation and answered: "It is my wish." The Cardinal replied almost in a threatening tone: "You must not think of it! This is not the time for such gestures!" In the King's antechamber it was whispered: "The Keeper of the Great Seal fancies he'll walk out through the door, but he'll go through the window instead." The urgency of the difficulties in Court and Government circles now paled before the international danger.

Richelieu had retained the authority of a viceroy of the King of France over the armies in Italy. The news from Italy was bad; the forces there were quite inadequate. Once more, as during the English attack, it was the gallant Thoiras who had to defend the threatened fortress of Casale. Spinola, the greatest contemporary expert in siege technique, sat down before the walls whose fall must destroy the last hope of French help for the Duke of Mantua. Spinola was a very different opponent from Buckingham. While he was investing Casale, Collalto, after crushing a feeble resistance, swept with his German troops into Mantuan territory. The French troops in Suze, a small force under the command of Maréchal de Créqui, were refused permission to march through by the Duke of Savoy, in spite of the agreement made a year before. It was a difficult position for Charles Emanuel. Hapsburg seemed omnipotent, a success for French arms impossible; the time must come when this foolhardy attempt to resist the Spanish system would lead to a collapse of the French monarchy. Of Richelieu's achievements till now only the suppression of the Huguenots could be regarded as genuinely successful; all the rest seemed to be lost; more, Richelieu's foreign policy was now judged in most of the European Courts as a definitive failure which could never be made good again, while the inner difficulties of France were by no means ended; the country, which had been involved by the ambition of Richelieu in such hopeless complications, was not even firm on its own feet. If the Huguenots were crushed for the moment, the great feudal nobles were still to the fore, and Gaston of Orléans, the successor to the throne, was once more at their heads.

If Gaston had only conspired in Paris, it would have been easy to deal with him. But he had fled the country before his brother's return, which completely changed the position.

This treasonable act came about as follows. When Marie de' Medici sent Maria Louisa of Gonzaga a prisoner to Vincennes, the King and Richelieu had recognized that hasty deed, although it was a violation of the relations between France and the Duke of Mantua. While he was with the army, Louis XIII had no wish to exasperate his mother. But when, at Gaston's bidding and that of the blundering Bérulle, she now as suddenly set the Princess free and let her come to Paris on the condition that she did not marry Gaston, thus hopelessly compromising her, Richelieu could no longer conceal his displeasure at such senseless conduct. The Cardinal wrote at length to Bérulle pointing out the disastrous effects of such interference.

But Gaston wanted to be paid all over again for his renunciation of the marriage. First he had demanded money and a high military command. Now, prompted by his chancellor, Jacques de Coigneux, and Puylaurens, his favourite, he asked for much more, namely, the governments of Champagne and Burgundy. His object in choosing these great and rich frontier provinces was transparent. But even to this monstrous proposition the unsuspecting Bérulle gave his support, and the

Queen-Mother insisted upon it with violence. Richelieu replied to Bérulle that reasons of State made the fulfilment of such a request inconceivable; the lands that Gaston wanted bordered on the Empire, Lorraine, Spanish Franche-Comté, Switzerland, and Savoy, and if the persistent disobedience of the Prince were rewarded in such a fashion, his supporters would quickly make further demands. Bérulle informed the Queen-Mother of the Cardinal's message.

Marie de' Medici's next step was in her usual theatrical style. As often before, she drew up a written secret agreement with her closest friends. She put her hand to a solemn promise to bring down the Cardinal, while Gaston pledged himself in writing finally to renounce his plan of marrying the Mantuan princess. Mother and son entrusted the two documents to the Comte de Bellegarde, who carried them from that day next his skin in a golden locket attached to a chain round his neck.

But Gaston fled to Lorraine, where the Duchesse de Chevreuse had prepared the way for him. He was to be the centre of a conspiracy depending on Imperial aid. Richelieu did everything he could to induce the fugitive to return; he wrote that the King offered him the governments of Amboise and Orléans; he promised him 100,000 livres at once, and 50,000 talers in two instalments. Such means always worked with the heir-apparent; he returned. For how long? That was the question; he was not to be pinned down and he was difficult to watch; everything the Cardinal attempted against him must recoil fearfully on him if he ascended the throne; the King was ill and still childless; there lay a perpetual, almost open danger in the mere existence of Gaston. His residence in Lorraine had signified nothing more nor less than a treasonable attack on France with the help of the feudal nobles of that province and foreign assistance, and that meant the mighty army of Ferdinand II, which filled all Europe with alarm.

Richelieu left Paris as Commander-in-Chief on December 29th; he was accompanied by the Duc de Montmorency,

Cardinal La Valette, and that great soldier, Schomberg. He had had a hard fight to prevent the King from taking part in the campaign. He regarded the outcome as much more uncertain than in the previous year; it was a matter of life and death, and the superiority of the enemy was great. Louis XIII's health must not be endangered. If Gaston were to succeed, it would be the end of the monarchy. Before leaving, Richelieu had persuaded his master of the necessity to remain in the country and keep a vigilant watch in Champagne on the Emperor's movements on the Rhine. These precautions were all the more essential, since there were reports of plague and dysentery from the battlefront. Shortly before setting out, Richelieu had obtained from the Curia a dispensation which absolved him from his daily duty of reading the breviary; the Papal act of grace was of great importance to him in his increasingly enfeebled state and his labours far into the night; he had exerted himself hard to obtain it, and now he begged the Holy Father not to make it public, at the same time saying how grateful he would be if he were permitted in certain cases to mention the privilege, so that he might not cause any scandal among those near to him.

Now Richelieu was completely the soldier again and in the element which he had chosen in his early youth as most suited to him. He arranged that the army, twenty-two thousand men strong, led by Créqui, La Force, Schomberg and five masters of ordnance, should be under his supreme command. The troops were to be divided into two forces, the one to advance through Savoy, the other through the Dauphiné.

With a large escort Richelieu appeared at Lyons on January 18th. He took lodgings with his brother Alphonse, in whose stead he had once become a bishop; immediately after his first rise to power, in 1626, he had forced Alphonse to leave the Carthusians and had had him appointed Bishop of Aix and in 1626 Bishop of Lyons. Since 1629 Alphonse had actually been a cardinal; Louis XIII had on his own initiative endowed him with the cardinal's hat. But Richelieu did not feel at home in the archiepiscopal palace. His queer brother was like a reproach to him, and besides he could never bear to live for long in towns; wherever he happened to be, he had to have some open place with gardens. His daily walk after dinner, no matter what the weather, had become a necessity to him. This time he chose the garden of Ainay, so famous at that time, at the junction of the Rhône and the Saône. Here he consulted with the high command; here he worked out again, as before La Rochelle, the whole technical question of the campaign down to the last detail.

The Duke of Savoy offered to negotiate regarding the march through. His brother, the Prince of Piedmont, had crossed the St. Bernard pass and suggested a meeting on neutral ground to the Cardinal. Schomberg advised against it; they should march, he said, and bargain no longer with these people; La Force inclined to his view; Bassompierre was for the diplomatic solution. At this point an agent of the Pope appeared and offered to mediate. Richelieu shut himself up with the man for three hours. Strangely, the agent of the Vatican made a strong impression on him; he returned to the fact again and again during these winter days. "The finest intellectual equipment," he said, "that could be conceived, a gifted mind, which can master with ease the nature of political affairs and the arts of negotiation." He felt in the man something almost amounting to equality with himself, and with quick decision refused to consent to the armistice offered him. People were surprised that the Cardinal should waste so much of his time on a young cleric attached to the service of the Nuncio in Turin; no one had ever heard of him and his name did not waken any associations: it was Giulio Mazarini.

After his conversation with the obscure priest who fifteen years later was to succeed him, Richelieu decided to take Schomberg's advice and attack. He sent an exhaustive memorial to the King, in which he said that he had come to no clear agreement with the Duke of Savoy, and that that Prince had assembled an army of fifteen thousand men in Avigliano, where he was requisitioning everything, so that nothing would be left for the French army. Thereupon he gave his orders, briefly and clearly, allotting to each commander the objective he had to reach. Since February 1st the Cardinal had been in Grenoble, as the year before. On March 15th the Duke of Savoy received an ultimatum; he tried to save himself by further shilly-shallying; during the night of March 18th the attack began: the French forces crossed the Doria and the army of Savoy withdrew almost in flight to Turin. Next morning the Cardinal crossed the river along with the rear-guard. A Monsieur de Pontis tells that he saw him riding into the water on his horse, his doublet rust brown with golden embroidery, his armour water-coloured; two pages rode beside him, one bearing his gloves, the other his cardinal's hat. Richelieu rode at a gallop up the opposite bank out of the foaming mountain stream, and in the light suddenly breaking from behind a cloud he seemed to his troops like the god of war himself; it was as if he had always lived in armour. During the morning it grew as warm as summer; the troops sang as they marched; they swore that they would take Turin straight away; there would be rich booty. But in the afternoon a storm broke such as is known only in the southern foothills of the Alps; snow, hail, and wind drove the soldiers on in the direction of Rivoli, and Richelieu, who was once more driving in his carriage, could hear with his own ears his men's curses and imprecations. He called Puységur, who commanded the Guards that day, to the carriage. "Do you hear the impudent devils?" he asked. Puységur answered: "They do this now; to-morrow, if the sun shines, they'll pipe another tune and shout long live the Generallissimus!" "It must be stopped," said the Cardinal curtly; the Major bowed from his saddle and accepted the order. In the evening a soft light was spread over the landscape, cleansed by the storm. As Richelieu drove to the castle of Rivoli, perched on one of the three hills of the place, the troops cheered him from every window. When Puységur appeared in the evening to receive his orders, Richelieu asked him: "Has your rebuke taken effect already?" "No," replied the Major, "I shall wait for the roll-call to give it." Richelieu smiled. "Don't say anything," he said and dismissed the officer. This trifling incident exemplifies the touchiness of the Cardinal, which often interfered with his capacity to impose his will, and in the most diverse ways; he always took back such errors again, but often it was too late.

Nobody knew his plans. "To Turin!" shouted the troops; but their officers considered that an attack on the capital would be senseless and not in accordance with the Cardinal's usual cool judgment. Besides, negotiations had been resumed with the Duke of Savoy. The State Secretary Servien was sent to him with the message saying that the French army had no hostile intentions, but had acted purely out of concern for its own safety. But the Duke refused to receive Servien; he forbade his subjects to exchange even a word with the French; all that could be got out of him finally was that he would send an ambassador to the Cardinal in his own time.

On March 20th, quite unexpectedly, Richelieu ordered the army to march, and on the 21st he appeared with his assembled forces, which were greater than anyone expected, before the extensive fortress of Turin, to ride round whose walls took an hour and a half. Charles Emanuel, who had foreseen other plans for his opponent, at once ordered a relieving army stationed near Pignerolo to turn back again. Richelieu had foreseen that error; leaving a small force to invest Turin, he marched off with his main army and on the 21st began to besiege Pignerolo; standing up to their hips in water, his men dug trenches up to the outworks; on the 22nd La Force and Créqui attacked; in the evening the place was captured except for the citadel. Eight days later the Cardinal wrote urgently to La Force: "You will save my life if you attack the bastion with every means and take the citadel. Make the impossible possible; everything depends upon that." The citadel surrendered on Easter Sunday of the year 1630. The possession of Pignerolo was decisive; the Cardinal's lines of communication with the Dauphiné were now secured. From here he could hold the Duke of Savoy completely in check; he ruled the plain of the Po; and even if Casale fell, he now held sufficiently strong pledges to have it returned again.

The army of La Force had crossed Mont Cenis at the end of February.

But the Duke of Savoy now extricated himself from his difficult position by taking a step which all French historians have designated as an act of treachery; he declared himself for Spain and the Emperor, as was clearly demanded by the interests of his house and his country. He called Spinola to his aid. The strategic position was now so much changed for the better, that Richelieu considered it advisable for the King to be with the army in order to give its successes the necessary weight; also he was perfectly well informed regarding the intrigues against his work and himself which were being busily carried on in royal circles.

As soon as the Duke of Savoy showed his colours, Louis himself had resolved to appear at the scene of action. Since February 13th he had been at Troyes in Champagne, watching Germany and doing nothing. The whole net of paralysing intrigue which surrounded him had grown denser than ever at his headquarters. He was torn between the senseless claims of his brother and the reproaches and sudden moods of his mother. Mother and son now worked along with Marillac; they had roused a strong popular movement, embracing even the lowest classes, against the policy of the King and the Cardinal, a pamphleteering campaign supported by the great feudal nobles and also by foreign powers. When Louis XIII set out for Italy with the turn of the year, the whole Court followed him to Lyons: the Queen, Marie de' Medici, Marillac; they tried to prevent him from proceeding farther; the attacks against his Minister redoubled in violence. If Louis gave way the Cardinal was lost and the campaign must end in disaster. They were all terrified of the name of war; they all urged that peace should be made, except for the lesser nobility used to war, who, however, saw more hope in fighting for the nobles, or even for the foreign powers, than in this highly precarious war against the Emperor and Spain under a completely new discipline which had never been known before the Cardinal's time.

But the position of the King was still worse. Richelieu had watched from the distance his every action, and each report had alarmed him. After the fall of Pignerolo he had counted with certainty on the King's full support in his further plans; his spirit was so positive that he always attributed a forward-striving effect to every genuine success. And indeed the King set out on his own initiative; he left Champagne and appeared in Lyons; but to Lyons his mother and his wife at once followed him, and with them the whole burden of confusing and inimical influences, discouraging prophecies and doubts, the vacillating and dizzy feeling which the King knew so well as soon as he was away from the source of his strength, the feared and longed-for Cardinal. The King was ill; his body was submitted to drastic treatment; almost daily he had electuaries; he had been bled some forty times in the course of one year. Richelieu was in constant correspondence with the royal physicians, and again and again he exhorted the King in his letters to follow the prescriptions of these learned men, even when they were unwelcome to him; he wrote to the Queen also in this vein. As if nothing had happened, Marie de' Medici still received from Savoy the regular reports which Richelieu had never failed to send her for years. In each letter one can feel a desperate struggle against the inevitable end of their relationship, towards which Richelieu had taken the first steps; yet still the Cardinal hoped for an adjustment of the difference. A relaxation of the tension would mean for him a great saving of nervous energy, for the break with her which he was preparing for was a matter of life and death; whether the King would survive it was questionable. The bond between mother and son was tragically intimate, and Richelieu always turned to the Queen-Mother when he wished the King to follow the doctor's orders. It was characteristic of this great man, who prepared the way for so many of the achievements of the nineteenth century, that he believed firmly in the medical science of his time and had little use for natural remedies or any other form of miracle-working.

Louis XIII arrived in Lyons on May 2nd. On the 5th the two Queens appeared; he left them and grimly set out on the 10th for Grenoble, gloomy, dispirited, "perhaps the saddest man in his kingdom," as a chronicler reported; but he was able to prevent the Court from travelling with him. Since the 9th Richelieu had been in Grenoble. Louis greeted him as if he were his saviour. That the King had succeeded in reaching him was for Richelieu a victory greater than the fall of Pignerolo; it meant reunion, the possibility of taking a free breath; but he had staked everything upon it; before Louis's arrival courier after courier had come with letters from Marillac demanding an immediate peace on no matter what conditions.

On May 10th a council of war was held in Grenoble; at last the King found himself in a different, more invigorating atmosphere; the marshals, the masters of ordnance and the Cardinal took counsel, and the secretaries who had accompanied Louis heard with amazement a different tone from that to which they had been accustomed in Marillac's circle. Richelieu gave a detailed account of the state of operations and the general political situation; like the others he was for a vigorous prosecution of the war; to treat with the enemy at the moment, he considered, would be disastrous. The standpoint of the Cardinal was unanimously approved.

The King was still uneasy; he knew the state of things in France, the daily growing campaign of libels and inflammatory sheets, and the many people who counted on his weakness, his downfall, his death that they might undo the structure of which his father had erected the most glorious part. Past and present were vividly before the eyes of the King; he was deeply bound, by a shy, admiring love, to his dead father, whom he did not hope to follow or equal but yet of whom he tried to be worthy in his gloomy, almost ruthless defence of the throne, and to whom he never felt closeer than when, set free from his doubts, his illness, his melancholia, he hunted the deer or faced his enemies.

His combination of weakness and responsibility involved him in the tortures of that love mingled with hate which again and again brought him under the influence of his mother, who had wept so few tears on Henry's coffin and by virtue of that fact possessed a strange mystery, a strength capable of defying the dead ruler, and for her son something incomprehensible in which at times he sought refuge from his perpetual self-reproaches at the thought of his father. Marie de' Medici knew how to deal with him; when, summoning all his resolution, he tore himself away from her, she was always able to repair the breach; a last riddle remained for Louis to solve, and it drew him back.

Immediately after the council of war at Grenoble, the King begged the Cardinal to go to Lyons and explain and defend his war policy in person, which he, the King, had only managed to save by leaving at the right moment to join his generals and fortify himself with their resolution.

Richelieu set out on his hard road. In Lyons he spoke before the Queen-Mother, Marillac and Marshal Montmorency. There was only one choice, he said; either Savoy must be conquered and Casale saved, or by a shameful peace they would have to suffer a heavy loss in power and prestige. Marillac's opposition, which hitherto had been marked by a certain obsequiousness, now appeared in full force; he was scarcely polite; Richelieu stood alone against his opponents. The people were murmuring and would not endure their misery much longer; dreadful would be the responsibility of anyone who asked these wretches to embark on another war. Marillac warmed up old history; wars in Italy had only brought misfortune to the French kings; the hardships of a campaign were bound to be injurious to the King in his delicate health; the fact that they held Suze and Pignerolo would not prevent the inexhaustible reserves of the Emperor from maintaining hold of the mountain passes, so that an ever new flood of German troops could be poured into Italy; nor would the trifling successes scored by France save the Duke of Mantua; it was the nature of the French to become careless as soon as half the battle was won and to give away in the end, one after another, all the advantages they had won.

The Keeper of the Great Seal was sixty-seven. Richelieu remarked of him almost with pity that he was still actuated by personal ambition, and that what he brought out was "a stale concoction of dead and gone things."

The Queen-Mother's response was remarkable; passionately on Marillac's side, yet unwilling to oppose the King directly, she too spoke of the honour of France which must not of course be sacrificed, and of guarantees for the Valtelline and the French soldiers shut in Casale. Empty, senseless phrases, which Montmorency supported, thus sealing his subsequent fate. Richelieu never forgot that hard hour; he was so roused that he saw through everyone present and could read their thoughts. He too knew the dreadful suffering of the French peasants; it remained a fundamental axiom of his thought; but he considered that it could be alleviated only through an active foreign policy, not, as Marillac wished, by shaping the European policy of the State to merely contemporary domestic political and economic requirements. Foreign policy was for him the highest manifestation of the State, and had to take precedence of all its other functions, since in the last resort it decided over them all; also it was for him the one field of human action in which, often by the slightest and almost imperceptible means, a word, a sign, one could move and change great tracts of future history. Richelieu replied to Marillac with coldness and an undertone of cutting impatience. Monsieur de Marillac, he said, had told them that this war could not be waged without bringing great hardships with it. "That applies not only to this war but to all wars," he continued, raising his voice, "but it can be no reason why we should deliberately choose a peace on the most feeble, wretched and scandalous conditions! The complaints of the people must not induce us to make such a peace; they complain over necessary evils as over unnecessary ones; they are as ignorant of what is vitally essential to the State as they are ready to grumble at some hardship which is indispensable in order to avoid a great disaster."

In the present case Richelieu emphasized again and again the share which the will of the King had in the prosecution of the war; after the fall of Pignerolo all the despatches from headquarters had made clear the disadvantages and dangers of continuing the campaign, but Louis XIII had replied with the dignified resolution of a soldier by commanding the army to attack Savoy. About the intrigues behind his back the Cardinal said not a word. The Queen-Mother dismissed him graciously with the assurance that in the circumstances which he had outlined she was convinced that it was necessary to prosecute the war. Richelieu could not have read more from her words than that formal assurance. It was quite clear to him that Marillac represented the opposition in France and that he would at once begin to work on the Queen again; he also knew Marie de' Medici, and that her great influence with her son might make any single whim of hers dangerous to the State. As for the impulses which moved her, Richelieu has described them in their commonplace reality. He wrote: "What moved her was her hatred of the house of Gonzaga, her ambitious love for her daughter, the Princess of Piedmont, and her own need for peace and comfort, which she wished to enjoy in her Luxembourg Palace." Women of that kind have only one measure: themselves and those most closely connected with them. In this they remain so close to the sources of all strength that neither logic nor enthusiasm can affect them for long. Richelieu reckoned with all these imponderables, not imponderable to him; his incorruptible sense of reality judged all human motives not by their intellectual value, but by their actual calculability.

When he returned to Grenoble he received news that Thoiras was holding out as stoutly against Spinola as he had done against Buckingham. Louis now ordered the attack on Savoy. Créqui took Chambéry with six thousand men, the King himself marched into Anneçy, and the Savoy troops withdrew into the valley of Aosta.

But the King's uneasiness over the Court intrigues behind him, the machinations of his mother and Gaston, would not give him a moment's rest; his fancy turned them into a nightmare. He now wanted the Queen and his mother to see the position with their own eyes, to talk to the military commanders, to listen to his own reasons; and he begged them to come to Grenoble. Richelieu did all he could to prevent their finding an excuse; it was important that he should have them at hand, under his eyes and his influence. But Marie de' Medici declined; she was not feeling well and it was too hot, she said. Vizille was proposed instead of Grenoble, equally without success; nothing could be done. The King's uneasiness grew morbid: it was like a sort of dread of this first direct passage of arms with Spain, in which he outdid even the daring of his father; something he could not name drove him to seek the advice of that incomprehensible old woman who had never felt the thrill of great decisions.

Richelieu had to do with a sick man. He himself called the year of 1630 the year of tribulation. When at last the King suddenly resolved to leave the army and return to Lyons, giving up everything, spreading discouragement in his own army and confidence in the enemy, the Cardinal wrote: "Never before have I been in such a wretched position. How gladly would I be out of this world and upraised into the mercy of my Lord." Marillac went on daily working on the Queen-Mother with his thousand and one reasons; she greedily swallowed his arguments, only too glad to have their support. The King wished to go to Lyons for six days, not a day longer, he swore. Richelieu did not let him travel alone, and Louis himself commanded him to be present at the consultation; he needed strong support; he was afraid of himself. And so the Cardinal appeared once more before the intriguers, who listened to what he said as if they were a court trying him. He emphasized again that Casale was lost if the French army did not appear in Italy. Now that the King was present, Marillac concentrated on putting the whole responsibility for the war on the Cardinal. Unlike his contemporaries, who considered that Marillac was moved merely by selfish advantage, jealousy and ambition, Richelieu held that the spring of his actions was lack of perspective and a wish to make himself important; considering his capacity to hound to their death men whom he regarded as a danger to the State, his indifference to Marillac was a sign that he despised him.

While he was in Lyons news came that the departure of the King had had the effect which he had feared; six thousand men had deserted.

But even that did not move Marillac. He kept repeating that they were risking the life of the King, and what Louis never liked to hear, the "childless King." They were embarking on a European adventure, he continued, for which he could foresee no issue; think of the fearful consequences if a general war against Spain and the Empire were to involve the frontier countries of Savoy and Lorraine, and the much dreaded change of the crown were to occur at the same time. Someone suggested a *via media*: the King should accompany the army only to the Italian frontier, not to the scene of war. Marillac seized on the suggestion and gave it an unfortunate rhetorical turn: "If I had the intention to send your Majesty to Italy, then this is the way I would choose . . ." Louis XIII sprang up. "If I wished to cross the frontier, even alone, I should do so, and no one would prevent me!" he cried, leaving the room. On June 21st he left Lyons alone; on the 24th he was in Grenoble.

Richelieu now endeavoured to separate Marillac from the

Queen-Mother. He ordered him to come to headquarters at once. Marillac was deeply alarmed; he hesitated, complained that he was old and ill, but finally had to obey and set out by slow stages; when he arrived the King was already on his way to Italy. Marillac refused to go any farther.

Scarcely had Louis XIII arrived with his army when news came of a severe epidemic of plague in Piedmont and Upper Italy. The two Queens grew still more bitter against Richelieu. Louis's headquarters were in St. Jean de Maurienne. Marillac pulled every wire to have him brought back again. He worked now from Grenoble. Louis had said: "If I make the ill old man follow me he'll die on the road, and then they'll say I wanted to bring him to his death." Marillac worked on the King's physician Bouvard. But Bouvard replied that the King's quarters were healthier than those in Lyons; they were airy and cheerful, new rain had fallen, and the place was cool. At that time people prayed for wind when there was a pestilence.

But even Richelieu could not conceal from himself now that the danger was great. The plague was spreading. Public opinion was no longer to hold or bind. The Duke of Savoy published everywhere that the war was solely the work of the Cardinal. Riots were breaking out all over France. It was said that the Parlements were no longer answerable for the King's authority. Reports from the front were alarming; the pestilence had reduced the number of troops by a third. Military reverses came on the top of this; on the 18th Mantua fell into the hands of Collalto, the Imperial commander, and there was looting. "This is nothing, only the beginning of worse things," Marillac triumphantly declared. And again, in letter after letter, by messenger after messenger, Richelieu was implored or ordered with threats to see that the King returned.

Everyone who came near the Cardinal at that time feared him. He seemed to be turned to stone by his bitter and immovable resolution; everything depended now on him alone. But as the pestilence silently spread, he began to be anxious about the presence of the King. The choice for him

was a hard one: if the King died, the French State which he
served and he himself would be ruined; if the King returned,
the army would melt away; the six thousand deserters had
been a mere prologue. He wrote to say that His Majesty
might encounter mishaps, might fall ill anywhere; everything
depended on whether he could hold out now for a little
longer. The enemy, he said, were suffering from the pestilence
as well as the French. But now a new and decisive difficulty
appeared; the generals, as before La Rochelle, were disputing
over questions of precedence, and those who felt offended
by the Cardinal's decisions turned to his enemies at home.
The prospects of success were so low that the Cardinal, as if
he were signing his own death-warrant, decided to advise the
King to return to Lyons. He himself remained in Saint Jean
de Maurienne. There was one other man as unshakable as
himself, a man prepared to do or die: Thoiras in Casale.
Couriers kept coming and going between him and the Cardinal. "Hold out," Richelieu wrote to him, "I know I can
depend on your heart and your head!" Thoiras withstood
the great Genoese Spinola, the conqueror of Breda and Spain's
greatest commander, who now began to fight for his reputation. In spite of the pestilence, Richelieu ordered the afflicted
army to advance; three points on the Po were occupied,
Panealieri, Vigone, and Villafranca. The fresh troops arrived
in Suze on August 17th. Schomberg, that dependable man,
the most reliable of the generals, was given command. But
the pestilence climbed the mountains; the new troops were
already infected; and presently the plague began to demand
its sacrifices in Saint Jean de Maurienne itself, where Richelieu
was posted. Louis XIII showed again that when he was in
command of his faculties he always knew how to value the
Cardinal. His order to Richelieu to return at once to Lyons
could not be ignored, and was couched in a fashion which
betrayed deep agitation. On August 22nd the Cardinal
arrived in Lyons to pass through the bitterest experience of
his hard life.

CHAPTER XIX

FRANCISCAN INTERLUDE IN REGENSBURG

The deepest desire of the strange Franciscan priest whom Richelieu in his correspondence called the "tenebroso, cavernoso," his real earthly vision, was the union of France and the German Empire in a crusade against the unbeliever, a sort of enormous adjustment of all differences in a common mission. Ferdinand II's intervention in Italy had rudely torn the web of his dream. Now all the more immediate problems came into their right: the question of the Mantuan succession, the freedom of the Alpine routes, the Dutch, Venetian, and Swiss alliances, the attitude to the Catholic League in Germany, to Wallenstein and the policy of Bavaria, above all the crucial question whether the alliance with the German Protestants would be a permanent necessity, and in what way the Scandinavian countries could be brought to strengthen it.

It was a world-shaking conversation which took place between Father Joseph and the commander of the Imperial army, Wallenstein, in a tent in the camp at Memmingen on the warm summer night of July 23, 1630. A light as from the eyes of the chimera lies on the encounter between these two men.

Wallenstein, the star-gazer confident of his fortunes, trusting to the powers which upbore him as with great invisible pinions, yet certain of himself to the very edge of the precipice: the monk so essentially different in nature, who went step by step, pausing, listening, soundlessly pursuing his way by night and never to be seen by day. Wallenstein wanted for the German world what Father Joseph sought for the French:

unity. And each in his own way strove to bring back the vanished synthesis of the Middle Ages, a unified Christendom. Though Father Joseph went to Regensburg as Wallenstein's keenest opponent, to weaken the ties between the Elector and the Emperor, because he believed that France should lead Europe and considered that the realization of a unified Christendom could be reached only in that way, he did not find himself, curiously enough, in pure disagreement with the great soldier; the strange and equivocal nature of Wallenstein, which could not be reduced to any clear Latin formula, met him half-way. Wallenstein certainly wished the Emperor to be all-powerful, but only so that he himself might achieve power. He dreamt of uniting the German lands, and in that solitary talk with the priest of Rome he contemptuously flung aside all caution and confessed his plan: to set up in Germany an empire of his own. Then his dark and penetrating glance turned to other things, and he, the Slav, began to dream aloud of Constantinople, of Byzantium. Joseph listened with amazement, though no change of expression betrayed his feelings; but as soon as he returned he informed the Cardinal of everything, and furnished him with still deeper insight into German strength and German weakness.

On the Mantuan question, too, Wallenstein expressed himself without caution. He was a personal friend of Gonzaga, and was resolved to leave him in peaceful possession of his inheritance; moreover he hated Spinola, who was always being played off against him as a master of the military art, and this private enmity he now flung into the scales. He said that France would be given satisfaction; the enemies of the Emperor must not be increased by such a powerful opponent on account of Mantua. From the Emperor's correspondence it is shown that Wallenstein's ambitious plans were no mystery to his master at this time.

Father Joseph had heard enough in one night to foresee correctly the more remote developments that must follow. Along with Brûlart de Léon, the French ambassador to

Switzerland, he took his leave of Wallenstein and set out by way of Ulm and Donauwörth for Regensburg.

Seldom have the powers and instructions of two ambassadors formed such a perfect diplomatic unity as in that mission of Brûlart and Joseph. Everything was vague and floating, yet for the initiated of a precision of intention which excluded any possibility of error. The Ambassador appeared on an extraordinary mission; he could make and listen to proposals, but he was not empowered to enter into any definitive agreement. Father Joseph's credentials from the Cardinal described him as a scholar with only a watching and advisory brief; but this contradicted the fact that he was accredited with Ferdinand II, and that all Europe knew him to be Richelieu's right-hand man; and though he was plausibly subordinated to the Ambassador, the inner hierarchy of the relation was so clear that nobody could misunderstand it. Brûlart had also received his instructions; but these official ones, like the private ones entrusted to Joseph, had been inspired, more, drawn up, by Joseph himself in accordance with general lines laid down by Richelieu. Joseph mentioned these general lines to his close friend, Father Mortagne: the Electors were to be set at odds with each other, and estranged from the Emperor by various means, and prevented from uniting among themselves; any attempt by the Emperor at centralization or union was to be designated as Hapsburg tyranny; the struggle for independence by individual German princes was to be supported by every means, and any who resisted were to be assured of French support against the Emperor. An ancient ambition of France can be seen in this policy; a policy which finally displaced the German centre of gravity from the West and South to the North and East, causing centuries of German division and misery, yet involuntarily producing positive effects as well as encouraging the cultural life of the German lands, so that far into the nineteenth century the variety and the indigenous development of the different parts of the German nation were maintained. The exhaustive instruction which Brûlart was given showed exact knowledge of the country and the people, and above all of the princes; there was precise advice for the treatment of each separate German Court. The chief aim of the French mission consisted in weakening the Emperor wherever possible, in obstructing him and paralysing him in all his undertakings, in making the house of Hapsburg hated by the Germans, and in gaining French influence at every point when there was any sign of resistance to the Imperial authority. The Germans, as usual preferring the particular interest to the general, responded to these efforts in a way which caused amazement beyond the Rhine. At a time when the great nations were establishing themselves as States and beginning to divide the world among themselves and found their vast colonies, the Germans turned against their ruling house, which had opened for them the road to Asia Minor, and had submitted large stretches of Slav and Hungarian territory to German influence, and by a collaboration with Spain could have achieved, granted internal unity, a position in Europe far more powerful than that of France. Yet as Ferdinand II said at the Regensburg Reichstag of 1630, the French Franciscan priest bore off the German Electors' hats in his cowl. In the name of freedom, and especially of religious freedom, countless Germans now helped to advance the policy of France. Richelieu's Grey Eminence put his hand to the work which ended in the Peace of Westphalia, when he betook himself to the Reichstag in the fine old Danubian city of Regensburg.

Regarding the Mantuan succession, which was of course in the forefront, there was no mention whatever in his instructions; concerning it and it alone the Cardinal left his negotiators a free hand and full powers. Here Richelieu's sense of proportion can be clearly seen. It was obvious that any political conversation with the Imperial authorities must at once raise the Italian question; more, that that question would be considered the cause of the special mission. But for that very reason the negotiators had to treat the dispute as a secondary matter and pretend amazement that so much importance was attached to it. The position in which Richelieu found himself must also be taken into account. Everything for him depended on the success of his enterprise in Italy: the difficulties at Court, as will be shown, had sharpened alarmingly; but he refused to give the Italian incident any undue importance abroad. It was the external occasion of Brûlart's and Father Joseph's presence at the Reichstag, but nothing more; the Cardinal laid real weight only on the secret dealings of his ambassadors.

Actually, the Mantuan succession was of course a matter of dispute between France and Spain. Madrid must not hear of France's need for peace by way of Vienna. Besides, that need was such as anyone not in the innermost circle of French policy could not estimate; nobody knew this better than the Cardinal himself. He steadily and calmly pursued his foreign policy, even after he believed that his position in France was lost; that moment was not far distant.

On the other hand, the whole Italian question could be used as an argument with the Electors. What could be more convincing as a proof of the ruinous dependency on Spain of the Imperial House and its policy than this Italian dispute which had broken out between France and the Empire, a dispute into which Olivares had dragged the Hofburg when, as everybody could see, there were only reasons for peace between Germany and France, and no cause for irritation, no grounds for opposition, except it were the disinclination of the French king to look on at the destruction of German freedom?

On August 2nd Brûlart and Father Joseph were received by the Emperor; on the 3rd Father Joseph was given a second audience. For Richelieu that interview meant much: he himself was its unspoken theme. Father Joseph fought in the Danubian city against the domestic enemies of his master, Marillac in particular, and he had to overcome a deep prejudice in the Emperor. Marillac and his followers had exposed Richelieu's anti-Hapsburg plans in all the Courts of Europe as a world danger, and had claimed to know his intentions; Father Joseph took up all these insinuations, asked for details, and demonstrated their flimsiness; he drew a picture of Marillac and his supporters, disappointed climbers who were in league with the rebellious nobles; more, as no elector was present, he informed the Emperor that the aim of the Bourbons was precisely the same as that of the Hapsburgs: a unified sovereign State. On the second day Father Joseph, with his uncanny assurance in treading the mazes of his own tortuous policy, was certain that he had convinced the Emperor of Richelieu's peaceful intentions. The real negotiations only began now.

The circle on whom Father Joseph had to work at the Reichstag was a large one. The Electors of Saxony and Brandenburg had merely sent representatives; but all the others appeared in person; also almost all the Catholic States of Europe, along with England, were represented by their ambassadors. On July 3rd the Emperor requested the electors to consider the reorganization of the Imperial army, and to provide for the payment of regular subsidies. But before anything should be decided the electors pressed for Wallenstein's dismissal; Father Joseph was behind this demand, for he had made prudent use of the commander's imprudent words; he had also hinted to the Emperor the dangerous plans which Wallenstein was nursing. So Wallenstein was sacrificed for the first time. Ferdinand announced his decision on August 13th; in September he sent Werdenberg and Questenberg to Wallenstein at Memmingen. Wallenstein, who obeyed the Emperor's command without resistance, knew that he would soon be needed again. He counted on the quick advance of the Swedes.

What Richelieu feared most was that his two representatives would do their work all too well. The Emperor did not attach much importance to Mantua, where he was merely Spain's seconder; but it was obvious that his representatives would try to use the Italian dispute to secure a general peace, perhaps even an alliance with France; and of that Richelieu would have nothing.

"If peace could be concluded between the Emperor and France," Richelieu wrote to Father Joseph, "the King would gladly act as mediator between the Empire and Sweden. . . . But great care must be taken to mention no such thing in the agreement." Richelieu wished to make a separate peace with the Emperor in Italy; but in every other respect he wished to keep his hands free. In these circumstances the work of the French representatives at Regensburg was of peculiar delicacy. If they went too far in agreement, they ran the danger of being sacrificed by their master at the last moment; also, they would annoy Venice, Holland, and Sweden. On the other hand, if they were too backward, the Emperor and the Catholic electors must see clearly that France was consistently supporting and inciting Sweden. Also Richelieu was negotiating in Italy directly with the Imperial commander Collalto; the Pope and his agent Mazarini had helped him with every means in their power; and on September 4, 1630, the armistice of Rivalto was signed over the heads of the Regensburg negotiators. It was high time, not only because of the state of the French forces, enfeebled by pestilence, but above all because of the domestic position in France itself and the apparently hopeless predicament into which Richelieu was being more and more deeply driven. It was Richelieu's position that Father Joseph kept most closely in mind during his further activities in Regensburg.

CHAPTER XX

THE DAY OF THE DUPES

Richelieu had left the sick army and arrived in Lyons on August 22, 1630. On the 13th the royal physician Bouvard had given him good news regarding the King's health. When he arrived there was no longer any cause for anxiety; Louis XIII seemed to have withstood the hardships of the campaign and escaped the risk of infection. For a month the Cardinal was able to work together with the King again, though at a grave disadvantage; much of his energy had to be wasted in repelling the indefatigable intriguers. Marie de' Medici treated her son's counsellor as if he were air; any concessions which Richelieu made she did not even deign to notice. He entrusted Louis de Marillac, a brother of his enemy, with a high command in Italy; he received no thanks; the gesture was read as a sign of weakness.

On September 22nd a consultation took place between the King and his mother, who was living outside Lyons. Louis, who felt obliged to honour his mother according to the scriptural precept, once more discussed all his State affairs with the old princess. On leaving the consultation on that September day the King was suddenly seized by a fit of shivering; it was at two o'clock in the afternoon; Richelieu, who was present, was deeply alarmed. He at once had the King taken back to the town in a boat and installed him in the palace of the archbishop, where Louis went to bed, shaken with a severe fever. He was bled; the fever increased; the King grew weaker and weaker until the 25th of the month came. Then violent dysentery broke out. On Tuesday, September 30th, his confessor Suffren prepared him for death. The Archbishop of Lyons celebrated the Mass in his room; Louis was given the sacraments; then he requested in a feeble voice that the doors should be opened. More than a hundred persons pressed into the room; the King apologized for not being able to speak because of his weakness; he was dying, Father Suffren would speak for him; of everyone he had wronged to ask forgiveness. The crowd knelt down; Richelieu, kneeling between the Queen and his brother, the Cardinal of Lyons, burst into tears.

A few hours later the Cardinal wrote to Schomberg: "I have been more dead than alive since early this morning I saw the most excellent prince and the best master in such a state that I never expected to see him alive again. God in His mercy has now been pleased to relieve us of our heavy anxiety, an abscess in the King's body has burst, and his condition is so much improved that the doctors now believe they can say that he will recover. But in spite of the words of these learned men I have not yet recovered from my deep apprehensions."

As soon as she heard the news of her son's illness, Marie de' Medici had hurried to Lyons, where she never left him during his sickness. Day and night she remained in the sick-room, as if she had only now discovered her real nature; she surrounded the suffering man with such an abundance of loving care that he once more became completely hers. Once he managed to whisper: "I am twenty-nine to-day; I have always tried to be a good son; if I have not always succeeded, forgive me." And all their relations were penetrated with a feeling of forgiveness and endless harmony.

Now, after the sudden turn for the better mentioned in Richelieu's letter, days began which seemed exempt from fate; all earthly thoughts were banished, and death seemed to have no more terrors; in the subdued light of the sick-room mother and son were more and more securely rapt in a delusive euphoria of boundless understanding in which every obstacle vanished.

For Richelieu it was a question of all that he lived for, and to few could that word "all" have meant so much as it did to him then. The possibility of a rude reverse of his fortunes had never been so terribly near. If the King died, he would find himself quite alone against an opposition filled with enmity and hatred; even friends such as Bouthillier would not be able to withstand the outburst of universal loathing.

The full blame for the King's sickness was now ascribed to Richelieu. He was made to feel this daily, and Anne of Austria said to him in the presence of everybody: "This is what comes of the journey to Saint Jean de Maurienne that you forced on the King!"

Among the enemies of the Cardinal were now Bassompierre and the Guises; they went over to the party of Marillac and the Queen-Mother. The impartial rule of the Cardinal had lain too heavily on the nobles, and on no one more than the happy-go-lucky Bassompierre, who hated equality before the law, the State, and the King worse than death itself. Plans were hatched. It was decided that Richelieu should be executed immediately after the King's death; Gaston, who would then reign, would marry his brother's widow. A d'Epernon, even a La Rochefoucauld, were for the immediate execution of the Cardinal. They decided that the moment that Louis closed his eyes, a certain Troisville with twelve musketeers would seize the Cardinal and put a pistol to his head. Everyone was in favour of arresting the hated man at once. The Governor of Lyons, asked whether he was prepared to perform that grave act, replied cautiously that when the time came he would order the Swiss Guards to carry out whatever the Queen-Mother should decide.

Richelieu knew of all these plans; only the inner necessity to continue his work, perhaps also a grim wish not to give his enemies such a rich satisfaction as his death would provide, sustained him. His friends denied the truth of the reports regarding the counter measures which he had taken; but he himself knew only too well that if the King died he would be irretrievably lost. It is certain that he made preparations to flee to Avignon, the city where he had once known the bitterness of exile, and where he now thought of putting himself under the protection of the Pope. It was whispered that the Duc de Montmorency had promised to conduct him to safety with an escort of five hundred noblemen. This was also denied by Richelieu's friends, and his apologists assert that Montmorency, who was executed two years later by the Cardinal as an enemy of the State, had never made any such offer; the story had merely been invented to brand with the odium of inhumanity Richelieu's harshness towards Montmorency. Yet there was something in the Cardinal's nature which must have made hard for him the thought that he had shown weakness before a Montmorency and been reduced to accept a Montmorency's magnanimity. Here we touch the darker nature of the lonely man, who admitted about this time that he could trust the fidelity of only one friend: the German Schomberg. He actually thought once of summoning him from Italy to Lyons with a strong force.

With the betterment of the King's state the immediate danger was past; but now another, less immediate, danger arose to torture his nerves still worse, since he had often experienced and often dealt with it before.

Richelieu's opponents began to work on the enfeebled King. They tried to cut him off from the Cardinal. Louis's illness prevented him from seeing anyone who even reminded him of State affairs. Daily and with increasing urgency, Marie de' Medici impressed upon the helpless, exhausted mind of her son that all the evil came from Richelieu, all the uncertainty on the frontiers, all the party hatred in the nation, all the rage and apprehension in the Court and among the nobles, even the constrained, unreal, unendurable relations in the royal family itself. At first Louis tried to make some resistance, but the slightest effort exhausted him; he told his confessor that he would die of this persecution, now that God had been pleased to save him from his illness; he could not endure it. But the others did not relax; with a horrible and petty obstinacy, with a flood of never-ending words, they assailed the exhausted King for hours on end. In August, when the same charges were made to him against the Cardinal, when they had said: "Richelieu is a devil: he created this conflict with Spain and the Empire simply to make himself indispensable," Louis had replied, shortly before he fell ill: "The Cardinal is not almighty; only God could have averted what has happened. But if Richelieu were an angel of heaven he could not have shown more foresight and prudence on every side, and I must confess that France has never had a greater servant." Counting on the King's weakness, they redoubled their efforts. Marie de' Medici was perhaps no longer his most dangerous enemy; the quiet Anne of Austria, hitherto so far from his affections, now assailed him too. Behind all the agonizing repressions which rise from natural energies ill-guided, husband and wife found themselves in the security of a maternal tutelage. Louis confessed to his wife how heavily he was troubled that he had lived estranged from her, and that he had been so harsh and unsympathetic towards her; but Anne replied gently, took all the blame upon herself, and assured him that the misunderstanding between them had arisen solely because of that evil and dreadful man, the Cardinal, the cause of all mischief, who paralysed her will and terrified her heart; his shadow would always lie between her and the King, if he could not be finally got rid of. Marie de' Medici felt that victory was near; she redoubled her efforts, for the King had given his wife what almost amounted to a promise. But her fresh attack produced the opposite effect from what she had hoped. Louis told her definitely that he was too exhausted and could not see things clearly enough; it was neither the place nor the hour for such grave decisions; he would not decide until he was back in Paris. To the Cardinal, whom he summoned to his sick-bed, he said: "Her Majesty the Queen, my mother, is displeased with your Eminence; I urgently advise you to seek a reconciliation." He refused to listen to any answer; he spoke as the sovereign; and his words contained a threat.

On October 6th it was decided that the King must leave; the autumn mists of the Rhône at Lyons were unfavourable to his recovery. After another conversation between the Cardinal and his master, it transpired that Louis refused to part from him during the journey; Marie de' Medici was to remain behind for some days with Bouthillier. Everyone recognized the hand which had contrived this solution, and acknowledged the minor success which Richelieu had won. On the 19th they set out; Louis journeyed with his Minister as far as Rôanne, but there news reached them which changed the situation gravely for the worse.

A courier brought the news posthaste from Germany that the King's ambassador extraordinary, in consideration of the alarming reports of his sovereign's health, had signed a treaty of peace with the Emperor on October 13th, and now requested its ratification.

Everybody breathed freely; in Lyons there was great elation; the nightmare had been lifted; past was their dread of the incalculable danger of a conflict with the German Empire and its endless reserves of strength. Bouthillier at once sent the text of the peace agreement to Richelieu with the observation that he hoped this solution would satisfy the King.

Father Joseph, the prime agent of this sudden *démarche*, saw from the distance the gravity of Richelieu's position; he knew that the full responsibility for a great European conflict now rested on the Cardinal's shoulders, that that responsibility must crush him if anything happened to the King, and that, even if Louis recovered, it could scarcely hope to survive the popular fury in France.

And now, in this unexampled predicament, Richelieu revealed the strength of his inexorable political passion as never before; his character became his destiny, and the super-personal in him took precedence of every other consideration. He tore up the agreement in a rage. "The Ambassador," he cried, "has exceeded his powers. This peace agreement is

375

completely useless!" And he showed the King that by Brûlart's arrangement the whole policy of France would be ruined; they would sacrifice everything they had achieved, and would have to return to the courses of Sillery and the Regency and direct dependency on the House of Hapsburg. Louis was silent; he had only one wish now: to return to Paris as quickly as possible and get the reins of power into his hands again. He commanded Richelieu to remain at Rôanne and defend his policy before the Queen-Mother and Marillac; he, the King, was still too weak to oppose the desire of his people for peace.

Richelieu had to obey. He curtly informed the Queen-Mother and Marillac: "The ambassadors were empowered only to observe and report; they were at liberty to treat only regarding the local Italian dispute; they have exceeded all their instructions; they have arranged for a general peace; more, they have gone the length of making an alliance with the Emperor, sacrificing at the same time all our other allies; we will have to give back to our enemies all we have won; we are left with nothing." Marillac jumped up; it was quite incomprehensible to him that Richelieu had the insolence still to stick to his policy; he became violent. But Richelieu went on, without being deflected from his course: "We must not ratify this agreement; the commanders of the army in Italy must be ordered at once to prosecute their operations with renewed vigour." There was something so powerful, so absolute in his bearing that day, that he carried the majority of the Ministers with him; the Queen-Mother and Marillac remained alone in opposition. But what was the King's Ministerial Council? It had been created and constituted by Richelieu himself. The refusal to ratify the peace treaty caused great bitterness at Court, and the news ran like wild-fire through the country from town to town, until it reached the lowest among the population; "The dark Cardinal, the King's evil spirit, has prevented peace!" Instead of with the son, Richelieu now set out for Paris with the mother; they sailed down the Loire slowly and with great pomp; troops escorted the great boats on either bank. Richelieu himself organized the journey to the last detail with all its entertainments, its delightful surprises; he sailed with his arch-enemy down the great river which mirrored the castles and gardens of the very nobles who, like Marie herself, had resolved on his downfall. Never had Marie been more amiable towards her creature, the Cardinal. She flung all her tough energy into dissimulation, which came so natural to her race. Bassompierre was amazed at the familiarity of her relations with the Cardinal, but Richelieu did not have any doubts; behind all these amiabilities the bitter fight went on.

The King was himself again. It was said that he did not trouble his mind much now with State affairs; he listened to music whenever he was not occupied with the hunt.

Scarcely had Marie settled herself in the Luxembourg, when she at once resumed her campaign against the Cardinal with extraordinary persistence. She conferred with Marillac one day and with her son the next. All Paris spoke of nothing but the approaching fall of the Cardinal. Father Joseph, who, after the sacrifice of his work at Regensburg, was once more in Paris awaiting orders, wrote soon after his return that he could not bear to contemplate the deep depression shot with apprehension into which Richelieu had fallen.

Louis was staying for the time being in his hunting palace at Versailles, for the Louvre was under repair. The Cardinal followed him out to the woods; he had learned that the King was moving on his behalf and persuading Gaston of the great Minister's indispensability. "How did the journey go? How did you get on with Her Majesty?" Louis asked him on his arrival. But when Richelieu hastened to reply that everything had gone excellently, against all his expectations, Louis answered: "You're mistaken." And again he broke off abruptly; he refused to listen to the Cardinal; he imposed an unusual distance between himself and his Minister.

During these days Richelieu aged greatly. Strangers who saw him in Paris for the first time were surprised by the painful spirituality of his looks. Many thought that death would forestall his downfall.

His friends, who feared the worst for him, now also began to advise him to discontinue his impossible Hapsburg policy and withdraw to the ostensible position which he had taken during the siege of La Rochelle. They urged him to get the support of the Catholic party; recently he had gone very far in that direction, had sacrificed Fancan, the best journalist who ever served him, to the *dévotes*; Fancan had died in the Bastille. But to all these proposals he turned a deaf ear; he refused to yield by an inch. He lived now in his growing work as in an element; he could no longer escape from it; he was one with it; and it is at this stage of his life, at the moment when, before the final conquest of all obstructions, his whole part in the destiny of his country was once more at stake, it is here that we may consider once more what it was in the spirit of the time that determined that he should come to the front.

In France the Counter-Reformation had set in a whole generation later than in the rest of Europe. The inner reform of the Church had been held up not by external circumstances merely, but by the resistance of the Gallican movement, so decisively characteristic of the whole of French history, against the promulgation of the Papal will. Like all other reforms, it was postponed until the religious and civil wars had been fought out, until it was possible to see things in proportion, and to regulate external policy according to the process of inner reconstruction.

Because of the late beginning of French Church reform and the prolonged vigour of French Protestantism, the spirit of the Renaissance, hostile to Church and faith, never took root in France as it did in England. The Catholic Church developed in France, in contrast to other countries where it had to battle for itself, freely and without hindrance under State protection. The powers of French Catholicism had been redoubled in the religious wars of the sixteenth century, and now that they applied themselves to internal reconstruction, to conscious affirmation, these wars, thanks to Richelieu, were over; the Catholic Christianity of France therefore embodied organically, without any division, a truly religious genius which Nietzsche, from the distance of another age and another philosophy, was one of the first to recognize. But it blindly passed over the danger of the revolt preparing underground, and from the moment of the revocation of the Edict of Nantes it fell into impotence, because it no longer had that opposition which every power requires for its own preservation. Nevertheless the spiritual mould in which the French were cast, and which persisted them in all their manifold secular activities as well, was formed in the period which begins with Henry IV, reaches its zenith under Louis XIII and Richelieu, and declines under Louis XIV: a theological discipline was its foundation. Even during the Revolution that mould endured secularly and has endured to our day, and in spite of the profound difference between the theories it has served since then and any Christian creed, every violent convulsion of the life of France has always been followed by a revival of Catholicism, in accordance with the law that any mould, once shaped, tends to recall to the spirit which created it. The "Gesta Dei per Francos" remained unforgotten, and between French and Catholic thought there exists an affinity, no matter how far removed may be the objects with which they are concerned.

The difference between the French and the Spanish-Hapsburg Counter-Reformation is shown unmistakably in their architecture. It is the difference between the Baroque style and the rational, measured, Cartesian style of French seventeenth-century architecture; and Richelieu clung to this truly national difference even at times when a compromise seemed to most of his collaborators the only possibility.

By the work of Richelieu the century was given that political method which Descartes describes in his *Discours*. A methodical formulation of all provinces of life from politics, through art, philosophy, and literature, to religion, can be clearly seen in France during the first sixty years of the century. All the great theologians, even all the mystics of the century—strange as it may sound—were men of method. Pascal's apologetic fragment reflects a sublime system of thought; and from the clear sense of the age for lucid categories followed also the creation of a social *élite*. Reason as the guardian of method enjoyed royal favour; this was shown most clearly in the theatre.

These observations may suffice to indicate the powers of growth which, manifested in all the departments of French life, bore the Cardinal victoriously in the end through all the dangers, enmities and treacheries which surrounded him. He was like an incarnation of the collective unconscious of the epoch. In the great leaders whom a people flings up can be read the inner value of the task to which it is called in a given age. There is a strange contradiction sometimes between the temporary outward circumstances of such a man's life and the deeper powers which make him invulnerable. And now we can turn to the powerlessness of all hostile influences against Richelieu's fate.

After the Cardinal's return to Paris no one would have betted a penny on his survival. In the beginning of November 1630 he begged for an audience with the King to discuss the intrigues which were on foot against him; but Louis refused to receive him. The King had moved to the neighbourhood of the Luxembourg, so that he might be able to talk more easily and frequently with his mother. It was said everywhere that after a hard inward struggle he was resolved to restore complete harmony between himself and Marie de' Medici.

But the air of the city was not good for the King. He suffered from sleeplessness; for hours in the night he would try to come to a decision; and he would waken after heavy, unrefreshing slumbers asking himself whether he should really sacrifice the Cardinal. He wanted to have time to think, and longed to withdraw into privacy again; riding through the autumnal woods at nightfall, his thoughts became clearer. He declared that he proposed to go at once to Versailles. But first he resolved to have another, quite private talk with his mother.

On November 10th, at eleven o'clock in the morning, he went to see his mother. As soon as he reached her apartments she ordered the doorkeeper to bolt every door and admit no one.

Now they were alone, and the final battle began. As if she were assembling every weapon which her former love and her present hatred of the Cardinal gave her, all that remained in her mind of deadly remembrance, all that she knew, had heard, had guessed, had invented; as if she were resolved to fling all her passion and disappointment into the battle for the soul of her son, and had summoned every spirit to her aid, she impetuously assailed the King. It was a fateful moment in which she, half a Hapsburg, tried to defeat the Bourbons. She tried to snare Louis by his given word; she put before him the promise given on his sick-bed in Lyons that he would treat with her after his return to Paris. She slowly set herself to subjugate him; he shrank back against the wall; he felt dizzy; his resistance crumpled. As if his years, one after the other, had been lifted from his head, he sank into the unresisting helplessness of a tormented, apprehensive child. All the bolts had been driven home; the outer world was far away; there was nothing but this voice from which he had once crept into the dark corners of the Louvre, and this glance which had once fallen on his cradle.

Then suddenly a never-used door opened; it led to a low windowless passage which connected the room with the chapel. Richelieu stood before the King of France and his mother; her words broke off abruptly. Marie had forgotten one bolt. Her privacy with Louis was over for good; the three of them were there again.

What an unexampled event, that appearance without announcement before the King and his mother, after orders had been given that their privacy was not to be disturbed! It must have been an act of desperation.

And now, just as abruptly, there followed a response which was equally insupportable to Louis. Marie de' Medici lost her head; she gave her son no time to intervene or utter any command; she began to shout. She flung at the Cardinal's head the outrageousness of his behaviour, his intention to put the King aside and set Gaston on the throne, and marry him to his niece Combalet, or rather not Gaston, but the Comte de Soissons; she was beyond herself; she screamed that Louis should avoid him like the pest; he was a traitor, a liar, a creeper; he wanted to declare his sovereign a bastard. This man, half-knave and half-fool, had cost her millions; he owed everything to her; he had fawned on her like a dog; but now it was over; she never wanted to see him again, or anyone belonging to his accursed line; she would fling out the whole wretched pack, neck and crop. Until the last trace of Richelieu's influence was rooted out she would not lift a finger to help the King with her counsel.

During this uncontrollable outburst the two men had remained silent. Then without a word the Cardinal sank on his knee before the King. He did not know, he said in a low voice, in what he had offended, but he begged for mercy and forgiveness. And twice, in a breaking voice, the Queen-Mother screamed at him: "No! Never!"

From that point things went very quickly. Such behaviour in the presence of a crowned head was quite unbelievable according to the ideas of the time. "What are you doing, Madame?" said Louis. "You offend, you insult me!" But Marie would not let him continue. "Do you prefer a lackey to your own mother?" she cried. But that shameless question was too much for Louis. In a dry voice he commanded his Minister to rise. Then he bowed coldly to his mother and hastily left the palace and entered his carriage. He did not deign to give a single glance to Richelieu, who had followed him.

The King at once changed his arrangements; he did not go to Versailles, but proceeded at once to his rooms in the

Rue de Tournon, where he flung himself on his bed and forbade anyone admission. He felt almost stifled by disgust and
humiliation. Everything, his dim recollections of the last
days of his father, of his joyless childhood, of his shameful
position before Luynes's intervention, rose up in him: everything that he had achieved hitherto, everything that he was,
the majesty that rested on him, the tasks he had accomplished,
the victories he had won over himself, the pious desire for
atonement which had moved him in his dealings with his
mother—all this was suddenly gone, killed at the moment
when his mother had dropped her mask, pushed him aside as
if he were less than nothing, as if he were still the tormented,
insignificant child of former times. He saw her before him, with
her purple face which had grown still stupider with age, as if
filled with passions which had turned sour, shouting down
everyone with her loud voice, without dignity herself insulting the dignity of his person, and giving free rein to the one
attribute which had endowed her with the strength to bear
the tragic greatness of Henry IV and outlive it, to sacrifice his
work and with her concessions and pleasant shifts to direct
the policy of France according to the expediency of the
moment, as if it were a bank: her vulgarity. The days of his
sickness and of her tender care for him were forgotten; that
had come merely from her lust for power and possession; at
any time during these days in Lyons she would have been
prepared to play off Gaston against him; and the shameless
subjectivity of her nature deeply repelled him, her dishonesty,
her inability to lend by love durability to her relations with
others, which began with hymns of praise and ended with the
destruction of the persons praised, who became less than air
to her, or merely the image of her own boredom. Her policies,
taken from this one to-day and from the next one to-morrow
and fought for with blind obstinacy, yet without any sense of
responsibility, any courage in the face of danger; her perpetual
appeals to the sentimental judgments of the public; her melodramatic outbursts—Louis could no longer endure them; his

inner conflict had with one wrench been ended, and now he would be hard and free himself completely, for it was clear to him how little all these confused, private, merely psychological considerations, including his own attachment, mattered compared with the great and impersonal aims which at moments he divined in his Minister. At the right moment, again as a saviour, Richelieu had entered the room; he had broken through everything, the express command of his prince, etiquette, convention, and dispelled the humiliating charm. But in the world which began at the threshold of the King's room everyone considered that he was lost, and even he himself was near the point of giving up the fight and fleeing the country.

He had sent for Marillac, and Marillac had replied that he was unwell; but as he left the Luxembourg in deep agitation he met his colleague, who ironically saluted him and went on his way to the Queen-Mother, now assured of success. Marillac had already begun in his mind to distribute offices and favours; all day the fluctuating crowds of self-seekers streamed to him; he had an hour's consultation with the Queen-Mother; the matter of the conversation was unknown. Marie, too, received countless suitors; she was radiant; she held court; she felt herself, more than ever, the hub of the kingdom. She told everybody that she had flung out Richelieu and all his crowd as ignominiously as they had deserved it for a long time.

Richelieu himself thought of flight; he coolly made his preparations; he expected every moment to be conducted to the Bastille. Avignon seemed to him now too uncertain and too difficult to reach. He decided to take horse hastily to Le Havre and get away by boat. His niece Combalet and his old friend Bouthillier completely lost their nerve and raised no objection. But Cardinal La Valette gave him heart again. He judged the position more coolly, and thought that the King would stand firm and resist the cabal. Since Richelieu had had the courage for such an unheard of act, he continued, he must not give up everything now; he must go at once to Versailles, for news had just come that Louis was leaving the Rue de Tournon and was to hunt that very day. Some gentlemen of the robe who chanced to be present supported La Valette. While this matter was being discussed in great agitation, young Saint-Simon, the father of the author of the Memoirs, suddenly appeared with a message from the King; he asked to see the Cardinal, and was told that his Eminence was in conversation with Cardinal La Valette. Saint-Simon requested a few words with La Valette, and informed him that the King commanded Richelieu to follow him at once to Versailles. With a shining face La Valette brought the news to Richelieu, the saving news which promised a turn for the better without guaranteeing anything. Then he at once followed Saint-Simon to the King, who was on the point of entering his carriage in the Rue de Tournon. "Are you surprised?" asked the King. "More than I can say," said La Valette. Louis answered: "Monsieur the Cardinal has a good master; tell him that it is my will to speak with him at once; he is to follow me."

When the Cardinal stood before his master, he again sank on his knee. The King, deeply moved, took him by the hand to raise him; he told him that he knew how to treasure what he possessed in him, and assured him that he would protect him; he knew also the reverence and gratitude with which the Cardinal had always surrounded her Majesty the Queen-Mother; if it had been otherwise, he would have withdrawn his favour from him.

Every time that he had had something decisive to demand from the King, Richelieu had offered his resignation. This time, when Louis assured him of his protection and trust, his request to be relieved of his offices had quite definitely the aim of bringing about a final settlement of the situation.

Louis was unusually frank; he declared that many of his ancestors had suffered because, under the pressure of their Courts, they had sacrificed excellent Ministers. If the Queen-Mother were capable of assisting him with wise advice in affairs of State, he would feel happy to work along with her;

N   385

but she was incapable of that. It would mean a grave loss of authority to him if he were to give up such an excellent servant, and no one in the future would trust him; but it would also be a sign of cowardice in Richelieu himself if he now forsook a master who was prepared to go to such lengths for him.

Richelieu asked: "How will the world judge Your Majesty's decision, seeing that I am charged on every side with grave ingratitude towards Her Majesty the Queen-Mother?" "It is not a matter of the Queen-Mother, but of the intriguers who have driven her to such lengths," Louis replied, and he added: "I honour my mother, but my obligations to the State are greater than towards her."

After this Louis acted quickly and decisively; whether of his own will or under pressure of Richelieu's, we do not know.

In the Luxembourg nothing was yet known of the real position. When the King sent Michel de Marillac the command to proceed to a village half a mile from Versailles, the old man was convinced that his enemy had fallen, and that he would now be given his place; everybody congratulated him.

On the evening of the same day the Ministerial Council was summoned; Marillac could not leave his village; for the first time he became anxious. The Ministers assembled; the King declared that for a year a cabal had existed which held up and confused State affairs in an insupportable manner; indeed the intrigues of certain persons had almost succeeded in transforming the Italian campaign into a disaster. The proceedings in Lyons had been beyond endurance. Marillac was deeply implicated in all these events. Because of his age, his services, and his exemplary private life, the King would not proceed to extreme measures; but he would deprive him of his office and banish him to a place from which he would never return.

While this was being decided, Marillac proceeded to the village church quietly to await there the misfortune he had begun to fear, and gain strength and comfort to endure it. He was engaged in prayer when the messenger who brought the

King's letter entered the church and tapped him on the shoulder. "Will you not hear the divine service to the end with me?"' asked Marillac. Then he rose, acknowledged his King's command, and without any attempt at resistance handed over the royal seal in its casket, which he had always to carry with him. He followed the guard which was sent to escort him, travelled day and night without knowing the end of his journey, and was at last conducted to the castle of Chateaudun, where thenceforward he was a captive. As a stoical son of his time, he has described his ill-fortune. "What a sobering thing life is!" he said, looking back over his career. Two years later he was dead. That resistance to the Cardinal's policy, made great by circumstances, ended quickly and silently. Marillac was a rigid, narrow-minded, and honest supporter of a policy which opposed to Richelieu's national idea something of the universality of medieval thought.

After the sudden and unexpected outcome of the grave State crisis, there still existed the danger of a revolt or a *coup* by the army. Marillac's brother, the Marshal, commanded, along with Schomberg and La Force, the French army advancing into Upper Italy; judging by his daring and violent character, it was not outside the possibilities that, when the news reached him, he might return across the Alps with his army and march on Paris.

But Richelieu was again at his post and made the necessary provisions. A courier was sent posthaste with a letter to Schomberg; the Marshal was given along with La Force the hard order to put his colleague Marillac in preventive custody and conduct him back to France under a strong guard, without advancing any reason except that it was the King's will.

The courier arrived at the camp in Falizo at the moment when the three Marshals were sitting down to dinner. Puységur, who was present, has described the scene. Schomberg stepped into a window niche and broke the seal of the royal letter. He began to read; La Force looked over his shoulder and with the words: "Read that alone!" suddenly took him by the arm. Schomberg left the dining-room and went into another room. He returned visibly agitated, and said that he could not take part in the meal. Marillac impatiently urged him to sit down at the table; Schomberg excused himself formally, and begged him as soon as he was finished to read the King's despatch along with La Force and himself. While Marillac ate, Schomberg summoned to him the officers of the Guards. He reminded them of their oath, and informed them of the King's order; he added that he relied upon their fidelity and prudence in carrying it out. Shortly afterwards the three commanders assembled. La Force said to Marillac: "I am your friend, and as your friend I beg you to accept without resistance the command of His Majesty our King and master. Perhaps all this will be cleared up and come to nothing." Then he handed Marillac the letter. Marillac turned as white as a sheet; then he bowed and handed over his sword.

Fourteen days later he was conducted to St. Menehould. He was still without apprehension; he assured the King of his devotion; he imagined that he stood well with Richelieu.

But Louis XIII had feared him during the brief days of the crisis, and that sufficed to seal his fate. As nothing palpable could be charged against him, his past was raked up. Marillac had once had to supervise the erection of the citadel of Verdun; now it was discovered that theft and embezzlement had occurred during that operation. An extraordinary commission was formed; the new Keeper of the Great Seal, Chateauneuf, a supporter of Richelieu, presided. Twenty-three judges had to decide the verdict; ten were for letting Marillac off, as there was no proof that he benefited from the incriminating irregularities; thirteen, obeying the voice from above, voted for Marillac's death. Till the end Marillac was convinced that the Cardinal had no say in the course of the trial. His relatives and friends bombarded Richelieu with petitions, but he answered evasively that it was entirely outside his competence; they should apply to the King: the outcome of the trial alone could decide. He asked Louis XIII once if it was not possible to save

Marillac by a general amnesty, but Louis refused to consider it. On May 10th Marillac was beheaded in the Place de Grève in Paris.

The Queen-Mother had replied to all these sudden blows of fate with measures equally violent and foolish. At last, when, as if startled out of a deep sleep, she recognized the truth, she ordered her carriage in order to go at once to the King, try once more on him the power of her words and her presence, and daunt him with the imperious compulsion of her loud, commanding voice; but her friends dissuaded her. Her whole Court in the Luxembourg went about as if stunned; by back-stairs they forsook the ageing princess; there was a perpetual coming and going; goods and chattels were smuggled away in the night. A nobleman resolved to put everything to the hazard sat dumbly by her as she wept and cursed and confusedly drew up cunning or daring plans. He raised his hand with a gesture of complete despair. "It is the day of the dupes," he said. The phrase has remained.

But in spite of her weakness, Marie de' Medici retained the inconquerable strength of defiance; her rage hardened into a capacity to resist; ambition and thirst for revenge gave her the strength to endure anything. The King sent her an interme-diary, Bullion, a supporter of the Cardinal. Marie shouted at him: "You're surely mad to dare to appear before me!" Then she asked how Richelieu was, how he looked, what he was saying; a thirst to hear everything about him remained at the centre of the whirlpool into which all her feelings were sucked. Bullion replied that her former superintendent the Cardinal had suffered so much that people could hardly recognize him. She did not believe a word of it, and burst out crying again. Bullion spoke of atonement, means of accommodation. "What means?" she shouted at him. The King, he replied, could not dispense with the Cardinal; he could not let him go; nobody could supervise the affairs of the State but Richelieu. "That's just it!" cried Marie, quite beyond herself. "That is what this fox, this creeper, has done: to confuse everything, leave everything in a muddle, hide himself behind everything and make himself indispensable!" But Bullion went on soothingly to say that only her anger made her think such a thing; if she no longer saw Richelieu and his supporters in her own house, but only in the council chamber, the position would surely be endurable for her, and both the King and the State would benefit. But she lost her temper again, shouted that she would die first, she would not give way an inch to that traitor, her own creature, who would have been nothing but for her. After a short sullen silence, she declared that she would never set foot in the council chamber again; no, she would rather die on the spot than meet that arch-villain the Cardinal; the day must come when God would open the King's eyes and ears. "God," she added, "does not pay a weekly wage; He pays at the end, the very end, and all at one time. I will bide my time, I will wait my hour," and then with uncanny spite: "I would sell myself to the devil rather than forgo my revenge!"

During these days the King suffered like a man tied to the wheel. Inwardly he had settled with his mother, but the mystic bond, the dread of the curse remained; dare he lift his hand against her? There were hours in which he vacillated again, in which he would have been glad to escape from the problem into obliviousness; Richelieu was threatened every moment by an inner capitulation of his master; even now the ground might open and suddenly swallow him. He wrote to all his relatives, to his niece Combalet and his cousin De la Meillerays and his old uncle La Porte, imploring them to be very careful to utter no word of complaint or criticism, to be silent and endure everything the Queen-Mother might do to them. Louis XIII was tormented by these terrible events in his immediate circle which were to decide the fate of thousands of people, more, of centuries of future European history, and yet could be decided only in the dark grounds of his lonely and sick spirit. By her nature and her resources of strength Marie was more powerful than he; if the Cardinal did not fill and support him constantly with his strength, then in spite of all his reluctance, all his accumulated resentments, he would break down and give way along the whole line. How hard he was pressed was shown by the fact that he spoke to everyone about his quarrel with his mother; he could not keep the bitter thought to himself. In November he referred to the quarrel before a delegate from the high courts; another time he told the president of the Audit Office that he was in a terrible dilemma. It was as if he were resolved this time to get public opinion on his side, public opinion which had once condemned him in the days of Luynes's harshness to Marie.

And the Queen-Mother naturally heard of all these talks, of all her son's vacillation; everything was brought to her, and much was added to it. Eager enough already, she was hounded on by others. "Everywhere," they told her, "the Cardinal's sly whispering voice can be heard; everywhere his soft and evil hands have set their snares." Richelieu counter-plotted; through priests he tried to make Marie believe that he had nothing to do with the whole business, and stood quite aside from it.

The Nuncio, Cardinal Bagni, was approached as an intermediary. Marie received him with a flood of complaints. He listened with the patience of the practised confessor, let her say what she wanted to say, then in her mother-tongue quietened her with words of a remote and yet familiar ring, at the same time maintaining all his curial dignity. She became more gentle, she seemed to give way; finally she gave her promise humbly to seek a reconciliation as a Christian. At once a meeting between her and Richelieu was agreed upon. But at that first encounter her hatred broke through her equivocal resolve, and she would have liked to scream all her loathing into the Cardinal's face. Her friends reproached her, pleaded with her, and the second time she was all lamentation, all sorrow. "Well, yes, perhaps it can be done," she admitted at last. On his side Richelieu humbled himself; he was resolved to endure anything, to attempt the impossible, if it would only put an end to the lying fiction that he had ever done anything against his mistress. Yet they parted, behind all their fine words and fine promises, inveterate enemies. The Queen-Mother was one of those people who cannot keep an agreement; for she knew only one law, which was rooted not in her mind but in her whole constitution and obeyed all her moods. In a few days Marie's private physician spread the rumour that the ostensible concession was a mere trick.

It seemed that the whole business might drag on still for a long time and end in a state of slow, empoisoned hostility. The most irresolute, volatile, frivolous of the participants in the tragedy brought about the solution: Gaston of Orléans.

A few hours before Richelieu set out for Versailles, Gaston had hurried to his mother, borne on the jubilant stream of Marillac's supporters. But scarcely was Marillac's arrest made known than he lightly turned on his heel, appeared before Louis XIII, completely renounced his mother and her party, and pledged once more his obedience and fidelity. He informed Richelieu that he had certainly hated him from the bottom of his heart, but that now he saw how grievously he had been mistaken; and in future he would love him as heartily as he had once loathed him. Gaston's intimates, Coigneux and Puylaurens, demanded rewards in money, land, and honours for their master's change of mind; these paladins asked the King for dukedoms, no less, and Coigneux actually demanded a cardinal's hat. As time passed, and a reconciliation was attempted between Richelieu and the Queen-Mother, and the King seemed to show a corresponding disposition, these gentlemen became extortionate. The Government, they declared, was negligent; they were resolved to get what they wanted with more expedition, and to force Richelieu's hand they tried to incite Gaston against him again and reconcile him with the lonely, bitter old woman in the Luxembourg. They threatened and translated their threats into acts; the heir-apparent was again, it seemed, to become the centre of a conspiracy, was again to call up the threat of foreign interposition. No sooner said than done. Gaston appeared before the Cardinal, declared that the promise solemnly given to him no longer bound him; he therefore withdrew his favour, and would himself find means to acquire power; and thereupon he left the Court and proceeded to Orléans. And once more it was a choice between the King dismissing the Cardinal, or Gaston raising all the discontented elements of the land in revolt.

Confronted with this ultimatum, the King at once decided to remove his mother from the neighbourhood of the conspirators; between her Court in Paris and Gaston's quarters in Orléans ran the thread of revolt; it must be broken. With his wife, the Queen-Mother and the whole Court, Louis removed to Compiègne. He was resolved not to let Marie de' Medici out of his sight. No sooner had they reached the castle buried in its woods than a last attempt was made, at the instance of Suffren, the King's confessor, to reach a friendly understanding with Marie. Schomberg was induced to have a talk with her private physician. The Marshal found it hard to bow his proud head to such intrigues and serve his master in such clandestine ways. Vautier, the busy pill-monger, as Schomberg called him, was flattered. In the evening, when he was alone with his mistress, he made one more attempt, but achieved nothing. She wished to live in friendship with the King, but the Cardinal she absolutely refused to see again, and not until he was gone would she take part in the royal councils. Thereupon Louis sent back the Marshal along with Chateauneuf, the Keeper of the Great Seal, in person; in vain; she stuck to her resolution, which was nourished with new hopes by Gaston's intransigeance.

In the Ministerial Council Richelieu rose last to speak on the situation which had been created by the Queen-Mother's behaviour. His speech was like one of those garden mazes which were so popular at the time, in which by labyrinthine ways one was forced to reach the point determined by the architect, but could hardly leave again without the thread of Ariadne. It was the final battle in the campaign begun years

N*

ago against the fateful woman who had once made possible his rise to power, and who now by virtue of that claimed the rights of an abysmal jealousy to bring him down and destroy him.

All the neighbouring States, Richelieu began, were once more spying out pretexts to foment division and discontent in France in order to destroy it. The Queen-Mother and the Heir-Apparent were embittered; all the discontented elements, the nobles, the Parlements, the masses with their sudden moods, were waiting for a standard to be raised, under which they might assemble to the detriment of the royal authority. Not many years ago such conditions had brought France to the verge of ruin. Never had the situation been more dangerous than now. If it developed further, they would lose all possibility of making an honourable peace with their foreign enemies. There were four possibilities. First: they could seek an accommodation with the Heir-Apparent, but that was impossible because of his own and his followers' faithlessness and lightness of mind. The second possibility was an accommodation with the Queen-Mother. But what difficulties faced them there! She was wily, deceitful, and revengeful. She would not be really satisfied until the day when she was once more in full possession of power and could destroy everyone against whom she nursed resentment in her dark and retentive memory.

There was a third possibility: for himself to vacate his office: this was the only decisive solution, and therefore the best; it must be chosen. Here, certainly, they had to face the question whether, even if he went, there would be an end of the intestine conflict. Might there not be an attempt to wrest the sceptre from the King, and after the dogs were killed, to attack the herd and even the shepherd himself?

A fourth possibility was still left; namely, to dissolve the new cabal. But how was that to be done, how could such a thing even be embarked upon? The Queen-Mother herself was the centre of the conspiracy, from which it derived its life. No, such a measure seemed hopeless and unworkable, unless a very ticklish measure were carried, and Her Majesty were induced to reside in some place in which she would be cut off from all communication with the rebels. But enormous caution was required for such a course, for it was greatly to be feared that it would appear inhuman in the eyes of the public. He himself could on no consideration recommend it; coming from him, it would only be interpreted as an act of base revenge. No, only if His Majesty the King himself, putting aside all considerations, decided that here lay the only possible way, would he consent to it; but at the same time he must implore His Majesty finally to grant him leave to resign.

Richelieu's speech was a longish one, and naturally all the Ministers, his colleagues, voted for the fourth and last course, and Louis at once took measures. He gave orders that the Court was to set out for Paris at once, but that Marie de' Medici was as soon as possible to betake herself to the town and castle of Moulins; as during the period of her first banishment, she would be entrusted with the government of the province; Condé, the present governor, would be indemnified.

On November 17th the Venetian ambassador wrote: "The Queen-Mother and the Heir-Apparent are far too powerful and important elements in the State for me to credit that the Cardinal will succeed in bringing them down."

The Cardinal was working at full stretch, and then, quite suddenly, he relinquished everything. That duplicate relation between ruler and servant which was later to be so effective was more and more definitely taking shape. It consisted in an unbending will, the Cardinal's, the infallible execution of which was guaranteed by a faulty but in moments of resolution immensely reliable personage, the King himself, armed with all the powers of absolute sovereignty. From all that happened thenceforward the Cardinal showed a conspicuous detachment. Many of his critics have concluded that because no letter can be found to prove his share in the final battle with the Queen-Mother, he stood quite aside from it. He would have been unwise indeed to write any such letter; "scripta nocent";

and the real decisions of life do not take place on the level on which words can furnish proof; for this reason the task of historical knowledge is a very different one from that of the interrogating magistrate.

In executing his harsh design Louis XIII chose the method of surprise. Before dawn on the morning of February 23, 1631, he set off; his wife was quietly wakened; the departure resembled a flight; the mask was kept on to the last moment; there was no consultation with the Queen-Mother. Not until well on in the morning, when the Court was on its way to Paris, was Marie wakened by Marshal d'Estrées, and confronted with the accomplished fact: the King and the Court were gone; eight companies of the Guards had arrived; sentries were stationed before the castle and at the town gates; she would be conducted to Moulins by an escort; a letter from the King would inform her under what conditions she would reside there.

To the surprise of everyone present Marie received this announcement in silence, and as if she had now entered into a new inner chamber of herself, she quietly folded the letter and said: "The mother of the King and subject to the man who rules his mind." Then she added: "I am innocent." She burst into tears, rose ceremoniously from her bed as the daily usage prescribed, but this day without saying a single word: after she had dressed she wrote to her son that what he designed would have the approval neither of God nor man. To those who were with her she is supposed to have said: "How small a thing can change the course of one's life! If I had not forgotten one bolt in Paris that day, the Cardinal would have been lost."

And, indeed, through the door that opened that day a new age had entered. The hour had come when the proud upholders of the past were to fall; the freest, the most fearless and open-hearted nobleman of Henry IV's time, the great Bassompierre, the friend of kings, who freely gave his fidelity but would never grant it on compulsion, was among the first. There was something in him deeply averse to the hard schematizing mind of Richelieu: unspoilt enjoyment of happiness and danger and privilege. In December 1630 Richelieu had already noted: "The letter (Marillac's) which he wrote Bassompierre from Italy, though it is always said they are enemies, gives us proof of the contrary, and this understanding between them is certainly not without some purpose." Compromising correspondence had been found; what more was needed? Immediately after the return of the Court to Paris the great Lorraine nobleman was seized and flung into the Bastille. His goods were confiscated, his castles razed to the ground. Now began all over the country a great breaking down of the walls which had enclosed ever since human memory the nobles and the life they led; that great builder, the Cardinal of the Roman Church, began his work of demolition, and while the towers and fortifications, mined with black powder, fell with a loud crash, there slowly grew up, as if blinded, a nameless and oppressed people, the peasants, of whom there was still so little rumour in a world whose fate was decided in four or five splendid palaces by the same few persons. Bassompierre vanished, a man so filled with the fullness of life that he had been accustomed to greet death like an intimate friend, so that more than a century later Goethe still delighted in certain pages of his memoirs. He retired from the stage; he grew so poor and lonely that he burst into tears for the first time since making his great renunciation for Henry IV, when his last companion, a young ragamuffin, died.

A few days after Bassompierre's arrest Princess Conti, to whom he had been bound by a life-long friendship, was sent into exile, shortly after which she died a mysterious death. It was the beginning of the great assault on the feudal nobles.

But for the time being the Queen-Mother still withstood the attack. Louis XIII cautiously prepared public opinion for the final settlement of his house; he explained the position to the guildmasters, so that his point of view might reach the masses in the capital; but the people of Paris had never loved the Queen, and were quite indifferent to her fate. Meanwhile

Marie refused to budge from Compiègne. Louis had the eight companies of the Guards relieved by twelve companies of the Navarre regiment.

The last intriguer in the grand style to stick to Marie was Vautier, her physician. He provided her with a pretext for not leaving Compiègne: she was without money, she wrote, her horses were lame, she had a severe cold, she had learned that they intended to send her by force to Florence, where she no longer knew anyone, and where none of her near relations were alive. Louis replied more sternly, and finally commanded; but in vain, she would yield only to force. The son sent his mother messenger after messenger, and finally Schomberg himself. But she held on with her nails, with her teeth, deeply insulted; surrounded by troops, she felt like a captive enemy of the State. Richelieu advised the King to withdraw the guard.

About highly-placed persons whose fortunes have sunk there are always to be found shadowy figures who believe that with a reverse of fortune they, too, will be elevated to a position at least worth striving for in comparison with their present one. Two men, Joachim de Cérisy, Marie's almoner, and De La Mazure, a lieutenant of the guard, spun the new plot, which was modelled on Marie's flight from the castle of Blois. Richelieu had constant reports of mysterious visits to Marie, strange encounters, clandestine removal of valuables; but he seemed to attach no importance to these things. He waited with crossed arms; he had left open a way to disaster for his old benefactress and enemy, and he hoped she would take it. On Friday, July 18th, at ten o'clock at night, witnesses saw a carriage with six horses standing before the gates of Compiègne on the road to Soissons. On the same evening a gentleman and a veiled lady were seen walking on the walls; they left the town through a little gate; the porter shouted that he was going to lock it: the gentleman replied: "You can do so; we are not coming back." The pair reached the carriage, entered and drove away. A small escort joined them to protect the mother of the King in her flight through the sleeping country.

Marie's intention was to proceed to the fortress of La Chapelle, where she would be safe and near the frontier, and where, with the support of the Spaniards, she could treat with the King. The Governor of the fortress was the Marquis de Vardes, but at the time he was represented by his son, an enemy of Richelieu. Strangely, no sooner had that young man received word of Marie's intention when he was imperiously ordered to attend at Court. He obeyed, but at once rushed back again without asking leave, so as to be at his post in time. Before he arrived his father, who was staying on his estate in Normandy, quite unexpectedly received a command to return at once to La Chapelle, re-assume his duties, and order his son to leave the place. The Marquis obeyed without asking any questions. Marie travelled all night. At Sains, next day, she learned that the fortress was closed to her.

She burst into loud lamentations. She did not want to leave France, she said; only the treachery of young Vardes was forcing her to do so; her enemies would rejoice if she fled over the frontier. In that she seemed to be speaking the truth. Quietly, without fuss, she was manœuvred out of France. At any moment troops might appear; she must reach Avesnes as quickly as possible, the next large town, which was near the frontier of Spanish Flanders. She took up her quarters in the "Feu de France" in Avesnes; she stayed there for ten days; then the approach of cavalry was reported, and on July 30th the widow of Henry IV crossed the frontier of the country which she had bullied for so long, and set out for Brussels. She did not know that she would never return, that from now on, a tired and sick old fool, she would wander from one country to another without rest, welcomed nowhere, treated with cold reserve, divested bit by bit of the honour she had so long been accustomed to, hatching mouldy conspiracies, spinning bootless intrigues of her own, trailing from Court to Court, accumulating debts, in vain trying to summon back her vanished splendour, without a gleam of hope. As soon as she reached Brussels, her friends incited her to write a violent letter to the King, in which she put the blame for everything on Richelieu, and once more implored her son to separate himself from his accursed adviser. Louis ordered his mother's enormous possessions to be confiscated. Henceforth he showed no trace of pity for her. When, after years of misfortune, she ended her days in Cologne, grey, broken-down, almost in destitution, the King of France, who was then slowly approaching the end of his own life, seemed to be quite unmoved.

Now, that heavy and strange parting having been accomplished, it was almost child's play for him to bring his brother, the Heir-Apparent, to his knees. On March 11th Louis set out with a strong force for Orléans, where Gaston was stationed. Gaston fled, at the same time publishing an open letter in which he made those charges against Richelieu which were to determine the attitude of coming generations to him. Gaston described him as a gloomy, ambitious man who treated the infatuated King like a puppet, and ruled the State for his own mad vainglory, proceeding from one revengeful act to another in the cold-blooded pursuit of his lust for power. Thereupon Louis XIII requested the Parlement of Burgundy to issue a proclamation in which all his brother's supporters were declared guilty of *lèse majesté*. Gaston fled to Franche-Comté, then to Lorraine, bombarding his brother with insulting letters from every halting station. His sheets circulated everywhere; they broadcast the charges that Richelieu had for years refused to terminate the Italian war simply to maintain himself in office, that he contemplated regicide and the seizure of the crown, that the King's mother had only escaped him by flight, that he seized men and executed them at his pleasure, that he had respect for no one, and that he would ruin the country, where the people were miserably dying of hunger.

But Gaston was not a doughty enemy. We can leave him here. Richelieu had now broken through, and he was free.

Now began his work, prepared for with such prodigious circumspection, such an incorruptible sense of reality; and out of it was to issue the new European state system. His personal biography here must yield precedence to his operations on European history; they will therefore be described later in a more general form.

With the day of the dupes that triumph announced itself which, resting on the principle of all-embracing masculine rule as Richelieu and the perfect absolutism which he achieved reflected it, prevailed against the dying world of the Middle Ages and the impure and self-seeking maternal rule of adjustment and accommodation embodied in Marie de' Medici. Through the complete reversal of her original feelings towards him, she had become the most stubborn and radical enemy of his free activity. Now she was finally overthrown. Now stroke by stroke his work could be realized, his far-reaching, violent European aims executed in Germany, bringing disaster to the German people.

One will never understand the Cardinal if one regards his European policy or his deadly struggle in the intimate circle of the royal house as animated by rational, soulless calculation. Everything that he achieved was purchased with constant suffering; he was possessed by his task, and was its slave. Seldom has the accomplishment of a superhuman task shown so convincingly that here a born fulfiller was at work, who greatly took upon him the full burden of his destiny. But what must strike us most of all is that Richelieu, though he felt the sublime compulsion which carried him irresistibly on, never subsided for a moment into a passive reliance on his star, into an irrational blind sense of his mission, but at every point of his work relied on the full employment of the human reason. Through a strict use of the capacities given him, which he employed with absolute precision, as if no other resource were available, his nature, which inclined to excess and had something demoniac in it, always returned in the end to measure and balance. The circumstances in which he worked, in which all that he did had to test itself upon and prevail against the resistance of a traditional form of society and of the problematical but in essence noble character of the King, kept him from ever estimating too highly the spirit of the age, or losing himself in it, and always led him back in a double sense to the reality of the national norm, first through the sobering influence of the King, who never fully trusted Richelieu's dreams, and secondly through the continuity of the monarchical institution itself which, irrespective of its temporary representative, was set above every individual rank or station.

Like all the great creative forces in history, Richelieu was a great destroyer. He tore down as much as he built up, yet it was not his fault but that of his successors that they did not grasp the profound lesson of his work, the lesson that no wall must be removed unless another and better one is erected, and that one must always build as if one were building for eternity.

INDEX